A HARD HAT IN HELL

A HARD HAT IN HELL

SUZANNE SZUCS

BOOK DOMAIN LLC

CONTENTS

The Heat Is On 1

WTF! 97

Critters 363

Funny and Absurd 414

Challenging and Just Plain Scary 459

When It's Good, It's Like Flying a Kite 515

Hasta La Vista, Assholes 525

This book was handwritten when I finished it at over one thousand pages. It was clear that I had a lot to say on the subjects I was writing about. It was brought to my attention that a handwritten manuscript is NOT what you present to publishing companies. Being an older lady now, I found it easier and quicker for me to type the book directly into my cell phone after narrowing it down to around five hundred pages.

There are two mottos I live by, and although they are both similar, they each set an intention in your mind to succeed in attaining your goals. One of them is "If you keep your feet moving, you will eventually get to where you want to go." The other is "If you want to build a brick wall, it's best to do it one brick at a time."

These two mottos are so meaningful to me that they are worth repeating. To say that I've finally finished after the last decade is a relief beyond measure and hopefully will exorcise a few demons for me. I hope that the women who read my book will gain some insight, learn of a nonconformist craft, and hopefully find some entertainment. Thank you for your interest in my memories of the wild ride that my life has been—"Surf's up, bitches!"

I've written this book for three main reasons. The first is to allow a little insight into the ways and meanings of men's behaviors and to be of assistance to all women who have daily dealings with them; the left-brain/right-brain differences, not to mention the hormonal ones. Second, for the women like myself who think "out of the box" and like a hands-on experience in a more unorthodox career choice—the examples left behind from your hard work, making a difference, and the right and union way of entering the construction workforce. Third, the most important to those dealing with constrictive, challenging, and emotionally draining relationships: "There is light at the end of the tunnel." If I could survive a regretful situation in which freedom seems an impossibility, so can you. You can change the progression of your life to a loving, safe, and secure way and be a positive example for others that are lost.

These memories of my experiences as one of the first women to drive pile, sheeting and to set iron as a union crane operator closely relate to three movies that I've seen throughout those years. I remember seeing them and feeling a close understanding of the messages they were extending to their audiences. To describe my book, I will use the titles of those three movies as my story holds elements that closely relate to those ideals. It's a little bit of Goldie Hawn in *Private Benjamin;* a fish out of water, so to speak. It's a lot of Charlize Theron's performance in *North Country* as a woman in a predominantly male workforce and also in an extraordinary career choice. Of course, it holds true to include Sally Field's movie, *Norma Rae,* supporting the inclusion and beneficial results as a member of a strong and powerful union.

Unfortunately, my story also holds close ties to two movies that it took me several attempts to watch in their entirety because I myself was living in those same circumstances for sixteen years; twelve of those years trapped, legally bound, physically and mentally enslaved. Those two movies are Tina Turner's *What's Love Got to Do with It?* NOTHING. In a nonconclusive ending compared with Farrah Fawcett's *The Burning Bed,* I still mentally rehearsed my first husband's demise thousands of times over within the confines of my mind.

The title of my book is *A Hard Hat in Hell.*

THE HEAT IS ON

"Get a real job or stay home with the kid!"

Those words were repeated to me on a daily basis over the course of about two years by my ironworker husband. I was a manager in the shoe department of a well-known retail store at the time. I also organized the lamp, candy, and gift departments there. Even though I dressed very nice to look professional while working in the main areas of the store occupied by the customers, I also drove the delivery van. I set up the furniture, delivered to the customers' homes—I liked having the variety of jobs to perform and I liked being busy.

Unfortunately, my paycheck paled in comparison to the amount of money my husband made each week as an ironworker. I had originally started college to become a chiropractor but had run out of funding to pursue that dream any further, at least for the time being. My husband's idea of a "real job" meant that he wanted me to jump back into the construction trade in one form or another. He wanted me to join a union trade here in Wisconsin in order to make decent wages, have good health insurance coverage, and to also earn a pension for myself. He knew that I was capable of doing the work involved because when he met me in my home state of California, I had just ended a three-year stint as a Union Cement, Lime, and

Gypsum Laborer. I had worked at a cement plant that existed north of the small beach town that I'm originally from.

During the two years he'd begun to nag me about joining a union trade, the only school I'd be able to attend in order to become a Chiropractor was located in Oregon. He was not willing to uproot with myself and our daughter in support of my career choice. I had sworn that I would never return to work in construction due to all the bullshit I had endured throughout those three tumultuous years. My reasons for leaving my job at the cement plant far outweighed the few that had kept me at it for as long as I did. By the time I decided that I couldn't be a laborer anymore, I had severe tendinitis in both of my shoulders, an elbow, and a wrist. I also suffered from peptic ulcers that would pop up now and again in my stomach as well as migraines that were due to stress. In fact, when I finally pulled the plug on that job, it was as if a huge weight rose from my shoulders and I could breathe again.

I had been seventeen at the time and was so bored with high school that I was barely attempting to keep up with appearances there. I was too busy surfing mornings and most afternoons as well before my nearly nightly karate classes. I also had horses to care for and ride.

The huge cement plant was located up the coast outside our town. They were informed by the state at that time they would be required to hire some female employees. They had a little over two hundred men working there and, other than the women who were employed as secretaries in their office, had entirely male employees. They were to hire five women to satisfy the new state requirements and they were not the least bit happy about having to do so. That began my first journey into a *"hard hat hell"!*

I decided to write about my experiences as a lesson for others as I know that I'm not the only woman in the world who loves to build and create. I've seen books that are titled *How to Live with a Man* or *How to Think Like a Man.* My lessons for you are how to "work" alongside men and how to deal with whatever *shit* they throw at you. How to understand where they're coming from and how to work accordingly with those men that you really "don't" want to work with. Now I'll explain to you what it's like to be a seven-teen-year-old girl thrown into the midst of two hundred plus men who think that the sole reason for you entering their workspace is for their own amusement. Most of them approached us as adversaries and with the intention of forcing us to quit as soon as possible. Those men had never before encountered a stubborn Swedish girl such as myself. Throughout all the years of my life, if someone ever told me that I couldn't do something, I'd set out to prove them wrong.

All five of us females started out in the yard. Working in the yard involved dealing with all aspects of maintenance and new construction performed throughout the entire cement plant. All the other employees there worked throughout the mills. Employees working in the mills pushed all the appropriate buttons to keep the various parts of the plant operational. They were also responsible for keeping their individual areas they worked in free from any spillage of cement product that occurred. It was relatively easy work, and it also paid more money per hour to the employees that worked there.

The big drawback for me was that the work hours in the mills were split into three alternating shifts—first, second, and third. You would work first shift one week, the second shift the next week, and the third shift the following week. You would continually be working that routine of alternating shifts each week. The reason the shift work was out of the question for me was because I attended karate classes four of my weekday evenings and half of the day each Saturday. I taught a karate class before the one in which I attended Wednesdays and had a sparring class after my usual class on Fridays.

I attended a four-to-five-hour class on Saturdays that were a long duration of time because I was fortunate to be able to train under a master in Chinatown. It was a timely drive up and back along the coast from my beach town to Chinatown in San Francisco.

I have two black belts. I began in Taekwondo. I trained for six years before my instructor or "sensei" relocated to Hawaii. I had to start over in the only remaining martial arts offered in my town at that time. It's a Japanese Shotokan style called "Serenji-Roo," which I hold a second degree black belt in. I trained in that style for six years also. When I moved to Milwaukee, I had intended to open my own dojo (studio), but when I found myself using it nearly every day to defend myself against my first husband, I was no longer interested in doing so. I didn't even attend classes here in Milwaukee; I'll write more about this issue later on in the book.

I surfed as often and as long as I possibly could as I was growing up in California. If there were no rideable waves to be found, I would be riding my horse. I had trained and ridden horses for years in exchange for the ownership of two horses. I had no time for "shift work." My only choice was to refuse my promotion to go up into the mills at the cement plant after my two-week introductory period.

Most women quit before the two weeks were up because the work was so hard to perform. Our yard foreman was a *beast* of a man to work for. His face was constantly beet-red in color as he was always yelling at everyone. I found him to be a ridiculous caricature of Archie Bunker who was a male chauvinist pig of a man portrayed on a television show at that time. I would respond to him in a quieter tone so that he'd have to bring down his own vocal volume just to hear me speak, and also just to piss him off! He was and still remains one of the biggest assholes that I've *ever* encountered.

I assigned myself to be his instant karma and remained under his command as a member of his yard crew. He tried like hell to get me to quit or to move me up into the mills. It seemed that he hated the sight of me and couldn't stand me polluting his atmosphere. I hung in there for three years, refusing to do either. That was the beginning of the war of wills, and to that, I said, "GAME ON!"

Of course, I was given the worst jobs you can ever imagine doing. One of the first jobs assigned to me was to use a pickax, a shovel, and a wheelbarrow. A large rectangle was marked out for me on the pavement next to the railroad tracks in front of the main office. That was located in the main entranceway into the plant, and all of the head honchos had a clear view of me as they looked down from their picture windows. I felt like a bug under a microscope. I was to use the pickax to break through the asphalt and then use the shovel to put the pieces along with the soil into the wheelbarrow. I then walked the wheelbarrow a good distance away into our dump area to dispose of the materials there.

It was hot, filthy, and sweaty work. I looked upon my job as being paid to work out instead of me paying a gym to work out in. The work was hard enough, but I had an audience the entire time I was digging that deep trench by hand. I was surprised to see how many of those days passed with the head honchos monitoring my every movement from their offices above me rather than tending to their own work. If that wasn't bad enough, I had wives driving to the cement plant out of their own curiosity to see the young woman their husband's had been forced to work with. I thought about the few other women hired who had gone up into the mills to work the various shifts and thought, *Out of sight, out of mind.* Those jealous wives had no idea that I was not the only female who was new to the plant's attendance. I felt like I should have worn a T-shirt that read *"I'm only here for the money, honey!"*

After I'd been at that dog and pony show for almost a week, I had just about reached the required depths and measurements the foreman had marked out for me to excavate. I was surprised when he removed me from that project just shy of its completion to send me to work elsewhere.

The next morning, as I walked into the plant, I noticed that the huge hole I'd dug out had been completely filled in. I assembled with the rest of the crew to receive our assigned tasks for the day. I asked the guys if they knew what happened to the huge hole I was digging. One man who operated the big front-end loader at the plant explained to me that the foreman told him to fill it back in as if it had never been dug out in the first place. I was HOT! All of that work, shoveling over my head to toss the soil out of that deep hole I'd dug. He had just given me that job in order to keep me out of his hair. It had taken me nearly a week to dig that hole by hand and only about half an hour to fill it back in with a big front-end loader bucket! Did it ever piss me off to realize all my hard work was a waste of time.

As a young girl back then, I took those macho games played against me personally when I should have looked at the job for what it was—an opportunity to make some really good money. I WAS being paid to work out, and he was just a clown in disguise.

I was also assigned to assist the on-site demolition expert whenever he was in need of assistance. No one else would work with him because IT WAS SCARY! Some idiot engineer designed the giant two-hundred-foot-tall set of silos with "flat bottoms" inside them. They didn't have a cone shape interior to help eliminate the concrete powder held within them so that it would slide down into the pump located at the bottom. The pump progressed the material through a series of augers and conveyor systems that loaded up the tanks. The tanks filled the endless stream of semitrucks that delivered to various cement suppliers all across the country.

The cement dust would accumulate along the walls of the silos and would stick there until the demolition man would "blow" the interior contents. This would get the powdered cement to flow down the sides of the walls into the pump. The problem with that was that it caused chunks to form which would not pass through the pump. I then had to stand on top of a platform that reached up to the ceiling. It was placed directly beneath the silo we were imploding. I had to strike the chute that housed the pump above my head with a sledgehammer. It made for a very long day and eventually became a key factor in the development of acute tendinitis in my shoulders.

The scary part of working with the demolition man was during his preparation period. He would hand me the blasting caps while he unspooled the wires needed to charge the explosives. He would always say to me, "No matter what, keep those two wires AWAY from each other!" Once he placed the dynamite and wired the charges to it, he would wind the two ends of the wires I was holding onto the "blow box." We'd both get behind a makeshift barrier, and he'd cry out, "FIRE IN THE HOLE!" It was so loud even with my earplugs in.

I could hear and see cracks running across the ceiling above me. Someday that ceiling would become a safety issue and start coming down. Who knew when that would happen? I was always so relieved when the demotion man would head back up into the quarry in the mountains behind the plant. That was his general work area where he blasted apart the sides of the limestone quarry walls. The limestone was loaded into giant dump trucks and then driven to one end of the plant. The dump trucks released their contents into crushers located there.

Every Monday, I was given the most horrible job to start my work week with. I had to assist the man in charge of the dust collectors. The cement dust was such a fine powder that you could not see it floating throughout the air. It was not healthy to breathe or have on your skin. In most of the areas, we were required to wear dust masks and long-sleeved shirts to protect our skin however we were able to. There were dust collectors everywhere and were all connected to these giant dust collectors up on the hill behind us by a vacuum system.

Inside those huge dust collectors, it was extremely hot. The amount of dust running through them would cause the long tubes that were their filters to randomly blow apart. Those tubular filters were made out of a special cloth material and attached to both the ceiling and to the floor. They were held in place by special hoops that were tightened or loosened by screws.

Our job was to enter the huge dust collectors first thing Monday mornings after the dust collectors had been shut down over the weekend in order to allow them to cool off somewhat and the cement dust circulating within to settle on the floor.

It was still so hot inside of the dust collectors that we brought rags inside with us to kneel upon while removing the bottom portion of the tubular filters that had blown apart. It was like working in a hot sauna, and the dust would stick to whatever parts of your sweaty skin were exposed. We then swept up the spilled dust into the uncovered hole before attaching a new filter over it. I would work along the floor and my buddy would stand up on a ladder and work on the ends attached to the ceiling. There were usually quite a few broken tubes in each collector from week to week. That job would take up almost the entire day to complete. The dust caused caustic burns on your skin due to its limestone component, and it caused you to itch all over also.

The dust would permeate all the layers of clothing that I wore. It was like water in that when I removed my bra and underwear when I got home to take a shower, there wasn't any outline left on my body from wearing those garments. The dust had permeated the cloth and was all over my skin. The only time that phenomenon did not occur was when I was required to wear rain gear for a particular job, but who the hell can run around wearing a rubber suit all day? By the end of the work day at that cement plant, all of us workers looked like a band of weary ghosts—a ghastly ash gray in appearance. The only areas of clear skin visible on our faces was around our mouths and noses from where we had worn our dust masks.

The only good thing about working in the dust collectors was that we got through the most difficult job right away. No matter how hard the jobs would be throughout the rest of the week, they generally paled in comparison as far as the rate of difficulty was concerned. The man I assisted in the maintenance of the dust collectors became a good friend of mine, a partner in crime so to speak. We would dare each other to do silly stuff in order to pass the time in a more pleasant and challenging fashion.

One of those dares had to do with his nasty chewing tobacco habit. One afternoon, I asked him, "What is it with the chewing tobacco? Every time I look over at you, you're spitting that god-awful juice on the ground!"

He told me it freed up his hands by not having to hold a cigarette. Then he got a gleam in his eye and a smile crossed his lips as he said those magic words, "Hey, kid (everyone called me 'kid' because at the age of seventeen, I was the youngest person working at the cement plant), I'll bet you fifty dollars that you can't keep a pinch of tobacco in your mouth for five minutes."

"Five minutes? Who can't do something for five minutes! I've got this one in the bag. You better get your wallet out," I said with great excitement at the prospect of becoming fifty dollars richer. I was already envisioning the beautiful pair of shoes I was going to buy with my prize money. I no sooner put a pinch of the pungent foul-tasting tobacco in my cheek when my poor mouth, in agony, began salivating like hell, and my vision of my new shoes began to fade.

My buddy said to me, "I forgot to tell you, do NOT swallow the juice no matter what happens. You must spit out the juice."

Seeing as how I'm *not* a spitter, I was doing a terrible job of trying to spit the juice out of my mouth.

I was operating a little Bobcat skid-steer loader at the time, and I had splotches of brown juice from the tobacco staining my clothing and dappling my machine. I could feel my face turning green! My stomach was trying to churn its way out of my body. I immediately steered toward our dump that was located a short distance from where we were working. I barely made it there in time to exit the machine before I puked my guts out—was I ever sick. Eventually, I made my way *slowly* back to where we were working. As I reluctantly climbed out of my machine, the vision of my beautiful new shoes vanished completely like a balloon pricked by a pin.

My buddy took one look at my green face and my brown stained clothing and busted up with laughter. Realizing that he had just beat me out of fifty dollars, he merely held out his upturned palm and said, "Pay up, baby sister!" That was the one and only time I tried chewing tobacco—YUCK!

The guys at work thought it would be funny to surprise my girlfriend and I by decorating our hard hats for us. When she and I arrived at our lockers one morning to put on our safety gear for the day, we noticed the new additions they had added. They had taken the insignias off two different men's colognes and cemented them to our hard hats. The emblem glued to my hat said "Savage," and the one they glued to hers said "Brut." We tried like hell to pry off our new *"decorations"* from our hats without any luck and were stuck wearing them for our duration of employment there.

All the guys we walked past that morning immediately cracked up with laughter upon seeing us; it was an entirely new humiliation. When I asked my screaming foreman if I could have a new hard hat, the answer was, "Hell NO! I find that one you have on to fit you perfectly."

Anytime we placed padlocks on our locker doors to achieve a little privacy for ourselves and our belongings, we'd find them cut off by bolt cutters the following morning. We had to be careful to leave our purses and anything of worth locked up in the trunks of our vehicles if we wanted to retain them.

There was a handful of guys that I enjoyed working with. One of them was the buddy I previously mentioned who I assisted with the dust collectors. He was a lot older than I was, but I enjoyed his wicked sense of humor and our daring challenges. Another favorite of mine was a sweet old-timer of Italian descent. He had a very strong Italian accent and called me "Suza" instead of Suzanne or Susan. He'd also had a bad accident at some point in his past that had caused deep compressions in his forehead area. It looked as if someone had struck him in the forehead with a very large hammer and it had left his skull broken with serious dents remaining. Those fissures in his forehead caused one of his eyes to be a bit cockeyed (no pun intended here) so that he could not look straight at you with both eyes.

He always requested me to be his assistant whenever he was called for any emergency repair or if he had specific jobs pop up here and there. He was the plant's head carpenter. He taught me "framing" which is the skeletal structure of a wall, box, or building out of lumber. He also taught me to mix, pour, and finish concrete.

Every day that I had the honor to work with him, he told me a new joke that he had heard. He also gave me his bag of peanut M&M candy that his wife awarded him within his lunch box every day; it was his favorite candy of all time. I knew how hard it was for him to part with his bag of candy, so I made sure I did the best job for him to earn it. I would tease him that he must have done something very special for his wife in order for her to be giving him candy every day.

Wednesdays were killer workout days for me; it was always a ten-hour day. Two guys and myself would load fifty-pound bags of cement as they were delivered to us rapidly down a conveyor belt. There was a certain pattern to stacking the bags onto the pallets. Two of us would stand on either side of the pallet and be responsible for stacking their side. If a bag were to break while stacking, you rapidly brushed it off to the side and quickly resumed your stacking rhythm. The conveyor belt did not stop its progress unless it was a dire emergency. As soon as a pallet was completed, a skid-steer loader would move it out of our way, and we would proceed to stack the pallet that was at the ready underneath it. Semitrailers would pull in to have the pallets loaded onto them. They were then driven to various retail stores to be sold.

That proved to be very hard work, lifting and maneuvering fifty-pound bags of cement for ten hours at a rapid pace—it felt like boot camp.

What was worse was when I was the person chosen to operate the machine that filled the bags with cement, the machine looked like a large church organ, and it was located at the beginning of the conveyor belt. It had foot pedals like an organ does, but it also had levers that allowed the cement powder to fill the bags that I slid onto nozzles. The levers were then shut off long enough for me to slide the full bag off the nozzle and lower it onto the conveyor belt below me. You couldn't just drop the bag beneath you or it would break open. The seat I sat on allowed me to slide from side to side because it resembled a large organ bench. There were either three or four nozzles that I used simultaneously, constantly filling the bags. It was quite the coordinated effort to operate the machine.

Your legs were spread apart so that you could reinsert new bags onto the nozzles while carefully placing the full ones below you. Bags would blow apart every so often due to the high pressure delivering the cement dust into the bags. That pressure assisted on quickly filling up each bag. The hot dust would blow up all over me when a bag exploded as I filled it. It was a macabre surprise to be completely covered with the dust, and I never knew when one would burst when filling it up. I HATED that job. I ended up with infections on my hoo-ha from the hot dust when the blow-ups occurred because the dust particles would penetrate all my layers of clothing. I began wearing rain pants that were essentially plastic bib overalls.

My choices were to either be sweating from the sauna effects of wearing the rain gear or take a chance on getting a nasty infection by not wearing them. It was a lose-lose situation. All day long, we moved at an exhausting fast pace in order to finish loading the necessary pallets within a ten-hour day. If we failed to do so, we were expected to continue the next day until we completed the amount of pallets needed—NO thank you!

The bastard foreman did not like me joining the guys for our coffee and lunch breaks. I don't think he liked the fact that we all got along well together and were able to work with each other free of drama. We all took our breaks in the yard office which was, in essence, his glorified shack. One day, I noticed a trailer being towed into the yard by a truck. It was intended to be used by the women working at the plant.

It was parked in a place far from the foreman's shack (office), yet it was within his view so that he could keep an eye on it. I thought, *That is fine with me because the men will not be able to invade our lockers.* I didn't mind being sequestered from the men because I was used to being alone all day anyway for the most part. I would sit in there by myself for all of our break times. The girls that worked the other shifts would leave little notes for me to say "hello" and to warn me about which men to look out for. They enlightened me as the youngest female among them about all the assholes working up in the mills. I would leave messages for them as well. Once in a while, we'd meet up at the bar in the tiny town that the cement plant was located in.

One of the women lived in that tiny town. She was the eldest one of us and was married to a much younger man who was very handsome and of Spanish descent. She was the raunchiest woman I'd ever met. She would tell the nastiest jokes that even made the men blush! I got an idea to surprise her. I'd been getting the *Playgirl* magazine for some time. I cut out all the photos of the naked men and taped them up all over the walls and ceiling of the trailer. I wanted her to be "pleasantly greeted" when she showed up to work her shift that evening. She loved it! She left me a note stating so along with her latest joke she had for me.

The only person who didn't care for my interior design style was our male janitor who had to clean our trailer for us. Although he was the janitor for the entire plant, it really irritated him to have to clean up after us women. He was a very old-fashioned Sicilian (don't call him Italian!) and was used to women cleaning up after *him!* He also did not like the fact that all five of us were making A LOT more money than he was.

He was constantly complaining about us and about having to clean our toilet and trailer, even though I always thanked him and was kind to him. One morning, as I walked into work, I noticed a bright orange sign posted on the open door of our trailer. I then noticed the trailers entrance had been corded off with a sign hanging from it that said "Do Not Enter." When I asked the bastard foreman why I couldn't go into the trailer to have access to my locker, he informed me with a big smile that it had been fumigated. That lying weasel of a janitor had told the foreman that he heard one of us women had crabs!

The janitor tore down all of the pictures of naked men that I had decorated our trailer with. He removed all our clothing and other items from our lockers, except for our hard hats. He had thrown all our belongings into the garbage. He had then hosed down the entire trailer with a very strong cleaning solution. I couldn't believe the asshole mentality of the foreman and the janitor. The janitor had found a way to not only eliminate the male nude photos I'd supplied but also humiliated us women in the process. He seemed very pleased with himself with what he'd accomplished. I was beyond aggravated with having to deal with him. I told him that his services were no longer needed in the maintenance of our trailer, that we were perfectly capable of cleaning up after ourselves. I also told him that the gloves were off and that he'd better watch his back and to stay the f——k out of our trailer!

Another one of the jobs I dreaded there was when I had to be tied to a rope and dropped through a porthole near the top of our two-hundred-foot-tall silos. A partner and myself made the scary climb up to the highest porthole by using a series of elevated platforms. One of us would remain on the outside holding onto one end of a long rope. The other would tie the opposite end of the long rope around their waist and put on goggles, a respirator, and put in earplugs. Those measures would help keep the dust you would become engulfed in from invading those areas of your body.

You had to struggle to fit through the porthole opening and be dropped down by the rope tender until you could find an area to plant your feet. You would also take a utility light that was attached to a long extension cord so that you could see the interior of the silo. The cement dust would collect and compact along the walls of the silo. Some genius of an engineer (NOT) had the brilliant idea of putting flat bottoms in the silos. The walls were straight when they should have been cone shaped. If they were cone-shaped, then perhaps it would have aided the cement dust to flow toward the bottom and into the pump to carry it out.

I had to take a shovel and chip away at the stuck cement dust until it would *WHOOSH* in an avalanche fashion toward the bottom. When that would inevitably happen, it caused total darkness until the dust would settle somewhat. The light bulb would need to be dusted off in order to have visibility once again. You had to be very careful not to slide down into the pump along with all the cement dust. It was a very scary, filthy, and dangerous job—IT SUCKED! You had to hope and pray that your partner sitting outside that porthole was hanging on to your rope tightly.

Whenever I sat on the outside while my partner took his turn chipping away at the dust on the inside, I could not hear any sound from within the silo. I could feel a great tug on the rope whenever a portion of the dust slid down the wall because he would slide a bit along with it. It would have been so easy for someone to become buried inside; no one on the outside could hear the person on the inside yelling because the concrete walls of the silos were so thick. If one of us had an emergency on the inside, the rope tender on the outside would have to climb all the way down to the ground and then run to find someone to help. If there were an emergency involving the rope tender on the outside, the person on the inside would have no knowledge of that fact and would have been left in a precarious position. Remember, this was way before cell phones, pagers, or even walkie-talkie radios. That job was so dangerous that at that time, I thought of a million ways to improve how it could have been done, but hey, I was just a teenage girl—what did *I know?*

We used to place tape around the cuffs of our shirts, binding them to our wrists and also around the ankles of our pant legs. This was done in order to help in keeping the dust out, but after I share this next memory with you, you'll find that in all actuality, it did us little good. After having to perform that job one day, I found myself so exhausted that when I got home from work, I laid down immediately upon entering our home that I shared with my mom and my two younger sisters. I just needed to briefly rest before taking my shower to wash off the job for the day. I lay there longer than I anticipated and ended up falling asleep.

When my mom awoke me for dinner, and I arose from her black Naugahyde couch, my mom and sisters began laughing and pointing to where I had taken my nap. On the couch was a complete white powdery outline of my entire body. I had left behind what looked like a crime scene outline of a dead body that you see on crime drama television shows! All the cement dust I carried with me had been left behind on my moms' couch. She said that it looked as if a ghost were lying there.

The lime in the cement dust was so caustic and burned your skin. It would eventually break down the leather in your work boots and erode your boot laces. It was because of that we were issued two pairs of work boots every year from the company. After painting the ghostly picture on my mom's couch, I kept a robe in the garage. I would undress out there and enter our home in my robe to keep the dust outside. I also sat on a towel in my truck on the way home from work.

I was given one job that I actually enjoyed, but to make sure that the bastard foreman kept giving it to me, I pretended to hate it. Whenever he assigned me to it, I would say under my breath but loud enough for him to hear, "Oh God!" in a defeated tone of voice. I would cast my gaze downward and add a slight shake of my head "no" as if I actually dreaded the idea of it. It was given to me once a month and lasted no more than a day or two. I had to walk through the entire plant and check the fire extinguishers. If I came across a used one, I had to swap it out for a freshly prepared one.

I updated each extinguishers tag as I came upon it to prove that I checked it for that month. There were hundreds of extinguishers provided throughout the plant. Once I finished going through the plant, I walked along the beltline up into the mountains and checked the extinguishers located periodically along the way. At the top of our beltline, there was our quarry. The beltline carried the limestone from the quarry down to the crushers. Up in the quarry, there were giant dump trucks and front-end loaders. The stone was separated from the mountain with explosives.

Whenever I arrived at the quarry, I felt like I was entering the land of the giants. It reminded me of a television show I watched as a kid called, you guessed it, *Land of the Giants.* The tires on the machines reached way above my head in height, and I stand at five foot, nine inches. I was fascinated by those giant machines! It was a workout for me to climb up the tall ladders of the machines to check the extinguishers located within the cabs. I had to be careful as I stood off to the side and waited for each operator to complete his assigned task before he could drive his machine over so that I could check his extinguisher. Those men in the quarry always greeted me warmly and with big smiles. I got to say hello to the demolition expert while I was up there also. I think that my visits to the quarry broke up the monotony for the men working there. I liked to think that they enjoyed a friendly visit from a surfer girl rather than another grizzled older guy.

The reasons I liked that job was because it was easy in comparison to the usual hard labor I had to endure. I liked working alone and didn't have to feel any resentment or hostility emanating off most of the men I had to work with. I also didn't have to come up with any excuses as to why I didn't want to date anyone who asked me out. It's a very delicate situation to find yourself in when you don't want to hurt someone's feelings. You don't want to deal with their embittered backlash or revenge tactics if they feel somehow emasculated.

A lot of the men I worked with did not understand or want to hear the word *no.* Using humor made them feel like they were joking with me in the first place and therefore allowed them an "easy out." It left them feeling as though I didn't take them seriously in the first place. In that manner, they did not feel rejected and had lost nothing in the process. Here is an example of what I'm saying: if a guy asked me out, I'd say, "Now you know my boyfriend wouldn't go for that, but your wife probably wouldn't mind a break—ha-ha!" Then I'd give him a little shove as I laughed it off. That was using male humor reversed back in his direction. If I could make it into a harmless joke, they would seem to be willing to forget about it and move forward.

However, if a guy grabbed my boob or pinched my butt, I'd flat out punch him. Then I'd say something like, "Do it again, and I'll drop your ass!" Then they'd stay clear of me.

You must set absolute boundaries and demand some respect from your male coworkers. If you don't show them that you respect yourself, they will not respect you either. I'd also remind them that they would not want a man to behave that way to their girlfriend, wife, daughter, or mother. Once in a great while, a guy who I would say that to would offer me an apology and tell me that I was right. It would upset them greatly if a man were to behave in that manner to the important women in their lives.

I also carried a small screwdriver in my pocket just in case a guy had any ideas that he'd corner me in one of the many secluded dark places I was sent off to work on my own. I was (and am) always aware of my surroundings. I'm glad I was trained about awareness at a young age and also for my safety because it served me well throughout my entire lifetime so far. It's also saved my life a few times.

As for acting as though I did not like the job of checking the fire extinguishers each month, the bastard foreman was only satisfied if he could make every day that I worked for him pure torture. If I enjoyed doing something, I found that I'd never be sent to do it again. The only reason I got to work with the nice carpenter was because he specifically requested me, and the bastard foreman had no choice but to comply. The carpenter had way more seniority with the company and held a way more important position. That man was my godsend at that plant. I acted like I didn't like checking the fire extinguishers and therefore got the job assigned to me on a regular basis.

The men did not like checking the fire extinguishers because there were rattlesnakes everywhere up in those mountains. You would see them warming themselves in sunny areas. There was also a resident mountain lion that lived up there that no one wanted to mess with. I had gone hunting for wild boar every year with my dad as a kid. We camped outdoors and came across rattlesnakes often. He had given me my own snakebite kit and had taught me how to use it. That snakebite kit joined my keys and my screwdriver in my pocket. I think the bastard foreman was hoping that I'd cross paths with the mountain lion or a rattlesnake. In fact, I think his hopeful thoughts of my encountering one or both of them was a major factor in the reason he assigned the job to me. Who knew that men would fear those two creatures so much?

They should have been introduced to a wild boar and see the damage it could do with its tusks. The first time I saw one when I was a little girl on a hunting trip with my dad, I thought it was the devil! It was super early in the morning and still dark outside. I saw a creature with huge curling tusks strutting out from its jaws, and I could see its breath that looked to me like smoke. He was grunting and snorting as he ran across the roadway in front of us. With a flick of his curly tail, he leaped over a barbed wire fence as graceful as a deer. At seven years old, that was the scariest thing I'd seen so far in my short life. My dad turned to look at me and said, "That's what we're hunting for!" I could have crapped my pants then and there! Instead, I remained as cool as a cucumber because I wanted to keep going on hunting trips with my dad. That was my very first lesson to "never let them see you sweat."

One day, the bastard foreman found a way to keep me out of his mind for a very long time. I had my usual shovel and wheelbarrow with me when he introduced me to my two new companions, "Big Bertha" and "Little Buck." I named them because I would be spending enormous amounts of time with them for the remainder of my career at the plant. "Little Buck" was short for "Little Bucking Bronco."

Little Buck was a forty-pound jackhammer. When I used him, it felt like I was riding a "bucking bronco." I knew what that felt like because I broke and trained horses for many years. "Big Bertha" was his big sister, weighing in at eighty pounds. Just lugging those two tools around along with their air hoses was a workout. I'd transport them from job to job in my wheelbarrow.

The bastard foreman escorted me and my new friends underneath the office and parking lot to introduce us to the underground tunnel system put in place there many years ago. There were twelve tunnels; each one was one hundred feet long. Conveyor belts ran through each of the tunnels. The conveyor system carried the finished cement product from the plant to a building that supplied the semitrailers equipped with tanks.

When a truck pulled in, a hatch would be open on its roof, and a fabric sleeve would be dropped into the empty tank to fill it up with the powdered cement. Once again, a "genius engineer" had the conveyor belts built in a flat design rather than a concave one. A concave or V-shaped design would have aided in containing more of the material on the belt as it traveled over the rollers beneath it. I swear that it most have been the same genius engineer who designed the silos with flat bottoms in them rather than cone-shaped bottoms. Since those tunnels ran below the ground and we were directly beside the ocean, it was always damp within them. It would even be wet at times with condensation dripping off the walls and ceiling. Puddles of water would appear on the narrow pathway that ran next to the conveyor belt. That would occur if the evening before brought in dense fog from the ocean. When I looked down the tunnels, they were narrow and separated by a stone wall between them. I could see towering mounds of cement dust that had fallen to the sides of the conveyor belt. The mounds had hardened into concrete due to the dampness.

The man in charge of maintaining and greasing the rollers of the conveyor belt could not walk beside it in order to do his job. That was where Big Bertha, Little Buck, and myself came in along with the help of my wheelbarrow and shovel. I had to shovel whatever material I could off of the floor and place it in my wheelbarrow. When it was full, I had to take it to the end of the tunnel and tilt the wheelbarrow up to the railing to shake out the material held within it. When I came to the concrete that had hardened, I had to use the small jackhammer (Little Buck) to remove enough of the concrete for me to be able to fit in the big jackhammer (Big Bertha). It took me SO LONG to clear away the hardened concrete from the tunnel. It was dark in the tunnels with only a caged light bulb overhead every so often to light the way. It was cold and wet; I could see my breath in the air sometimes. The condensation dripped from the stone ceiling onto me all day long as I worked. It took me about three weeks to clear one tunnel of its congested pathway. Unfortunately for me, when I completed one tunnel, the bastard foreman would have me clear the next one, and so it went tunnel after tunnel. I jackhammered and shoveled material into my wheelbarrow eight hours a day in the dark wet tunnels for months at a time. By the time I cleared all twelve tunnels, it was time to begin all over again. I had to go back to the first tunnel I cleared, and it looked as if I'd never cleared it in the first place. If nothing changes in the situation, you get the same result. In that situation, the cement dust was still spilling off the con-

veyor belts and hardening on the floors.

At my age now, looking back at the hideous assignment, I'd say, "Bring it on, asshole! You can pay me to work out all day—easy money!" Back then, at seventeen, eighteen and nineteen years old, I took it that the bastard foreman was showing me how unimportant I was by burying me down in those dark tunnels day after day. In the mornings, he wouldn't even speak to me. He'd just nod his head in the direction those tunnels were located. I felt he was trying to break me, to get me to give up being in the yard crew and move on into the mills to work. Every day, he made it very clear that he wanted me gone.

I became very depressed working by myself in the dark every day. I knew I wasn't alone in feeling that way when I found a pint of tequila hidden far back in one of the tunnels; it was almost empty. I wasn't the only person not feeling a welcoming atmosphere down there. Perhaps it had belonged to the maintenance guy. No one had been able to reach that bottle for a very long time, so my bet was that it belonged to the man before me who had to jackhammer his way through that tunnel. He probably had become depressed as I had become, and it drove him to drink.

(As I am presently writing about these past memories, I wonder if the winter depression I deal with every year has something to do with the trauma of the duration I had to spend in those tunnels. The wintertime here in Wisconsin has very dark gray skies, and it's cold and wet. It's as if in my subconscious, I'm back in those tunnels. Hmm.)

I learned a valuable lesson that I'd keep learning throughout my career. If you do something really well and quickly so that you don't have to do it anymore, it can sometimes come back to bite you in the ass. If you perform a task better than someone else can, they may keep "you" as the person to perform that task (as in from tunnel to tunnel to tunnel).

I still had to help my buddy maintain the dust collectors on Mondays until the task was completed before heading down to the tunnels. Every morning, a super loud whistle blew to start the workday and the change of shifts in the mills. That thing was so loud it was obnoxious. Heaven help you if you came to work with a hangover and had to endure that "devils' horn"! On some mornings, the man in charge of pulling the lever to sound that whistle just hung on that lever so the sound continued for an eternity. I always said that if I ever found out which asshole—I mean, guy—was in charge of sounding that whistle, I'd break his arm off and beat him severely with it!

One morning, I'd had enough of that earsplitting torture. I'd broken one of my eardrums surfing big waves one day, so maybe it hurt my ears more than the guys. I didn't know and I didn't care. I looked over at my dust collector buddy who liked to place bets with me (that were more like dares) and said, "I'm going to STEAL that son of a bitch! A hundred dollars if I do?"

He looked over at me and chuckled, then he said, "You're on, kid." We made a rule that I had to do it within a week's time.

As we set off to change some damaged dust collector sleeves, I asked him if I could borrow some of the long lengths of rope he had in his shop. He was happy to help me in the great adventure I was about to embark upon. He also loaned me a couple of his GIANT pipe wrenches. That "huge" whistle had been up on the roof at the highest point of the mills since the buildings had been erected many years ago. I made sure to stash the safety belt that I used to be lowered into the silos along with the rope I borrowed from my buddy. I knew that I would need both of my hands to disassemble the whistle from its mounted position and would need to tie myself to something so that I wouldn't fall from the roof. I had never been up there and wasn't sure what to expect after making the climb to get up there.

I had a laborer buddy I'd been partnered up with on a lot of my most miserable jobs. We had become friends, and he was my first choice to be my accomplice. First I had to invite him to join me in ingesting a few ice-cold beers after work in order to ask him to go on my excursion with me. Lucky for me, he accepted to be my partner in crime. When I then asked the cost for his services, he asked that I pay him with more beer (cheap labor! I could afford the cost of a few more brewskis).

On our specified evening after work, I wore dark clothing and drove back up north to the tiny town the cement plant was located in. I met my buddy at the tavern there and downed some liquid courage. We entered the plant through the woods on the plant's southern boundary. We made our way to the mill that had the whistle mounted on the roof. That building was where we located my stashed pipe wrenches and safety belts with ropes. The climb up to the roof was rough. That building was equal in height to a five-story building.

Since the metal structure was so old, we used the worn areas in the exterior wall for footholds. We also used whatever railings and skeletal structures and machinery to climb up to the roof. The pipe wrenches were heavy and cumbersome to climb with.

Once we had made it onto the roof, we had to be very careful where we stepped so that we wouldn't fall through the weak and eroded areas.

Trying to unscrew the whistle from its mount proved to be much harder than I thought because in all the years it had perched there, the fog and rain had caused the cement in the air to harden onto the whistle. In fact, it was entirely encased in cement. However difficult it would prove in being removed, I did not make that hair-raising climb for nothing and was not planning on doing it again. The whistle was coming home with us one way or another.

It was a good thing that neither one of us was afraid of heights because we were up there for quite a while. We finally just wrenched the whistle off of the pipe it was screwed onto the best that we could. The threads were completely trashed, and they would not be able to screw another whistle onto that particular pipe, but I couldn't have cared less about that; in fact, I considered it to be a bonus. We tied the long ropes to the whistle which was about four feet tall, eighteen inches in diameter, and was heavier than hell. We lowered it over an area below that was vacant of any machinery. We hung onto it until it became too heavy to hang onto anymore and then let it fall to the ground. We did the same thing with the two heavy pipe wrenches.

After we carefully descended to the ground, we carried the pipe wrenches back to the dust collector shop and hid them from sight until I could return them to their proper place during work hours. The whistle was so heavy that we rolled it out to the parking area and stashed it into the bushes until I could walk back and retrieve my truck to come pick it up.

The two of us had a hell of a time picking it up and blocking it in place so that it wouldn't roll around in my truck bed as I drove home. We drove home to catch whatever shut-eye we could before returning to work the next morning. I rolled the whistle into my mom's garage and hid it underneath all the plastic that surrounded my potter's wheel. There it remained for a few years.

The following morning is one of my favorite memories out of all three years I endured working in that hellhole. All the crew gathered together in order for the bastard foreman to dispatch us to our duties for the day. My dust collector buddy was in attendance. We all waited and waited for the whistle to blow so that our work day could begin…to no avail. The longer the silence grew, the redder the face of the bastard foreman became. "Why, that son of a bitch!" he yelled as he became totally unglued. I wanted to laugh so hard that I was crying with joy inside myself.

My accomplice and I just stared straight ahead with bored, impatient, and neutral looks on our faces. I glanced over at my dust collector buddy, and he was looking bored as well. When he glanced over in my direction, I winked at him and rubbed my forefinger and thumb together as if to signal *"Hand over MY money,"* He caught my wink and gesture, then his whole face contorted into an utterly shocked expression. Then he shook his head, faced the ground, and a huge smile broke out all over his face. He couldn't believe that I'd actually stolen that damn obnoxious whistle!

We got a little longer to hang out before we had to begin our workday because the bastard foreman was completely beside himself that no whistle had been blown. He stomped off in a rage to the main office to find out what in the hell was going on. That was one time where my being a female worked to my advantage. I was viewed by most men there to be the "weaker" sex and not even considered to be a culprit in that prank.

The men assumed the whistle was to have broken somehow. No one at that time was willing to climb up onto that roof (and wouldn't for a very long time). They figured out that it was due to a malfunction in the lever or the air valve that caused the whistle to be silent. They had no clue that it was no longer perched on top of the roof.

Later on in the afternoon, I found the time to return the borrowed ropes and pipe wrenches to my dust collector buddy. He smiled broadly when he saw me approaching and said, "That's the best one hundred dollars I've ever spent. Just to see that motherf——s face as red as a beet and angry as a snorting bull!" The next day, when he handed me that one hundred dollars, a revised vision of the new pair of shoes I'd had my heart set on but lost in our chewing tobacco bet reappeared.

Since there was no whistle to blast our eardrums out every morning, we were dispatched in a much less rude fashion. The bastard foreman actually had to "act" like a foreman and "ask us" to gather around himself so that he could tell us what our jobs would be for the day.

Months passed before an article appeared in our town's local newspaper about the missing whistle. They had investigated the top of the roof to see if it could be repaired and had found it missing entirely. The cement plant offered a reward for its return. It turned out to be an antique whistle made entirely of brass, and it was off of a well-known ship from many decades ago. It had quite a historical past that increased its value. There was also an award offered for any information into its whereabouts. I didn't want to end up in court over a silly teenage prank that I'd played, so the whistle remained hidden in my mom's garage for a very long time.

Later on down the road, I met a lot of ironworkers who came to the cement plant to erect the iron portion of a new building being constructed. One of the ironworkers named Tank (he was a really BIG guy!) was from a state in the Midwest. Upon his returning trip home, he took the whistle far away from California for me—*WHEW!* Looking back, I wish I would've kept it. It had needed to be acid dipped to remove all the years of accumulated cement that coated it (and made it so goddamned heavy!). An antique ship's whistle made of solid brass would be worth a small fortune. It was too bad I didn't know what was underneath all of that cement when I absconded with it.

The pulverizing of stone and mixing it with other ingredients was done in these huge kilns. There were four of them and they were lined with special bricks that could withstand extremely high temperatures that it took to successfully combine the products. Golf ballsized steel balls would tumble inside the rotating kilns, pulverizing and combining the materials within them.

The kilns were giant cylinder shaped tubes with steel doors at both ends. They were lined on their interiors with special bricks made just for them. They had a unique shape that were basically a wedge. The cement plant employed masons that had been trained on how to replace all the worn-out bricks with new ones. It didn't take long for the steel balls tumbling constantly on those very hot bricks as the kilns rotated to destroy them.

The masons tapped the bricks into place with their uniquely designed hammers so that the wedged shaped bricks held each other in place. Also used were thin steel cards that were tapped into any space in order to keep the bricks held tightly together. Once one side of a kiln had the eroded bricks removed and the new bricks inserted, the kiln would be rotated to the next portion to proceed with that process of removing the old bricks and tapping in the new ones.

That process would take about a week to complete. In the first place, the kiln to be worked on had to be shut down for a couple of days in order to cool down enough for people to safely enter it. As laborers, it was our job to remove all the expired bricks. We picked the bricks up by hand and filled our wheelbarrows with them. We wheeled them down a ramp we made with planks of lumber and dumped them over a railed edge of the floor we were working on. A Bobcat skid-steer loader scooped up the bricks with its bucket and drove them out to our dump area. We also brought in the new bricks to be inserted into the kiln with our wheelbarrows.

The temperatures were so hot to work in that it was as if you were working in a sauna all day. You had to be careful not to touch any exposed iron such as the door of the kiln or you would incur a nasty burn. The poor masons would sweat bullets all day working in there.

There were four kilns, and if one was down, the other three were still rolling nonstop and were hotter than hell to walk among them or be anywhere near them, for that matter. I dropped pounds off my body by sweating all throughout each day that I worked on those kilns. I drank water as much as possible in order to replace as much moisture as I could. I never had an appetite while working in that extreme heat.

Each of the four kilns was around eighty feet long. When you walked inside one, you could not touch the ceiling overhead; those things were massive. In the mornings, when you were given your assignments for the day and you heard the bastard foreman mention the word *kiln,* the men would utter a dreadful groan. Some of the men would be joining me in the hell called a "kiln" because I was always the first on the bastard foreman's guest list of attendees for the day. I think he was hoping that I'd melt away into oblivion in there.

Women would be hired in the front office and then join us in the yard to be given their assignments. The bastard foreman would give them a super hard laborious job for the day, and then they would quit at the end of it. I'll never forget one girl who showed up naive as to what she was in for. He took her for a tour of the cement plant in his truck and then drove up into the quarry in the mountains behind the plant. He always drove so fast, like a bat out of hell. Those dirt roads were very rocky and bumpy. At a fast clip, you were bouncing up and down in your seat. Anytime I got in the truck with him, I wore my hard hat due to the crazy amount of bouncing his driving caused his passengers. I remember hitting the ceiling of his truck with my hard hat, grateful that I was wearing it.

That poor girl didn't put her hard hat on (nor did the bastard foreman suggest that she wear it). She hit her head so hard on the roof of his truck that she had to be driven into town and taken to the hospital emergency room. It took forty-five minutes just to drive back to town. She had severe whiplash and, due to her neck injury, quit the job immediately and sued the company. I never found out if she was successful in her court battle or not. My guess was that since she didn't have her hard hat on that her court case was dropped.

From all the jackhammering I'd endured, my fingers rattled around loosely in their sockets. I had to tape my fingers together before I could squeeze the trigger and jackhammer any further. I had developed acute tendinitis in both of my shoulders, my right elbow, and left wrist. The tendinitis was most likely from striking an iron pump over my head with a sledgehammer. Whenever I was assigned that job, I had limited movement because I was balancing on the top of a rolling ladder. It had a small area of platform on its top for me to stand on while I worked. That job always needed to be performed after the demolition expert blasted the silos in order to release the concrete stuck to their interior walls. I was to pound the chute in the hopes of assisting the cement chunks to travel through the pump. I would pound on the chute for the entire workday and sometimes well into the following day also. It was a very unnatural position to hold your arms and shoulders in, especially for that length of time.

The worst issues concerning my health that I had to deal with were the migraine headaches I began to get and the sharp stomach pains. I was screamed at for three years by the bastard foreman before all the health issues came to a head. I had to take about a month off of work in order to calm the inflammation in my shoulders and my arms. I was already wearing an elbow brace as well as one on my wrist. Way before the month break I had to take, I'd begun carrying a bottle of Pepto Bismol in my overalls pocket. I'd feel stabbing pains in my stomach as soon as the bastard foreman started screaming at me. His face would turn beet-red and he'd get real close to my face before he began screaming. He absolutely hated my guts (looking back, I think it was what I represented and stood for). It didn't matter how hard I worked or what a good job I did. He never behaved in that manner with a man unless he screwed up royally, but as for me, it was a daily occurrence.

I ended up being diagnosed with peptic ulcers in my stomach. I was only nineteen years old at the time. At the end of the month that the doctor had me take off from work to heal my tendinitis, I felt like a new person. Although I couldn't surf and could only teach my karate class without participating in my other karate classes, the stress was relieved, and therefore, my stomach was able to heal too. Butting heads with the bastard foreman everyday was not good for my physical and mental health—I'd had enough.

I was really going to miss the good wages I was making, but my body was deteriorating rapidly at a very young age. I should have tried the shift work and scrambled my karate schedule accordingly, but instead, I quit. Wouldn't you know that when I drove up to the cement plant to speak with the bastard foreman about terminating my employment, he spoke to me for the first time without yelling at me? His face didn't turn red. I thought I could have worked there for many years if he'd only treated me in that humane manner.

Those three years were very hard for me to endure at that very young age. As I write this chapter about my experiences at the cement plant, I realize that I would've rather spent my hours there with the rattlesnakes and the resident mountain lion than with the men I was working with. If I were to go back in time with my present knowledge and wisdom, I would have RULED that place. A few years after I had left my employment there, an ex-boyfriend of mine accidently stepped into one of the channels of augers that carried the cement dust through the plant. He lost the lower portion of his leg below the knee. The moving augers were covered only with pieces of plywood, grating, or lumber so that workers in their various areas of the plant could sweep any of the spilled cement dust into them (waste not, want not, I guess). We always had to be careful crossing over the covered augers with our wheelbarrows so as not to dislodge them. He was offered a settlement and a job for a lifetime there. OSHA would have had a field day with that place; there would have been fines left and right.

Little did I know that the experience of working at the cement plant was training for the career I'd end up with in my future. As for the bastard foreman, he was an "amateur" asshole in comparison to the first man I would eventually marry. My first husband was a booming ironworker who was from Milwaukee, Wisconsin. A boomer is any tradesman transplanted to an area located outside their local jurisdiction to work a job. This occurs when work is lacking in a tradesmans area. To make a living, they must travel away from their homes to do so.

I should have stuck with my initial gut feeling. When I first met my future first husband, I couldn't stand the sight of him. He had come into my town to erect a new iron structure at the cement plant. As time grew on, he wore me down with his charms. On our first date, I showed up with a hell of a purple shiner and seven stitches in my eyebrow above it. I'd gotten both in a full contact karate sparring match a few hours beforehand. I only had to wear a closely matching eyeshadow on my healthy eye to try and match my purple shiner one. Back then, in karate classes, there were no safety pads or helmets; no mats on the floors we fought on. Little was I to know that my future husband would give me so many black eyes that I couldn't count them all. It should have been a clue to myself when he had no qualms about my appearance when I showed up for our first date.

It was due to the three years that I'd spent in cement plant hell that made me swear that I'd never have another job like that one ever again. You know how the saying goes, though: "Never say never."

I'd joined my first husband in Milwaukee (he was my boyfriend at the time) after he'd gone back to his home there and sent me a oneway ticket. Moving past a lot of history, I'll just say that we ended up getting married and having our daughter. My mom mailed me clippings from our town's local newspaper that had articles about two women who had been working at the cement plant; they were almost killed there.

They were creating a lot of friction by bringing the abusive treatment they had endured there to the media. In particular, they acknowledged the actions of the bastard foreman. The men working at the plant wanted those two women gone. They were not meshing with the men there whatsoever. One afternoon, as the two women were driving a vehicle up into the quarry, a bulldozer on top of the cliff above them pushed huge boulders over its edge. The boulders fell from the cliff top and crushed the vehicle the women were in. They were lucky to have survived and were suing the cement plant in court. If the men had succeeded in killing the two women, it most likely would have been believable as an accident. They were way up in the mountains with no witnesses other than the bulldozer operator.

As I read the newspaper clippings about those two women's ordeals at the cement plant, it was clear to me that the atmosphere and the attitudes of the majority of men remained the same as they were when I worked there.

My ironworker husband wouldn't let up with his idea of me joining a union in the trades of construction. There was no other work I could do that was a good enough job in his mind's eye. I had bartended and been a bouncer in two different bars. I'd worked nights cleaning one of our huge medical colleges. My final job I had before I caved in to his daily nagging about it was as a manager in the shoe department, lamp, gift, and candy areas of an expensive retail store we once had here. I personally couldn't have afforded to shop there.

Yes, I wanted to be paid more money. Yes, I wanted good health insurance. And, yes, I wanted a pension. Therefore, all of my husband's nagging wore me down. He had actually begun that crusade of his while we were in my home state of California. He told me about all the facets of ironwork, such as rod busting (which I was definitely NOT attracted to). Rod busters are the men you see bent over all day, tying wire around the iron rods to hold them together on bridges before the concrete is poured to encase them. They also tie rods for columns and walls for structures. That work is incredibly hard on your back, knees, and wrists.

There is structural ironwork which I thought would be exciting but extremely dangerous. My husband was involved in the structural aspect of ironwork. He was a "connector"; that's the guy you see way up in the air, grabbing the piece of iron the crane swings into place and bolts it to the piece that, in the past, he would be standing or sitting on. He and his partner, who is located on the opposite side of the iron piece being set, slowly piece together the entire structure. It's the two connectors along with the rigging crew on the ground that piece together a giant puzzle which is the structure they are creating.

You must remember that back when he was an ironworker, there were no lifts that you see the men standing in today. They were not tied off with safety harnesses on and there were no safety nets set up below them. They had a special gift of balance that allowed them to walk across iron beams that could be as narrow as six inches wide, and they did that high above the ground. Needless to say, they didn't suffer from a fear of heights, and if they fell from their beam to the ground, they died—talk about living on the edge.

He let me try on his tool belt he used when connecting iron. It had pockets of strong canvas to hold the nuts, washers, and bolts that were used to hold each piece of iron together. The belt also had holders for him to carry his sleever bars. Those are the unique bars made of a heavy steel. It is the ultimate ironworker's connecting tool. One end is in the shape of a wrench, and it's used to tighten the bolt and nut once it's through two pieces of iron being connected to each other. The other end is tapered to a point and looks like a ring-sizer (which is one of the ways in which I use mine). The tapered end is put through the bolt holes on both pieces of iron and assists in lining up the pattern in order to insert the bolts in their proper position.

My husband's tool belt weighed about forty pounds. The belt rides on the hips and rides offset due to the weight of the sleever bars carried in the holster portions. It causes you to compensate for carrying more weight on one side of your body, making it very hard to walk erect and not lean to one side. That makes the connecting job a lot harder than it looks (as if the heights involved didn't already make the job more difficult). Most ironworkers develop major back issues and many end up needing back surgery. I know of two neck surgeries and three back surgeries that my ironworker husband had performed on him.

The job of "connecting" as an ironworker sounded hard but exciting to me—a real challenge. I had skydived a couple of times and was not afraid of heights. Before I moved from my beach town in California, I was preparing to try hang gliding for my next adventure. That's a sport where you run off a cliff, holding onto a piece of equipment that looks like a glorified paper airplane! You jump from the cliff, hoping there are wind currents there to assist you in a graceful flight to the ground below. I'd surfed waves up and down the coast of California and into Mexico for over a decade. My adventurous side was intrigued by the idea of being paid to remain up in the air all day.

Then there is "ornamental" ironwork. Ornamental ironwork is a much safer division of ironwork. It consists of creating the beautiful and ornate gates and fences that you see incorporated into building construction. I met an ironworker in California who had an ornamental iron business with his father. He had informed me of a welding course that I should take, and after I completed the course,

I would be hired on to work in his shop if I wished to do so. That offer was contingent upon my acceptance into the local ironworker's union.

I took the welding course at our local college as my buddy had suggested. I have a funny story about what transpired during one of my classes. When I arrived at the classroom, I recognized the instructor as one of my father's longtime friends. I had my welding hood down over my face and was practicing welding when all of a sudden, I felt hands on my chest. I couldn't see anything through the extremely dark welding lenses that had been inserted into my welding hood. Then I was knocked to the ground while I felt hands tapping on my boobs!

I wrestled the man (there were no other women in the class other than myself) off of me and jumped to my feet as I ripped the welding helmet from my head. I screamed, "What the hell?" as I stood in a karate stance and prepared to defend myself. The instructor jumped back to distance himself from me and said, "I had to put the flames out! Your chest was on fire!" I looked down at my chest and saw that my shirt had a huge hole burnt in it. I must have had a funny and shocked expression on my face because all my male classmates started roaring with laughter.

I hadn't smelled my shirt as it was burning and had a T-shirt on under it, so I didn't feel the heat from the fire either. I had to first thank my instructor for putting out the fire on my chest, and then I had to apologize for nearly slugging him in the face. He said to me, "If you catch on fire again, you're on your own!" When my dad heard from his buddy (my instructor) that I almost kicked his ass for putting the fire out on my chest, my dad thought that it was hilarious.

I was invited to Wisconsin before I was to be sent out of the ironworkers union hall as an apprentice. What I ended up doing after the constant nagging about rejoining the construction work-force was to go through all the listings of local unions in the phone book. I called each one and asked if they were accepting applications for apprentices.

I also asked if I could fill out any required forms right away and if they had any testing they wanted me to complete. If they answered yes to my questions, I asked when and where they wanted me to go. I ended up filling out applications for the unions of electricians, steamfitters, boilermakers and glaziers. They are the installers of windows called "sash" and glass that is used in the construction of buildings. I had high hopes of joining the elevators and escalators union because it was clean work, you were out of the elements, and therefore were not interrupted by the weather conditions. The list was very long, however, for their apprentices waiting to be sent out to work. If I had joined that particular union, it could have been years before I was sent out in the field.

The ironworkers put me on their apprenticeship list right away. What I had going for me was that as a woman, I was considered a "minority," and the state was making it mandatory for the unions to expand in hiring them. My husband had been an ironworker since he was a teenager, so that helped me get into that union; his older brother was also an ironworker. My husband had been nicknamed Goldie as in Goldie Locks because as an apprentice, he had very long blond hair.

Most of the ironworkers I had met I knew mostly by their nick-names. They had given each other some very odd names such as Tank, Skidrow, Crazy George, Hog, Drifter, Helicopter Pad—I could go on and on. When I ended up working on future construc-tion projects with them, the nicknames they came up with for me were Suzy Q or just Q for short. Another was HB for Heartless Bitch, which was my nickname in high school when I bothered to show up there. I'm pretty sure my husband leaked that one out to the men. Then, of course, there were Bitch and Cunt on occasion.

My husband also told me to sign up with the operating engineers union because there were no construction jobs without the heavy equipment used to make them possible. In all iron erection projects, they needed at least one crane on the premises. When I asked him how I'd learn to operate one, he told me that all of the big cranes were run by the operator who was assisted by an "oiler." The oiler learned from the operator how to operate the crane while maintaining the crane. The oiler performed most of the maintenance on the crane by greasing, oiling, and cleaning it. The oiler was on the jobsite one half hour before the other workers. They earn "grease time pay" by unlocking the crane, removing its window covers, checking its fluid levels, greasing and oiling it. They had the crane running so that it was warmed up and ready to go. The crew and operator would show to the jobsite, and work would begin for the day.

He told me to ask for an oiler's position. However, after filling out an application to enter their apprenticeship program and taking their written test, they told me that they never heard of an oiler. I told them that was funny because my ironworker husband worked with them all the time, and he was the person who told me to sign up for the job. I was then told that they would get back to me with a date and a time for me to drive north to their school. I was to take a field test in one of their pieces of equipment. Apparently, they were not as excited as the ironworkers to have a female minority in their midst of thousands of heavy equipment operators. In fact, later on, when I was accepted into their union, I was only one of five women at that time.

I will mention at this time that I had already tested to enter the apprenticeships of the steamfitters and the boiler makers. They had simple tests to do such as what shape fits where, tests that reminded me of the toys I played with as a small child, such as stacking blocks or braiding cords. Easy enough, I thought, that I'd passed those tests with flying colors. Instead, I was informed by both of those unions that they didn't find me "coordinated" enough to perform their work. That was a crock of shit. I'd been crocheting, knitting, doing karate, surfing, making jewelry, sewing, and making pottery for decades. They just didn't want any women among them.

I had an out and out threat delivered to me from a Glazier I'd served as a patron in one of the establishments I bartended in and was a bouncer for. I'd signed up for an apprenticeship in the Glaziers union he'd been a long time member of. He told me that I would most likely have an "accident" on the job if I was accepted into his union. That's a long fall to the ground if you happen to be installing windows in a skyscraper.

I ignored that asshole's comment and was placed on the list of apprentices waiting to be accepted to work on a jobsite. Although an ironworker's son had signed up after me to go out on a jobsite to work as an apprentice Glazier, they sent him out before me. He was an Indian, and I was a woman, so we were both minorities. I never received a phone call from that union offering me a job. Trying to get hired in a male dominated industry was like banging my head against a brick wall.

I finally received a phone call from the operating engineers union to set up a date for me to field test at their school up north.

I was asked if I had any experience with heavy equipment, and I told them of my work as a laborer many years ago. I told them that as a laborer, I operated a Bobcat skid-steer loader from time to time. When I arrived at the school, I saw that it was built on many acres of land. I was driven out to a level area with a Bobcat parked nearby. The instructor who had driven me out there pointed to a large square that had been painted on the soil. He wanted me to dig a basement within the painted square down to a depth of six feet, using the skid-steer loader. He would return in a couple of hours to check on my progress. I was surprised to find myself at ease in the seat of the Bobcat because it had been years since I had operated one.

I did the best that I could, and when the instructor returned, he took a few measurements of the depth in various spots of the "basement" that I had dug. He told me that I'd done a good job and that he wanted me to fill the hole back in so that it looked as it had before I began the excavation. I knew that it would take me a lot less time to fill it back in and would also be a lot easier to do.

He seemed pleased with my results when he came back to pick me up and take me back to my vehicle. He told me that after discussing my results with the necessary men who chose the apprenticeship candidates, someone would call me with their decision. Within two weeks, I received the call notifying me that I was selected as an apprentice for their union and also told me the contractor who I would begin working for.

My ironworker husband was ecstatic when I told him the news. He would no longer have to leave town to find work or go out of state if he chose not to. He set me up with some of his old work clothes and safety attire. He also loaned me some of his tools until I could purchase my own.

I had no idea what I was in for as I headed off to begin the first day of my new career. I worked alongside a foreman and his crew to separate the boom sections of a crane that were to be loaded out on semitrailers and taken back to the yard of our contractor. They had just finished a piledriving job. The foreman was quite good-looking, charming, and he readily explained to me what we were doing so that I could understand. It was easy to learn from him; he was a good teacher. It's very strange how life surprises you because neither one of us knew on that very first day that we would go on our first date eleven years later! Until that time, I had developed a crush on him that I kept privately to myself because we were both married back then. I think it was my mind's way of taking me somewhere away from my abusive marriage mentally.

I ignored those feelings and plundered on through my difficult marriage. I focused on doing the best that I could both in my personal life as well as my newfound professional one. After my first day of work, I was exhausted. Everything I lifted or carried that day seemed to weigh a ton. I felt as though I'd been lifting weights at the gym all day. I was also filthy, dirty, and had grease all over me. When I arrived home after work, I told my husband that I understood why he sat in his recliner and took a nap immediately after his workday ended (on those rare days when he didn't stop at the tavern before coming home). I resolved never to nag him about his napping after work ever again. Of course, I received the "I told you so" speech on how construction work takes such a toll on you.

I may as well tell you right off the bat that my marriage was a "war zone" from day to day. If I hadn't had my martial arts training, my marriage wouldn't have lasted the sixteen years that it did. I had left several times and had tried to divorce him as well but never had the proper resources or funds to finalize a divorce and go our separate ways. Having a child with him made it impossible for me to leave. I did not want to leave her with him. Without me there, she was defenseless. In fact, what finally terminated our marriage was when he was trying to climb over my downed and injured body in order to most certainly harm her, but I'll write about that later on in this book.

Every day at work, I learned new ways of taking care of myself out in the elements. I kept extra clothing in my vehicle in case the weather changed. I added first aid products to my very large lunch box. The size of my lunch box made it a handy seat or table if I was working out in the middle of nowhere. It was also large enough to contain extra food and water in case I had to work overtime unexpectedly. I had extra safety gear in my vehicle such as gloves, sunglasses, and rain gear. As a crane operator, I carried various greases, solvents, and lubricants for whatever machine I was operating. Grease guns, rags, and tools were also in my vehicle. I had Gojo to take a "whore's bath" at the end of each day to remove the grease from myself before entering my vehicle to leave for home.

I've always been interested in how things came to be, how they worked, and why. For what purpose were they invented? How things get from point A to point B. I can't imagine the thought process someone has to go through to put their thoughts onto paper in manufacturing plans, architectural designs, and engineering schematics. The cranes I learned to operate were the old friction rigs. Those cranes were Manitowoc, Americans, Linkbelt, Lima, Komatsu, and hydraulic cranes. I also learned to operate Lieberman tower cranes which were electric.

The older Manitowoc models had long levers that resembled plow handles that you would see on old farm tractors. My feet were the only things holding the brakes. Nowadays, cranes are equipped with hydraulic assist. In cranes such as those, you flip a switch that turns your crane from friction to hydraulic. That scenario relieves your body from having to keep constant pressure on the brakes. Toward the end of my career, those cranes were becoming the norm on the construction site. They were designed to eliminate aspects involving human error.

Whenever I operated a crane of that design, I couldn't believe how much better I felt at the end of the day.

I've also operated the big red Manitowoc cranes that you see everywhere, erecting large tall structures. Although those larger cranes appear more intimidating because of their size, they are actually easier to operate. They are capable of lifting enormous weights due to the rigging required to make those picks; they also move a lot slower. Cranes are also equipped with computers now. They calculate your lifting capacities and the radius you can safely work in. They tell you the proper boom angle in which to hoist or lower your load. Those cranes have sensors located in various areas connected to the computer. If you enter into any unsafe territory, the computer will then shut you down. Once again, those measures are taken to reduce operator error.

Throughout the years of my career, I had no computers to provide me with information in any of the cranes I worked with. During the years I worked, we operated by "the seat of your pants." You had to know the weights of the loads you were picking. You needed to refer to your load charts to configure your boom angle for each pick. If you were pushing the limits, so to speak, and the ass end of your crane began creeping up off the ground, the squirming sensation in your gut or the puckering of your asshole (thus the moniker "by the seat of your pants") was the "sensor" you had that told you enough was enough. In my day, those limits were tested fairly regularly on jobsites, forcing me to think, *Why the hell didn't you get a bigger crane for this job?* The answer to that question was always the same: $$$$$! They didn't want to spend any more money than was absolutely necessary. You will find that reoccurring motto throughout jobsites today. Another practice that I dealt with time and again was the question of "What can we get this little lady to do for us?" Meaning, "What can we get away with here?" or "What can we talk her into doing?"

The answer to all that bullshit was easy: NOTHING. If you know your stuff, you stand your ground. It was my ass on the line, not theirs. My motto of "boobs are bigger than balls" came into play on those occasions where they thought I could be intimidated into pushing the limits of safety and logical thinking. When learning to operate a crane, I was taught that the ultimate decision to make a pick or not was determined by the operator. A few times, I was told to "do it or they'd find someone else who would."

I would respond by saying, "Good luck with that," and then I'd explain why the pick couldn't be made in the manner they expected. I'd also provide an alternative plan of action.

It's easy for people who have never sat in the seat of a crane to seek the impossible because they have no knowledge of how the machine works. It could be very aggravating at times but understandable. I had no idea what it was like to stand around all day, twiddling my thumbs and barking out orders while everyone else busted their asses all day either.

I will tell you about our operator's school. As an apprentice, you are required to have scheduled classroom time where it is explained to you how to perform maintenance on your equipment and why it's necessary to do so. Safety first is pounded into your head, and dangerous scenarios are played out while informing you on how to react in an appropriate, safe, and calm manner. First aid and CPR are taught as well.

The first year I was scheduled for my classroom education, I figured it was a good opportunity for me to add to my growing work of body art. I figured that I would be sitting indoors, so the large tattoo I was getting on my back would have time to heal before I had to return to the great outdoors to work.

After getting the tattoo, I cut a huge hole in the back of my flannel shirt so that the material would not stick to my freshly inked design. The guys in my class thought I was nuts, but that was only their beginning introduction into my personal style and character I was bringing into their future.

All was well until we had to go walk a picket line out in the frigid cold, ice, and snow of winter! I had to reluctantly pull on my one-piece Carhart coveralls and pray that my new ink didn't stick too badly to the material when I peeled them off at night. "Ouch!" is all I will say to that, even though there were a lot of other four letter words thrown in.

The other half of apprenticeship training each year is held outdoors. Those apprenticeship classes are held during the winter months when work is slow for everyone. It not only taught you how to deal with a giant frozen machine but how to remain outside in *all sorts of weather* conditions. By the time I'd been in construction for five or so years, I could easily handle temperatures well below freezing. If it dropped below fifteen degrees, I'd have had a harder time being outside all day. The windchill factor was the true temperature that you needed to dress for. The wind drops the temperature significantly.

My first year at the school, learning outside was tough for me because my old fart instructor didn't want to be the guy with a girl in his class. When he took us out in the back forty to where the practice cranes were parked, he made sure to stick me in the oldest piece of shit crane they had there. It was so old that it looked like a huge metal box on tracks. It had a boom and big long plow handle levers to operate it. I had to use both of my arms to push or pull its levers. I also had to literally stand on the brakes in order to lock them into place. It had a "live" boom, which means that if you were not paying attention, it would run. That means that it would start booming down on its own, gaining speed along with its descent. I had to grab the boom hoist lever and raise it back up ASAP! Later on in my career, I operated an old Manitowoc crane mounted on a barge that had a live boom also.

You can hear a boom running. It makes a high-pitched whirring sound. The sound is made from the cable that holds the boom up as it unwinds off of its drum at high speed. Learning to operate that old piece of shit crane up at the school prepared me to be able to operate that barge mounted Manitowoc.

We performed different functions in those cranes at the school and became familiar with what we would be dealing with on a jobsite. When I asked the instructor why we were learning on those older model cranes, he replied, "If you can operate those old machines, you can operate anything!" He was absolutely correct. Those words stuck with me throughout my career.

Most of the cranes I encountered to operate were a piece of cake in comparison to those old contraptions I'd learned on at the school. I recited the instructors motto to the young men and the couple of women I passed my knowledge on to.

I was given a two-year apprenticeship. They took one year off from their usual three-year term due to my prior three years I'd spent as a laborer. That was because I'd learned to operate a few pieces of equipment during those years. It's to your advantage to become a union apprentice if you are considering a career in the trades. They find work for you, and you have business agents that protect your rights on the jobsite and monitor them to make sure that those rights are not violated. If any concerns arise for you, they are there to correct and manage them. My business agents helped me time and time again throughout my career.

The school the operating engineers have now is outstanding. When I went up there for my apprenticeship years, it was only a barracks type building that we stayed in. It held many beds and only had one bathroom. They turned a large utility closet within the building into a small room for me to sleep in. Directly outside my room was the television viewing area. There were rows of chairs set up so that we could watch television in the evenings if anyone desired to. That made it hard for me to get a good night's sleep with all the noise from the television and the men talking.

I had noticed that a majority of the men had come up to enjoy time away from their families. Those guys hit the taverns as soon as class ended at three-thirty. They came in late at night, drunk, and were hungover the following morning. I myself brought up my snow skis, workout gear, crocheting, and even my shotgun to hunt pheasant on the nearby public hunting grounds. One night, as I was attempting to sleep on my cot, I heard my door slowly opening. I said to the man who had entered, "What the hell are you doing in here?"

He told me that he had made a mistake, thinking that my door was the bathroom entrance. *Right,* I thought to myself as a red flag popped up in my head. After that, I pried a chair up under my doorknob and slept with only one earplug instead of two so that I could hear anyone attempting to enter my room again.

Sure enough, a few evenings later after the intrusion, I could hear my doorknob turning once again as I tried to get some sleep; the chair I'd propped up there seemed to do its job as a barricade. That man continually invited me to join him for dinner or to have a drink with him. I always declined and reminded him that although I wasn't wearing a wedding ring, *I was a married woman.* That never seemed to hinder his advances at all or kept him from attempting to enter my room during the evening hours.

I began to notice him at the stores or gas stations I went to after class. I had become friends with a couple of guys who were my age and also apprentices staying in the barracks building with me. They had noticed my unwanted admirer lurking around my closed door at night and remained in the television viewing room after all the other guys had retired for the evening. They had even noticed him following me around town while I was shopping.

They told me that I was more than welcome to join them when they went to dinner after class. They were so nice to have my back and they were both perfect gentlemen. One of them was so shy that he hardly spoke a word, and his married buddy told me how upset he would be if a man were stalking his wife; that was why they decided that they would look out for me.

I didn't take my problem with that man to the authorities at the school because I realized that by being one of the first women in the union to stay at the school, I represented all the women who would join in the future. I had to make it clear that women could handle themselves in a calm manner and could troubleshoot their way through any problem that arose. I didn't want to give them any reason at all to question whether women belonged in that business or not.

I had worked hard through the years to prove beyond a shadow of a doubt that women brought attributes that were unique, team building, soothing, and complimentary to the jobsite. I also made it clear that we would *not take any shit from any man at any time.*

When I went home on the weekend, I informed my ironworker husband about my "fan" who had become my stalker. He gave me this advice: "Kick his ass, but don't do it on the school's property. When this happens on a jobsite, because it's going to, you wait until you're in the parking area. That way, the school or the jobsite won't be liable for any costs for damages or legal charges that the man might incur." Trust me when I tell you that I put that advice to use on several occasions.

The following Monday, I was back at the school and found my shadow following me around the grocery store after class once again.

I went up to him in a calm manner and said, "I don't need your uninvited attention. I told my husband about you, and his advice to me was to *kick your ass* if you continue to follow me around. I've got two black belts, one in each of two styles. That means that I know countless ways to break both of your arms and keep you from operating anything for a long time. If I hear you attempting to enter my room at night again and I don't feel like breaking a sweat, my shotgun I hunt pheasants with up here is right next to my cot. I may mistake you for an intruder trying to rob us all while we're asleep and have to put it to use. I think you can figure out where I'm going with this. Now FUCK OFF!"

At the end of school that first year, I decided to inform the instructors about the stalker's behavior. I told them about that particular man stalking me the entire time I was there and about him trying to enter my room at night. I said that I could take care of myself but that another woman may not be able or willing to do so. They seemed shocked that I had dealt with that behavior and thanked me for bringing it to their attention. They apologized and told me that if I had come forward with that information sooner, they would have expelled the man from our school. I told them that I wanted women to be welcome there without any concerns about having to give them special treatment. I assured them that us women were perfectly capable of entering the men's workforce (and dominating). They told me that they would be keeping a close eye on that operator if he returned to the school in the future.

At the end of that winter season, I was attending a union meeting when an instructor from the school approached me. He told me that a short time after I'd left the school, the asshole operator enrolled in another one of the classes offered there. A young lady was up there taking her required apprenticeship course at the same time. He immediately began stalking her as he had done to me. This time, the instructors were watching for his disturbing behavior. He actually scared the young woman to the point in which she chose to attend her apprenticeship class at another time and left the school. The instructors decided to ban him from attending any further classes there (good riddance!).

I met and got to learn alongside some really awesome guys up at the school. One night, we were having a rare ice storm in the area. We all stayed off of the slippery dangerous roads and hung out in the television viewing room for the evening. An instructor entered the room, and with him were a mom and her young daughter. The road had been too slippery with ice for them to complete their drive home located in the next town.

The instructor asked me if it would be okay with me if I shared my room with them for the night. I was the only woman up there at that time, so I said, "Of course!" The guys brought two more cots into my room for them to sleep on. There were no cell phones back then, so the instructor took the mom to his office to use the phone to let her husband know where they were and that they would be staying with me for the night. The guys brought them whatever food they had left over from their lunches. They also carefully ventured out to locate the mom's vehicle and brought it to the school so that the two of them wouldn't have to walk all the way back to their car the next morning.

They were so helpful and made the mom and daughter feel safe and comfortable that I've never forgotten their outstanding behavior. It proved to me that there really are some good guys out there. Shortly after, the school received a thank-you card from the mom and daughter. The instructor told me that they expressed their gratitude to me for sharing my room with them for the night.

Without our help that night, they would have been stuck in their car throughout the freezing cold temperatures and the pitch-black darkness of the night. If they had attempted to continue driving, they most likely would have slid off the icy road and had an accident. We were all happy to have been able to help them.

The next year I was up at the school, I had the enjoyable company of one more girl in the classroom. The school had worked out cheap rates for students to stay in the hotels of the two nearest towns; one to the east and the other to the west of the school. She and I would visit each other from time to time in one of our hotel rooms. When returning to class one Monday, we found out that she had gotten engaged over the weekend.

I asked the guys if they would be interested in throwing her an engagement party, and they were all in. Everyone brought food and plenty of beer to my room. I had decorated a bit, and we surprised her when she came to my room for a visit. The guys were really great about it, and I took photos of the festivities to give to her later. Once again, I had reinforced proof that not all guys are bad news. I would need all my memories of men's positive behaviors to carry me through the shitstorm of assholes I would be encountering through my career and the one I married at home.

Nowadays, our school is the epitome of what a training center should be. It is a state of the art facility that caters to a long list of learning opportunities. It's huge in size with a very large shower room, bathroom, changing and locker area for women. The men have the same setup. There is a huge cafeteria with food catered to feed everyone for lunch so you don't have to leave the premises to do so.

It's even equipped with a massive indoor training area that even cranes fit into. Now the students learn inside to operate heavy equipment without having to brave the arctic chill of the winter months. I did bring up the fact that training people inside neglected to prepare them for the realities of operating out in the winter weather conditions. As one of my karate senseis (instructors) used to say to me, "This isn't a tea party!"

The equipment operated on the jobsites today are very up-to-date and modern compared to the old friction cranes that I operated. Now you have heaters, defrosters, windshield wipers, and some even have air conditioners. Some equipment such as backhoes and fron-tend loaders are even equipped with stereo systems and comfortable seats that support your neck and back.

All the equipment have computers in them to inform you if you're level, your working capacities, and radius in which it's safe to do so. In cranes, they tell you your boom angle, and there are safety sensors that shut down your machine when entering dangerous ter-ritory. I could count on my hands the new pieces of equipment I operated. I usually had to figure everything out myself.

As for the mechanical part of my training, I learned more from "hands-on" experience than I did from reading books. I asked a lot of questions. Remember this: the only stupid question is one that isn't asked. Whenever I heard a sound that was out of the ordinary, I would ask a mechanic what it could be that was causing it. I usually tried to make the sound I was hearing and describe it to the best of my ability. I frequently heard, "That's the way my wife describes the sounds our car is making if she thinks something is wrong with it." I was lucky that the mechanics I usually worked with took the time to explain to me what they were doing to my machine for maintenance or what they were repairing so that I could possibly do it myself in the future.

I became very involved in the union right away. My motto was I had to work twice as hard as a man to be considered half as good. That's the way it goes when you're trying to pioneer into a new realm of consciousness. The vast majority of men did not welcome my presence among them, and it made me feel like a stranger in a strange land. I'm a stubborn, hard as nails Swedish woman, and I wasn't going anywhere but onward and upward. My ironworker husband always told me, "Give them eight hours of work for eight hours of pay, and they'll keep you working." I took that to mean no screwing off!

My first two years, I worked a lot at our cities sewage treatment plant. It's located in an area called Jones Island, and it's built along our lakefront. I wanted to learn to drive pile, and that's exactly what we were doing there. A very long pipe pile is driven deep into the ground by a big air hammer. Once driven, it is filled with concrete and has rebar embedded within it. Rebar forms are tied into the embedded ones and the structure emerges from there. Iron bolts can also be embedded into concrete, and pillars of iron are connected to those, and the structure is bolted together as it rises in other structural designs. The integrity of the structure, such as piling or sheeting, is underground and invisible to anyone after the building is complete. When I began driving pile, the cranes were equipped with three drums of cable. One drum catered to the "leads" in which the hammer rose up and down inside. The main drum was equipped with "power down" to assist in easing the heavy hammer into place. In the cranes I operated that did not have the advantage of "power down," I would throw out the master clutch. All the cranes functions were able to maneuver when the master clutch was engaged. When a heavy load is being lowered and you throw out the master clutch while pulling in the hoist lever, it makes all the machinery turn backward, and it's a little easier to lower the load slower.

All our pile driving cranes also had a third drum of cable that hoisted the pile to be driven. There were three levers and three brakes involved in picking (hoisting and lowering). There was a swing lever and a brake and a boom hoist lever and a brake. Your mind was kept occupied by whatever functions you were performing with the crane—it was mental gymnastics! Also on our cranes were big air compressors mounted on the roof with fuel tanks to boot. The only item missing on the crane was my personal port-a-potty. I'm kidding, I had my own personal coffee can in the back of the crane for that—ha-ha!

Whenever I was an oiler on those cranes, I was like a spider; I was all over it, barely touching the ground on some days. The operator has a lever mounted on the catwalk that shut off or opened up the valve delivering air to the compressor that ran through air hoses to the hammer. That required a lot of multitasking. The operator manipulates all of the cranes functions, all three drums of cable, and also the hammer. Operating a crane in ordinary circumstances eliminates one of those drums of cable and the hammer. It was important when I was operating a crane for my mind to be crystal clear and free of any access thoughts other than what I was making it do. There was a lot at stake and lives to be accountable for.

I went up to the school for my third winter as an operator to take an advanced crane course. I was to learn how to drive sheeting. That was one of the many services the main company I worked for provided in the construction industry. Sheeting are corrugated sheets of steel and are driven into the ground in the same way that pipe pile are. They have a locking chamber on each side of the sheet so that they can slide into the other when driven. That creates a wall once complete.

A sheeting wall retains the soil once excavation is complete within the walls. Sheeting walls are what keep the soil from falling into rivers and lakes. They are the initial forms for basements of large buildings.

Once again, while up at the school that freezing cold winter, I was the only female. The old antique instructor chose to ignore me the best he could. He had a guy there who became his "teacher's pet" (which I referred to as a "kiss-ass"). The kiss-ass was always the first student to sit in the crane to get some hands-on training while the rest of us worked out in the ice and snow as his crew. At least while we were seated in the crane, we had the heat from the engine providing a little warmth. If you closed the cab door, it would cut off the bitter cold wind. We *all* wanted to take our turn in the seat of that crane, but the *kiss-ass* spent the majority of each day sitting in it.

I was always the last to get in that seat and would only get to spend about forty five minutes in it. That was not cool at all with little ole me. I was sick and tired of freezing my ass off and being part of "the crew" doing the grunt work! The moment that clown climbed down from that crane, I said, "MY TURN!" and hopped right into that seat. All of the guys looked up at me with pissed off expressions on their faces. I said, "Hey, I actually have to do this on jobsites and need to learn how to do it the best that I can. I'm not up here at the school to take a vacation from my wife and kids. I'm not up here to hit the taverns every day after class. I'm here to learn."

They didn't say a thing to me in response, but they were not happy with an aggressive female in their midst, and I didn't give a shit how they felt about it!

One class I attended up at the school I will never forget because they showed us the shocking actual videos of fatal accidents involving heavy equipment. Those videos were taken from the first responders on the accident sites, safety inspectors from OSHA, and anyone involved in determining what had caused the accident to happen. Upon seeing those videos, I noticed they had the actual time recorded in the bottom frame of the scene you were looking at. They were horrible to witness and were shown to us in order to sear the images into our memories in the hopes that we wouldn't make the same mistakes as those deceased operators.

One man had placed a cable around a tree and attached it to the front of his skid-steer loader. He was backing up in reverse to pull that tree down when the cable snapped. The tension on the cable was so great that when it broke, it recoiled back toward the man and cut him in half. Whenever I had to cable something in a similar situation, I made sure my body was in the clear of any harm.

The accident I recalled most often was when an operator got into his large front-end loader after lunch break and backed out of where he had parked his machine, running over and killing a worker. The man had nowhere to sit for lunch and decided to lean against the rear tire of the front-end loader. He had fallen asleep, and when the engine of the machine roared to life, he was not quick enough to get out of the way as it rolled over him, crushing him to death.

We were taught as apprentices to do a morning walk around of the piece of equipment you were to operate that day. You were to notice if there was any fluid underneath from leakage. Were there cracks in the mirrors or windows? If you had tires, was there enough air in them? All fluid levels had to be checked before starting up the machine. Were there any objects blocking your machine?

That same walk around the machine to check for obstacles was performed once again after lunch break. I use that same walkaround for my own vehicle before I get in it. In this way, I know if I need any air in my tires, if I have a leak underneath, or if there are any obstacles I don't want to drive over.

I was letting my business agent know when the members of other unions were stepping over the line by operating our equipment, taking our work from us. The sewage treatment facility enlargement was a huge long-term project. There were a lot of men employed to perform all aspects of the job. There was a lot of equipment on-site to monitor who was operating what, so they made me the union steward for the project. I then had to also deal with different issues men were having working there.

The union also would come to take me off of the project to attend meetings from time to time. They were seeking more minorities to join our union. I would tell the interested parties what to expect out on the jobsite and describe to them what it was that I did. I would answer questions at the end of my talk. I also belonged to a group called "Hard Hat Women" at the time. That was a support group consisting of women working in various trades. We would get together once in a while to check in with each other and try to enter women who came to us into the union they desired.

Some men were happy that I was there on the jobsite to help keep our union affairs in order, and the rest of the men resented it. Working alongside the men all day long and every working day of the week, I found that some men developed a crush on me. I think the reasoning behind their misconceptions was because I understood what they had to go through each day. To other men, I merely appeared to be a challenge to conquer. They did not care how many times I mentioned that I was married, they would continue to ask me out anyway.

I found that if I just said "NO," they would make my life hell because I rejected them or they would start rumors that we had a sexual relationship anyway! I learned to diffuse the situation by using humor. I would answer, "Now you know my ironworker husband might drop a spud wrench on your head if he knew you asked me out." Then I would laugh a little and leave it at that. Usually they'd just walk away thinking that the whole conversation they had started with me was taken as a joke. In that way, it was a "no" answer from me and yet not a rejection to them. Their male egos were fragile, and working with those men could *make or break* my day.

I had many years ahead of me in construction and had to secure my presence within it because it was my workspace also. At times, I came across an individual who thought that they could wear me down by asking me out every time I saw them. To those men, I spelled it out for them by saying, "No means NO." I think it comes down to men wanting what they can't have. The work itself was difficult and very stressful, so when I added the attitudes of egos and assholes, it made it that much harder.

My first two years, I worked almost exclusively at that sewage treatment facility, and during that time, I was an apprentice. When I first walked into that plant, it was like entering an obscene carnival. There were huge tanks of fluid with giant wands circulating, constantly stirring the liquid human waste held inside. On top of the wands were seagulls perched in a row. They were enjoying the "ride," all the while absorbing the germs and bacteria rising up out of the liquid—YUCK! It was hard to find your appetite while working inside the plant. My body embarked on its own private diet, not waiting for my mind to decide to eat or not. I most definitely lost weight on that project!

I also lost my voice about once a month due to the invisible bacteria permeating the air. I ended up on major allergy medication while working there, and that also included weekly injections.

When I saw the ironworkers erecting a tower crane on the project, I realized that it was the crane for me. I could sit in its cab way up in the sky far above the jobsite. I would be able to remain up there, away from the men. My only contact would be my radioman on the ground to signal me and also state vocally the functions I needed to make the crane perform. I also wouldn't have to worry about parking because I could fit my Harley I was riding back then onto the concrete slab the tower had been erected on. No one would know a woman was operating that tower crane.

It appealed to me because I had spent money a couple of occasions to jump out of an airplane, skydiving. If I operated a tower crane, I would be paid to stay up in the sky all day. I brought up my desire to be a tower crane operator at my next union meeting, and the president matched me up with the tower crane operator assigned to the one they had erected on my jobsite. He would be my mentor and agreed to have me climb up on my lunch breaks, rainy days when the job shut down for the day, and also after work two days a week.

It was a hell of a climb, two hundred feet up the ladder to get to the cab of the crane. The interior was small with a seat in the center. The front half of the cab was all windows, and there was a large rectangular window in the floor where your feet were when you were in the seat. It was only designed to be used by men, so there was a urinal built into the wall. It looked somewhat like a funnel, and a tube ran from it to the outside of the cab for the urine to exit. As for me, if I had operated a tower crane all day on a jobsite, I would bring a coffee can with a lid along with me. There was just enough room behind the seat for me to utilize the can. I would throw a rain poncho over my head to create a "tent" effect so no one would know I was peeing into my coffee can. No one can see you when you are so high up in the air anyway.

It was very hard on my neck to view the jobsite below me. I would observe through the window in the floor between my feet. It always reminded me of the same angle my neck was in whenever I washed dishes in my kitchen sink. I swear a man (who DIDN'T do dishes) designed the height in which a kitchen sink and countertop are. If dishes were washed daily by a man, the sinks and counter tops would all be built a little higher to take some of the strain off your neck. It was weird in the fact that when I was up in the tower crane, I had a strained neck from looking down, and in a crane on ground level, I received a strained neck by looking up skyward. The sessions I trained in the tower crane during the wintertime were tough as I'd been wearing insulated coveralls to help me retain my body heat, but I needed to drop out of them at the base of my tower crane ladder so that I could climb up to get into the cab quicker.

Sitting in the tower crane was as if you were playing a video game. In each hand, you held a joystick. The left one swung the cranes jib from left to right. The right joystick moved your trolley in and out by moving it from side to side. If you moved the lever in your right hand forward and backward, it dropped or raised the block with the hook on it. You would trolly and move your block at the same time.

The views from high above the ground were stunning. I could see storms moving in or going out from the horizon. I could watch the sun rising up out of the lake if I was operating a tower crane in the early morning or see the beautiful sunsets in the evening. I always wanted to see all the fireworks displays going off in all directions of the distant counties, but I was never allowed to climb up into one after jobsite hours due to insurance coverage reasons.

I was taught tricks to use when operating a tower crane that proved to be very helpful. On sunny days, while lowering your load or rigging toward the ground, you paid close attention to the shadow. When the shadow was close to the ground, I would start slowing the descent of my load because as the shadow and ground united, I had reached my destination. I had five speeds defined from a "click" I felt within the lever I held in my right hand. When I pushed the lever to its furthest click away from me, the load flew down rapidly. As I eased the lever back toward myself, it slowed down the speed.

When I learned to swing the cab attached to a very long jib that was well over one hundred feet in front of me, I used landmarks to begin to slow down my swinging direction in order to not overshoot my destination. It takes time to halt the continual momentum of the swing by bumping the swing lever in the opposite direction it's moving to be able to stop it. I used the wind direction to move the jib for me. I would move my lever into a neutral position and let the wind push the jib until I had to begin braking against it.

Stopping the swinging motion of the tower cranes jib was tricky. The first time I began training how to swing the jib while taking as much care as possible to not stress the tower holding it and its cab startled the hell out of me. There are special bolts that hold each section of the tower together. They are torqued to an engineered measurement and can only be used once because of the tremendous strain they endure. What freaked me out so much was that when I swung the jib, I could see the tower twisting a little between my feet whenever I looked down.

Worse than seeing all that iron twisting was the sound it made. It sounded like a cat snarling and squealing as if it was in a fight— "EeEEOOoo!"

It was so scary I thought that the sound I was hearing coinciding with the tower twisting meant that the whole tower crane was going to crumple to the ground, and I would meet death there on the jobsite!

I was taught to prepare myself if a worker on the ground crew was not familiar with working using a tower crane. When pouring concrete with any crane, as the cement emptied from the concrete bucket, I needed to gradually keep lowering it as it became lighter. The flex in the boom would retract along with the lightening load. That assisted in keeping the bucket within the workers reach as they hung onto it. The problem with a tower crane was noticeable if a worker slammed shut its opening hatch abruptly. Men would do that in the hopes that the vibration the slamming effect caused would bring down the concrete hanging up on the sides of the bucket. Unfortunately for the operator in the cab of the tower crane, it caused the entire tower to sway back and forth. It's easiest to think of a fishing pole bending as you catch a fish and then straightening back out as you remove the fish from the line.

I've mentioned that when I swung the tower crane's cab and jib that it caused the tower to circle. So when someone cut me loose from a load on the ground, I would be swaying forward and backward along with rotating in a circle. I felt similar motions sitting on my surfboard, waiting for rideable waves of size to roll in and catch. That constant motion was a major factor in keeping most men out of a tower crane, along with a fear of heights. I knew an operator who regularly operated tower cranes all over the country. He told me that on a hot summer day, he had his windshield open outward to allow some fresh air into his cab. A worker far down below him let the concrete bucket hatch slam shut. That motion caused his tower to rock back and forth in such a severe fashion that he had to hang on tight to the window's frame to keep himself from flying out his front window!

A major factor I learned was that men had a concept drilled in them their entire lives about "women drivers." They firmly believe that women do not drive a vehicle as well as they can. Now magnify that belief of theirs by one hundred, and you'll know how they feel about a woman operating a crane. If you magnify that belief by one thousand, that should give you an idea how they feel about a woman who is operating a crane over one hundred feet in the air over their heads—THEY DON'T LIKE EITHER PROSPECT! That was the mentality I had to deal with over and over, every day, for over two decades (nearly three!).

Every day I walked onto a jobsite, I just wanted to make money like everyone else walking onto that same jobsite. But for myself, I had the additional task of changing people's minds. Not any minds, MEN'S minds. Those were the doubtful, stubborn, neanderthal minds. Minds that emanated, "What the f——k do you think YOU'RE doing here?" and "Blah, blah, blah." It was a great challenge to conquer, a burden to bear, and a humongous PAIN IN THE ASS!

As soon as I began operating and they could see for themselves that I knew my shit, I could see the cautious and fearful expressions melt away from their faces. It drove me crazy that I had to prove myself time and time again when that never happened to any man that I saw walking onto a jobsite.

The tower crane that I first learned to operate happened to be on a jobsite full of ironworkers that I knew very well, long before I became an operating engineer. I was the only wife of an ironworker to join the construction trade for a career. Throughout those previous years, a lot of those ironworkers had pissed me off immensely by drinking in the tavern with my husband after work and into all hours of the night.

They knew what an asshole he became when he was drinking, so when they had enough of him, he came home to fight with me. My husband saw a guy wearing a T-shirt one day that read "Add alcohol—instant asshole," and he said, "That's me!" Did that message occur to him to stop drinking? No, it did not! He became such an asshole for me to deal with that if he was in the tavern for two hours, I had to be prepared to deal with his drunken tirades. If he wasn't home by eight o'clock in the evening, I usually had to defend myself physically when he showed up. I used to ask God, "Why is this happening to me?"

Then I would remember something I had read in a piece of Al-Anon literature that said, "God doesn't give you more than you can handle." That would make me think that if I hadn't been training in karate for most of my life that I wouldn't have been able to be married to that guy. In his worst moments, if I hadn't dealt with his addiction issues, he wouldn't have had a wife and kid. It finally made me realize that dealing with all that for sixteen years was A BUNCH OF CRAP! So my advice to anyone at all living within the confines of alcoholism or drug addiction saturating your loved one—get the hell out now! My relationship was both mentally and physically abusive, and it almost killed me. I will go into more depth on how my first marriage finally ended in another chapter.

I've struggled for years with keeping my temper locked up and chained, but every so often, the beast has broken those chains, and unleashed anger has burst forth. It became exceedingly harder to hold back those evil forces when my husband began staying out all night. The later he stayed out, the angrier I became. That was way before pagers and cell phones were introduced. I worried myself sick about his physical and mental health. I also worried about how mean he would be when he finally came home.

One night, I lost it! I heard a car pull up in front of our house after the bars had closed, around three in the morning. I ran out of the house like a crazy person and demanded to know who that woman was driving him home. Since the car was pulling away as soon as my husband had exited the vehicle and shut his door, I began throwing rocks from our driveway at it. I couldn't possibly catch the bitch by running after her car, so I was hoping at the very least to break her back window. Also, I was naked under my robe I had on, and if I took off running after the car, my robe could have dislodged, and I would have streaked through our neighborhood!

My husband slurred in his drunken voice, "Thaatz no womaann (hiccup), thaatzz Mark (burp)." All I had seen was the back of the driver's head as the car sped away. The hair on the driver's head was shoulder length and flipped upward at the bottom as if curled purposely that way. I said to my husband as I marched past him, "Well, tell him to get a haircut, he looks like a woman, goddamn it!" So the ironworkers thought I was one of the "crazier wives" they'd have to look out for, and now I was a crane operator on their job. It was my *pleasure* to lower all the ironworkers that would climb into my man basket at lunchtime to ZIP them down to the ground level so that they could head for the tavern for their half-hour break. The first time they all jammed themselves into my man basket, I hollered out my window, "Payback's a bitch, boys!" I flew them down to the ground so fast they'd thought they were on a ride at Six Flags Great America Amusement Park! I threw the hoist into fifth gear, and I could hear it whistling. It makes me smile to this day as I write this, remembering the shocked fearful expressions on their faces. Their eyes were as big as pumpkins and their mouths were in the shape of Os as they flew to the ground. I'd used my trick of when the man basket met its shadow to slow them down at last minute, then I set them ever so gently on the ground. I'd see some of them shake their heads in disbelief as they exited the man basket. I could see the glare of other men's upward gaze and read their lips as they mouthed, "You bitch!" to me.

"Ha! Ha! Like I hadn't been called that a million times," I'd chuckle to myself. It was fun for me to see them step gingerly back into the man basket after their lunch breaks in order to return to their jobs. Their facial expressions made that climb up and down that extremely high ladder worth it for me every time.

As much as I loved operating the tower crane, I had a hell of a time getting a regular job running one. Not only did the men not want a woman working over them, they did NOT want a woman making more money than them. They did not want a woman in a more powerful position than them. It was okay to pack a lunch for them and clean and mend their work clothes, but to work alongside them proved to be another story.

There was a skyscraper being erected in our city along our main thoroughfare. The operator in the tower crane was caught intoxicated on the job. When you are that high up in the air, the danger increases tremendously. It's very easy to hurt or kill someone or many. I was sent to that jobsite to be that fired operator's replacement. When I showed up on the job instead of climbing up into the tower crane, they assigned me to replace their material hoist operator instead. That piece of equipment moved up and down along the side of the structure. It carried both materials and workers from floor to floor. The operator I was replacing on the material hoist (or elevator) was on a two-week vacation.

When I inquired as to why I was not operating the tower crane as planned, I was told that the operator had pleaded with the superintendent on the job for another chance and was granted it. Back then, there were only a handful of tower crane operators due to lack of interest among our union members. The only means you had to learn how to operate one was the manner in which I learned to have a mentor willing to train you personally. Nowadays, there are simulators that resemble large video games that work really well as far as showing you the views and movements you would deal with once inside the cab of an actual tower crane. You don't have to make the intense climb up the ladder to breach the cab either.

The other unusual tower crane tale I will tell about was on the night shift of yet another extremely tall building being erected along our lakefront. They didn't require too many picks for the crane to make at night since their lighting consisted of a few light plants and the lighting system mounted along the tower of the crane. Since the tower crane operator had a lot of time on his hands between picks, he had taken up the hobby of spying on people in the nearby condominium windows with his binoculars (I know—pervert alert!).

While not paying attention to anything other than who he was spying on at the time, his arm accidentally pushed his hoist lever forward. That position of his joystick (No! Not *that* one!) caused the large heavy tower crane block to quickly rush toward the ground, crashing through the ceiling of their jobsite trailer. Unfortunately for the tower crane operator, his crew were having their evening dinner break. Fortunately, no one was injured (I'm sure some bladder or anal leakage occurred, but at least there were no bones broken). He had been fired on the spot. Since the other couple of tower crane operators we had were employed elsewhere, I was approached at work early the following morning to see if I could possibly rearrange my work schedule to take the fired operator's place. I discussed the situation with the jobsite superintendent I was working for and called our company office. They agreed to send a replacement to take over my seat in the crane I was operating. I went home and prepared to work the second shift that evening as the replacement tower crane operator.

I was getting excited to see the city lights that evening from my view from high above. I dropped my daughter off at her grandparents for the night since I wasn't sure exactly when my shift would end. I made my way down to the lakefront and found the parking area for the jobsite. What I also saw that startled me was the tower crane in operation! *What the hell!* I thought.

I approached the jobsite trailer carrying all my gear, along with my lunch box (complete with my portable toilet, the coffee can). When I announced to the foreman there that I was his new tower crane operator, he looked at me with a shocked expression on his face. "Didn't anyone call you?" When I replied no, he explained to me that the fired tower crane operator put on his best display of groveling while pleading for a second chance to remain on the job.

His apologizing worked, and that was him up in the tower crane, putting it through its paces.

I was screwed. Not only was I not needed on that jobsite, but I had been replaced that morning on my previously established jobsite. Where the hell was I going to be able to earn a paycheck? I was pissed off once again. Instead of putting me up in the sky, they were willing to put both a drunk and a pervert up there—WTF (the initials do not represent any wrestling affiliation)!

Fortunately for me, at that time, there were hundreds of pipe pile to pound into the ground at our sewage treatment project. There were two pile driving cranes set up and working, and there was a "service" crane to unload pipe pile trucked in for the job. The service crane moved equipment for the two crews when needed and supplied both cranes with the amount of pipe pile they would be driving in each specific area required. You had to really be on the ball and pay attention to all of your surroundings when lowering and swinging loads of pipe from the semitrailers down into the deep basement the cranes were working in. Taglines attached to the bundles of hoisted pile allowed the pile drivers to help ensure they were free from making contact with anything else upon placement.

The operator assigned to run the service crane began showing up late for work was extremely tired and irritable and was caught napping in between truck arrivals. He began calling in sick for a couple of days at a time, and a replacement was sent from our yard to fill in for him.

When he didn't even to bother to call in to the office, there was no replacement to be found at the last minute to fill in for him. Without the aid of the service crane, our production of driving pile ground to a halt.

As time is money, that didn't sit well with our office. I was told to climb up out of the hole we were working in and operate the service crane. It was scary for me because that was the first time I would be unloading the heavy loads of long pipe pile. It was an exhilarating challenge, and I did a good job. I didn't drop any pipe, and I didn't bump into anything as I swung them down into the hole. I ended up operating the service crane the following day also.

The next day, the operator finally returned to his crane. When I spoke to him regarding his absence, he told me that he was going through a divorce and having a tough time dealing with that. I told him that he needed to inform the office if he wasn't making it into work so that they could send a replacement to the jobsite. I mentioned to him that I had to leave my crew without an oiler for our crane so that I could take his place. I felt bad that he was going through a difficult time, but he still continued with his disappearing act and not bothering to call in on the mornings he wasn't showing up to work.

One afternoon, the vice president of the company made an appearance to see how the job was coming along. On his way out, he called me over to his vehicle. He asked me if I'd be interested in operating the service crane full-time since the assigned operator was missing so many days. As much as I wanted to operate a crane of my own, I explained to him that the operator was going through a rough period in his personal life and as the jobsite union steward, I was there to help him, not to take his job from him.

That decision sucked for me because it would have launched my career as a crane operator that much faster. It also sucked because I knew that a guy wouldn't have given a shit about anyone but them selves and would have hopped into that crane without a second thought about the operator he was replacing. I had to think about how women would be perceived in the future and didn't want guys thinking, "Watch out or that bitch will steal your job!" I sensed every day that I was there they thought I was doing just that.

The following day, I returned to oiling on the pile driving crane I'd been working on. I noticed a new operator climbing into the service crane. A semitrailer load of pipe pile pulled up in front of the service crane to be unloaded. As the pile drivers began unloading the pipe, the semitruck driver approached me. He told me that I'd done such a good job unloading the trailers of pipe pile that he and the other semi drivers made a request that I would be the permanent service crane operator. He also told me that when he was in the office, he heard them talk of firing the crane operator that was so frequently absent and not calling in to say he would be. If I knew the operator was going to be fired, I would have taken the position as the service crane operator. Things would have turned out a lot differently if the vice president of the company asked me if I wanted to do it and he were to explain that the operator was going to be fired. Instead of taking the man's job as I thought, I would have been filling an empty seat.

I worked steadily on that sewage treatment plant expansion for most of my two years as an apprentice. I did the best job that I could, and I always worked hard. I was absolutely devastated when I was laid off for the first time. I asked, "Why me? What did I do wrong?" I was told that it had nothing to do with my performance at work; it just came down to money. I had just become a journeyman (journeywoman) operator, and therefore, I was to be paid a lot more money. The company I was working for also went by seniority, and since I was the last to be hired, I was the first to be laid off.

Work slowed down during the winter months back then, and I had to go on unemployment. I found out that unemployment only paid about one-third of the wages I made. That caused me to have to live off all the money I'd managed to save when I was working. That was to be a vicious cycle throughout my career whenever work slowed down for me.

The day they laid me off happened to be my birthday. I was so upset and depressed because I was thinking that all of my hard work had made no difference to the powers that be in the office. I felt easily dispensable, underappreciated, and unimportant. I went home, put on my pajamas, and went to bed. I was crying when I told my ironworker husband that I'd been laid off and was in no mood to do a damn thing for my birthday.

It was a Friday and one of my worst birthdays ever. My husband and my daughter wanted to cheer me up, so they gave me my birthday present. It was a tower crane block made out of gold, and it slid along it's chain in the same way that an actual block slides along the rigging of a tower crane cable. It was a very unique and special necklace and remains to be one of my favorite pieces of jewelry to this day. I had a collection of model cranes, and one of them was a tower crane I was trained on but miniature. It was a gift from my mentor on that crane as a symbol of my completion of training. About a week before my birthday, I noticed that the block of my tower crane model was missing. When I asked my husband if he knew what happened to it, he told me that he noticed the crane lying on its side one day and figured that one of our dogs must have bumped into the shelf it was displayed upon.

My husband and daughter had removed the block and taken it to a friend of ours who was a jeweler. As much as I loved my new necklace, I still climbed into bed (mentally, I climbed under a rock).

I was laid off every winter during my beginning years when our pile driving and water work would slow down. I was a better worker and a better operator than a lot of the men, and yet I was always the first to go. It was brought to my attention from several of the guys that I had enough money coming into my household due to the fact that I was married to an ironworker. Most of the men I worked with were the sole providers for their families. Their wives stayed home, raising their kids.

That sucked for me because I needed my own money. I needed to save up for an emergency evacuation fund for my daughter and I. We'd been known to have to flee on a moment's notice. My husband was guilty on numerous occasions of walking into our home and stating that I had five minutes to grab what I could and get the f——k out. If I didn't comply with his wishes, I'd have to prepare for battle that sometimes involved weapons. I couldn't have my young daughter be a witness to that behavior. I'd come home on too many occasions to count to the sight of my belongings thrown out of our home and strewn all over our front yard for the neighbors to view as well as all the traffic driving by. I lived under the constant stress over what I was walking into when I came home from work every day.

Every time I was laid off, I'd burn through every penny I'd saved. I had to use it to pay for bills, groceries, and childcare (when working). I paid for half of all our bills unless he failed to pay his half, which was low on his priority list. Topping his monetary list were drinking, drugs, and gambling.

I had been diagnosed with endometriosis years before and had several surgeries to remove it. After clearing the disease briefly by surgery one time, I miraculously became pregnant with my daughter. As my husband's alcoholism became more apparent and contributed greatly to his violent behavior, I adapted and shared this motto with him: "Do to me what you will, but I will dish it right back to you. Touch our daughter, and you'll be in the hospital or the morgue."

After becoming an operator, the endometriosis would come back every year. I would deal with the pain until I couldn't press down on the brake pedal in my car anymore. If I couldn't hold the brakes in my car, then I surely couldn't hold the crane brake pedal down, not to mention all the weight that brake was holding. That would be when I'd have to take some time off in order to surgically remove the spiderwebbing of endometriosis that glued my insides and organs together. I'd have to take the time to recover and regain mobility before returning to work.

I could actually feel the webbing resume about three months after having surgery to remove it. It was an extremely aggressive disease and felt like a demonic spider was spinning webs of great pain and misery inside my abdomen. I had it removed four times, and the fifth and final surgery I will write about in another chapter.

I did not share any bank accounts with my husband, so during layoff periods from work, my finances would become depleted. When I married my ironworker husband, I was unaware of the huge amount of money he owed to the Internal Revenue Service for unpaid taxes. When I took his last name, they took all of my money, which was how that knowledge came too light—SURPRISE! That was when I opened my own bank accounts and had to work out payments with the IRS.

You may "think" that you know someone, but their true colors are shown once you've signed your name on a marriage license. That gives your significant other the "license" legally to be who and what they really are. It may take only ten minutes to hear your vows and get married, but it takes years to get divorced, so I hung in there with my marriage. My husband went to rehab three times while we were married. It was court-ordered due to circumstances I will not get into. It was not his choice to go and therefore did not work for our family. However, it did lead me to Al-Anon.

This is a group for the significant others of members who are in Alcoholics Anonymous or who will hopefully attend AA meetings at some point. The principles and reading materials apply to everyday life and situations. You are basically taught to be nonjudgmental and to focus on improving your own flaws of character while loving the good in those around you. I use their reading materials and ideals in my life every single day. I used those principles while dealing with the thousands of men I worked with throughout my career.

I learned how to be at my best and to set a good example. I reinforce good behavior to get more of the same. This also helped me with dealing with bouts of depression then and now. I also learned that laughter is the best medicine and found that a good sense of humor was essentially a key in dealing with men's behavior. Men "are" their jobs; women "do" their jobs for the benefit of their families. There is a big difference between the two. That is why men head to the tavern after work, and women go home to be with their children and prepare dinner for their household. It's a completely different mindset.

After a few winters of trying to survive unsuccessfully on the meager payments from unemployment compensation, I returned to work for a few different contractors until the work returned for the company I mainly worked for. I preferred working for them because they were very family oriented. One day, I was operating a bulldozer, clearing a huge field down by our lakefront. I came back to my machine after coffee break to find a note on my seat. The note told me to leave and pick up my daughter from her school immediately. They would send a replacement for me to work the remaining hours of my shift. I was told to call the office in the morning if I needed more time at home with my daughter.

I frequently reminded the men I worked for that I didn't have a wife at home to take care of everything while I made money. I WAS the wife and mother who took care of everything AND made the money. I could see the light bulb going on in their eyes that said, "Oh, that's right." That was not the only time I was relieved of my operating duties in order to go and pick my daughter up from her school. I was oiling on a crane when the superintendent pulled up to me in his vehicle on the jobsite to tell me the school had called the office, requesting that I pick up my daughter. I made a mad rush to the school and found her sitting in the office, awaiting my arrival.

I said, "I got here as fast as I could. What's wrong with my daughter?" It was all I could do to keep from flipping out when the woman in the office explained to me that my daughter kept drawing on her hand no matter how many times her teacher told her not to. The teacher washed her little hand only to have her draw on it again. "Are you insane?" I was pissed off! I had just lost my wages for the rest of the day over a battle of wills between an adult teacher and a small child.

I looked daunting in my filthy work clothes, wearing grease on my arms and face. I said, "Now that I've been replaced by a GUY on my job for the remainder of the day, I'm taking my daughter home with me. For your information, if she wants to look like her mother, it is fine with me!" I rolled up my left sleeve so she could see the tattoo of flowers and vines that ran from my hand up my arm. I finished our conversation by telling them "not" to call me unless it was an emergency.

That didn't last long. I was operating a crane when my foreman instructed me to pick my daughter up at her school; my replacement was on his way. When I arrived there, she was sitting in the office once again. I asked her if she was hurt or ill in which she replied, "No."

"What's going on here?" I asked the office personnel.

"Your daughter is flipping off her teacher with her middle finger and saying, 'Bitch, you!'"

I was caught off guard by what she said, but I was not shocked by any means. I tried to remain calm as I told the woman that both her father and I worked in construction. "Swearing is the native tongue of our trade. She must have picked it up from us. She's just a little girl, and you are all adults, so I wouldn't take it personally!" Then I reminded them once again that I had to be replaced by a MAN in my crane seat and would be lucky to get that seat back in the morning. I told them that I would take my daughter home with me and explain that swearing was for the construction site.

I also explained to them that there was nothing I could do about her father's swearing but that I would tone it down on my part when I was at home. As soon as she and I were in the car and headed for home I said, "It's f——k you, not bitch you!" Then I proceeded to enlighten her on exactly the definition of each of those words. I think she was more than a little surprised because as I was telling her about the "birds and the bees" at her young age. Her eyes became as big as saucers, and her little mouth took on the shape of an O. That was the last time my daughter swore at school (elementary school, that is!).

The third and final time I was dismissed from my crane to go to her school, I'd had it. That time when I got to the school's office, my daughter was crying as she sat in the chair, waiting for me. I'd recently bought her an expensive pair of glasses that she needed to wear in order to see correctly. They were cute, they were pink, she had picked them out herself, and they were now BROKEN. It was the first time I learned that a girl had been bullying her ever since she had begun wearing them and that the girl was responsible for breaking them. I demanded an appointment with the girl, her parents, and the school principle. We set up a time for all of us to meet, and I informed the woman I was speaking with that my daughter would be absent from school until I was satisfied with the outcome of the situation. She would be in the company of her grandparents while I was at work.

I was not in a friendly mood when I showed up to the meeting in my filthy work clothes, coming straight from my jobsite. I flat out told everyone present in the room how I had to work my ass off to pay for her glasses. I explained that she needed those glasses to see clearly and that I expected the parents to reimburse me for them. I said that I also expected disciplinary action to be taken against the girl responsible for bullying my daughter from both the parents and the school. I was willing to take legal action if my requests were not met. I expected an apology to my daughter from the girl, and my daughter was there to learn without putting up with the asinine juvenile behavior of a child devoid of manners. The girl was suspended for two weeks and did apologize to my daughter.

On my way out, I stopped at the school office for a chat. I told the woman there that every time they called me in, I had to be replaced on the crane I was operating. The men complained to me that if a man was in that crane seat, he wouldn't have to run off to the school—his wife would. I told them that the next time they needed a parent to come in if my daughter wasn't sick or hurt, her dad would be coming in. I explained that I sat in a crane and raised iron up into the sky to him. "He's the one who bolts the iron together to construct the building. He will have to come down from that iron to see you about mundane bullshit and will lose his wages for the remainder of the day. You will be in for a real treat when he shows up," I warned.

I explained further that when a crane isn't running, the jobsite shuts down. The daily budget is upset, and so is the building sched ule. Men lose money when they can't work, there are big fines when schedules are not met, and the big money contractors won't be happy along with the banks supplying the funds. "Call her father's employer to call him to the school," I reminded them on my way out the door. It turned out they never did.

Men do not have the same priorities that women do. Even though I was operating the key piece of equipment on any jobsite, I felt as though I wasn't taken as seriously as the men were. Never once was I asked if my husband was able to go to our daughter's school. It was always assumed that the wife and mom were to go to the school if necessary and care for the children, period.

Men developed a camaraderie while bonding at the tavern after work. Jobs were given to buddies of whoever had any authority to give them while they were imbibing in alcohol at the tavern. I knew of this from my ironworker husband who himself had been placed on many jobsites in that manner. I did not take part in those after work activities. I picked up my daughter immediately after work to spend time with her and run our dogs before I made dinner.

I knew of one woman who stopped with the men regularly after work to drink with them. All I will say is that a lot of bad decisions were made due to the atmosphere, and she lost respect among the men she had to work with. Men always comment that women are queens of the rumor mill, but I have firsthand knowledge that men are worse by far. I kept my work habits on a professional level and, after a long while, was usually treated as one of the crew. That kind of acceptance was one of the main reasons I chose to work mainly with the family oriented company unless work was slow and they had to lay me off.

In the winters when I was laid off from that company in which I mostly drove pile and sheeting, I worked for structural contractors raising iron for the ironworkers. I worked with the Millwrights on shutdowns, putting new machines in place. I worked for large contractors who specialized in erecting hospitals and another who specialized in building bridges. I swung a lot of concrete buckets also.

Toward the end of my career, I became disenchanted with going through the same damn bullshit from proving myself to new guys that I just took the layoffs as time to work on the things at home that were shelved while I was working. I've found that it's true what they say. "You either have time or money but rarely both (whoever the hell *they* are)." I would remain at home until my usual pile driving company hired me back to work. I'd worked alongside the men there for so long, and we worked so well together that I trusted them to not try to have me do something stupid with the crane. I also didn't have to worry as much about making it home at the end of the day in one piece; I felt that we had each other's backs. I didn't have to "babysit" those guys the way I'd had to while working with other contractor's crews.

Before my daughter entered elementary school, I had to put her in day care while I worked. She was extremely intelligent and could read, do some writing, and even some math. Our family members and some friends continually suggested that I place her in a Montessori School so that she could continue learning in preparation for elementary school. That school was the most expensive among the day care centers, but I thought that we would give it a try for her. On bad weather days in construction, it's customary to go into work and wait for two hours, called "show-up time," to see if the weather improves or not. That could include rain, snow, or strong winds. All bad weather has negative effects on the working structure of the brakes in friction cranes. The main concern is for the workers, to keep them safe from working on slippery surfaces. If the weather remained on issue after our two-hour waiting period, we were usually allowed to return home and deem it a rain day, snow day, or whatever. Wet brakes on a friction crane allow for the slipping of loads and causes a great danger to those working around it.

Whenever I was released due to a bad weather day, I would immediately pick up my daughter upon my way home to spend as much time as I possibly could with her. I went to the Montessori School and didn't see her anywhere upon entering. I began to question the woman in charge as to her whereabouts when the children behind her became rambunctious and were getting a little loud. All of a sudden, the woman turned to the children and yelled, "SIT!" just as if she were training a dog. Those children sat down and clammed up so fast that it alarmed me. Once there was silence in the room, I could hear my daughter crying from somewhere outside the room we were standing in. "Where the hell is my daughter?"

The woman took me to the kitchen where I found my daughter sitting alone in the dark room. She was sobbing hysterically as I asked, "What the hell is she sitting alone in the dark for?"

The Gestapo woman informed me that my daughter was being punished for NOT EATING HER BROCCOLI.

I informed the woman that my daughter had been eating broccoli every day at her grandparents' out of their garden and had no doubt become sick of it. I asked if she had offered her any other vegetables to my daughter, and she told me that she had not. I told her that I felt her punishment over a vegetable was ludicrous. Gestapo told me that her own son was there as well (he was one of the trained dog children who sat silently there like a good puppy), and he had spent some time alone in the kitchen also.

That was it for that place! How could I possibly keep my mind focused on operating a giant machine, lifting heavy loads over the heads of men when there would be a part of my mind worrying about my daughter's welfare? I took my daughter out of there and stopped by her grandparents' house to see if they could watch her while I worked until I could find a new day care facility. I was lucky in that my in-laws' house was only three blocks away from my own.

As soon as we arrived home, I notified the administration office of the Montessori School to tell them why I was withdrawing my daughter from their school. I insisted on having my costs refunded and informed them that the woman in charge of the facility my daughter had attended would make a better dog trainer than to be in charge of the welfare of children.

A friend of mine had recommended a day care provided by a church in our area. It was far more reasonably priced and seemed to have a nice atmosphere when I checked it out after work. Things went well for my daughter there until my next rain day. I showed up early in the day after my show-up time at work. As I gathered her belongings, I asked the woman working there to please bring my daughter to me so that we could leave for home. She informed me that my daughter could not leave until she "was done with her math." I left the woman behind as I marched through each room in search of my daughter. I finally found her seated at a tiny desk with a paper in front of her. There were long columns of numbers that she was expected to add up at her young age. I said, "That's enough of this crap, let's go!"

My daughter stated that they would not let her leave her desk until she completed her paper. I said, "Oh, yes, they will!" And that was the last time we stepped inside of that church.

I was done leaving my little daughter with people that I didn't know. I stopped off at the grandparents to see if they would be willing to keep her during the week while I worked. I would rather be paying them the money anyway. It was an enormous weight lifted from my shoulders when they agreed to watch M (my daughter's first initial) for me.

I've mentioned that my first marriage was a volatile one; in fact, it was like a war. If you have ever seen the old *Pink Panther* movies with the late actor Peter Sellers in them, you will be able to picture what the similarities were to my life. In those movies, Peter Sellers plays a detective who has a man in charge of running his household. Out of the blue, when he's not expecting it, the man leaps out at him from wherever he'd been hiding and attacks him. It's a full on assault in which the two men become engaged in a karate fueled fight (in my home, it was karate against street fighting, learned from his many barroom brawls). In my home, I never knew which flipside of my ironworker husband would present himself when he walked in the door.

The degree of physical fighting that would undoubtedly ensue would depend upon how much alcohol he had ingested. I could almost clock how drunk and mean he would be depending on what time he came home from the tavern.

It's difficult to leave your home life dramas when you head into work each morning, but it's vitally important that you do. As an apprentice, you are taught that if there were to be an accident on your jobsite, it could be considered "operator's error" if the machine you were operating was involved in any way. As a crane operator, it was their choice whether to make a pick or not when rigging, obstacles, and weather were involved.

I actually had to suck it up on a few different jobsites at times and admit to my superintendent that I'd had a rough night at home and was having a hard time concentrating enough to operate a potentially deadly massive machine. At the time those rarities occurred, it was obvious to those I worked with regularly that I was involved in a difficult marriage. I hadn't spoken words to members of my crews about my circumstances, but it hadn't taken a rocket scientist to figure that out when my black eyes made it obvious (or fat lip or bruised face, etc.). I'd had to not only step down and LET A MAN TAKE MY PLACE, but I also had to take an enormous pay cut for those days. I'd also had to reduce myself from running a big powerful crane that was a necessity on the jobsite to operating a mind-numbing air compressor that caused the hammer to drive the pile.

Men didn't do that. I'd seen them hop into a crane sick, hungover, puking, and practically on their deathbeds. I couldn't take the chance of injuring someone; I couldn't live with that.

My husband usually won our fights. If it was a stranger who confronted me, I would have undoubtedly kicked their ass. When it's someone you love and the father of your daughter, you want to avoid fighting with them at all costs. I never wanted my daughter to ask me, "What happened to Dad's face?"

And I'd have to answer, "I punched his lights out!" I bore a lot of guilt for having to fight with him at all. Just because he was being an asshole at times didn't mean that I had to be one as well. I used that theory with all the men I worked with too. I wasn't about to let anyone ruin my day on a jobsite.

There is only the present in which to live your life. In the martial arts, there is a Japanese word we use, *Satori.* It means to live in the present moment. Yesterday is gone. There is nothing you can do about your past but to learn from it. Tomorrow is not here yet (if we are lucky enough to see it), so it is a waste of time to project ahead with worry. There are too many assholes in the world; we don't need to be additions to their population.

A lot of men I'd worked with knew what assholes some of the ironworkers could be, especially my husband, because they drank together after work. The men would get into fistfights once intoxicated. They had been known to give each other bloody noses, black eyes, and even knock each other's teeth out. Then they would move on to becoming the best of buddies and buying each other drinks in the minutes following the fighting. I had witnessed that crazy behavior many times when picking my husband up from the tavern to take him home.

A superintendent in the main company I worked for seemed to relish in making everyone's day a total misery. Every time he laid me off, he chuckled when he told me. Every time he sent me to a shitty jobsite or to do a job he KNEW I didn't want to do, he laughed after giving me the news. I couldn't stand that guy. He was one of those people who, when you see him walking toward you, a feeling of dread would wash over you.

He had a very bad habit (or hobby?) of calling me very late at night to tell me to drive to a different jobsite early the next morning. I had been laid off for a very long time and was in my bed, SLEEPING on a Sunday night, when my phone rang. I thought perhaps it was an emergency call from a member of my family; all of us lived in different states and different time zones. To my astonishment, it was that superintendent waking me up. He was calling me to tell me that I was needed to operate a crane in the morning. I informed him that I needed to set my daughter up in day care before I could arrive on the jobsite. I reminded him that a day or two advance notice would allow me to have day care set up ahead of my work schedule. That news must have gone in one ear and then out the other because he continued his frustrating last-minute notifications throughout the many years I worked with him. Perhaps he forgot in those moments that he was dealing with a WOMAN who was a MOM or just didn't give a rat's ass either way (I opted for the second reason).

I was feeling resentful the next morning as I got my daughter situated in day care for the week and paid accordingly for her to be there. I was annoyed that I had missed my overtime pay of grease time on the crane I was to operate and hadn't been informed on what the hell I'd be doing.

I apologized to my crew for my tardiness but explained to everyone of the late notice I'd received and that I'd had to set my daughter up in day care in order for me to make it into work.

The men were understanding and told me about their own experiences of being redirected to various jobsites late Sunday nights, disrupting their sleep. What the hell? It was generally known what was going on work wise Friday afternoons in order to set up for work on Mondays. Whenever he pulled his late night Sunday antics after that, I would think, "It's late, go to bed, get a life!"

We had a productive day, even though we had a late start. I loaded semitrailers with materials and pile driving equipment that was leaving for a jobsite the following morning. At the end of the day, the superintendent pulled up to where we were finishing up loading. He came up to me and said, "Well, that's it for you for now, ha-ha. Work is still slow. I just needed to send the operator assigned to this job elsewhere for today, so I don't need you anymore. I'll call you when work picks up, heh-heh."

"WHAT?" I had abruptly woken my daughter out of her bed early that morning, placed her in day care, and paid for her to be there the entire week.

It hadn't been worth it for me to work only one day. That screwed me up with the unemployment I'd been receiving during the time I'd been out of work. I had to refile and wait two weeks before my next check from them would arrive. I wouldn't get my one day's pay for another two weeks either. He had screwed me over royally. I learned to shut off the ringer on our phone before going to sleep at night. Back then, there were no cell phones, so when I was asked why I hadn't answered my phone when I was called *super late at night,* I told them I'd turned the ringer off so my daughter could sleep undisturbed. I didn't bother asking why I wasn't called earlier in the day because I already knew the answer to that question—it wasn't as FUN for him to do so.

When cell phones were introduced, my main company handed them out to the foreman and the operators; I declined one. I told the office that I needed to keep my personal phone in case my daughter had to reach me in an emergency. It wasn't conceivable for me to carry two phones with me, so I gave my phone number to my yard foreman only. He could tell me what he needed me to do throughout the course of the day. I didn't give my number to the office since they were not paying my personal phone bill.

As for that superintendent, he proved to be an asshole over and over again. I heard endless stories from the men I worked with; they all supported that statement. All I can say about people like that is it's real easy to be an asshole; it's a lot harder to behave in a courteous and respectful way and to use your manners. The other thing I have to say is that karma is a bitch!

Now get prepared for A LOT of swearing in the next chapter. No, the rest of this book won't be as bad. Yes, this is a necessary title for the next chapter. It's titled "WTF!" for a reason (a *million* reasons, actually) as I am writing an honest account of what I went through in the world of construction. I said that question many times out loud and millions of times to myself throughout each day. Between my three years working as a laborer and twenty-five years of operating heavy equipment, I probably hold the world's record in asking that question. The jobsite experiences and just dealing with the "other" set of chromosomes will explain why that question eventually became my mantra. Bear with me, readers, and I'll make it up to you with the following chapter, "Critters," a much more enjoyable topic (and also more vocabulary friendly).

Inside one of the tunnels

The silos

Underneath a dust collector

A cement covered plant; the base of the silos is shown far right

The silos at the far right side of the road

*One more vision of the many tunnels before I
cleared out the overflow of cement*

One of the roads through the gray and dreary plant

*The faint line on the roof is the infamous ships
whistle (or I should say "WAS")*

Up at our school learning to drive sheeting

Tracking our crane into place before connecting the hammer, leads, hoses, and air compressor preparing to drive pile

The first tower crane I learned to operate
Placing the huge pipes that material would flow through using
the tower crane and also the Manitowoc crawler on the right

View of the crane I oiled on and learned to drive pile from above in the
tower crane view from my cab; the jib is in the top of the photo and the
pile driving crane on a different jobsite in the lower left of the photo

Top photo shows the view from my cab of another jobsite with a pile driving crane

View of crane on a barge working from the river and other cranes on the left on another area to erect a structure; I took the photo from my cab in the tower crane

WTF!

I know you will be asking yourself this question while reading this chapter, "Suzanne, what is up with all of this swearing?"

To that, I answer, "Swearing is the native tongue of construction." With all the nonsense I found myself dealing with constantly, I made that statement to myself at least once a day (usually more times than that!). I promise to reward you for dealing with my *"sailor's mouth"* in the next chapter, "Critters," by using much cleaner language.

I'm going to start off by telling you of an incident involving myself that I am ashamed to have happened at all. During my first marriage to the ironworker, we made excursions to the northern woods whenever possible. We would stay up at my brother-in-law's place. It was a nice break from the bustling city life.

After work one Friday, when my daughter was a young girl, I took the two of us up north for the weekend. That Sunday, we set out early for the five-and-a-half-hour drive home. I was an apprentice at the time and needed to prepare for work early the next morning. I was very hungry when we set off for the long journey. There was only one restaurant in a small town we drove through, but I could see a long line of people waiting to go inside and be seated to dine.

I thought, "Screw it, I can make it until the next town." WRONG! Alarms were going off in my head. *DANGER! DANGER! Body is in need of nourishment—NOW!* People will driving along a two-lane highway in the country, out in the middle of nowhere, when I ended up behind an old couple crawling along on their Sunday drive. They were very SLOW. Since I had a clear vision up ahead and we were the only two cars on the highway, I didn't see any harm in passing the old couple, even though there was a solid line dividing the two lanes.

I drove along for quite a while, still searching for a restaurant or always tell you to listen to your gut, and they are right; I didn't, and I was wrong. I was a gas station to purchase some food. I was frantic for anything to eat at that point because I was in shark mode and ready to chew my own arm off! As I passed a state trooper parked on the side of the highway, he turned his flashing lights on. Since I was the only driver on the road in either direction, I thought that something must have been wrong with my car that I was unaware of.

I had been driving the speed limit, so that couldn't be the reason he was pulling me over. When he approached me in my car, he told me he was writing me a ticket for a traffic violation that I'd made. There had been only my car and the one the old couple were in on the road for the last hour, so I denied having made any violations. He told me that he'd had a witness and that if I wanted to contest the ticket, he was writing me that I could show up in court on the date provided. I would be working overtime hours on the construction site all week and had no desire to take a day off to drive all the way back up north. I didn't want to lose a day's wages either. That was when my pot boiled over and the shit hit the fan. I said to him, "You are full of shit! You are just using me to fill your ticket quota! I'd been the only driver on this highway for some time now."

He pointed at an airplane circling overhead and explained to me that the pilot had seen me crossing the solid line dividing the lanes of the highway when I passed the slower car miles back. He told me that they employed farmers in the area who flew planes on the weekends to assist in monitoring the traffic. How in the hell was I supposed to know that?

It is here that I will prove "hangry" is not just an expression; mix that with PMS, and it creates a devastating composition. My mouth took on a life of its own as it burst forth with, "I'm starving! If you want to give me a ticket so badly, you can do it at the nearest restaurant I can find! You look like Dudley Do-Right in that ridiculous hat!" That was a cartoon character I watched on television as a kid, just the complement any state trooper wanted to hear—NOT!

I rolled up my window, threw my car into gear, and stomped on the accelerator. I took off down the highway and now had a state trooper tailing me with his lights and siren blaring away. I thought to myself, *What the hell? I may as well get there as fast as I possibly can since I have an escort.* Since we were still far to the north end of our state, there were no exit ramps and no other traffic. We flew along at high speed for quite a while until I could see a roadblock of several police cars up ahead of me—all with flashing lights. Did the sight of them bring about a dose of sanity to my PMS-ing nutrition-starved brain? NO, IT DID NOT.

As I was forced to a stop, I felt like the Hulk as I practically ripped my door off in the process of opening it. Marching up to the nearest police officer who was addressing me as "Ma'am," I quickly transitioned into a scene out of the *Exorcist* movie where the demonized girl is levitating above her bed as her head is spinning around. Instead of the green vomit projectile from her mouth, words I didn't know I even knew were spewing from mine like a rapid-firing machine gun.

The red curtain of anger descended as I yanked the shocked cop off his feet and shook him like a rag doll as the verbal assault pummeled him from my mouth. My internal voice was screaming inside my head, saying, "Put him DOWN. For God's sake, woman, you've lost your mind! What the f——k are you doing? STOP! STOP!"

I could see his face turning beet-red and his demeanor changed from shocked to "forget this shit"! The fellow officers were quickly advancing to where our twisted tango was in progress. I set him gingerly back down on the ground and finally was able to shut my demonic mouth. Then came the embarrassment of being abruptly spun around and being handcuffed in front of all the ongoing traffic that was allowed to pass the cop cars and worst of all, in front of my young daughter observing the mayhem from my car.

I was put in the back seat of the police officer that I'd riled up (a nicer way of saying "assaulted"). My daughter was placed beside him in the front seat, and off we went to the town's jail that held jurisdiction over the area. My daughter thought it was great to get an unexpected ride in the police cruiser and appeared to be having the time of her life. I, however, was slowly regaining my composure as the reality of my actions struck home. Boy, had I ever f——ked up and screwed myself royally! How was I ever going to undo all the bad decisions I had just made?

When we pulled into the jail, the officer deposited me in a chair directly at the desk of a female officer. My daughter was at my side. My daughter was the first to speak, "If you put my mom in a cage, can I go in too?" As if we were at the fun house at the fairgrounds! She was so excited and happy at the prospect like it was some adult fort that adults hung out in for kicks.

"Oh my god," I groaned internally.

"So what exactly happened here?" the female officer asked me.

I explained that I was starving and had terrible PMS. I also told her that I thought the state trooper had been trying to force an unnecessary traffic ticket on me which I declined and that the situation had snowballed from there. After she finished writing her report, she rose from her desk and disappeared. Apparently, it was ham dinner at the jail that Sunday because she returned with not one plate but two plates of food and set them in front of me.

After finally ingesting some substance, the reality of my consequences were coming sharply into focus. The female officer told me that I was indeed heading into a jail cell until someone could come to collect me. My daughter was to be taken elsewhere until I was released. She told me, "You know that you need to apologize and explain yourself to the officer who arrested you, and the sooner, the better. We have impounded your vehicle, suspended your driver's license, and you will be leaving here with a number of fines due to your traffic violations."

I reluctantly walked into my new digs for the day (dare I say "jail cell") and asked the female officer to send over the man who arrested me. I bit the bullet and humbly apologized now that the demons had been exorcized by the not one but *two* ham dinners. I explained that it had become apparent to myself that hangry and PMS were a deadly combination for me. He told me that he could understand the PMS part since he was a married man, but that the rest of my behavior had been scary at best and that I needed to address my anger issues *(you think?)*. He added that I was being charged with speeding, eluding the police, resisting arrest, and assaulting a police officer (in other words, I was in DEEP SHIT!). He told me that I had one phone call and that if someone didn't show up to claim me by midnight that I would go before a judge in the morning, and my daughter would be taken by child services.

As difficult as it was for me to apologize to the officer, it was even harder for me to call my husband. When he answered the phone, I told him that I needed him to make the long drive north to get me out of jail. His reply was, "Oh, hell no! I'm watching f——king football!" and hung the phone up on me. So much for my one phone call (so much for the "better or worse" portion of the vows!). Needless to say, I ceased being a fan of football from that moment on. I told the officer that my husband wasn't coming, and he stated that he could understand why. I pleaded with him for another phone call, and he said, "Anything to get you out of here."

I had no other option than to call my in-laws, another tough phone call to make due to my embarrassment. They told me that they were on their way.

I was sweating it out when they finally showed up ten minutes before the deadline. I couldn't get out of there fast enough! As we were walking out the door with my half asleep daughter in tow, my husband showed up. When he saw that his parents had made the long trip to retrieve me, he was livid! "Why did you have to drag my folks into this?" he yelled.

I told him that he made it clear to me that he wasn't coming. He asked me where my car was, and when I told him it had been impounded, it was as if I'd poured gasoline onto an open flame!

My in-laws told us that they would drive our daughter back with them and that she could sleep at their house that night. It was obvious to them that we had *issues* to work out. I was so exhausted from the bizarre events of the day that on and off, I dozed while my husband ranted and raved on and on about my shortcomings, and all I heard was a bunch of "Blah, blah, blah." Zzzzzz.

When we finally walked into our house and set down the belongings removed from my vehicle I was forced to leave behind, I said,

"I'm exhausted and can't wait to go to bed and get some sleep. I'm going to call the office right now and let them know that I won't be able to make it in today." It was four o'clock in the morning, and if I were to work, I would usually leave the house around five. The job I was on at the time was along one of the main streets in our city. "Oh, hell no!" my husband yelled at me. "You're not going to miss work due to your obnoxious behavior. Now I have to leave earlier than usual to drop you off at your jobsite before going to my own."

I was f——ked! I was tired! WTF! It just so happened that he was connecting on a huge arena project that I had previously driven pile for. Now I was across the street from that project, oiling on a crane. We were driving pile for the parking structure to accommodate the patrons for that arena. At least it wasn't far out of his way to drop me off at my jobsite. With neither of us getting any sleep, it was a tense ride into work.

I was so tired that I lay across the tracks of the crane to briefly close my eyes during our coffee and lunch breaks. When the men asked me why I was so tired, I told them that I'd barely slept the night before. That brought on the jokes about me having a wild night of sex with my husband, that I should leave the partying to Friday and Saturday nights, not Sunday. Ha! Ha! Ha! On and on it went, I was glad I could be their amusement for the day—NOT.

The male rumor mill exceeds at an extremely rapid pace. If I thought I could keep my embarrassing arrest a secret, I was dead wrong. As soon as my husband began working on his jobsite after dropping me off at mine, he told the men he worked with, "You'll never believe what the bitch did now!" It wasn't long before those rumors crossed the street onto my jobsite. An ironworker I knew on my jobsite told me what my husband had said. In his enhanced version, I'd beaten the cop half to death!

I had to tolerate a whole new set of jokes like, "We've got a first-class bitch on our jobsite!" and "You better be careful what you say to her or she'll kick your ass!"

In some circumstances, the rumors caused some men to keep their distance from me, which I was fine with. Others, however, felt they had to challenge me. They'd say things like, "What are you going to do about it?" or "Are you going to cry about it to your ironworker husband?"

To that I would respond, "No, dickweed, because boobs are bigger than balls!" and I would just walk away.

Why have I shared this deep, dark, and "not so secret" tale of woe with you? It's to prove that "What the f———k!" moments don't just pertain to the actions of others but also of yourself as well. Yes, I can be an asshole, too, even though I try my best not to be one. My mom raised me, saying, "Live and learn" and from my actions on the day of my arrest, *I did.*

I learned a lot of life lessons as well as work lessons throughout my nearly three decades of working exclusively with men (thousands of them). I found that at work, it was like falling into a wild animal enclosure at the zoo—proceed with caution—and to "never let them see you sweat!" I adopted the habit of wearing mirror lensed safety sunglasses early on at work. They never knew if I was angry or amused as I matched that accessory with a poker face. It always kept them on their toes, guessing "Is she? Isn't she?"

I had observed that trick when I was an oiler for a certain crane operator. He had a dairy farm at the time, so he was up early enough to milk his cows before making his long drive into work. When I pulled onto a jobsite or our company's parking lot, if I was working in the yard with him, he'd be sleeping in his truck. He had mirrored lensed safety sunglasses on, and the only way I knew he was sleeping was because his seat was tilted back. The crane seats did not tilt back, however, so whenever I noticed that he wasn't reacting to the foreman's hand signal, I would go tap him on his shoulder to wake him up. There would be a lull in between driving a pile bottom and then welding the top extension set on top of it, so I knew how hard it would be for him to stay awake during those times.

From outside the crane, it looked like he was alert and attentive in his seat behind those mirrored lenses. I had some foremen ask me why he wasn't taking the hand signals, and I had other foremen who knew him discreetly ask me to go wake him up. I never slept behind my own mirrored lenses, but I did use them to disguise any emotion displayed in my eyes. If I was shooting daggers at someone with my gaze or if I was laughing internally at someone's stupidity, they never knew it. If someone's insults or hurtful remarks brought a tear to my eyes, no one knew that either. Thus the nickname "Heartless Bitch" followed me like my shadow (sticks and stones—blah, blah, blah).

Another lesson I learned was "it takes two to tango." It takes two people to be in an argument or disagreement. Personally, it took me a long time to work on that one. As soon as I learned that we could proceed through the day's jobsite requirements a lot smoother and faster if I kept my comments to myself, I kept my mouth shut *(HELLO—jail, anyone?)*. It was my job to take the signals given me and make the machine do what was being asked of it. It was the foreman's job to tell the crew members what needed to be done. Could I have rigged, strapped, chained, hooked, and secured my loads better than a lot of the ways I was seeing it done? Oh, hell yes! Would they listen when I explained the reasoning behind my suggestions? That would be a hell no! So I learned not to make a mountain out of a molehill. WTF, it wasn't going to matter to me ten years down the road so I wouldn't set precedent on it then.

Another lesson I learned that I try to use in everyday life is, *"Don't Be a Dick!"* It's so easy for everyone to act like an asshole. That to me is the ultimate in laziness! To be nice, decent, and respectful is hard; it takes work. To behave in a friendly supportive manner when I had to deal with men acting like a bunch of juvenile delinquents used to make me feel like I was babysitting!

Being nice can be a disarming tool. I've calmed many an irate man down simply by listening calmly and speaking in a much lower and quieter tone of voice. That would cause them to have to lower their own voice in order to hear me. They would be ranting and raving because they wanted to be heard. In a lot of cases, I found that if they weren't capturing my attention with good behavior, they were sure to get it with negative behavior. I learned to complement the good actions and behaviors I witnessed in order to develop more of the same.

As far as the worst behavior I saw, I treated it as a man would; I would lean out the door of the crane and yell, "Don't be a dick!" loud enough for everyone to hear.

That statement would usually bring on outbursts of laughter from other crew members such as, "Yeah, quit being a dick!" and jokes about the behavior at hand which could turn it all into a joke, and we'd all end up laughing about it. That would turn a negative into a "reset" for the remainder of the day.

On the other hand, at times, my "dick" statement could inflict enough humility into the man having a temper tantrum to stop by realizing it wasn't an attractive feature for a *female* to witness.

It's hard to keep bringing your attention back to the moment you are living now. It's especially hard to do when you're in a daily battle of being on a difficult jobsite day in and day out. I often felt like I was wishing my life away, waiting for my job to be over for the day or the duration of a job. It was as if I was postponing my life until I could leave work. My thoughts would project to the future when I could retire and no longer have to deal with the stress of my career. As I did that, I realized all the nuances I was missing through-out the hours of my day.

I refocused on a concept I learned long ago as a martial artist and a Buddhist. The Japanese call it "satori," and it means to *live in the moment.* We must remember that tomorrow is not guaranteed. I know that for a fact because I've almost died several times. Two of those incidents I will cover in the chapter, "Challenging and Just Plain Scary." There were a few near drownings while surfing and my first parachute jump from an airplane where I smashed down on the runway. Twice I had dangerous health issues occur, and if it weren't for my now husband, I wouldn't be here.

Yesterdays are gone, and the only thing we can do from past mis-takes is to learn from them. There is always room for improvement in our day-to-day existence.

Throughout my career, the safety standards kept getting tougher. The chains that were required for the uses with a crane magnified until I had to drag them to the crane instead of being able to carry them. Whenever I was laid off, I would lift weights at the gym in order to be prepared when I returned to work.

My endometriosis grew worse. Due to its invasion of my body, it caused severe PMS. I would feel so bad at work that when it cast its wicked spell, I would often go right to bed once I arrived home. I would warn my husband and daughter to save themselves by staying clear of me as I isolated myself in my bedroom. I would then tell them to enter at their own risk only if necessary. I would feel like a shark swimming in dark waters, searching for anything I could sink my teeth into. It was an absolute nightmare to live with that disease. The fifth time I went to the specialist to have the endometriosis surgically removed, he told me that he couldn't cut away at me any further. Every time a surgery to remove it was performed, scar tissue would develop and could cause irritation in the future. Everything had to come out. I was forced to take the time off work and have a total hysterectomy performed.

When I woke up after the surgery, I felt like I was trapped in an alien body; I was ON FIRE! There were no "hot flashes." Instead, I was ablaze in hell! From that point onward, I've had to wear replacement hormone patches to douse the internal flames. When I had to deal with future issues at work, I'd reminded the men that although I no longer had any female organs other than boobs, they were still bigger than balls ever would be! Ha! Ha!

Now that I've written about one of my most WTF moments, I will tell you some of the millions of WTF moments brought on by the opposite gender of our species.

When I was an apprentice oiling on a crane that was driving pile at our sewage treatment plant, the operator would not pay any attention to the hand signals I was giving him. I was the eyes of the crane when we needed to track it from one area to the next to work. Although it was my job to maneuver the crane around corners, avoid manhole covers, and to not make contact with anything, it couldn't be done without the operator's cooperation. When the foreman came over to see what the hell was taking so long for us to walk the crane into place, the operator would take *his* signal. It was very frustrating for me to be ignored while trying to perform my duties.

We needed to work on a Saturday when the majority of workers would not be working. It was going to be a very hot summer day. I thought, *What the hell, I'll wear a tank top because it's going to be very hot outside, and we will be the only crew working.* Wouldn't you know, that old operator took every signal I gave him! It must have been because when signaling, your hands are held in the vicinity of your chest, in my case near my boobs! I thought, *What the f——k? I'm not wearing a damn tank top everyday just to get you to pay attention!*

Monday, when I came to work in my usual attire, he wouldn't take my signals once again. I was done putting up with his bullshit. I yelled up at him sitting there in his seat and said, "If you don't want to take my signals, hop down out of there and I'll operate that crane!" He sat there, glaring at me, so I took a hike to cool off. An ironworker I knew had been watching me struggle with that operator throughout the job. He walked up to me without saying a word and handed me a cup of coffee, then walked back to where he was working. It was such a kind and thoughtful gesture to do for me at that moment that I've never forgotten it.

From that point onward, not only did that operator take my signals, but he requested that I be his oiler on his crane wherever it went for quite a while until I operated cranes myself. He became one of my mentors in pile driving. I must have passed his warped test to see if I would stand up for myself. WTF!

The next tale is from the same jobsite. We were still driving pile for the huge building being erected, and I was still climbing up the tower crane for training during lunch breaks. It was summer time and a nice day to be working outside. A florist van pulled up next to the jobsite. As you can imagine, that was a very unusual sight to see on a construction site. Everyone was watching to see if the driver had taken a wrong turn and was lost. No, he wasn't. He got out of the van and took a large vase of flowers out from the back and started walking onto the jobsite.

He walked up to me in front of all the men and handed me the vase. He said, "You're the only woman here, so you must be Suzanne." I stood there, shocked as he told me to have a nice remainder of my day and made his way back to the van. That was not something that I could ever imagine my husband doing, and when I read the card, it said they were from a "secret admirer."

WTF! Alarm bells were going off in my head. The crane operator asked me who they were from, and I told him that I didn't know. I felt like a bug under a microscope as all the men who witnessed the floral delivery stared at me with expressions of shock or anger. They would have a lot of suspicious innuendos to pass on to my husband at the tavern after work that day. Needless to say, the shit hit the fan when my husband arrived home that night. In his intoxicated state, he accused me of screwing around with someone at work.

I wasn't foolish enough to bring those beautiful flowers home with me, even though what woman doesn't love seeing a beautiful bouquet of flowers on her kitchen table? I offered them to my crane operator mentor. I told him it was a win-win opportunity for him to take those flowers home to his wife. She would be elated by the thoughtful surprise, and he would win extra brownie points for doing so. Then I added that maybe he would "get lucky" that night. It only took him a couple of seconds before accepting my offer. I hid them inside one of the buildings nearby to keep them out of the dirt and sun.

The next morning, a very cheerful operator hopped into that crane seat with a big smile on his face. You would have thought I was his best friend, for that day anyway, ha-ha! Now that experience was unusual in itself until it happened again about a month later. Some man on that jobsite was going through a lot of time and money to impress me, and I never had a clue as to whoever it was.

One of my buddies who was on the excavation crew there had a good idea as to what to do with my latest bouquet of flowers. He told me that even though his shy crew member hadn't sent me the flowers, he did have a crush on me. He was married and had small children at home. He was a quiet guy and a gentleman to work with. Anytime I needed assistance, he always helped me out, along with my buddy.

The prank involved me walking over to the shy operator who was running a large frontend loader, with the new vase of flowers in my hand. I said, "I know that it's been you sending me these beautiful flowers, and I LOVE THEM!"

His face immediately turned beet-red, and he had the expression of a deer in the headlights. The embarrassed operator began stammering, "But, but, but…I…didn't…send th-them to you, I'm so sorry!"

His buddy about fell out of his backhoe. He was laughing so hard, and then I started laughing too. The shy operator figured out that his buddy had set him up, and he seemed more relieved than mad and joined in our laughter.

I told my buddy to take the flowers home to his wife as a reward for coming up with his bright idea that made the day a fun memory for us three. Sure enough, my buddy got lucky that night! At least both of my bouquets didn't go to waste.

The bouquet incidents proved to me that men didn't care if you were married or not, they were still going to make their moves on you. You may not notice it in the form of bouquets of flowers being delivered to you, but you will take notice of it.

We took some time off from that building to track the crane all the way to the other end of the island. We were to drive piling to make foundations for huge tanks to be built upon. The ramp that had been constructed was very narrow and steep to walk the crane down. A deep hole had been excavated for us to work in.

It's a hairy experience to walk a crane up or down a steep incline. The way in which you do it is similar to loading or unloading a crane minus its boom, off and onto a lowboy semitrailer used for transport. Usually, you back down the ramp while keeping your boom as low to the ground as possible. That action acts as a counterweight to keep your crane from flipping onto it's back. The counterweights that are bolted or pinned to the back of the crane weigh many tons a piece. Those are necessary to hold up the boom that stands high into the air. As you climb a crane out of the hole, it's usually done in the reverse position.

We had an air compressor mounted high on the back of the crane, and the leads with the hammer inside were still attached to the boom. The operator kept the hammer a few inches above the ground and used it as an anchor to keep the crane from tipping over. It took us quite a while to get our pile driving crane down that ramp and into the hole.

Our service crane was there to unload the pipe pile off of the semitrailers and lower them down into the hole for us, along with our welders, toolboxes, and other equipment. When the service crane needed to join us down in the hole to move our pipe pile and equipment to another part of the jobsite, it was like something out of a comedy routine. The operator lined up his crane to aim straight down the ramp, and then he might as well have made the sign of the cross like in a religious ceremony because he flew down that ramp on a wing and a prayer!

The foreman and the other men on the crew told me to get ready to throw huge timbers in front of the crane tracks to help it slow down. I remember thinking, *What the f——k are we throwing large timbers in front of the crane for?*

Sure enough, as soon as that crane breached the tipping point at the top of the ramp, there it came, faster and faster like a runaway locomotive, *KA-CHUNK, KA-CHUNK, KA-CHUNK!* It came clambering wildly down the ramp crushing all the hardwoods we were throwing in front of it into sawdust. Two pile drivers carried a heavy light post over that had been taken down for the duration of our project. "Screw it!" they yelled as they placed the big-ass log in front of the rapidly approaching out-of-control crane. WTF! We nearly had a disaster on our hands. We would have to replace the sacrificial light post once our job was done.

That introduction in how to maneuver a crane up and down a steep ramp had always stayed with me. It taught me what NOT to do. I refused to appear like something out of a *Flintstones* cartoon with a bunch of cavemen throwing various debris in front of my crane to make it stop; WTF kind of nonsense was that?

As we were driving pile in that location, winter was upon us. We'd been working on the site for quite a while, and I'd used the port-a-potty so many times that the path to it was embedded in my mind until a full-on blizzard hit our city! I could barely see it as it blended in with the blinding snowfall. Once I reached it, I had the additional burden of trying to open the door with the mound of snow rapidly piling up against it. I thought, *Holy f——k, I better pee fast before I'm snowed into this port-a-potty!*

After that fiasco, I decided to stay on top of the crane, back behind the air compressor. If I stood inside the doors, it would block a lot of the snow pelting me, and I could use the heat from the engine for warmth. I decided to pee in a bucket up there if I had to because I couldn't see shit and, therefore, no one could see me either! It was too dangerous to leave the crane; it was too dangerous to be there at all. The blizzard reminded me of an icy winter I spent up at our Operating Engineer's School. It was super cold outside, and I was in a crane class there. All of the cranes were parked in rows that lined both sides of a roadway. There were obstacles such as tires and barrels for us to practice dropping our headache balls into. We were also moving items with our cranes from place to place while taking hand signals from our partners. The port-a-potty was placed at the end of the road from where my crane was parked.

I regretted the idea of using the port-a-potty in that frigid weather because I had to remove the many layers of clothing I had on to do so; it was like peeing in a meat locker! I "skated" my way down the road as if I were on an ice rink. After using the facility, I was attempting to wrestle back into my many layers of clothing and my cumbersome coveralls when I slipped on the icy floor. Out I slid, naked from my waist down, I shot out the door of the port-a-potty sliding on my ass in front of two rows of crane operators! I was so EMBARRASSED!

"WHAT THE FUCK!" I screamed. I somehow managed to stand up and dress myself in record time. After a moment of shock as to what they had just seen, the men all erupted with laughter. I knew that I must have looked hilarious, so I gave it to them right back. I said, "You motherf——kers! You act like you've never seen a half-naked woman out in the middle of nowhere before!" Then we *all* started laughing. As I made my way *slowly* back to my crane, I said, "Boy, does my ass hurt!" They told me that I had really bounced off the ice.

Anyway, with those memories in my head during that blizzard, there was no way I was leaving the roof of the crane. I could barely see the headlights of our vice president of the company's vehicle as he pulled up on the road above us. He informed us that the entire island was being evacuated because the snowdrifts were becoming so high that cars were barely making it up the on-ramps to the over-passes connecting to the surrounding area.

The foreman yelled out that we would finish driving the pile we were on before leaving. What the f——k! Everyone but the fore-man wanted to leave as soon as possible because we all had to drive home in white-out conditions. The foreman was an old man who had been with the company for many years. He was one of the few old-timers who would make you work right up to the minute it was break or time to go home. My theory was that number one, they were "ass-kissers," and number two, they were insecure about all the younger foreman coming up in the company and felt they had to prove that they were still a useful asset. When you were sent on a jobsite to work for one of those foreman, you knew what you were in for, and it sucked! It always made me think, *WTF! Grow a pair!*

Sure enough, I was pushing snow as if I had a plow on the front of my car as I precariously made my way off the island. I was barely able to drive up the ramp and barely made it into my driveway when I finally arrived home.

Once we finished the tank area of the island, we moved over to the brick stack that towered high into the air. We were to drive piling next to it in order to withstand the weight of very large pipe that was to be connected to it. The connection would be from the new building we'd been working on for the majority of our time on the project and the big stack. The pipe would lay in an iron cradle that would bridge over the main road through the sewage plants interior.

The closer we worked to the stack, the harder it was for me to breathe the air. Human waste was processed and "baked" into fertilizer called Milorganite. It's sold in various garden centers. The air on the island was abundant with bacteria. The air would appear ordinary during our days, but in the evenings, smoke could be seen billowing rapidly from the top of the smokestack. When I arrived on our jobsite every morning, there was a brown fuzz covering our crane. The top portion of our cranes were painted white with the lower half painted black. When I would attempt to clean the walls of the crane, the brown fuzz smeared around before I could wipe it completely away. I told the men, "WTF! We are literally breathing *shit!*"

I kept losing my voice while working and coming down with bronchitis often. I had to go on a couple of allergy prescriptions and get weekly injections while working near that toxic stack spewing God only knew what. All the men around me at work and my husband were thrilled when I lost my voice entirely for two weeks.

One very scary accident happened to me while we were working by that smokestack that no one was aware of. Winter had begun once again during our long duration of work at that sewage treatment plant. All the pile we had previously driven into the ground on our jobsite had been covered with a plastic film to keep the water out. It had snowed the night before and therefore, those pile were invisible underneath the icy carpet.

As work began, the operator I was oiling for had to track the crane in reverse to pick up a pile and then track forward to the position in which it was to be driven. We had laid down mats for the crane to move in both directions on. The mats ensured that the crane would be level for driving the pile. As I was walking, I fell onto one of the plastic covered pile. My leg went down the pipe, and as I lay in great pain on the ground, I worried that I'd broken it. My leg was totally encapsulated in the pipe pile, and I was in too much pain to try and get it out.

I was yelling for help, but no one could hear me above the roar of the crane engine. A scary observation became clear in my mind. *If I don't get out of the way, the crane could possibly crush me when it moves in reverse! WTF! I am screwed!*

I stopped yelling and began concentrating on lifting my leg out of the pipe. The pain had ebbed enough for me to know that it wasn't broken—thank God! I managed to maneuver my leg out of the pipe finally and rolled out of the way of the crane's path.

The crane was so loud that no one had heard me as I had laid on the ground, and the crane also blocked the vision of my crew from seeing me, so when I finally rejoined them, it was as if nothing out of the ordinary had happened. Instead of raising alarms, I thought of a way to keep that accident from reoccurring. When the head superintendent stopped by our jobsite to see how we were progressing, I asked him to have some of our safety spray paint in a different color than we were using to mark where our pipe pile were to be driven to be sent out to us. I explained (in a far more toned down manner) that my foot had punctured the plastic covering on a pipe pile and had sent me to the ground on my ass. I told him that I wanted to color the tops of the driven pipe pile in our neon spray paint so that someone didn't incur a serious injury due to the present invisibility of the pipe pile.

He thought it was an excellent suggestion for safety and from that afternoon, when the paint arrived to this present day, that is how driven pile are identified. The safety colors of spray paint used on jobsites are so bright that they can be detected, even through a light blanket of snow.

Unfortunately, I had the biggest and most unusual (painful too!) bruising around the top of my right thigh area for quite a while, but at least I hadn't broken my leg.

I was getting a lot of serious headaches while working on "Bacteria Island." I kept thinking that it was because my hair was up underneath my hard hat all day. At that time, my hair had grown down to my hips. Usually, by noon, it felt like the band on my hard hat was tightening up on me like some medieval torture device.

I had noticed that after wearing their hard hats all day, the men would take them off at the end of the workday and replace them with baseball caps. I also had noticed that almost all of them were *bald on top*. "What the f——k? I didn't want my hair being rubbed off by my hard hat!" I silently screamed to myself. After I had that shocking awakening, I began wearing a bandanna in pirate fashion over my hair so that I'd have a cushion between my hair and my hard hat; in other words, I had a lot going on up there.

Then came the comments, "Who are you? A pirate? A gypsy? a hobo? A Viking?" I'm telling you, those guys were looking for anything to fill the void of amusement in their day. They were so lucky that I came along into their drab careers to brighten things up for them!

I pulled the trigger and chopped off my hair to my shoulders, thinking for sure that it would cause my headaches to subside. I don't like my hair short; I just don't. After a few tears were shed, I put on my bandanna and then my hard hat and went off to work. What the f——k, it didn't make one bit of difference! All the years it had taken me to grow my hair long ended up with handfuls of it lying in a trash can; I cried some more.

That was the last time I cut my hair other than to trim the ends once in a while. Throughout the rest of the years I worked, my hair grew on the top of my head to the point where I looked like Marge Simpson of *The Simpsons* cartoons, or one of the coneheads in the old *Saturday Night Live* skits. As for the headaches, I realized that two drawbacks to my job were bringing them on: the stress of the job itself and *THE MEN*. Somedays at work, I felt like I was running a day care center for children! The only relief was for me to take an aspirin for each.

It was a reasonable assumption to forget how dangerous my job was because I did it every day for years. I had to keep reminding myself that I literally held the lives of many in my hands each day when I climbed into a crane. As for the men, the stress lay in dealing with the ones that hated that I was there and what that represented (a woman doing exactly what they had been doing for years and, in a lot of cases, did it better!). The men that behaved like assholes and the ones that acted like little babies needing to be coddled all the time (mama's boys). There were the men who felt as if they were God's gifts to the world (and especially to women). The men who knew *EVERYTHING* and the ones who didn't know SHIT! There were men who love/lusted for me (I always thought, *WTF is wrong with you?* I was always wearing greasy and filthy bib overalls for God's sake and usually had grease on my face smeared into my makeup. I didn't understand the attraction. Kinky maybe? Was it the money I made? That must have been it.).

I also had stalkers; I wrote about one of them when I attended my Operator's Skill Center. I will be writing about more later. The funny thing about the men I worked with was that I'd seen quite a few of them in passing while wearing my normal attire outside work, and they didn't recognize me. In my everyday appearance, I was incognito, hiding from them in plain sight, ha-ha!

My hair got so high on my head that if I bent over while wearing my hard hat, it would spin. I began parting my hair down the center of my head and creating two buns instead of just one. That hairstyle caused the men to come up with a few new nicknames for me (my, how that list was growing, especially when you added the curse words). Those names were Cindy Brady from the old television show, *The Brady Bunch,* and Princess Leia from the *Star Wars* movies. WTF! I'd been called a lot worse. At least each bun fit between the webbing of my hard hat, and then it didn't budge from my head at all anytime I leaned over.

We moved our crane back to our initial jobsite on the island. The only time that I hadn't worked with my "now husband" was on the portion of the island sewage expansion project that we were just leaving. I realized that he was the only man out of the hundreds I'd worked with so far in my career that I had missed being around. I had developed quite a crush on him. He was very good-looking, charming, and could be quite humorous. We were both married then, and I chalked that crush up to being around a man who was nice to me and was charismatic by nature. I was sure that sort of thing happened in all areas of work when two people spend so many hours each day together.

Apparently, I smiled more often in his presence than in anyone else's. I hadn't realized that until my crew came up to me at the end of the day as we were walking to our vehicles and said, "Don't even think about it!"

I said, "What the f——k are you guys talking about?"

"We see you smiling at the foreman. You'd just be another notch in his bedpost. He's out with different women all the time, so forget it! We don't need any drama on the jobsite."

"I'm a married woman, motherf——kers! A little smile is just that. Christ, I smile at you guys, would you rather that I just be a bitch?"

"You don't smile LIKE THAT at us!" was their cocky reply.

I was embarrassed by that conversation but would never forget it. I pushed my "sunny, not a cloud in the sky rainbow" thoughts deep down into my gut. I locked them away there and said, "Sayonara" and got back down to the business of being the best crane operator that I could be. I planned on proving to every man I came across on every jobsite that I walked onto that, yes, there was room for us women to have a place there as well, so move the f——k over, moth- erf——kers! My feelings stayed put where I stashed them for eleven years. I'll write more on the outcome in the chapter titled "Funny and Absurd."

On a rain day we had during our "Island Residency," I had for- gotten my thermos in our jobsite trailer. I had already taken off my bib overalls that kept my work clothes clean underneath them. I'd removed my hard hat and bandanna to let my hair down. I fig- ured that since everyone on the jobsite had cleared out due to their "tavern warnings," I would just walk back in and quickly retrieve my thermos. I was passing a group of ironworkers that were late in exiting the plant. "Hey, honey, you want to come have a beer with us?" one of them said to me.

"No thanks, you guys, I'm on my way to pick up my daughter." "Where are you working here?" one of them asked in a friendly tone of voice.

"You guys see me over by that crane every day!" "Oh shit, Suzanne, we didn't know it was you!"

"You look so different with your hair down!" another guy added. "What the f——k, you guys, you're not even drunk yet!" I joked as we all started laughing.

That was a good lesson for me to be able to remain incognito whenever I saw a fellow worker in the grocery store. I could sail right past them, and they would not recognize me in my girl clothes and with my hair free of a bandanna and hard hat. I also had a hard time recognizing them without a hard hat as a great deal of them were bald on the top of their heads. The last thing I felt like doing after the workday was to rehash the daily grind of the job; I had better things to do. The few times I had gone to the bar with my ironworker husband before I entered construction, I noticed that was all they usually talked about—work.

I had a couple of traumatic events happen to me while I worked on the island project. One of them occurred one evening at my home. I was alone there with my daughter when there was a loud knocking on my door. My husband was drinking his dinner at the tavern. When I opened the door, I was shocked to find a guy I knew from the jobsite, standing before me, DRUNK! Another worker was with him, apologizing profusely. The seemingly sober man said, "I'm so sorry, he insisted that I bring him here."

I didn't give him a moment to explain what business he had being at my home because there was no excuse for his behavior. I said, "Are you out of your f——king mind? Get out of here and don't ever come back. My husband will kill us both if he sees you here and he could come home any minute now!" I looked at the guy who had driven him to my address and said, "Take him and get the hell out of here now!"

I don't even know how that guy got my address. I found out that he and his wife lived in the near vicinity of our neighborhood, along with their children. I'd seen him drive by my house occasionally in his work truck, presumably on his way home from work. However, I never caught him acknowledging my residence in any way. Perhaps he was the admirer sending me those floral arrangements at work; I never knew for sure who the culprit was.

A few days after his devious interruption of my privacy, he approached me at work. He apologized for his unwelcome appearance at my home. I told him that his action didn't set well with me at all, and if he did it again, he would be extremely regretful about doing so. I asked him to think of his wife and how she would feel about his inappropriate behavior.

He told me that he wanted to see me outside work and had ingested liquid courage in order to show up at my house. I let him know how my husband would respond to his unwanted advances and informed him also that my brother-in-law was working on the same project we were along with many of their ironworker buddies. I mentioned that I had many ironworkers armed with their sleeve bars watching my back there. I reminded him that he was married with small children at home and he was the one who should have "their" backs. That turned out to be our final conversation after he promised to never show up at my house again.

One of the cruelest things anyone has ever done to me occurred one Saturday afternoon. My brother-in-law had not only been working on the same island project, but he was living with us at the time in order to work there. His residence was on the northern border of our state, and on that particular weekend, my husband joined him in a fishing excursion up there.

My young daughter and our two dogs were keeping me company while I tended to chores around the house when I received a phone call. The woman said that she was a nurse and that she was reaching out to me for a doctor who would be with me shortly. She told me that it was an emergency situation and that I needed to stay on the line until the doctor could speak to me; she needed to put me on hold momentarily.

After a short waiting period, the doctor came on the line. He informed me that my husband and the man he'd been traveling with had been in an accident. They must have been climbing on an old iron bridge and fallen from it because they were both found on the ground below. He asked if I knew who my husband had been traveling with because he had been found without any identification on him. When I told him that he was his brother, the doctor told me that he was sorry to have to inform me that my brother-in-law had landed on a piece of farm equipment when he'd fallen. He'd been nearly decapitated, and the fall had killed him.

My husband was unconscious and needed surgery immediately. He informed me that when my husband fell, his legs were crushed by the impact. Also that a gun he'd carried in his boot had gone off and demolished one of his legs. The doctor was requesting my permission to amputate the leg that received the gunshot. He would try to save the other crushed leg, but he could not promise that he wouldn't have to amputate them both. He told me to stay on the line and the receptionist was going to set up a flight for me to get to the hospital as soon as possible.

I was needed there to sign all of the necessary paperwork and to identify the deceased body that was brought in with my husband. The doctor told me that until a positive identification was made that I should not notify any other family members at that time. The receptionist came on the phone and told me that she would call back with the arrangements for me to fly into the airport in our far northern area. She would also make arrangements for transportation for me to get to the hospital from the airport.

I hung up the phone in shock and dismay. I stopped what I had been doing and began throwing a few items and pieces of clothing into a bag so that I would be ready to leave. I was thinking of who I could call to watch my daughter while I was gone. That weekend had become very stressful and complicated with that one phone call.

I heard a knock on my door, and it was my husband's cousin who lived one block away from us. He had stopped by to see how my daughter and I were doing. He took one look at my face and said, "What's wrong?" I told him about the phone call and that I was packing to leave. He told me that he and his wife would watch my daughter and that he would drive me to the airport. He told me to see if the woman called me back because it sounded to him as though someone was pulling a mean prank on me.

He told me that it was a known fact that my husband carried a loaded handgun in his boot on occasion and that both he and my brother-in-law climbed bridges now and again. He reminded me that all the guys they were both working with on their jobsites knew that they had taken off to go fishing up north that weekend.

Not long before that weekend, two ironworkers had been drinking in a tavern and had bet money on which of them could climb to the highest point on a famous bridge we have here in our city. It crosses over our main river and is a main freeway that connects the northern and southern sections of our city. The two drunk ironworkers were given tickets by an officer waiting at the bottom of the high arch they had climbed. Neither ironworker was the winner that night. It was not unusual for the ironworkers I knew then to climb on bridges.

My husband's cousin told me to call the tavern in the small town my brother-in-law resided in. I could leave a message for my husband to call me when he showed up there in the evening hours. No one ever got back to me about a flight or for any other reason for that matter; it had all been lies. I received a phone call that evening from my angry husband, accusing me of "checking up on him," not for health reasons but for trust issues I had with him. He warned me never to call him, that if I didn't hear from him, he was fine. If I received a direct call from him, then it would be bad news.

He showed me just how unhappy he was that I had called for him the next evening when he arrived home. After that, I never called him again—EVER.

The female receptionist and nurse are who had sold me on the evil prank. In all honesty, if it wasn't for the two of them, I would have just hung up the phone immediately. I never recognized any of those three voices which was to their advantage because I was eager to match them up with their faces.

My husband told me that the men working on the island project didn't appreciate the fact that I was the union steward there. They didn't like the fact that a woman wielded the power to shut them down when they tried to sneak onto a piece of equipment and operate it instead of an operating engineer. I had notified the hall a few times about that sort of thing happening, and the men involved had been reprimanded. They didn't like the fact that as a crane operator, I made a higher hourly wage than they did. They didn't like my presence there, period. Since I had no plans on leaving, they'd have to attempt to wrap their brains around that fact.

My husband also explained to me that other male union stewards along with himself had been given grief on various jobsites as well but not to the extremes I had experienced. He told me that I should run for a *business agent* position and really be able to sink my teeth into monitoring jobsites and being proactive in protecting our work. I will write more on that subject in a bit. The event of that prank was so mean that I remember it as if it happened just yesterday. WTF! Who could think up bullshit like that? What women would willfully help a man to hurt another woman in that way? How vindictive! I had learned a hell of a lesson that weekend, and it was to always watch my back and to trust no one on a jobsite.

As far as my dream of becoming a tower crane operator exclusively, I was running into obstacles after obstacle. I had completed all of my training on my own time at no cost to anyone. I was trained by our best tower crane operator. He had spent his entire career specializing in that particular piece of equipment. Honestly, there were not a lot of high rises being built back in those years when I was aggressively pursuing that position. If I were to strictly adhere to operating tower cranes exclusively, I would have had long periods of time in between jobs in which to wait.

I had been sent to a high-rise being constructed in the heart of our downtown area. When I showed up there, I found out that I would be filling in for the tower crane operator while he went out of town, and once he returned, I would fill in for their material hoist operator. The material hoist operator had a sudden death occur in his family and would need to leave the state for a couple of weeks.

The material hoist was an easy piece of equipment to operate. It was so easy that I found it extremely boring. All that was required of me was to throw a switch to maneuver the hoist to go up or down. It carried both personnel and materials from floor to floor. Material hoists are visible as they ride up and down along the outer side of a tall structure being constructed. The operator I was replacing had a chair inside so that he could sit on his ass all day and simply throw a switch—not *this* girl! That kind of tedious boredom would have driven me out of my mind, so I decided to be the most helpful material hoist operator EVER!

I said, "Good morning" to everyone as I greeted the men each day when flying them up to their designated floors. I assisted them in loading and unloading all the materials and equipment flying up or down. I even helped roll the port-a-potties on and off the hoist. I boosted my riders' morale as best I could by displaying a sunny disposition. It was an easy job for me at a comparable wage to the stressful job of driving pile with a crane. I could see a pile driving jobsite in progress while I was operating the tower crane on that same jobsite. It turned out to be the company that I usually worked with driving in those pile. It was unique for me to have a *bird's-eye view* of watching them work.

I knew many of the ironworkers on that jobsite. My brother-in-law worked on the evening shift there as a welder. One of the funniest things I saw on that jobsite was a half a port-a-potty. I had never seen one like that before (and I never saw another one like it again). It looked like a rolling cabinet with the front being a door to allow a person to enter. It was waist high and was extremely embarrassing for the man who was taking a shit while sitting inside of that thing every time I threw open the hoist door to allow men to enter or exit.

One morning, I startled a guy sitting in there, and I could see his face turn beet-red before he shielded himself from my view with a newspaper he had been reading. We were both trapped within each other's line of sight; neither one of us wanted to be acknowledged by the other as to what we were witnessing. It was so hard for me to keep from laughing my head off at the vision of half a man sticking out of that port-a-potty, trying to hide behind a newspaper!

I looked away to give the poor pooper some privacy and said to the port-a-potty delivery man I was helping, "You're on your own on this floor." He chuckled, probably anticipating telling the story of my awkward encounter to his port-a-potty shop buddies. *WHAT THE FUCK more am I to see on these jobsites?* I remember thinking.

That building was so tall that I don't recall how many stories it is, even though I pass by it if I drive through our downtown area in present-day life. Wouldn't you know that by the end of that fateful day, every man working on that jobsite had heard of my embarrassing encounter with the worker taking a shit? Most of them had to add their two cents worth about it, each one thinking they were the comedian of the day. I just joked back with them, stating that I was pleased to present them with some humor during my stay with them.

That job, though very busy and with long hours, went well for me. The men treated me decent, and a few of them told me that they wished I could stay on. They told me that the regular hoist operator never offered to help in any way and sat on his ass all day long.

The contractor on that job was a big outfit, and their specialty was in constructing hospitals. They called me to work for them on many projects throughout my career. They would contact me for work during the winter months when they knew I would be laid off from my usual company. They were a good outfit to work for.

I will tell you about the only accident involving a material hoist that happened during my career. It happened on the jobsite that I've already written about, and it never left my mind the entire time I was operating that material hoist. It was at the sewage treatment plant. They had erected a material hoist onto the outside of the building we'd driven the pile for. Another female operator had come to the project to be an oiler for the crane, setting the panels of precast onto the outsides of the building. She was under the employment of the main contractor there and had been provided by our union hall. She and I had become friends quickly. It was nice for me to have the extremely rare opportunity of having another female on the jobsite.

One day, they transferred her over to the material hoist to be its operator. A laborer and a boilermaker who happened to be my husband's fishing buddy and was a close friend of our family climbed aboard the material hoist to be taken down to ground level. The material hoist operates electrically like a tower crane does, but on that day it free-fell. There are huge springs set at the base of a material hoist in case such an accident occurs. All three people inside the hoist hit the floor as soon as possible as everyone is taught to do in a free fall situation.

It was passing the lower third of the building when it fell. If the hoist had dropped immediately from where it began its descent at the top floor of the building, the three riders would have been killed. As it was, all three workers had serious injuries and were taken to the hospital in ambulances. There were displaced shoulders, broken ribs, and multiple bruises and contusions among them. All three suffered major nerve damage because they had been crushed somewhat on impact.

Our buddy was a tall and robust guy. He actually lost some of his height because his vertebrae were compressed. He was never able to return to work as a boilermaker again. The laborer also was unable to return to work. All three dealt with major pain issues from that accident due to nerve damage.

The hoist had to be raised and held in place by a crane so that the springs that had cushioned it's fall could be replaced. Once new springs were installed, the crane lowered the hoist's cab, and it was disconnected electrically so that the entire piece of equipment could be gone over with a fine-tooth comb. I never heard the cause of its malfunction.

The bolts used in erecting a tower crane and a material hoist are torqued to the specifications that an engineer for the project has calculated. As for a tower crane, the bolts are not used again after a job because of the twisting of the steel tower as it's in motion. I don't know if the reason for the malfunctioning material hoist was mechanically induced or electrical. That was a horrible "WTF!" moment, and everyone who was there the day of the accident were elated that all three of those workers survived their ordeal.

After the tower crane operator returned and the material hoist operator also, I was no longer needed to fill in for anyone. I returned to the sewage treatment plant expansion project on the island. The operator of the tower crane who had been training me was voted in as our area's business agent for our union. The crane we had been operating needed work done on it, and a technician specializing on tower cranes had been brought in. Since he needed to deal with the electrical panels that were stored at the rear end of the jib, they were looking for an operator to run the controls as required by the technician. I'd been authorized to leave the crane I was working on and climb the tower to assist him. As I was speaking with the technician, he told me that I should become an electrical technician specializing in tower cranes the way he had. He told me that I would be very busy for the duration of my career. He said that there were not enough tower crane repairmen to keep up with the demand.

He was a young guy and was flown all over the world to address tower crane issues. They paid him an enormous salary, and he had an equally impressive expense account complete with a great benefit package. He did not have a spouse or dependents at home, so he was able to leave at a moment's notice; I didn't have that luxury. He admitted that sometimes he would be gone for long periods of time. Occasionally, the repair of one tower crane would lead to him providing services to other cranes in that area or country.

He handed me a radio so that I could hear him give me instructions on what function he needed the tower crane to do. For the remainder of the day, I swung the jib left and right, trolleyed in and out, and lowered and hoisted the block upon his command. As soon as he was satisfied with the crane's operating status, he told me that he was off to another country to repair some tower cranes there. He also told me that he was even sent to war-torn countries to repair cranes needed to rebuild cities. He said that if it were up to him, he'd rather sabotage the cranes instead of repair them back to operational order in some areas.

As for the pile driving crew I was working with, we had been told to step it up or begin driving pile on two shifts instead of one. We had new crew members added to our day shift. The three men sent to us were our more "religious" employees of our company. They usually held Bible study amongst themselves during both our coffee and lunch breaks. They were forever attempting to "save" the rest of us.

Some of our *heathen sinner* crew members thought that it would be extra amusing to amp up their decorating style of our jobsite trailer in which we ate our meals and held our safety meetings, using their topless female calendars and posters. It became wall-to-wall boobs in there with a few beavers (and I don't mean the furry kind that build dams) included to add the ultimate visionary punch. Back then, the manufacturers of tools, oils, aerosols, and equipment would give out free calendars with topless women adorning them to their customers as incentive for their future business.

As I entered our jobsite trailer for coffee break one morning, I noticed the boob decorations had grown to cover nearly all surfaces inside imaginable. That didn't bother me at all because I saw the same calendars and posters at my home in the garage. My husband had calendars from various Harley dealerships that had naked women draped over motorcycles or sitting upon them in lewd positions. My husband and I both owned Harleys, and there were so many motorcycles in pieces scattered over my backyard at that time that it was referred to as our Harley garden.

When I next entered our trailer at lunchtime, the religious guys had used their flannel shirts to cover up the naked women adorning the walls in order to shield them from visibility. That began the vigilant covering and uncovering of the naked boobs for several days. I remember wondering, *When are they sneaking into the trailer to pull off these antics? They are supposed to be working.* I also remember wondering, *Are we in the seventh grade? Are we at work or are we back in middle school?* The welfare and safety of myself and others were in the hands of men whose minds were obstructed by naked boobs!

That bizarre war of wills rapidly became out of hand over the following days when the naked posters covered our entire ceiling, and then the religious guys followed that endeavor up by bringing in large beach towels and sheets to hang over entire sections of our walls until it seemed we were dining on our lunch inside of a giant quilt or a circus tent for that matter! "Guys, guys, GUYS! I have a pair of those myself. Mine just happen to be bouncing around here on equipment, earning a REAL living and not sitting stationary for a photograph. I know God gave all of your wives each a set of those, and she probably used them to feed your children when they were born, so relax—enough already!"

My speech went over like a lead balloon because that was actually an argument about religion and not about bustlines. It didn't concern my sentiments on the calendars and posters adorning the walls at all. I was raised to never discuss money, religion, or politics because like our DNA, we are all different. No one wins in the discussion of any of those three subjects. Each religion deems themselves to be the one and "only" religion, and if those zealots I was working with found out that I was a Buddhist, I'd be rated right up there with a voodoo priestess!

I had enough of being used as their pawn in the religious game they brought to the jobsite every day, so I began having my own private picnic for lunchtime; it was a lot more peaceful that way. I also kept my spare work shirts in my car instead of hanging them in the trailer to be used as pulpit drapery.

Eventually, the workplace congregation were incorporated into the second shift pile driving division of the project. One of the guys prayers went unanswered one evening when his nose and collarbone were both broken. The iron hammer pounds away all day on steel pipe pile. The hammer takes on more abuse as it's used for two shifts instead of one. The stress causes cracks and pieces are known to fall from the hammer now and then as repairs become necessary.

Unfortunately, the foreman was standing in close proximity to the pile being driven in order to count the blows between the marks he'd placed on it. He heard an unusual sound and looked upward to see what was happening with the hammer. The iron chunk dropped from the hammer so fast and with such force that after landing squarely on his nose, causing it to break, it then bounced onto his shoulder area, breaking his collarbone before falling to the ground. He was damn lucky it didn't kill him.

That was a lesson for all of us to keep our distance from the hammer when it was in operation. I learned a lot of other lessons about driving pile on that project as well. The pounding of the hammer all day long as you are working, or in my case, creating, would not stop within my own head. For the first months, I had the incessant ringing of *"ping-ping-ping"* going on in my head.

That constant noise nearly drove me out of my mind. It became almost impossible for me to sleep because I could not block out that high-pitched pinging of steel on steel. It was inside me and I noticed myself moving to its rhythmic beat, like a little soldier girl. I began "marching" instead of walking to the beat in my head.

To make those matters worse, on some jobs, I had to count the blows of the hammer. If there was money provided in the jobs contract to hire a *blow counter,* we were given one. On the lesser scaled monetary contracts, that job went to the crane operator driving the pile. I spoke out about that situation to no avail. I stated that those of us crane operators expected to count the blows of our hammers were in the control of three drums of cable, the air to the hammer, holding the adjustment of the pile as it's ridden into the ground, AND maneuvering the crane through all of its functions SHOULD BE PAID MORE MONEY! WTF! We were doing the jobs of three people on any crew you'd see on a jobsite using a diesel hammer—THREE PEOPLE!

We were required to be ambidextrous, very coordinated, and able to do mental gymnastics in our heads. I was juggling so many thoughts as it was—was my boom angle correct? Do I need to swing a touch to my right or left to keep the pile straight? Do I need to lower the monkey? (Sometimes I was operating FOUR drums. One cable would hoist and lower a bracket, called a "monkey," that's held inside the leads. That was a tool used in assisting the proper alignment of the pipe pile I was driving into the ground.) I had to be constantly prepared to shut the air valve off to the hammer as soon as the foreman signaled for me to do so. Sometimes, I even had to count the blows of the hammer.

When a pile nears the required depth it is to be driven, soapstone is used to make marks inches apart from each other. The increments in which the markings are placed become less and less. The blows driving the pile continue until the count requirement is reached. The foreman is usually counting blows alongside a designated "blow counter person" who is provided by the general contractor.

The count must be in agreement between them both before they can continue on to the next pile driving placement. All records are kept describing each pile that was driven for the day. Those records are proof that the jobsite's engineers requirements were met. All the pipe pile that have been driven into the ground are the bases of structures built from the ground up. It has always amazed me how it was figured out exactly what could hold up the tons of weight involved in the construction of the many tall and vast structures I was involved in creating.

If the foreman had to excuse himself for any reason from his counting process and there was no blow counter to assist, then he usually asked me to do the counting since I had a close eye on the hammer at all times anyway. I occasionally worked with old foreman who were just too lazy to count and expected me to do their job for them; WTF, that just sucked! As I was driving pile, it was my responsibility to "release and catch" the hammer cable as it was spooling off the drum. As the hammer was pounding, I was required to pump the brake for that drum as it dropped down. That kept the cable from spinning wildly off of the drum creating a "bird's nest." A bird's nest is what the excess cable would resemble if it were allowed to spool loosely.

I could not allow the crisscrossing of my cable because it would crush the many small wires that made up the cable itself or kink the cable. Damaged cable cannot be counted on to safely hold a load and must be replaced. That proved to be a costly situation to have any cable replaced on a pile driving crane. The job itself is put on a standstill in order to cut loose from all of the equipment that you have hanging from the boom tip. All the damaged cable is pulled off by the pile drivers as they precariously perch on top of the boom which has been completely lowered to ground level. Once removed, they walk the new cable up through the boom tip sheave and back to the drum. I was involved in that process too many times to count, and I can attest to the fact that it was a real pain in the ass! It would shut down our jobsites for a day or two costing a lot of time and money in the process.

All the pumping of the brake holding the hammer when driving pile was very tiring on my knee, hip, and lower back. Now imagine you're pumping away and counting as if you are a toy soldier marching endlessly onward: *"One, two, three, four, one, two, three, four, one, blah, blah, blah."* I found myself counting the ringing blows of the hammer while attempting to sleep at night. I caught myself counting my steps whenever I climbed down from the crane to use the port-apotty or walk to my car. Everything was *"ping, one, two, three, ping, one, two, three."* It drove me OUT OF MY MIND!

I asked other pile driving crane operators if this unwelcome phenomenon had happened to any of them. I received answers from all over the map such as, "Yes, it did that to me for several months" to "Yes, that's why I hit the tavern after work each day, to quell the demon hammer that pounds inside my head!"

Some operators told me that they still counted to the endless chorus of the pounding internal hammer. "No, thank you!" I told myself. I chanted internally anytime I caught myself mercilessly counting in order to break the vicious psychotic cycle. After a couple of years, it finally stopped but not before I developed an acute case of insomnia. I kept telling myself that the ringing of the hammer pounding was the ring of an opening till holding all my future paychecks. I turned the dilemma into a positive by turning the sounds I was hearing in my head into a mental vision of dollar signs: *one, two, three, $, one, two, three, $ one, two, three, $.*

A blow counter cannot possibly cost the contractor a lot of money. All that job requires is that they stand close enough to be able to see the markings on the pipe pile being driven in order to count the amount of blows between them. They then record the numbers onto the forms provided to them; that's it. Most of us are taught to count by the time we are enrolled in KINDERGARTEN! WTF!

I kept the jobsites I worked on as free of garbage and debris as possible. I got tired of tripping over pieces of wire cut from the ironworkers tying up their forms or our rebar cages. I would get my pants legs snagged on the wire feed remnants from our welders. I noticed the garbage circling around other cranes as the operator's discards were flung out their doors as they swung their machines around. If I had wanted to work in a dump, I would have done so. As I walked through the jobsites I worked on each day, I picked up the garbage and also recycled. I had a garbage bag hanging from the catwalk on my crane so that it was available for anyone to use. I also tied a garbage bag to our toolbox to make it more excessive to the men. I collected all the aluminum cans the men threw to the ground after emptying them. Once in a while, I would come across a discarded beer can or two, tossed after a mysterious cooler encounter from the evening before (Shhhhh!).

I also collected the pieces of aluminum plates that lined the bonnet of the hammer driving the pile. Those plates were alternated with composite plates that resembled wood, called magna carta. Those plates were the cushion underneath rounds of welded used cable. The lined bonnet was the connection piece between the hammer and the pile being driven. It allowed the hammer to hit the pile as hard as possible while maintaining a balanced rhythm.

Every so often, I would take all the aluminum that I had collected into the recycling center, and the money I made from doing so made it worth my time to keep my jobsites neat and free from accumulating garbage. I received more money per pound for the plates we used for our bonnets because they were made from a higher grade of aluminum.

One of the contractors I worked for loved the fact that my jobsites were clean and the materials organized. They began to expand on my idea by sending large garbage cans with liners to be placed inside along with recycling bins. They sent those receptacles to all of their jobsites from then on. My main contractor I spent most of my time working for and the one I drove pile for began including boxes of garbage bags in all their toolboxes being delivered to their jobsites. It was a win-win for everyone around.

One morning, as I walked onto our pile driving jobsite, I noticed a cardboard pizza plate wired to the pile we had set our hammer on the previous afternoon. We would begin driving it further into the ground as soon as the crane warmed up and the crew arrived. On the round piece of cardboard, it said, "HA! HA! I found your stash of aluminum plates. I took them to the recycling center and bought myself a pizza for dinner. It was really good. Thanks for collecting the plates for me!" WHAT THE FUCK! Now I had that little f——ker who worked on our second shift crew stealing my aluminum just so he could stuff his face!

He was an oiler, and as such, his job required him to stay with the crane and it's operator. He was driving off the island to the recycling center which was a good distance away, then driving to the pizza place and ordering a pizza. It then took him more time to drive back to work once the pizza had baked and then he devoured it. That entire time, he was absent from his job and he was being paid an overtime hourly wage. If I were running that jobsite, I would have fired his pizza-eating ass! WTF!

Thus began the war over the aluminum plates. I began crawling underneath the crane and stashing the discarded pieces of plates from our shift up inside one of the greasy, filthy manholes created for operators or oilers to grease the inner workings of the crane. He was far too lazy to crawl up underneath there. During his shift, the dinner menu remained the same—pizza. Every morning, one or two pizza cardboard circles stained with grease were wired to the pile in front of the crane. "HA! HA! Oh…that was SO GOOD!" or "You missed out!" were written on them.

I was not the only person reading those taunting messages. Our yard delivery guy had questioned one of our crew members as to what was going on with those pizza cardboards. He took his rumors back to the yard where, eventually, the office knew of them as well. Heaven forbid that they were not making enough money as it was, now they would also be beneficiaries of our recycling instead of us.

The company began sending the yard driver to all of our pile driving jobs every day, specifically to fetch the pieces of aluminum plates that had been cut out of the bonnets. Karma is a bitch, and she will bite you in the ass sooner or later. Both the pizza-eating thief and I ended up on the same pile driving job once again. We were both sent to oil on two separate cranes. I will tell you his tale of woe after my stories take us off the sewage treatment plant jobsite. We had many different projects there, so we may be awhile yet.

We finally had finished driving all of the pile required for that huge building we were initially hired to work on. There was zero room for a ramp to be configured to track our crane out of the excavation on. The game plan the head honchos came up with was to lease an even larger crane to lift out our crane in pieces. We used our service crane that was stationed up top to lift all of our equipment and materials out of the hole. We then disconnected all of our equipment that was hanging from our boom such as the monkey, the bonnet, hammer, and leads. We also lifted our compressor, air tank, and fuel storage unit off of the roof of the crane. Next came the more crucial picks done with the use of the larger crane.

Boom sections, counterweights, each track, and finally the main portion of the crane that encapsulates the cab and engine compartments called the "house." It was a unique experience for me to witness the complete dismantling of our crane.

From the rear of my tower crane a view of our port and the electric crane in the center; I will write about that crane in a couple areas in my book

*From the tower crane everything is miniature in appearance;
those two orange rectangles are actually two shipping containers
just to give an idea of how high up in the sky I am*

*Gradually the iron rises up to greet me in the tower;
it's like putting together an iron puzzle*

*From a tower crane downtown I can see my pile driving
company on a jobsite a few blocks from my own*

Setting a concrete form in place looking up my boom

Setting concrete forms in place

My hydraulic crane at a hospital expansion from the top floor

*Setting precast panels over the iron skeleton of a hospital
parking structure with a hydraulic crane*

Hooking up to a precast panel to raise and set into place

Putting the boom into the friction crane I would erect the iron for a local university's architecture building; we had to put the crane together in a busy city street; the bus passengers had an interesting view

Power plant setting the big iron with a big hydraulic crane

*Eventually, I drove the little Broderson crane underneath
the iron to set the smaller framework iron*

*The Broderson was so fun that I wanted one in my yard to move
rocks and trees. It was a neck breaker; the boom swiveled a complete
360 degrees. It just fit underneath the iron we'd previously set.*

It was as if I had found lost buried treasure once they separated the house from the "turntable" (the base of the crane that the tracks are connected to each side of and that holds the house pin on which the cranes swings in either direction). I found many lost keys and a few watches, one of which was my own, lying inside the turntable gear.

Items would fall from my pockets through the wide slots in the floor where my brake pedals protruded from. I quit wearing a watch because I lost too many of them through the crane floor or the por-ta-potty. I'd have to precariously balance when using a port-a-potty, hanging on to all my layers of clothes so that they didn't hit the nasty ass floor, all the while hovering above the toilet seat in order to pee. I may have appeared to the invisible eye like our great blue heron who lived along the riverbank in our company's yard perched on his or her leg as it hunted its prey. I had also realized that it was not as if I would have been going home anytime soon, so why bother looking at it? Glancing at my watch had previously made for a very *LONG* day.

Once we reassembled our crane above the hole on ground level, the foreman (my *now* husband) and I were to walk the crane and it's operator to a different location on the island. We were heading along the lake. It was a very foggy and damp morning on the day designated to make our move. All of a sudden, I saw a blue arc of electricity jump from the powerlines overhead to the crane boom. I instantly saw tufts of smoke puff out from the front and rear ends of the cranes track closest to me.

I was walking to the rear of the track and the foreman was walk-ing ahead of it, leading the way to our destination. Immediately, the foreman yelled to me, "Did you feel that?"

I said, "Yes, I had a minor shock run up to my knees." "It ran all the way up my legs!" he said back to me.

We were both the eyes for the crane operator. We were making sure that he cleared all manhole covers and the walls on either side of the crane as we passed through a rather narrow corridor that ran between two buildings. We had also been careful to maintain the proper distance from the high powered lines. Still the electricity had arced over to the boom, ran down it, and exited through the front and rear of the crane's track. We then had to inspect the crane for any damage the electrical strike may have made once we entered a clear area large enough to allow us to boom all the way down to the ground.

I had heard many arguments made between my union brothers as to whether electricity could arc as it had with us, even though a proper distance from its source was maintained. Other operators had experienced its occurrence while others believed it to be untrue. It was too bad that those nonbelievers hadn't felt the shocks run up their legs as we had; their minds would have been changed.

It was concluded that the arc we experienced was due to the high voltage carried in those particular lines combined with the heavy moisture in the air due to the thick fog lingering inland at that time. We were very lucky that we weren't shocked to a higher degree than we were.

I had remembered that when shown the "shock" videos of fatalities as apprentices that had been taken by insurance companies, the people nearest the crane that became electrified dropped dead immediately. We had been shown those videos to singe it into our brains to keep a safe distance from all power lines. We also learned that if you could hear thunder than the possibility of a lightning strike was a threat. If we heard thunder on a jobsite, I exited the crane, and the crew and myself either waited it out in our jobsite trailer or our cars until it had dissipated. I had to face the fact that my boom was sticking high up into the air like a lightning rod. I worked as an oiler on a big Manitowoc crane on a different jobsite, and it was hit by lightning. I will write about that experience in the chapter titled "Challenging and Just Plain Scary."

My mom told me as a child she had stepped in a puddle that was in close proximity to where a lightning bolt had hit the ground and it had knocked her on her ass.

I've had my own incident with electricity involving one of the tasers that I own. I have two of them and each one is capable of taking down an elephant; the voltage is so high. I figured when I purchased them, "Why mess around?" After work one day, I was in the tavern enjoying a brewed beverage with my girlfriend who came up with the title of this book for me. I was showing her how to use one of my tasers. I forgot to de-electrify it before putting it into my back pocket when WHAM! It gave me a hell of a jolt. I felt my barstool rock backward a little bit. "Whew, I almost peed my pants!" I stated matter-of-factly.

All of the bar patrons started yelling at me, "Your hair! You should see your hair!"

I went into the bathroom to take a look in the mirror and see what the hell they were talking about. Sure enough, I looked like I'd rubbed my hands over one of those magic electric orbs in a science museum that makes your hair stand straight out from your head. "WTF! I look like the bride of Frankenstein!" I hollered out the bathroom door.

Everyone began cracking up with laughter. At least I didn't end up with those white lightning bolts she had running up into her hair on each side of her head.

We continued walking the crane along the side of the lake. We were traveling such a far distance to get to our next destination to drive pile that we had to stop twice along our route in order for me to grease the tracks. When walking a crane, it's a smart idea to have eyes both in front and rear of the tracks to make sure the cranes rollers don't walk out of them. That is a likely hazard if a rock gets caught inside and throws a roller out of its guide or if the tracks are too loose. That can also happen while turning a crane.

That walk took us a couple of hours to make, and we chose to do it after work to avoid any traffic, people, or obstacles. We were halfway to our destination when the crane operator told me to go and find a phone in order to call his wife. I was to tell her that he would be home late and for her to go ahead and have dinner with their children without him.

WTF! I was talking to an iceberg on the other end of the phone. "Sure he is!" was the iceberg's chilly response, then the line went dead. The iceberg had hung up on me. I began having flashbacks to when I was a laborer. Specifically, I was taken back to the days I worked while the bastard foreman's wife, among other wives, were my unwelcome audience. If those wives could have obliterated me with their fiery glare, I would have resembled a pile of ashes.

I walked back to my now husband and the crane operator who I had made the phone call for. I informed them both that it was the last phone call I would ever make to tell the spouse of a fellow worker that her husband or boyfriend would be coming home later than usual from work. "Why? What's the big deal?" questioned the operator.

I asked him to imagine the voice of a young man calling him with the news that his wife would be home at a much later time than he was expecting her. The young man calling happened to be the one male working alongside only women. "What ideas would pop into your head?" I asked.

I told him that she was thinking, "Who is that woman? Why is she with my husband? What are they *doing* that's keeping him from coming home to me and my children?" I told them both that it was just a bad idea to instigate such questions from your spouse or significant other. I informed him that his evening agenda would most likely include a distressing conversation with his wife. "Oh shit," was his response.

Those thoughts had not occurred to me until it was too late to correct my mistake by making that phone call, although I was just a member of a crew, others not knowing that would not see it that way. I suggested that he might consider picking up some flowers for her on the way home for not being able to enjoy the dinner that she had taken the time to prepare for him.

Working next to Lake Michigan brought visions of beautiful sunrises as I drove to the jobsite in the mornings. It was always weird for me to see the sunrise up into the sky from the lake's horizon. I grew up residing along the Pacific Ocean. I've witnessed the sun disappearing into it during my numerous surf sessions at dusk.

One morning, as I drove to that particular jobsite, it was storming. Big waves were crashing up over the sheeting wall and washing over the roadway before me. Usually, I would see the early bird fishermen sipping from their coffee cups as they watched over the lines they had cast into the water. Patiently, they would wait, hoping to see a tugging motion at the end of their rods, signaling that a fish had taken their bait.

On that once-in-a-lifetime morning, Mother Nature had done the work for them. Fish were flying up over the sheeting wall, caught up within the waves. The men were sloshing through the water, covering the street, armed with their nets. It looked almost comical as they scurried around scooping the large lake trout up with their nets. It was so bizarre to see the fish flopping around in a frenzy. The men would measure their catch to make sure it was of legal length before stashing it in their coolers. If the fish came up short in length, back over the sheeting wall and into the lake it was thrown. Those men had a hell of a fishing tale to recite at the tavern that day! When I told my crew what I'd seen on the way into work that morning, they just said, "Sure, Suzanne, there were fish flying up over the sheeting wall and onto the road. What in the hell did you have in your coffee this morning?" or "*RIGHT!" and "Wow! Now I've heard it all!" I guess fish tales only worked when a *man* was telling it—WTF!

There was a unique asset to working on that huge sewage treatment plant job. There were so many men from so many different unions working on it that parking had become a big issue. Also for those men who didn't bring a lunch or liquid refreshments with them onto the jobsite, the nearest place to purchase either was off the island and a good distance to travel off the jobsite. Since we were only given a half an hour for our lunch break, the main contractor leased the use of a small ferry boat and a captain to drive it. They rented a vacant lot across the river from the sewage treatment plant for workers to park their vehicles for the day. The ferry then brought them across the river to the jobsite.

At lunchtime, the men needing to leave the jobsite for lunch, rode the ferry back across the river to dine in one of the three taverns that were located along the river's shoreline. The taverns were appreciative of the additional business the island jobsite was providing them. They added lunch specials for the workers as each opened for the day. The men went to those same taverns directly after their shifts ended, also providing bonus business for those establishments.

The ironworkers that I had known for many years and some new ones that I'd met on that jobsite were frequently inviting me to join them for lunch across the river. One day, I had eaten everything I had brought in my lunch box earlier than I had planned. Rather than risk another jail term due to a "hangry" attack, I accepted the offer from an ironworker buddy to join him for lunch across the river at one of the taverns. The ride in the ferry, though short, was very fun. It was a refreshing break to remove myself from the jobsite even for a short period of time. That was during the heat of the summer months and the ferry ride provided some necessary coolness as we moved swiftly through the cold river. I told the captain that I wouldn't mind taking a ride in the ferry, even though I brought my lunch to work every day and that my parking was provided for me close to the crane. He told me that I was welcome to do so at any time. Whenever I needed a pleasant break from the monotony to relax, that was what I did; I took a cruise on the river.

Some new safety rules were put into play on that jobsite, and one of the first ones was, in my opinion, stupid. I'm not sure how the subject came to the attention of those *rule makers,* whoever they were, or even why. It had been a boiling hot summer, and due to the size of the structure we were erecting combined with the buildings surrounding it, a breeze had been unable to breach them. We were surrounded by the river where it joined our lake since the plant had been built adjacent to it, yet we were stifled by the summer heat.

The men started wearing tank tops to work or T-shirts with the sleeves cut off of them. Some of the guys were even wearing those wifebeater tank tops (hey, I didn't give them that moniker) which were the tank tops men usually wore under their dress shirts. It was so hot outside, who could blame them? I decided to wear a tank top myself one day, and my decision seemed to cause the shit to hit the fan!

There was a woman who was in charge of running all of the operations at that sewage treatment plant. I thought she was a guy at first when she asked me out on a dinner date the first day I showed up to work there. I graciously declined stating the fact that I was married. I don't know if that had anything to do with her actions or not, but she approached me at my crane, advising me that she was there to measure my tank top's shoulder width!

To this day, I can't imagine what the fuss was about the width of the material of our tops' shoulder widths. Since the issue had become such a bug up her ass, I would have thought that she would have approached the "wifebeater tank top wearers" before me since the width of their shoulder straps were half the width of my own. After I stopped operating the crane momentarily so that she could measure my top's shoulder width, she informed me that while working on "her" island, the material would cover me from my neck to my outer edge of my shoulder. If my superintendent or the vice president of my company were to have stopped by at that time and not seen my hammer pounding away on a pile, that lesbian leader of the shit plant would have received an earful!

I was too busy back at work to notice how well her measuring of the men's shoulder straps went, but knowing them, I could only imagine all too well how the ironworkers took the news. The next day, in solidarity, ALL the men showed up in the narrowest strapped tank tops they owned. I did not see LL (Lesbian Leader) come out of her office that entire day. I remember wondering if my secret admirer had been her. She could watch me from her office window; that must have been how she noticed that I was wearing a tank top in the first place. It was so disturbing and also distracting to wonder how that could be a safety issue when there were so many factors of our industry that were far more dangerous at that time.

Back then, the men did not tie off to anything and walked the iron freely. I climbed up my boom to grease it without being tied off. In fact, we hadn't even heard of tying off to anything then. No one wore safety vests. We instinctively were aware of our surroundings. There were no nets placed every other floor of a building being erected to catch any dropped tools, nuts, bolts, or any other item. Those ideas had not occurred to anyone yet. If an ironworker dropped anything, he would yell, "Headache!" and that one word notified all workers below him to NOT look up. Instead, you were to run for cover or keep your head down, hoping that your hard hat would take the hit and protect your body.

My favorite T-shirt I ever saw on the jobsite at that time had the required width of shoulder covering but was looked upon with great disdain among anyone with authority over our jobsites. No one dared to approach our crew member in order to measure his shoulder. After seeing the commotion his T-shirt was making, he decided to wear it *every single day*. I think the only days we saw him without it were his laundry days. His shirt was black, and in large white letters, it read, "FUCK YOU, YOU FUCKING FUCKS!"

That statement on his shirt pretty much summed up his attitude. He was a young guy and big. He had tattoos on his arms and was shaving his head bald before it became a common choice among men. He had an angry expression on his face that was his natural appearance. He was quiet and kept to himself, preferring to work alone. He was usually welding boots onto the initial pipe piling that we would be driving.

When he was threatened to be let go for wearing his opinion to work every day, he kept wearing it. He was laid off briefly due to his defiance, only to be hired to work by a competing contractor. When he was eventually hired back to work for our company, he wore that same damn shirt on his the first day back!

We worked together on many projects. He surprised me while we worked on a portion of the island project. He was helping me to move the crane to our next pile driving area. As we were leveling the crane at our new position, I had asked him to search for more dunnage to use. I had cast aside a short four-by-four inch piece of lumber and used the longer ones to track the front of my crane tracks up on. The crane was finally leveled, and we were able to begin driving pile.

The next morning, when the crew walked onto the jobsite, he came up to me in the crane and asked, "Do you remember that piece of four-by-four that was next to the crane track yesterday?"

"I do," I answered him.

"Well, I made a candleholder for you out of it last night." I was stunned as he handed me a beautiful wooden candleholder that he'd spun on a lathe. It even had a small votive holder with a cool scented candle inside. I told him that I couldn't believe that the beautiful candleholder he'd made me had been a filthy section of wood the day before. We began discussing our knacks each of us had for turning something cast aside as useless into a piece of artwork. It turned out that working with wood was how he relaxed in the evenings after a hard day's work. WTF! Who would have guessed that a menacing-looking hard-ass guy was actually a shy introvert artist? It proved to me that I never really knew the people I was working with alongside of day after day. I keep that candleholder to this day as a lesson to how easily it is to cast judgment or make assessments about people without actual in-depth knowledge of them as individuals. Throughout my career, I had people making judgments about me based on my appearance alone.

The initial safety harness introduction into the construction world was an atrocity that proved hard to adjust to. The first safety harness designs resembled bizarre bondage attire or an item you'd wrap a dog into before escorting them for a walk with their leash. As unbearable it was for me to wear one, I could imagine my male coworkers thinking that they'd never be able to sire children after wearing one of those all day. When I went skydiving, I wore a similar garment, but mine had a parachute integrated into it.

We were to begin wearing a safety harness if we expected to work above six feet from the ground. I was used to climbing all over the crane like a spider. We were trained to have three limbs touching the surfaces we climbed at all times to avoid slippage. Whenever I was an oiler in charge of the cranes maintenance and lubrication, I was all over the crane while it was in motion. As a crane operator, I used the three-point contact climbing technique to get up and down from the cranes cab.

I was so used to NOT being tied off to anything that once it became a requirement, myself and so many others had difficulty doing our jobs. That proved to be true when I forgot I was tied off to the section on the crane's roof that holds the boom up into the sky. I took one step further than my safety lanyard allowed, and it yanked me abruptly backward. I was pulled from the platform I had been standing on. I was then dangling like a rag doll over a void between the counter weights. I was swinging back and forth helplessly as the crane was relocating our pipe pile from one side of the jobsite to another.

It was no use in yelling for help because I could not be heard above the roar of the crane's engine. The crane was unusually loud because the operator who generally traveled to jobsites with that particular crane had insisted on installing an especially loud muffler stack to increase the volume of noise to a ridiculous level. His excuse was, "Loud pipes save lives." In my case, the earsplitting engines roar was halting my release as a human marionette!

I felt both ridiculous and helpless as I endured the relentless swinging motion. Finally, the pipe pile must have been moved entirely because the crane stopped. I heard men's voices gather together and then became further and further away; I realized that they were going to coffee break! "WTF— *HELLO, I'M STUCK UP HERE!*" Ah, yeah, no one heard me.

A guy working on one of the many floors above us must have mentioned to my crew that their oiler was trapped in her safety harness on top of the crane. I heard a bunch of laughter as two of my crewmates climbed to the top of the crane, looking for me—finally. "Where the hell are you?" one of them yelled out.

"Back here between the counterweights," I feebly replied. The bursts of laughter from the two of them could be heard all over the jobsite when they saw the dilemma that I'd gotten myself into. I could feel my face turning red as a beet, and therefore, I was not going to entertain those two clowns any further by trying to explain how I'd gotten myself into such a predicament.

As they were trying to dislodge me, they were making comments such as, "We should just leave you up here, that would teach you to be nicer to us." The other ass questioned, "What are you going to do for us if we let you go? Ha-ha!" I had to pee really bad after being trapped up there for so long.

I said, "Just get me out of here, you assholes! I already missed coffee break and you've heard what can happen if I get too hungry. I'm already going to be the punchline of your jokes all day, so thank you and you're welcome." I climbed down off of that crane and made a beeline for the port-a-potty!

I witnessed a far more devastating reaction to the newly imposed wearing of the new safety harness on an iron erection job. We were erecting a large arena downtown in the heart of our city. It was a huge project, and a lot of ironworkers had boomed into town to work on the jobsite. I was oiling on a very large friction crane. We were working with the ironworkers, specifically the "connectors" and the "raising gang." The raising gang rigged up the iron columns and beams in the required order in which they were to be erected. The connectors caught the pieces the crane flew up into the air and bolted them into place as the crane lowered and swung them within their reach. A basic bolt placement held the iron pieces together until the bolting up crew who followed closely behind them could place all the bolts needed and rattle them into place. They used a torque wrench to do so.

After the bolting up crew moved onto their next section requiring their duties, a welding crew fused the bolts or plates to further ensure the irons stability. It was fascinating to watch a giant puzzle of iron pieces being put together to complete a major structure such as an arena.

One of the connectors who was tied off for the first time to the iron column behind him was walking out to the center of the beam he and his partner had just bolted into place. He was so used to walking iron beams high up in the air unassisted that he forgot that he was tied off to the column. All of a sudden, we saw him jerked backward as his lanyard tightened. He couldn't move forward another step, and due to the yanking of his safety belt, he fell off the iron beam he had been walking on.

He hung limply, having been slammed backward into the iron column he was tied to as he fell. He was unconscious for a bit as we hurried to hook up the man basket to the crane's headache ball (the headache ball has a hook with a safety latch that all rigging is attached to in order to be hoisted). He was high up where the ceiling was soon to be installed. Two ironworkers were hoisted up in the man basket and were successful in maneuvering him into the basket. An ambulance arrived just as the man basket was lowered to the ground. Off he went to the hospital and into surgery.

He had broken the bones in his shoulder and would miss out on a lot of work while he recovered and then went through his physical therapy. He had boomed into town to work on that arena project. He was the sole provider for his wife and their children as she stayed home to raise them. Their residence was far north of our city. Instead of bringing home a steady paycheck for the duration of our project, he would incur a lot of hospital and doctor bills. He had walked the iron successfully his entire career without incident until the tables were turned on the tightrope walkers called ironworkers.

Back in those years, before I became an operator and was on the list to go out as an ironworker apprentice, you knew when you signed up that you would be walking on iron beams high up in the air. If anyone had an issue with that or was afraid of heights, they would have signed up to be an electrician or plumber apprentice—work that would keep them on ground level.

I worked at the end of the "old school" method of construction and then during the phases of how construction work is done now. When I would set iron for the ironworkers with the crane, we would "tree" the iron pieces. I hoisted them in the proper order the ironworker connectors were supposed to bolt them together. The raising gang would rig up five or six pieces of iron and attach them to my headache ball and each other. I would slowly drop the end of the bottom piece close to one of the connectors so that he could grasp it. He would then swing the other end to his partner. One connector would throw in a couple of bolts to hold the iron while I slowly raised or lowered the other end of the piece into place according to the hand signals they gave me. After a few bolts were thrown into the last position, we would move on to the next area. We continued until all of the pieces were bolted into place.

During the minutes it took me to set those iron pieces, the raising gang would be rigging up the next set of iron I was to connect to. As I would be hooking up to those next pieces needed to proceed, the connectors would put in the rest of the bolts required to complete the pattern and snug them up using their sleever bar combination adjustable wrenches. We operated all through each day on an iron erecting project like a well-oiled machine. We utilized our time wisely wasting very little of it if any because there was usually a daily amount of iron expected to be erected.

All tasks to accomplish the completion in the construction of a building are planned out in order to schedule the arrival of materials, to engage the necessary permits, concrete arrivals, all trucking, employment from the various unions are budgeted. Even projecting an extra allotment of time for weather patterns should that concern arise.

A lot of thought and time are involved in the planning of a construction project, so it's of vital importance to have trained professionals onsite to perform the duties they are assigned to do. Nowadays, a crane operator is prohibited from "treeing" the iron on an erection jobsite. The chance of an ironworker being bumped off the iron is a risk that no contractor is willing to take as it is now against the OSHA regulations.

Nowadays, an ironworker or anyone else working above the ground must ride up in a manlift and remain inside it's barriers as well as being tied off to its appropriate brackets. Ironworkers are not allowed to stand solely on their spud wrenches when connecting on the iron as they once did. There are safety nets installed every other floor as a building is being erected. They are used to catch all tools, nuts, bolts, etcetera, that may be lost from a workers grip dismissing the use of yelling "headache" if an item is dropped. They eliminate *"receiving"* a headache if you were to be struck by a dropped item.

Another action that is no longer allowed that was a constant back in the day was "riding the headache ball." At coffee break and especially lunchtime, the men working up on the higher floors erected would congregate around the crane's headache ball. I'd seen as many as six or seven men jostling for a position to place their foot and grab onto the cable it was attached to. The operator would then fly the headache ball to the ground rapidly so that no one would slip from their precarious position. It was quite a sight to behold, all those men clinging together and taking the riskiest daredevil ride to the ground that you could imagine!

I've given workers that headache ball ride so they could head off to lunch, and it was no surprise to find them remarkably slower about their return to their jobs once lunch time was over. At one point in my young daughter's life, she wanted a specific pair of tennis shoes. After hearing a "no" from me once I learned the price tag, she asked her father for them. After listening to her plead her case to purchase the tennis shoes, he agreed. When he brought her home a pair of new and *expensive* tennis shoes, they were not the specific pair she had requested. Thus began the great war of silence between the two of them over that pair of tennis shoes.

Not only was I dealing with a bunch of babies at work, I was then coming home to my family's obstinate war of silence and fuming angry stubbornness. I was dealing with an adult child and a chronological child!

Their silence finally ended when I returned the expensive pair of tennis shoes my husband had purchased and took my daughter to buy a more reasonably priced pair. That long drawn out process was not going to happen again. I thought that if my daughter could see for herself what her parents went through at work each day to earn money that she would gain more appreciation for our time and for the money we each made.

As winter approached, I was laid off from work. I thought that it was a perfect time to take our daughter to her father's jobsite and we could have lunch with him. My daughter was on a break from her school, so off we went to see him on a frigid winter day. It was a cold damp day with dark skies threatening that more snow was on the way. I made sure that we showed up on his jobsite before his lunch break. She was shivering, even though she was wearing her winter gear as we stood outside the car, watching her dad work. "It's too cold out here, let's go sit in the car and wait for him," she said to me. "Your dad is cold, too, and he doesn't get to go sit in a warm car.

In fact, he's out in the cold all day long," I answered her. On that day, her dad was working up on the fifth floor of the iron skeleton of the building being erected.

She looked up to where he was working and asked me, "How is dad going to get down from there?"

"You'll see," I replied.

Lunchtime rolled around, and her eyes looked on in amazement as her dad wrapped his legs around the corner column of iron and slid down it to the ground. The look on her face said it all. "WOW." She didn't realize until that day that her father was the same as any circus performer; his clothing was just not as colorful.

After we ate some lunch, we took him back to his jobsite, and my daughter asked him where the stairs were that would return him back to the fifth floor where he was working. I explained to her that the building was in its early stages and that the stairways had not been put in yet. I said to her, "Your dad is going up the same way that he came down." With that said, we watched him shimmy back up the column just as if he was a monkey climbing up a coconut tree.

I never heard her complain about wanting something expensive like those tennis shoes ever again. When we had left the frigid jobsite that day, enjoying the warmth emanating from our car's heater, I said to her, "Your poor dad has to work outside in the cold air for the rest of the day." She left that jobsite with a new understanding of what an ironworker connector did to earn a living in order to feed and clothe their families.

From that day forward, my husband and I would periodically take my daughter to visit each of us as we worked on a jobsite so that not only could she be aware of our daily activities involving our jobs but also that she would strive to have a more profitable and physically friendly field of work for herself when she became of age to do so. I wanted much more for my daughter and was insistent upon her attaining much higher goals for herself. I've enclosed photos of her dad bringing her to one of my iron-erecting jobsites.

My daughter was able to see two published photos taken of her father's unusual daredevil high iron act. One was published in our city's main newspaper many years ago. He was the radioman for the tower crane operator. They had set iron arches as the skeletal ceiling of a huge high structure downtown in the heart of our city. Some of the iron was to be set below the arches of iron spanning the structure. Due to the difficulty that made for the tower crane operator to determine the depth those pieces of iron needed to drop down, they devised a plan that would assist the operator in delivering the iron to the connectors waiting below the arches.

They put my daughter's dad into a man basket attached to the headache ball of a large friction crane they had working there as well. The operator of that crane had a very long boom and was able to set the man basket against the high iron arch, allowing my daughter's dad to step out onto it. From that standpoint high up in the sky, he had a bird's-eye view from which to speak through his radio to the tower crane operator. The two of them worked together to successfully maneuver all the necessary iron components through the open sections of ceiling without bumping into any other part of the structure or, more importantly, anyone else.

The photo was cool. It was taken from the ground, and it's focal point was a small man visible high up in the air in the middle of the arch of iron. The higher up, the smaller he appeared. He wasn't tied off to anything because those rules were not in effect yet nor had the safety harness been invented.

The other photo of him was scary to look at, and my daughter viewed it at her dad's memorial service which I will write more about in the chapter titled, "Challenging and Just Plain Scary." The photo was shot out of a helicopter for a publication that I can't recall. It was before I had met him, so I don't know if he was dropped into position by that same helicopter or if he managed to climb the towering column and maneuver himself into position of standing on top of the column. Since he was standing slightly tilted due to the weight of his tool belt on one side and leaning into the brisk wind, my guess would be that he was dropped into place by the helicopter. The photo showed how windy it was because his hair was blowing off to the opposite side of his slight tilt. Either way, it was a sight to behold because there was a shot of a lone man standing on the top of a column that does not provide nearly enough room to do so comfortably, and below him, you could see the tops of many city buildings and *CLOUDS* surrounding both him and them.

I've previously written that a typical ironworker's tool belt armed with their spud wrenches, nuts, bolts, and sleever bar weighed in at about forty pounds. To see him balanced on a small square of iron with absolutely nothing around to hang on to if he lost his balance was really something to see.

I'd worked with a lot of men who complained to me that their children were always asking to have money spent on them for one thing or another. I've heard their complaints about their wives constantly wanting to spend their hard-earned money also. My advice to them was always to let them see what they did in a day's work. It would bring upon them a new perspective and appreciation.

We were not the only spouses who showed up on each other's jobsites, but these next two stories I'm going to write about come under the heading of some really WTF! moments on a construction site.

We were driving sheeting along a perimeter that had been laid out for us. We were putting in a sheeting wall so that the site could be excavated. We would then return to the site and drive piling that the city's new jail was to be erected upon. It happened to be one of the hottest summers I worked in. We had been starting work an hour earlier than our normal beginning time in order to leave an hour early to get out of the heat as soon as possible.

The only shade available to us was that which our crane provided. We would all huddle together on overturned buckets to eat our lunch in that small shaded area. The sheeting wall we were pounding into the ground prohibited any breeze to cross over our jobsite. It was even hotter inside of the crane because the engine was located directly behind the operator's seat, and with every push of the throttle pedal, hot air was spewed onto the back of the operator. He would periodically get out of his seat and lay down on the crane's catwalk until he felt well enough to continue. We were all miserable due to the heat on that jobsite. We were not as miserable, however, as our foreman was soon to be.

I was the oiler on that crane and happened to be up on the crane's roof preparing to fuel up the air compressor mounted there. We had a fuel tank secured up on the roof also just for that purpose. I was high up above the ground and observed an erratic driver speeding down the road that we used to enter our jobsite. Our gate at the entrance was closed while we worked each day to keep any spectators from entering.

I couldn't believe my eyes when that speeding car that was veering wildly all over the place turned onto our entranceway and blasted through our cyclone fence and gate! "What the f———k!" I hollered out as the car drove onto the jobsite and right up to the sheeting wall we were preparing to pound down with our air hammer. Our foreman scurried down the fortyto fifty-foot sheeting section on the rope ladder he had strung up for himself.

Back in those days, before the idea of tying yourself into a man basket and scoping yourself up to great heights in the air, the men scrambled to the top of the sheeting wall however they could get up there. Once they made it to the top, they sat on the wall with the iron sheets between their ass cheeks. They kept their balance by placing their feet into homemade stirrups that hooked over the top of the sheets to keep them held in place. It looked to me like some bazaar gynecologists bench. I would joke to the men about my thoughts on what those stirrups they made brought to my mind; they told me to "keep my thoughts to myself." Ha-ha! I told them that now they knew what their wives and girlfriends had to go through when they went to a gynecologist appointment, but at least they weren't in stirrups forty feet or so up in the air! They usually made those stirrups by heating up a small diameter rebar rod and then shaping a hook in one end and a circle for a foothold in the other end before the rebar cooled. They used a torch to do it, and now those stirrups are obsolete along with the practice of sitting on top of the sheets.

Those poor guys would be sitting up there all day long and could have easily fallen off their perch at any time. They caught the bottom of the sheet as the crane operator very carefully swung it into them and then guided the sheet through the groove on the edge of each sheet as it dropped down to hit the ground.

Those grooves were manufactured into each sheet and were referred to as "locks" because they locked each sheet into the next, inevitably forming a wall. In that manner, the sheets could not be separated from each other. Eventually, they would be pounded or vibrated down to the desired height needed for the jobsite's requirements.

I'm sure our surprised foreman would much rather had made a run for the hills instead of join his crazy ex-wife on the ground below him, but he was pretty much trapped in the situation unfolding before him. Us crew members were all shocked when we found out his ex-wife was the crazed driver of the car. He told us all to take a break while he handled his dilemma of escorting his angry ex off of our jobsite. We could not help but observe the disastrous confrontation unfold since there was nowhere else for us to gaze; you might say we were a captive audience. There was a lot of yelling and arm-waving until suddenly she marched off to her dented up vehicle and sped off in a cloud of dust from our jobsite.

"Whew! That was a scary sight that I did not expect to see today," the foreman said to us.

Being the bold woman I am, out of my mouth came, "What the f——k was that all about? She destroyed our gate! Your ex-wife is a nutjob!" (I know, no tact or couth; just another woman verbally kicking him in the nuts!).

"Yeh, I should have figured that out when she showed up to marry me in a black dress. Our relationship went downhill from that point onward," he replied to my blatant questioning.

"Well, with that said, you're as nutty as she is! That black dress was the writing on the wall. You should have hightailed it out of the church when you saw her clad in that get up—WTF!" I added, pouring more salt into the wound.

We all had a good laugh before he climbed back up to his high iron perch above the ground but not before he called the office to tell them we needed a new gate—pronto! It was a long, dusty, boring, and very hot job to endure. There was no glory in it, and it was difficult to drive to it in the morning. I looked at it simply like "money in the bank." Apparently, I was not alone in feeling the boring monotony of our job because one afternoon, as I was fueling the air compressor on top of the crane, I happened to glance over at the sheeting wall. I saw an eye drawn and then a C and a U drawn in soapstone in big letters by the foreman. He was waving when he noticed me reading his message. That was no easy feat for a man with an iron thong up his ass! That brought a smile to my face, and his creativity and the "wild ride" by his ex-wife were the memories I took away from that jobsite.

I was working on another jobsite with that same foreman, but that one was at the opposite time of year; it was during an ass-freezing winter. At that time, I was living an hour and a half's drive away from our jobsite. I was trying yet again to make it through the long drawn out process of divorcing my first husband. I forget if it was my third or fourth time trying to complete that horrendous ordeal. I moved far north from our city in the hopes that it would deter my ex-to-be husband from talking me out of my pursuit of my freedom from him.

I was sick with the flu and had driven through snowy weather to get to the jobsite on the island. We were clearing an area of cargo containers and relocating them elsewhere. I didn't want to leave the foreman and crew without an operator, so I intended to show up, but when I'm sick, I sleep. That's just how my body seems to want to repair itself with rest. The frigid weather and all the clothing I had on to combat it were not helping me feel more energetic either.

WTF! I kept nodding off! I could not continue to work in that unhealthy manner for myself or the safety of my crewmates. I told the foreman that I had driven all the way down from my residence up north, thinking that I could make it through the day. I needed the money for my divorce attorney or I would have stayed home in bed. I told him that I was wrong in my attempt and that he needed to call the office and request a replacement crane operator. I confessed to him that I couldn't stay awake or think clear enough to be in a crane seat.

He told me that he couldn't have me getting in an accident on my way home due to falling asleep at the wheel. He gave me the option of sleeping in my car for a while, and when I woke up and still wanted to go home, that would be no problem. If I felt better after a nap, I could rejoin the crew. In the meantime, they could attend to other details regarding the job that didn't require the crane's assistance.

I could not climb into my car fast enough. I kept a sleeping bag in my trunk in case my car broke down on the long drive to and from my home. You had to be prepared for emergency situations in the frigid winter months by keeping a cache of warm blankets, food, light, flares, and whatever else necessary to keep you from freezing to death until help arrived.

When I woke up awhile later, I did indeed feel better and was able to resume working with the crew for the remainder of the day. I've never forgotten that act of kindness that foreman showed me that day, and it was important for me to include that story in this book. The WTF! question this story poses is, "Why can't there be more acts of kindness such as this on our jobsites or anywhere else for that matter?" It's both easy and lazy to be an asshole. It takes strength and cojones (or boobs) to project kindness.

I drove the test pile for our baseball stadium that now stands in our city with that same foreman. I will write more about the great service he did for me on that jobsite in the chapter titled "Challenging and Just Plain Scary."

The other spousal visit happened when I joined a crew that was working in a wooded area along one of our river parkways near a hospital complex. I was operating a forklift unloading a trailer filled with equipment and materials needed on the job. I was being cautious while unloading because traffic was steadily passing us where we were located.

A speeding car jumped the curb and almost ran into my machine. A woman jumped out of the car brandishing a revolver and was waving it angrily in the air. As she slammed her door shut, I recognized her. It was "One-eyed Rita," and that crazed woman yelled, "Where is he? Where's that son of a bitch, T——! I'm going to *kill* him!" We all knew who that woman was, and her boyfriend she was on the hunt for was in the woods, unloading the materials I had placed there. The superintendent was delegating duties to the foreman and crew as she was standing there with her gun, screaming obscenities.

"Can you wait to shoot him after his shift is over? If you kill him now, we're going to be shorthanded," the superintendent stated matter-of-factly. He was so composed while saying that. It was as if he dealt with that sort of crazy behavior day in and day out.

She halted and seemed to think about what he had said to her for a few minutes. "I can do that," she said calmly and marched back to her vehicle, got in, and drove away.

"What the f——k is going on?" I said in a surprised voice to the superintendent.

"I don't know and I don't care. I'm just glad that *I* don't live with her," was the answer I received to my question.

"Amen to that!" I replied.

The funny thing was her boyfriend had no clue that his pissed off girlfriend had just left the premises and that she wanted to shoot him. I said to my crewmate, "Man, you just dodged a bullet, literally!" To that, the superintendent and I started cracking up with laughter as our crewmember's face turned white as a ghost. "I'd be really careful when you walk through your door tonight when you get home. It wouldn't hurt to hold a bouquet of flowers in front of you when you do. I don't know what you did, but she is really pissed off!" Then I said jokingly, "If you're going to sleep with the One-eyed Rita, then you better sleep with one eye open!" The whole crew had a good laugh after that.

The next morning, I arrived at work early to unlock everything and check the fluid levels on our equipment like I usually did. I found our jobsite trailer already unlocked, and my crewmate was sleeping on a bench we sat on during lunchtime. "Rise and shine!" I said as I entered the trailer to put my gear and lunch box down.

He told me that after a huge fight at home, he had nowhere else to sleep but back on the jobsite. I didn't feel bad for him because rather than throw her out of *his* house, he allowed her nonworking ass to remain in the comfort of his home while he was stupid enough to attempt to sleep on a tiny bench! He was the one who had to bust his ass all day.

I thought to myself, *Clearly, I'm not the only one who lives with a person who had tendencies of behavior right out of the movie Psycho.* To confuse the hell out of myself as well as all the other crewmembers he worked with, he not only made up with that woman—he married her (WTF!).

Every year, our company would get the employees together for a dinner. It was a way for everyone to bond outside work and off the jobsite. The significant others in everyone's lives would be able to meet the people they spent most of their time with while working.

One year, the company paid great expense to hire a river ferry that provided dinner cruises. We were to enjoy a great meal together and libations from the bar as we cruised up and down the river that ran through our city. We all dressed up in our nice attire and boarded the ferry, looking forward to a fun Friday evening. That One-eyed Rita didn't bring her sea legs aboard or motion sickness medication either. She spent the entire evening puking over the ferry's railing as we cruised along our river walk. The people dining and drinking on the restaurant's patios that lined the river looked on in horror and disgust. It was very hard to enjoy the food provided for our dining pleasure with that loud retching as our musical accompaniment. *WTF! How much longer could the demonical notes go on?*

As soon as we pulled up dockside and exited, she was fine and then in the mood to party. "GOOD NIGHT, RITA!"

The next year, when all of us workers met at that same dock for our dinner cruise, there was an audible "Ooohhhh!" from the crowd. Here came One-eyed Rita once again on the arm of our fellow worker. I said to him, "I'm surprised she wanted to come aboard this ferry again after how sick it made her last year. Did she take any medication for seasickness?"

"I don't think so, but she wouldn't let me come by myself without her," he answered.

"What the f——k!" I said as I climbed aboard, thinking, *Here we go again.*

Once again, the sound of puking continued throughout the evening. That year, it seemed everyone had a remedy to drown out the disgusting noises emanating from that woman. Everyone got rip roaring drunk! We were all loud and obnoxious, I'm sorry to say. A few of our couples decided to rise above the puking atmosphere by taking their chairs up onto the roof of the ferry and partying up there. They had ripped off the "no entrance" sign that was supposed to deter people from climbing up there and threw it into the river! The line to use the women's bathroom was exceptionally long, so I took it upon myself to use the men's bathroom. "I have to share a port-a-potty with these guys anyway at work, so why the f——k *wouldn't* I use their bathroom now?" was my explanation when I saw all the shocked facial expressions with their mouths gawking open at me like a bunch of fish in an aquarium.

Once they saw how fast I got in and out of the men's room, they ran over to line up to use that bathroom like flies on shit! Eventually, one of the toilets stopped up and spilled over the seat, flooding the floor. "Good thing I've got high heels on," I said to my now husband as my feet kept dry, riding high above the floor (good god, my poor shoes!).

The staff enclosed with us on that dinner cruise had enough of us and all our shenanigans. From the puking to taking over the men's lavatory, to riding up on the roof of the ferry, we were banned from ever setting foot on one of their cruise boats again—*for life!* Shame on us, WTF.

The company came up with a new game plan for all of us employees to have a little bit of fun one night each year. We took one of our huge barges that we used to haul humongous rocks from our quarry to wherever the hell we were doing shore work along Lake Michigan. We had made beaches for the rich people who could afford it and wanted a beach on their lakefront property. We'd put up docklands and riprap to create marina areas.

The barge that was chosen for our party was fixed, resurfaced, and painted. Days before we were to be guided up and down the river by our biggest tugboat, the barge would be decorated. One year, the theme was western, so I helped paint stars all over the newly paved barge "dance floor." The paint proved to be rather slippery, however, because one of our foremen's wives landed on her ass while dancing after slipping on a star—-WHOOPS! Maybe she was just a little tipsy.

Another year, everything was patriotic red, white, and blue. My personal favorite year was pirate-themed and we all had to arrive at the barge in our pirate gear. One of the foremen I worked with quite a bit even had a fake stuffed parrot mounted on his shoulder. It was hilarious to watch that parrot smack into people whenever the foremen hit the dance floor. Of course, we all had to "walk the plank" when we exited the barge that evening.

In the beginning years, a live band was hired to play for us during our cruising hours. It was catered, and there was plenty of beer and wine for everyone to enjoy. We always held the barge parties on the Friday evenings of our yearly Italian Fest. We have festival grounds along the lakefront of our city. I've worked on jobs on those grounds as had many other members in our company. Each weekend, a different ethnic festival was held there. The best fireworks show put on during any of those festivals was hands down Italian Fest. That was the reason the barge party was held at the same time each year.

Our tugboat would push our barge out into the lake and hold us directly in front of the festival grounds where the fireworks were shot off. It was so much fun to turn off all the decorative lights on the barge and watch the fireworks display from the railing. After a few years, more and more contractors were invited on our barge cruise by the company's management. Instead of celebrating a year of hard work put in by the employees, it became more of a hobnobbing (kissing ass) with their business associates.

The barge party began dividing with the contractors on the front of the barge and us workers to the rear where the port-a-potties and tugboat were located. I guess the company thought that the port-a-potties were too stinky for their special guests to sit next to, and the tugboat was too loud—*boo-hoo!*

Of course, there were many drunken incidents that occurred. One of the contractor's wives was dressed in some pretty fancy duds to wear on a glorified barge and was extremely hesitant to use a por-ta-potty to tinkle in. I convinced her to use it by telling her that the only alternative was for her to hang her naked ass over the barges deck and pee into the river, but by doing so, she would be "moon-ing" the tugboat captain.

When she came out of the port-a-potty, she explained to me that her experience proved to be surprisingly pleasant. She told me it was so nice to see that there was a shelf in there for her to set her purse on. She strutted back to the *fancy* side of the barge, swinging her slightly wet purse as she walked. I didn't have the heart to tell her that she had just set her purse down inside of the men's urinal! I turned to the woman I was hanging out with and said, "WTF! Wait until I tell you where the hell that woman just put her purse! HA! HA!"

One year, we had a luau-themed party. There were palm trees everywhere! It was so beautiful with all of the colorful flowers and decorations. We all wore our Hawaiian shirts, dresses, and other beach wear. After a while, people became so intoxicated that they threw all of the potted palm trees overboard. WTF! They were intended to be raffled off at the end of the evening festivities and instead were laying on the bottom of the river—so sad.

Another year, everyone was pretty well-lit when we ran out of beer. Uh-oh, the shit hit the fan! The drunken voices began sounding off about how could expediters figure out the cost of materials and labor to build a structure but not be able to figure how much beer a barge load of people could drink? One of our foremen and his wife put on life jackets and stated loudly, "We're swimming ashore and going to the tavern!"

They stood on the edge of the barge, preparing to jump into our very cold and very polluted river. It took some convincing from one of our superintendents to change their minds. He promised them he'd call the liquor store to have a keg of beer delivered to the dock of a restaurant we would soon be approaching. As our tugboat pushed us further along the river, we spotted a man holding a dolly with a keg of beer on it waiting for us. I saw the alarmed expression on his face and his mouth forming the words "What the f——k!"

I bet it was the most unusual beer delivery he had ever made. It must have been quite a sight to see a barge load of loud drunken people being pushed up to the dock by a huge tug boat. As for my girlfriend who was ready to jump overboard with her husband in order to swim to a tavern, I told her, "Your boobs are so big that you don't need a life jacket, you come with your own flotation devices!"

She looked down at her chest and then over to me and said, "You're right! I don't need this stinking life jacket!" And with that statement, we all had a good laugh!

The last couple of years the company was in business, we didn't have any get-togethers between the office personnel and union workers. We were told that it was because they had too much work going on. All the barges were in use, and many of our men were working in other states. There had been a decision made a few years earlier to expand the size of our company by venturing into other states.

My "now husband" was one of those men chosen to travel out of state to work. One of the toughest jobs, he was the foreman on was North Dakota. He and his crew were there to work through the frigid winter months. The temperatures they had to endure dropped far below zero. It became dangerous for them to work outside for some of the days they were there because frostbite was inevitable.

My "now husband," being the foreman, had to drive to the jobsite regardless of those dangerous temperatures to fuel the equipment each day that they couldn't work. The equipment had to continually run. Otherwise, all the fluids would gel and it would be impossible to start them. Hell, they probably would have had to wait for the spring thaw for the equipment to deice. No one was going to steal any of the running equipment in those temperatures anyway.

Rumors were rampant that our company was going bankrupt. The authorities in the office kept assuring us employees that they were all bullshit and to put those rumors out of our minds.

Looking back, there were signs to prove that the opposite was true. The loss of the annual gatherings to ride on the barge, the endless time it was taking to get our equipment repaired, and the ordering of parts and tools that never arrived.

The crane that I operated in our main yard was an old friction all-terrain American. One of its front outrigger leveling cylinders was continually failing. It would slowly seep oil, and I couldn't count on it to keep the crane level. You must keep your crane level at all times to keep from tipping over when hoisting a load. In the yard, I was mostly loading extremely heavy items such as drill rigs, air compressors, or heavy iron air hammers. I will write more about some of the heavier picks I made with that crane in the chapter "Challenging and Just Plain Scary."

I kept writing my daily crane reports and checklists stating the problems I was having with that outrigger. I kept dropping off a daily repair request with the mechanics but to no avail. I was worried that I'd pick a heavy object, and the outrigger would shit out on me and I'd go over with the crane.

"What the f——k! I'll deal with it myself so that I'll feel comfortable knowing that I'm not going to dump over in this crane!" were my last words to the head mechanic. I acknowledged to him that I knew it wasn't his fault that he could not get the part that I needed; his hands were tied. The crane was such an old model that they were not made anymore. They had done a search with their computer over the entire United States. With some of our equipment, parts were shipped in from other countries. Due to the expense of those sorts of shipments, requests made to the upper echelon (the office) were usually placed on a back burner.

I took the biggest boom blocks I could find that were made out of hardwood and stacked them on top of each other. We used those blocks whenever we trucked a boom to a jobsite to attach to the crane to be used there. I then wedged them beneath my broken outrigger so that it was braced to my own satisfaction. I knew then that the crane was physically sound, and I wouldn't be tipping over due to the outrigger failing. Did that look like caveman tactics? Yes, it did, like something you'd see in a *Flintstones* cartoon perhaps but if it made me feel more secure than WTF!

As I was merrily swinging, hoisting, and booming away, I was noticing glances of curiosity from the many men coming and going out of the yard. I didn't give a shit, it might have looked neanderthal, but those boom blocks turned my crane into a functioning hoisting beast! The mechanic told me, "Hey, whatever toots your horn!"

So away I went, busting my ass loading trucks. WTF! Here came the head superintendent out of the office, who I went round and round about one thing or another constantly. "I want you to take those blocks out from under that outrigger right now!" he stated to me in his agitated voice.

"I won't risk dumping this entire crane over because the necessary part we need for repairs has not shown up in the mechanic's shop yet," I answered him back.

"Well, that just looks ridiculous!" was his response.

"It's better than this eighty-foot boom coming down and slicing through our yard trailer and the office. Not to mention demolishing all the equipment and trucks parked in its path," I pointed out.

"Well, could you take the blocks out from beneath the outrigger when you're not using the crane?" he asked.

"I can do that, no problem. Can you please find out what's taking so long to get the part we need to fix it?"

No answer was given as he stormed back to his office. The part eventually showed up, and I helped to put it in, but it was like pulling teeth to get your equipment repaired.

I'd also had issues with that crane's seat. It was built to sit on a pedestal with a hinge design. That allowed the operator to tip the seat forward to allow entry into the back area where the engine was. That particular seat just happened to tip you out of it entirely if your weight shifted to the front edge too much. The crane levers to operate the various functions had to be pushed far forward. The effect of doing so would cause the crane's seat to cast me out of the cab periodically.

One day, the seat pitched forward, and out the doorway I went. I missed the catwalk and fell ten feet to the ground. It was winter, and the ground was frozen like a block of ice. I landed squarely on my knee and felt an intense shot of pain where I had hit the ice. It hurt like hell, but I climbed back onto that damned crane seat because you can't be a candy-ass in construction! I already knew that I couldn't give them a reason to replace me because the only people around me to do that were men. Once I was replaced in my crane seat or any other for that matter, I would be lucky to get it back! It was a constant battle for me to get into a crane seat and to stay there. To this day, that knee feels like I'm on shards of glass if I have to kneel on it for any reason. When things such as that have happened to me, I always recall what my sensei (karate instructor) told me in class one day, "This is not a tea party!"

Another piece of equipment we had was so old that it was just scary. It was a truck-mounted drill rig. I had the unfortunate experience of having to drive it through the city streets to get it from the yard to its jobsite destinations. The fumes flooding the driver's cab would make me feel ill. I had to drive it with my head sticking out the window as much as possible because it made me sick to my stomach. The engine sat directly next to the driver's seat with only a thin wall of metal between it and the driver.

When I watched an operator drill a hole with that machine, I made sure to keep my distance. The operator had to swing the seat he was to sit on out from the side of the machine. His neck was craned in the direction of where he was drilling; that in itself was a guaranteed neck breaker. Also, as the operator was drilling, the seat he sat on flung him about as if he were riding on a bucking bronco in the rodeo! HA! I wasn't about to deal with that shit—WTF! If you've ever seen the awesome movie *Hatari!* that John Wayne starred in, the seat he sat in mounted on the front of his jeep he used to capture African wildlife reminds me of the seat on that drill rig. The operator was yanked and jerked in every direction. I expected him to be ejected from that seat at any moment.

Whenever I was asked if I'd be willing to learn to operate that piece of shit machine, I just said, "Oh, hell no!" without any hesitation. You could look at that machine in operation and realize you could decline to operate it without any additional explanation. The mast reached so tall into the sky that when chunks of metal broke off from it, they could hit anything within a wide radius of the machine, and that usually involved people!

I knew that if I learned to drill with that gargantuan dinosaur of a machine that I'd be shackled to it for my entire career because NO ONE wanted to operate it. In all honesty, it was a death trap. The operator could not dodge any parts of it that sporadically rained down from it from time to time. Whenever my "now" husband was the foreman working with that red devil beast, I'd remind him to stand clear of it while it was in operation so that he wasn't struck down from any of its metal meteors. When the company eventually went out of business (which I'll write about later), that piece of shit was the first piece of equipment sent to its graveyard. No one was sad to see it go.

There was a little mini excavator nicknamed appropriately "the Mini-X" that was fun to operate. My first thoughts when I cast my gaze upon it were, *I need to get one of those for my yard!* I operated it on too many jobsites to count. I drove steel rods called "chance anchors" into the ground. I will be writing about many of those jobs.

That machine had a crack in the armrest that was adjacent to the engine. The exhaust came directly into the small cab and fumigated the operator. I knew that I was breathing bad shit for air because it would put me to sleep. I'd get a bad headache and an upset stomach. I wrote up an equipment repair slip every time I did my daily inspections while I was operating it, but it never got repaired. It was a fun little machine to operate, even though it almost killed me one day while I was in its seat. I'll write more about that tragic day in the chapter "Challenging and Just Plain Scary."

I joked with the crews I worked with while drilling chance anchors that if I painted a spiral stripe on the anchor itself, we'd all be hypnotized while watching it spin down into the ground. I also joked that if I painted both a red and a white stripe, it would resemble a barber's pole whenever it spun. It was mostly a boring job while driving down those rods. It was also a risky job because the foreman was usually down in the hole directly next to the anchor I'd be drilling. If the torque head flew off the rod due to the extreme pressure required to drill it into the ground, it would cause him grievous injury. I had to pay close attention to what was happening each moment I was drilling.

That machine was impossible to operate without opening all of its windows and its door due to its exhaust problem. In the summer, it wasn't much of an issue to operate like that, but in the winter, I really had to bundle up. I was stuck in that seat and couldn't move my body enough to fend off the frigid winter air; I was screwed. The good thing about operating that machine was there was a lot less stress involved, and it was less dangerous work in comparison to operating a crane.

The first job I had to drill chance anchors with the Mini-X was in the weirdest place I could have imagined working. It was inside the company that manufactured vaults, also known as crypts. I didn't know beforehand that if you buried someone in a casket that it was further contained in a concrete "vault" (or crypt) in order to preserve the casket. The casket preserves the body, the vault preserves the casket, and the entire works are put underground where no one can see them and at great expense, I might add. I intend to be cremated and my ashes tossed into the ocean at my favorite surf spot myself: cheap.

It was the first time I had to take the cab off of the machine so that I could track it through the doorway provided to us in which to enter the building. It was also the first time *on that machine* that I had such a large audience watching me work. That would be a pattern I had to learn to adjust to throughout my entire career. Wherever I worked, men showed up to watch; every so often, I'd see a woman observing as well. It was those few and far between sightings of women watching the process I was performing that reinforced my beliefs that there were more women out there who, like myself, wanted to be part of the process of constructing buildings and bridges. They must share my enthusiasm for architecture and design. They were one of the reasons I decided to write about what it was like to be in the construction business. I also wanted to reach out to all women about the insights I've gained into male behavior.

My audience consisted of men who couldn't believe a woman was in the seat of the machine making their project possible. Some of the men were just waiting for me to f——k up so that their chauvinistic views would be confirmed. I wouldn't have been surprised in the least if they had bets among themselves as to exactly when I would screw up. Those audiences I constantly dealt with only fueled the drive for me to perform at the best of my abilities and show them all that—ha! I was capable of getting the job done, and ha! I didn't screw up.

I also learned on that job that it wasn't going to be the only time I was expected to do the impossible with the piece of equipment I was operating. It would prove to be a consistent challenge during my career to stretch a machine beyond its limits. We were to drive chance anchor rods deep into the ground in order to be able to hold up a massive machine that was being installed upon our exit. That machine was a humongous mold into which the cement would be poured into to set and then cure.

The hole that had been dug out for us was not the dimensions required for the job. Therefore, my first order of business was to excavate more soil from the existing hole. Since I was indoors, I could only dump my buckets of soil onto the floor next to me. It was very difficult to operate a small backhoe inside of a room and not hit anything around or over me, but I managed. The men who were sent with wheelbarrows to shovel up and discard the dirt I'd dumped were not thrilled with the menial labor I'd just provided them with. I then had to reach far beyond the machine's recommended limits in order to drive the chance anchors farthest out from my machine. It was so scary to realize that at any moment, I could have tipped over the edges of the hole and fallen inside it.

I was operating those scary points needing an anchor with my stomach up in my throat. At dangerous times like those, I wore my poker face with the attitude and motto to *never let them see me sweat.* If you showed that you were chicken to try and push your machine, no matter what kind of machine that was, that would be an excuse to not put me on certain jobsites, so I made sure to always attempt their requests. We used to call that "operating by the seat of your pants." There were many times that I had backhoes, forklifts, frontend loaders, and cranes standing up on the toes of their tracks or tires when making a heavy pick.

Nowadays, for insurance and safety reasons, there are sensors and computers in place to keep the operator from working the machine beyond its suggested limits. Your machine will simply block you by not allowing it to function in the capacity you're working it in. The levers and controls will cease to function, except to bring the machine back to capacities within its requirements. With a crane, you will have to boom back up and lower your load. That enables the weight hoisted to be closer to the machine. With a backhoe, you retract the boom which resembles a giant arm, casting some of the weight from its bucket if necessary.

Tower crane views of two different jobsites on Jones Island

Middle right is the view from my tower crane Jones Island, looking up our river through Milwaukee

The beginning of the Jones Island jobsite the tower crane would eventually be erected on

View of a pile driving job I would have been on if I were not operating the tower crane on the project in the middle photo

Setting the precast for one of the parking structures I worked on for one of our hospitals

Cranes up at our school to train operators

If you're afraid of heights, you soon won't be because your machine "needs grease to live"; I'm feeding the iron its supplements

Views from a tower crane are spectacular! Look how tiny everything looks below you; those iron beams being unloaded by that crane off the semitrailer look like tiny little toothpicks

Waiting to drive the next pile

Looking down over the "pools" at the sewage treatment plant, those wands spanning their circumference were the seagulls polluted merry go-round—YUCK!

Looking down over that island project, I realize we rebuilt most of that entire plant; I served nearly my whole apprenticeship on that project

From that two-hundred-foot height, I could see far north into our city

By completing the initial testing of *"Will she or won't she?"* they realized I had the *cajones* ("balls"; I mean "BOOBS") to at least attempt operating in the realm of the unknown. For me, once I accomplished something daring that was put before me, I felt thrilled that I was able to do it. I look back on my career now in partial disbelief at the things I accomplished, the adversity I was able to overcome, and hell, just being able to hang in there for a total of twenty-eight years is quite a feat to be proud of.

I had an unusual "captive" audience when I had to work far away from home at a senior citizens' retirement home. The building was sinking on one area of the property. We dug a deep trench along the brick basement, and I drilled chance anchors deep into the ground as close to the basement wall as possible. A "chair" was then placed on the tops of each drilled rod. A portion of that chair sat beneath the bricks, and the building was then jacked back up until it was once again level. It was a scary and tricky process to drill so closely to a building. It was even scarier because the foreman was in the trench directly next to the rods I was drilling. If my torque head would have hopped off of the rod as I drilled, the foreman would have been severely injured.

The pressure grew even more for me each day as the number of patients wanting to watch me work through the giant picture window before me grew as well. Instead of bird-watching through their window, they observed the *woman at work* for their daily hobby and viewing pleasure. I'd see nurses throughout the day pushing wheelchairs, carrying their inhabitants up to the window. Unless it was mealtime, there was a full house of mostly men sitting as silent foremen at the window. Every so often, I'd see one or two of them pointing at me as if to say, "*Now* what the hell is she doing?"

I know that it wasn't every day that they looked out their window to see a woman, filthy dirty, hauling heavy steel rods and augers back and forth before them. Their eyes really grew large whenever I hopped into the seat of the Mini-X to drive the rods down into the ground. I seemed to be more interesting to watch than their television sets, and I came with no commercials! WTF!

One job I was sent to, I drove to a woman's home to see if I would be able to crawl into her garage with the Mini-X or go alongside her garage to drill in an anchor or two on its corner. I realized as I drove to her home that I was in a very expensive neighborhood. Several beautiful homes had been built around a water fowl sanctuary; essentially, it was a swamp. The rear of their homes and their decks had been built on stilts so that they were over a portion of the existing pond. The front of the homes, although level with the rear, were on more stable ground. Although it looked cool upon first glance, I couldn't help thinking about the mosquito populations you'd have to endure while lounging on your back deck in the summertime. The woman had purchased her new home for a quarter of a million dollars.

She was showing me around the yard and exterior of her home, and I didn't see any problems as of yet. She opened the garage door and showed me the huge crack in the concrete that crossed the floor and a gap that was widening within it. She told me that the crack was growing in width and she could feel a tilt downward in the corner of the garage as she walked across her floor. I placed a level on the floor near the corner she was speaking of, and it was indeed sinking.

We came back to her home the next day with the Mini-X and drove a couple of chance anchors around the corner of her sinking garage. We were able to jack the corner back up into a level position with the rest of her garage floor. The gap in the crack closed, and she only had to fill in a regular looking crack in her floor that many of us have dealt with before. It was sad to see a young woman upgrade into an expensive custom home and deal with a problem due to its location and design.

There was a small building being erected in a city far to the north of us. Since it was a one story building and would not require any piling to hold it up, I was sent there with the Mini-X to drill in quite a few chance anchors instead. It was a very slow process of drilling them in. I was bored due to the long amounts of time each one was taking to drill. It was hard for me to stay awake since I was so bored, and it was taking so long; it was also hot outside being that it was nearly summertime. We were working long hours, and our drive to and from the jobsite took us two hours each way. Also, we had a lot of rain showers moving in and out throughout most of our working days.

It was only myself and the foreman for a crew, so I was more than happy to hop out of my machine and help him when I wasn't drilling, and while I was, he would go and do his paperwork for our job. Whenever a rod reached its required depth, I would search for old bottles and artifacts that I'd come across throughout our excavation. It was always a treasure hunt for me whenever I came upon a jobsite that hadn't been excavated before. Many decades ago, people cast their refuse somewhere on their own property. I'd been on several jobsites that used to be garbage dumps in the past. In some cases, the bottles I found were straight out of the old western days. I've found antique bottles, glassware, porcelain, and china dishes. I'd discovered old doorknobs, silverware, and pottery as well.

Although it was a fairly quiet run-of-the-mill job, it was so far away that I had to get up at three in the morning and out the door by four to arrive at that jobsite on time. I drove home in darkness, so I had to be on the lookout for the deer that ran across the highway every so often. It would be almost daylight when I pulled up onto that jobsite.

There was one thing I witnessed driving up to that jobsite one morning that has forever stuck in my mind. In fact, whenever I think of it, it's as though it happened just yesterday. It's a vivid vision in my mind. As I was driving, it had just rained very hard, and I was about to turn off my windshield wipers. I was far out in the open countryside, and as I looked over a field of green grass and the forest on the horizon, a perfect rainbow appeared. A full arch, I could see the point where it seemed to come up out of the ground and also the entry point back into the ground. As I stared in amazement by its beauty, another arching rainbow appeared in all its glory, above and over the preexisting rainbow! I saw not only one but *two* perfect rainbows in their entirety!

If I didn't have to be at work on time, I would have pulled off to the side of the road and watched them until they both dissipated. That was a very happy and positive awe-inspiring "WTF!" moment. I didn't have very many "WTF!" moments in my career that were positive ones. On that day, I learned a very valuable lesson: *"Find something GOOD in each day."* It may be small things to some people but significant to others. That was a beautiful and rare sight for me to see. If I wasn't on that long boring drive to earn a living on a jobsite that I didn't want to go to and prove myself to a bunch of men that I belonged there too, I would have missed that beautiful sight. I try to instill this lesson into my daughter to look for anything positive and of beauty during each day and to focus on it because the boring, sequential crap that occurs at work is just that—CRAP. I believe the double rainbow vision was a gift from God and an act of Mother Nature to prove that there is calm after a storm—and in life as well. When progressing through a mundane workweek filled with boredom, "people" drama, and WTF moments, I find it to be of utmost importance to focus on all the beauty and success each day offers—no matter how small or trivial they may seem to be at the time. It's the beauty and success you will remember, not the bullshit.

I was laid off from my regular company one winter, and I got sent out from my union hall to operate a crane for an out of state contractor. They had won their bid to work on a project for our power plant located in one of our southern counties. The power plant was expanding, and I would be erecting a new conveyor system using the crane they had rented. I would find myself in and out of that power plant many times for various projects throughout my crane operating career. The weather was a horrible mess of rain alternating with snow as our fall was turning into winter.

I was only making one or two picks a day as they welded and bolted pieces into place. It was easy money, but I was very bored. I would swing a piece into place and hold it while the crew did their thing. Once they had all of their primary bolts in place, I was free to do whatever kept me sane until they were ready for the next section.

I was told that I could go wherever I wanted to go and do anything I wanted to do as long as I could see the crane. If they needed me, someone would approach the crane in order to give me my instructions. We were working next to the lake, and the wind would blow off of the water and cause the frigid temperatures to be even colder where we were working. I found a small room filled with machinery constantly running that made the room warm with the heat it created. "That's where I'll be if I'm not in the crane," I told the men. There was more room for me to stretch out than inside the small cab of the hydraulic crane I was operating. There were several days that required no pick from me at all. In order to keep my brain engaged instead of nodding off to sleep with boredom, I brought projects to work on along with me.

I brought a small sewing kit in my lunch box. I sewed buttons on any of my crew members shirts who had them missing. I stitched up the tears, repaired zippers, and patched both the knees and elbows of all the clothing they brought in for me to repair. I thought I'd bring in a project that I could carry in my lunch box so that in my downtime, I could achieve something for myself too. I crocheted an afghan, one square at a time. I noticed that by completing all of those small projects kept me alert.

At the end of my career, I had made countless pairs of earrings, crocheted a lot of pieces, got in a lot of sewing repairs. I did a lot of beading, such as a lampshade and a small curtain. I wired rocks, shells, and marbles for mobiles that I've hung to decorate my home. I also developed exercises that I could perform while sitting in the cab of the crane. I did puzzles to keep my mind sharp, such as sudoku and crosswords.

Many of us know how scary it is to nod off to sleep while driving a vehicle, whether it was due to boredom or being too tired. That's a frightening feeling. You can magnify that feeling a thousand times, and you'll know the stress felt by a weary operator who is running a huge piece of equipment that's capable of taking out a city block or two if it collapses. It's imperative to stay alert and on your toes when operating a machine of that capacity.

The next job I was sent to work on by my union hall was back to the power plant. That time, I would be setting iron with a big mobile friction crane as well as a cute little Broderson crane to set the smaller iron. The Broderson would just fit underneath the big iron I would be setting. I loved the little Broderson crane so much that I tried to talk my ironworker husband into letting me get one. I tried to charm him into it by telling him that I could hoist his Harley motorcycles up in the air so that it would be easier for him to work on them. I also told him that I could decorate our yard with large rocks I found on jobsites with the little crane. To all of my ideas and reasons I came up with to sell him on purchasing a Broderson crane, he had one response: "What are you, nuts?" I guess he just couldn't foresee my vision.

I was setting all of the big pieces of iron with the big crane. We were erecting a new silo that would hold some sort of ash. I had to be very careful hoisting those big sheets of iron up to the connectors waiting on the iron beams high above me. There was usually a breeze coming off of the lake next to us. We hung long taglines on all of the iron pieces I hoisted so that they didn't bump into any of the men or any preexisting portions of the plant due to the breezy conditions. Even when connecting the iron, that motion caused the accumulated dust on the plant's beams to rain down on us crew members below.

I would hop into the Broderson and head up the hill to our iron yard. An ironworker from the rigging crew would join me; he had the plans that told him which iron piece we needed to erect next. The problem I had with the Broderson was that the iron pieces were too heavy for it to carry without toppling my little crane over. I boomed all the way up until the sheet of iron was directly next to the crane. It's boom spun three hundred and sixty degrees independently from the crane's cab. In operator's terms, we called that design "the neck breaker" because you had to wrench your neck around in ungodly positions like Linda Blair in *The Exorcist* movie.

I only hoisted those heavy sheets mere inches off of the ground. That was so the sheet of iron itself would keep me from tipping over in the crane. Then I secured the iron sheet by tying a long rope from the front to the rear of the crane, enclosing the iron sheet and keeping it tight to its side. I looked like Fred Flintstone at the introduction of the *Flintstones* cartoon when they put a giant slab of dinosaur ribs on the tray attached to his door. He's at a drive-in to dine, and the ribs are so huge and heavy that his car tips over sideways.

I would proceed ever so carefully and slowly as the iron sheet bounced up and down off the ground as my crane constantly tipped and then righted itself. I had quite a ways to travel back and forth in that manner from the iron yard. The dirt road I traveled on was littered with potholes and gullies; it proved to be a very rough ride. If the ironworkers were in a pinch, awaiting the next sheet of iron, they would send an ironworker or two to hold the sheet as I walked the piece down the steep dirt road.

I told the ironworkers that we'd take it real slow because the heavy sheet of iron was going to bounce off the ground and back up, also that it would rock side to side because of its weight. I told them to *make sure their hands were not holding onto the sheet,* to use their taglines instead so that the iron would not pinch them or hit them. "In one ear and out the other, WTF!" I no sooner gave them those instructions and had just begun my journey down the bouncy dirt road when I heard an ironworker scream out in pain!

He'd failed to heed my warning and held onto the sheet of iron with his hand anyway. Not only did he hold on to the sheet, but he held it on a direct pinch point where the iron sheet swung against my Broderson. His fingers were completely flattened like a pancake. The sides of his fingers blew out, and there was blood everywhere. I told the other ironworker to get back to the foreman and tell him that his partner needed to go to the hospital "NOW!" I elevated his hand and tried to keep the injured ironworker as calm as I could until his partner came back with his truck to make the long drive to the hospital.

Using my "female" perspective. I did not holler at him, "I told you *not* to hold onto the sheet of iron with your hand!" That was the first thing that I had seen "men" do. The guy already knew he had f——ked up in a major way. Maybe he thought he knew more than a woman in that business did—he was wrong. Now his mistake had cost him all the money he would have made on that particular job, and he would have surgery and therapy bills to pay for. He would miss months of work and not have the use of his hand. He already knew that it was his own fault and didn't need me to remind him of his mistake.

As for men who dealt with situations such as that, I'd seen them come unglued over and over. That only makes the entire situation worse. We all know when we've made a mistake, and it was a lesson learned. WTF!

The next quirk on that jobsite occurred when I was setting the huge iron columns that sat on the big bolts which were encased in concrete. They were in forms that had been poured into the floor. The rest of the iron structure would be bolted to those supporting columns. I was in the big crane, inching the column downward as a few ironworkers were guiding the holes in the columns base over the bolts. I would then hang onto the column until all the nuts were tightbrened down on the bolts, and the guide wires were secured to keep the towering column in place before they could cut the crane loose from the column. The guide wires would hold it plumb and erect so the crossbeams could be bolted between it and the previous set columns.

The problem happened just as the holes in the columns base plate began lowering onto the bolts. The computer in the crane shut me off and ceased to function. Computers were just being introduced into cranes at that time for safety purposes. The sensors had shut down my function to lower my load any further because not only did the weight of the column register, but also the weight of the cable extending downward. Every weight that hung below the tip of the boom was considered into the safety performance of the crane. To go beyond those accessed capacities risked the level of stability of your crane. To tip forward risked your crane going over.

The levers malfunctioned at a hugely inopportune moment. The ironworkers were wrestling against the great weight of that humongous column, steadying it so it would not mar the bolts ridges that the nuts would be spun upon. I only had an inch or two to go, and if the rear end of my crane came off the ground a bit, I knew that the column would hold me steady once it was in place. I could ease the crane back down slowly as I released pressure on my brake pedal. One ironworker came to our rescue by showing me a way around our computer dilemma. He had learned this on a previous jobsite dealing with a similar scenario.

He took a small vice grip and clicked it onto my computer's override key. That key, once turned by hand, snapped back into its usual position. With that vice grip attached, the key would stay in the override position without me having to hold it there. That trick freed myself and the crane up from our locked down position and allowed the column to be properly seated and bolted into place successfully. Nowadays, vast improvements have been made to those computers, and there are no tricks such as the one we used available to override those systems put in place. I'll say here that computers do not replace the proper training of heavy equipment operators. Whenever I see on the evening news that a crane has toppled over somewhere, I can usually see from the footage they are showing the reason it happened. Unfortunately, it is usually from a nonunion worker attempting to operate a huge piece of dangerous machinery without the due diligence of proper training such as found at my union's training facility. I was using the mini Broderson crane to connect the smaller pieces of iron to bolster the structure of the larger pieces once they were all connected to each other. I was lucky to creep the Broderson between the struts of a preexisting silo in order to get a better angle to install my smaller iron pieces. The entire plant remained in operation while we were erecting their new conveyor system. The power plant workers who were employed in the area we were working were supposed to lock out and tag out the buttons and levers used to operate the silo I was directly working under with the Broderson.

As I was holding an angle of iron in place while the ironworkers were bolting it, I noticed a female plant worker at the catwalk above me talking flirtatiously with a fellow male worker. They were directly next to the instrument panel that controlled all the mechanical functions in our area. The next thing I heard was a loud alarm going off, and then *WHOOSH!* The silo's trap door opened above me, and hot white pot ash came funneling down on top of me. The ironworker's both leapt out of the way as soon as they could slide off the iron.

I couldn't leave my seat. I was holding an iron beam in the air. I was held tight in my seat by the surrounding hot ash anyway. I sat as still as I could and held my breath as long as I could before slowly inhaling through my nostrils and shut my eyes to keep the fine hot dust out. The dust pile had grown to completely encase the Broderson and myself. The pile was up to my shoulders; the

Broderson and I appeared as a twisted inverted ice-cream cone with my head being the cherry on top of its opposite end.

As I was pinned in place by the mountain of ash, my skin was itching and burning. The heat from the ash was nothing compared to the rising heat of my temper—-*I WAS PISSED!* I looked up at the girl on the catwalk as soon as I could pull my arm up out of the ash and wipe the dust from my safety glasses. She was standing there with a look of shock on her face as she pulled her hand away from the instrument panel she was supposed to have locked out. "WHAT THE FUCK!" I screamed up at her. "You can see we're working here. If I could get out of this crane, I would come up there and KICK YOUR ASS!" She quickly took off and retreated back inside of her building.

The ironworkers grabbed what shovels they could find that were kept randomly around the place to clean up spills like the one encapsulating me in my crane. They dug me out as soon as they could so that I could find a proper bathroom to wash the toxic dust off of myself. Once I found a women's bathroom inside the plant, I stripped off my dust-laden clothes and shook them out the best I could. I washed my skin and had to put the clothes back on. It was one of those days that I just wanted to go home, take a shower, and put some aloe vera gel on the areas burned the most on my skin.

Instead, I had to push on and return to work. We couldn't set anymore iron that day because I had to dig out the Broderson from the looming dust pile it was immersed in. I had to clean up the area surrounding it in order to drive it under the iron pieces we had previously bolted in place. Once out of its iron erecting position, I drove it to an air hose and blew the dust out of it and then found a water hose to get the toxic dust off of its tires so it wouldn't degrade the rubber. The entire machine had to be re-lubed and the cables sprayed with penetrating oil. That was one occasion where I didn't hear one joke made about my situation from any crew member. I could have been buried alive that day and suffocated on the dust if more had been released from that silo. There was nothing funny about that.

I was working in and out of that power plant on too many jobs to count, and I worked for several different contractors there. There were always a variety of WTF situations that would pop up out of the ordinary that I would have to deal with. One job we did in that power plant was during one of our most frigid winters ever. We had to drive some pile so they could put in equipment to load semitrailer tanks with that same dust I'd had dumped on me—potash. They were also putting in a scale so they could regulate the weight of those tanks those drivers would be hauling to their destinations. We were working right next to the freezing waters of Lake Michigan once again. There were huge chunks of ice floating on the lake's surface, and freezing water was spraying over the sheeting wall. The spray of water covered our jobsite area as if we were in the middle of a lawn sprinkler service. The wind was howling off of that freezing water, making it more challenging and uncomfortably cold for all of us.

I had to get to the job for grease time earlier than everyone else because I was the oiler on the crane and I was also operating the big air compressor that supplied air to the hammer used to drive down the pile. We had to pass through a guard shack to get into the plant. Four uniformed men worked in two separate lanes that anyone entering had to pass through. You were not allowed to enter without an issued identification badge that had your photo on it, who you were working with there, and the duration of time your job would require your presence. They also searched the contents of your pockets, your lunch box, and anything else you were entering into the plant with. At the end of the day, you were required to go through that same procedure once again when exiting the property.

The guards refused to open their shack a half hour earlier to accommodate my grease time. They were already on-site, drinking their morning coffee in preparation for their day, so I never understood their reasons for not allowing me access. The colder the temperatures would get during the winter, the harder it was to get that old iron to turn over and start up. It was mandatory that oils, grease, and various lubricants were warm enough to flow throughout your machine; otherwise, it was like the Tin Man in *The Wizard of Oz*— all frozen up and unable to move (I've often felt my body is like the Tin Man's as well—unable to move from stiffness and in need of zerk fittings to apply grease and oil into my joints!).

It was putting us behind on those mornings we had to wait around for the equipment to warm up due to those lazy guards. Five days of grease time equaled two and a half hours of overtime onto my weekly paycheck. I would have thought that those guards would have jumped at the chance to earn a little more on their paychecks each week while we were working there. It wasn't as if they were teaching an aerobics class, for Christ's sake. Were their uniforms inflating their egos? Perhaps they weren't thrilled to allow a young lady whose wages were three or four times that of their own to make even more money than them. WTF, I didn't care. I wasn't there to make *"pals,"* I was there to make money, and I wanted mine. I wanted to get in there and do my job.

I decided, "Fuck it! I'm done with their bullshit." I threw my extra winter clothing over the tall cyclone fence next to their shack. I put a tagline on my lunch box and threw the end of the rope over so that I could hoist my lunch box up and over after I got to the other side of the fence, and I started climbing. It was very difficult to get a toe hold in the fence while wearing my work boots, but I made it to the top. On my way down the other side, I was not so lucky. I slipped and fell to the ground. My hand was on fire! I had a sick feeling in the pit of my stomach, sending signals to my brain that something was very wrong with my hand. My work glove had gotten caught on one of those spikes that stuck out on top of the fencing.

The metal spike had slid perfectly between my finger and the ring I was concealing under my glove. As I fell, the ring was stripped off of my finger, and my finger was a bloody mess as the result. I couldn't believe it had happened in that way as I scoured the ground at the base of the fence, locating my ring. My ring was bent in an ungodly fashion. I could fix my ring, but I felt like an idiot because I was very lucky that my finger wasn't dislocated from my hand! I vowed never to wear my rings to work again.

When you train as an apprentice, they tell you *not* to wear any jewelry because it could get caught in equipment or part of the machine you're operating. At union meetings, I noticed several men missing fingers due to being caught in machinery for whatever reasons. I didn't want to join their ranks! I liked wearing as much jewelry as possible when I wasn't working, so I appreciated all of my fingers allowing me to do that.

Some jobs were just one obstacle after another, and as I've previously mentioned, every job I'd worked on that power plant properly provided those obstacles every time. It was so cold on that jobsite during the winter that when we walked into work one morning, all of our equipment, machines, and hoses that air circulated through from our air compressor to the hammer were entirely encased in ice. The extremely cold lake water crashing up and over the sheeting wall were raining down over our jobsite and immediately freezing. That "weather phenomenon" (I'm describing it as nicely as I can) had progressed throughout the evening hours. We figured that to be the cause because not only was everything encased in ice—it was *thick* ice. It was as if everything were giant ice cubes! A big frozen crane, the big air compressor, and its attached hoses were frozen to the ground and encapsulated in ice. We couldn't open the toolbox because both it and the welder were giant ice cubes as well. It was a frozen popsicle nightmare of a jobsite.

The ground was an ice rink. Our winter boots were rubber soled, so we were all sliding across the ice rather than walking, and nearly all of us found ourselves on our asses more than once. "WTF! We're going to be injured just trying to get around here. It's obviously too cold for the equipment to run in that shit. If it's too cold for the equipment, it's too cold for our bodies!" I said and then added, "Let's go home!" I would use that statement many more times through the years when it was dangerously cold. Usually, my statements such as that fell on deaf ears, even though that statement was the truth. Since I've retired, I deal with the lasting effects of what those frigid temperatures do to your body and I deal with them EVERY DAY.

The foreman agreed that we needed to get out of there as soon as possible before someone was badly injured. The waves were crashing down on all of us. The ice was coating our bodies as we tried to chip the ice off of our toolbox so we that we could retrieve shovels and pickaxes. We needed to rid our equipment of ice in order to move everything away from the lake in case the waves didn't let up.

As we worked, I noticed that my jacket was icing up, and it was getting hard to move my arms because of the freezing of my sleeves. We were all icing up. The more we tried to move, the stiffer we became. It took a long time for us to dig everything out of its ice cocoon and move it a ways up the hillside to gain some distance from the lake. We were almost finished and looking forward to getting in our heated vehicles and heading home to our warm houses when the head superintendent of the company pulled up in his warm car.

He had heard that we were planning on heading home for the remainder of the day, and that information didn't sit with him too well. Since he was clueless as to how hard it was to function in the frigid temperatures, our foreman took it upon himself to enlighten the superintendent. He walked the superintendent from his warm vehicle to the cold edge of the lake where the wind was howling off of the lake's surface so he could experience the full embrace of winter's frigid hug. The foreman was wearing his insulated coveralls, but the superintendent was only in attire manageable for his cushy warm office.

As they stood in the cold discussing the jobs progression, I could see the superintendent begin to rock side to side and shuffle his feet as he was trying to keep the blood flowing to his extremities. He was freezing his ass off! It was amusing for me to watch because most office personnel had no clue as to what we had to deal with day in and day out as far as the weather was concerned, never mind the difficult jobs we all excelled at.

The superintendent finally nodded goodbye to the foreman and made a beeline for his warm awaiting vehicle. When the foreman returned to the crew and myself, he had a mischievous smile upon his face. "Yeah, the superintendent agrees that it's just too cold and wet out here today for us to work, so we'll all come back here tomorrow and try it again. Go home and stay warm," he said as we all scrambled to get the hell out of there. WTF, you didn't have to tell me twice!

Near the end of that job, I began having a toothache in one of my molars at the rear of my mouth. The dentist's office was closed by the time I got off work at night and drove back into town. I thought that I'd make an appointment once the job ended in a few days. We were working overtime, and I needed the extra cash. My molar had other ideas and began flaring up at a rapid pace. *Now*

WTF! I thought as I could feel pressure building up in my face. The side of my face was going from hot to hotter. As the day progressed, the pain went from bad to agonizing. I wasn't feeling so well when my foreman said, "You're not looking too good, and neither is your face!"

"What the f——k kind of thing is THAT to say to a woman?" I said (I was getting crabby as well). "It's statements like that one that are keeping men from getting laid in this world," I added, attempting to interject a little humor into our awkward conversation.

He said to me, "No, I'm serious, the side of your face is completely swollen. You should find a women's restroom and see it for yourself."

I did as he suggested and went in search of a women's restroom located in the internal maze of the power plant. I wasn't feeling well at all by that point, and my swollen cheek was in prominent view of my left eye. As I turned into the bathroom and approached the mirror, I startled myself. WTF! I was unrecognizable! My face was fatter than hell! In the movie *Hitch,* Will Smith is the lead character. He ingests some food with peanuts in it and has an allergic reaction. His face swells up so much that he looks like a goblin; the facial distortion is so bad. That's what *I* looked like! The side of my face was hot to the touch, and I had a hammering pain throbbing in my tooth. My molar had abscessed throughout the day as I worked.

Now I was in trouble. My dentist was long gone from his office, finished for the day. I went home, unable to eat, and had a fever going. The infection in my tooth was making me sick. The next morning, I couldn't make it into work but managed to get a dental appointment.

Unfortunately, I learned that until all the swelling went down and the infection cleared up, they could not work on my tooth.

The next day, I returned to work, feeling better as the antibiotics were working their magic, clearing the infection from my mouth. I ended up having to leave my job early on the day they were going to fix my tooth. That is something you have to prepare for in that line of work. You can't leave your machine on a moment's notice. The piece of equipment you're assigned to plays a vital role in getting the job done. If you needed to leave for any reason, then you must be replaced. The most likely scenario is that a man will replace you. When a man replaces you, you're very lucky if you get your job back. That was especially true when the man who showed up was somebody's buddy. If he joined them for a beer at the tavern after their shift ended, I was really screwed. They would get drunk together and share memories of past jobsite stories, and the next thing you know, it's "old home week," and they'd rather have their "buddy" show up than the "odd girl out."

I'd had that happen too many times to count. I would get a phone call at night to tell me not to bother going back to the jobsite the next day because they decided to keep "Joe Shmoe" there instead. I learned to take all my belongings with me to my vehicle after every shift in case I would be told not to return or transferred to another jobsite. Once again, as my sensei (my karate instructor) would say, "This isn't a daisy-picking class!" or his other favorite saying for me, "This is not a tea party!"

I was lucky to be able to finish that job, but because of the hours I'd lost due to my tooth and the dental bills, all of the overtime pay I made went to paying for those and not in gaining the cash that I'd planned on making. You'll find yourself working when you're ill too many times to count because it's always one thing after another on the unending obstacle course that is a career in construction or in any other career for that matter. *WTF!*

There were too many dickheads in that business; hell, there are too many dickheads, period. Too many men who had the opportunity to bring a positive and inviting energy to the table but instead chose to provide an intimidating and mean-spirited atmosphere to the jobsite.

There were too many mornings where I was filled with dread at what lay ahead of me as I faced the day driving into work because of who I had to deal with there. I showed up anyway, no matter what. I myself provided smiles and positivity to prove women would enhance the projects we worked on.

Those asshole types are what caused me to start swearing and questioning, "WTF!" in the first place. I found myself making that statement too many times of those same characters who had the lack of imagination, a lazy mindset, and a bleak black aura about them. I've said, "Oh, honey, you want to act like an asshole? You're only an amateur. My ironworker husband can turn into the biggest asshole you'll ever meet in your lifetime. He would chew you up and spit you out. That's what I go home to after working with you all day. You're just my warm-up, asshole. This is Candy Land to me, so don't flatter yourself, ha-ha!" Men such as those are just laughable.

My husband once pointed out a T-shirt a man was wearing to me. It said, "Add alcohol—instant asshole."

"That's me," he said and laughed.

"Yes, it is, so why don't you quit drinking?" I asked him but received no reply. After years in construction and forging ahead through a shitstorm of brick walls thrown up in front of me, I realized that changes to promote women's progression in my industry were going to move at a snail's pace. I had to apologize to my daughter that the changes I was working toward in breaking barriers as to what women can achieve would not come to fruition within her lifetime.

I may very well hold the world's record for having dealt with the most assholes in a lifetime. If that's not the case, I know my ranking is among the top ten of the list. Although that's nothing to be proud of, I am proud of the fact that it did not turn me into one of them. Now speaking of assholes, here's a story about another one.

I had been laid off from my main company one winter and had been sent out of the union hall to work for an outfit that was setting precast along the ramps entering and exiting our freeway system. It was a new contractor for me to work with, and I'd be operating a hydraulic crane. It was an all-terrain crane; it looked like a big truck with a crane mounted on its rear portion. It was to be driven onto the jobsite by the truck driver who was bringing it from out of town on his lowboy trailer. The contractor was leasing it from the company the driver worked for. I was mainly a friction crane operator, so that precast for me was like setting iron in the way that it was like putting together a big puzzle. Everything was great until after coffee break when it was time to move the crane ahead so that we could set the next area of precast.

I should explain to you here that "precast" is concrete poured into predesigned molds and is held together and made stronger by including a series of iron rods called rebar that is encased within its center. You see precast on bridges, along freeway ramps, on building structures, and on barrier walls that line some freeway systems.

I sucked in the stabilizers and outriggers on the crane after sucking in and securing the boom in preparation to move the crane. The truck driver who had delivered the crane was still hanging around the jobsite, watching me work as if he was my personal foreman—which he *was NOT.* He told me that he'd signal me to back the crane up to the new area where I'd be setting up. "Whatever trips your trigger," I said to the guy. We weren't going to be finished with the crane that day, so it was unclear as to why the truck driver was still there. Perhaps he had no other runs to make that day with his truck and trailer.

I went to back the crane up after releasing the air brakes, but it wouldn't budge. I thought it could be because I was backing that big beast up a hill, so I gave it more gas; it still wouldn't move. At that time, the truck driver grew impatient with me and started yelling, "Why aren't you moving? Give it some gas, for Christ's sake!"

"I'm not familiar with this crane, and I don't need to be yelled at! WTF is your problem?" I hollered back at him.

He was standing to the rear of the crane, and instead of walking up to the cab and talking to me in a normal tone of voice, he started screaming at me to "floor it!" over and over. He was now livid that the crane was not backing up. His face was beet-red, and he was clearly pissed off. My actual *real* foreman—*not that red-faced clown*— had given me instructions simply to back up the hill in the area he had pointed out to me. He told me to get the crane set up, and we would resume setting precast after lunch.

He and the crew had gone back to the precast we had set to bolt it together and properly weld it into place. That timeline gave me a couple of hours in which to move the crane and get it set up for further operations. The truck driver screamed at me to the point where I just said, "WTF! If you want me to floor it, I will!" I put my boot on the gas pedal all the way to the floor. The crane jumped backward, and then I heard a loud snap.

The crane would move no further, and the truck driver was screaming, "You broke it, now look what you've done!"

I got out of the crane and said, "What the hell are you talking about?"

He said, "You've broken the axle in two!"

I looked under the crane and immediately felt like a piece of shit as I could see that I had indeed caused the crane to break. I told the truck driver everything I'd done while inside the cab, the buttons I'd pushed, including the air brake button. He said, "You moron, there are TWO brakes to be released on this crane!"

I told him that was news to me because all of the hydraulic cranes I'd operated that were similar to this one only had *one* air brake. He didn't care. He was losing his mind at that point.

Then to add to my feelings of humiliation and embarrassment, that truck driver asshole took it upon himself to run up to anyone on the jobsite to say, "Did you see what that dumb broad did?"

I couldn't believe it. There were a row of dump trucks lined up to be loaded with soil from the backhoe that was excavating a basement for a building to be erected there. He made sure he stopped at every last one of those dump trucks to let them know how he felt about the "dumb broad" who broke his crane! I'm sure that the "dumb broad" title turned into "dumb bitch" as soon as he was out of earshot.

I told him to calm his ass down and call the company he worked for to let them know what happened and to send out a mechanic as soon as possible. The foreman came up to me and said, "Shit happens, we'll just lease another crane, and when it arrives, we can resume work." He was very gracious about it, adding, "Don't let him get to you, you're doing a good job here."

However, I was devastated that I'd made such a huge mistake and an expensive one at that. I'd also had it with that truck driver badmouthing me to any man in the vicinity and was trying very hard not to put my fist through his mouth. I couldn't stand him anymore and had to get away from him.

I called my union business agent and told him what had happened. He told me not to worry about it, that I had made an honest mistake. Most cranes had one air brake as far as the type of crane I was operating, not two. I also told him that I needed another operator sent out to replace me because it was all I could do not to punch that guy who was shaming me to everyone on the jobsite. The business agent told me that the job was mine and that the truck driver had no say whatsoever in the matter and shouldn't even be there in the first place. He told me that he'd be right out to put a stop to his asinine behavior. The job was clearly mine if I still wanted it.

I told him that I just wanted to get away from there. I would stay until another operator showed up to take my place, but I needed to keep my distance from that asshole truck driver. I was already fighting depression again as I'd been forced by my husband to move out of the house once more not by choice but to preserve the safety of my daughter and myself. I wasn't at my usual strong capacity to deal with ignorant behavior. I vowed to myself that if I crossed paths with that motherf——r of a truck driver in the future that I would give myself permission to deal with him as I saw fit at the time.

From time to time, I would come home to find all of my belongings hanging all over our hedges and strewn across our front lawn, my jewelry run over with the car in our driveway. It never failed to break my heart which, of course, was the clear directive. Other times, I'd be home, and he'd enter after leaving the tavern to tell me that I had five minutes to grab my belongings and get the hell out before he physically threw me out.

After working my ass off all day and arriving home to do housework and get the dinner ready after picking our daughter up, *all of a sudden,* I'd have to procure a living space for her and myself: a daunting task at best.

I can't explain the terror and heartbreak I felt at the cruelty of his behavior. Those feelings were compounded by having to uproot my daughter in all of that calamity, but I had no choice except to grab her and get out before chaos erupted into World War Three. Unfortunately, I couldn't afford a third arrest for assault charges. I was previously informed that if I incurred a third arrest, I would be put away for some time. As a mom, that would be intolerable. I couldn't afford to leave my daughter in the sole custody of her dad at that time due to his alcohol and drug use. Perhaps if my first assault charge wasn't against two police officers in California or the second against an officer in the state I now live in, the sentencing wouldn't be as bad. I've made it a rule not to find out either way. I must have been a Rottweiler in a past life or just had an aversion to their uniforms; I don't know.

That experience on that particular jobsite dealing with that asshole truck driver sent me further down the bleak black hole that was threatening to swallow me entirely. I was attempting my fourth course of action to divorce my husband at that time. I'd moved us to a town north of our city. It was about a forty-five-minute drive, and I'd made the move there to create some distance from my husband. He usually straightened up his act and talked me into giving our marriage another chance. It would work out for a while until he missed his daily gatherings with other ironworkers at the tavern. Sooner or later, the shit would hit the fan once again. That entire process of fleeing, seeking shelter elsewhere, reconciling, and moving back into our home caused me to withdraw into depression. We had moved in and out so many times that depression became my shadow; it followed me everywhere.

I was raised through twelve years of classes and training as a martial artist. I began when I was in sixth grade of middle school. Almost daily, I was in classes and taught to live life by our "dojo kun"; that is a code we must live our life by. They are made up of these laws: (1) seek perfection of character; (2) respect others; (3) endeavor (get off your ass and get busy); (4) remain faithful; (5) refrain from violent behavior.

Number four was one of the main reasons that I kept returning to my marriage to make it work…until it almost killed me. I'll expand more on that in the chapter "Challenging and Just Plain Scary." I'd struggled with number five for decades. I was confused at the concept that I'd trained in full contact karate (before they had helmets, gloves, shin and forearm guards, and mats lining the floor on which to fall on). I thought, *What was the point of learning to shred someone to pieces if you were not supposed to engage that knowledge?*

I was a successful bouncer in three different taverns for employment, due to my training. My knowledge of martial arts enabled me to defend myself when my husband Dr. Jekyll turned into Mr. Hyde. What took me a long time to realize was that the negative energy involving "violence does not dissipate as long as you participate."

I had finally quit fighting physically with my husband, but to stand there and take his physical punishment when I could clearly kick his ass into next week filled me with so much anger that I felt like a volcano ready to erupt and spew forth fire and violence everywhere. I learned from my therapist that keeping my anger inside was causing my depression. I was damned if I did defend myself and damned if I didn't. In karate, we call that *"kobiwashamaru"* which means "a no-win situation."

Nowadays, I'd have no problem whatsoever dealing with another jerk, but back then, in that state of mind, I just wanted to get away from that truck driver as quickly as possible. Sometimes it would become all too much to be in the constant company of the male species. I felt most often as if I were a stranger in a strange land. I couldn't possibly blend in because I was so very different. I could only bring a new opinion and a fresh breath of air into their midst. Some men liked me, some put up with me, and others tolerated me. There were a few who wanted nothing more than to see me fail, become injured, or give up entirely. Dealing with that atmosphere on a daily basis was exhausting.

My union had my back. My business agent drove out to the jobsite with another crane operator to replace me, but before I left, he'd asked me once again if I didn't want to finish that job. He told me that he'd have my back either way. I told him about attempting to divorce my husband once again and that I was going through a weak and vulnerable phase just then and that incident was another dagger of defeat for me personally. He told me to take some time for myself, and when I felt stronger, to give him a call and he'd find work for me. It was a nice feeling to know that there were decent men who had my back and that those men were my union brothers.

I got called from the hall to go and work for a contractor that's known for building mostly hospitals. That job, however, was setting forms and pouring concrete walls to build a trucking terminal. I would be operating a hydraulic crane that I could drive between the terminal and another jobsite to set iron for a building. WTF! It was all or nothing in that business.

I'd been laid off for some time, and instead of them hiring two crane operators for each jobsite, I was to set forms to pour concrete in the next day, then drive the crane several miles away to set iron. During the mornings, when I was not with the ironworkers, they were adding the additional bolts in each junction and torquing them to the specified pressure. Mornings after setting the forms, I would leave the carpenters to add all of the necessary clips to secure the forms so they wouldn't leak any concrete poured into them the next day. I was at both jobsites each day for a period of six hours each. I was a very busy girl!

Every day at the end of the shift, all these coolers appeared in the jobsite trailer. Our project manager brought cases of beer to fill them. Everyone on the jobsite had an open invitation to hang out for a while after work and bond over a few beers together before heading home. WTF! Drinking and driving are a big *NO-NO*. Yes, we lived in a city built around all the breweries that our city is known for, and I'm sure that saved many of the guys from having to stop at the tavern on the way home from work, but I'd never seen that happen on a jobsite before or since then. I was invited to join the guys to have a beer time and time again, but I declined because I wanted to pick up my daughter as soon as possible. I also wasn't drinking at the time. In fact, I didn't drink during the last eight years of my first marriage. I needed to be sharp, focused, and *fast* at all times. I previously wrote that I compared my marriage to the *Pink Panther* movies where the inspector had to be prepared to defend himself at any time.

In any given moment, the shit could hit the fan in the hours I spent in my home. While my husband hit the tavern after work, I was working out and lifting weights. I was in training, preparing for battle. Later on, when I sought help for my depression, I was diagnosed with post-traumatic stress disorder. That was because at any moment, a bomb could go off in my home, and that bomb was my husband.

I began to feel more like a mom to him instead of a wife because of the rules I laid down at that stage of our marriage. I told him that if he broke something, it would no longer be replaced. If he ripped the phone out of the wall (he would make sure that I couldn't make a call for help) once more, then we would no longer own one. Too many of our phones had been thrown out the front door. The last phone he threw out the front door made it all the way to the hedge that lined our driveway. There it lay, like an ugly garland. It stretched across our hedge for nearly a week so that all of our neighbors could view it as they passed by our house. They probably thought, "What the f——k is going on in there?"

*Setting up heavy concrete slabs for the load test needed
before driving pile for our present stadium*

*The forefront of the photo below is the hammer setting in the leads that are
attached to my crane; I was driving the test pile pre-jobsite requirements*

Another view of setting precast for one of our hospital's parking structures.

Beginning of arena down town in our city

Children's hospital being erected in our medical complex
That tower was a hell of a climb to grease the sheaves

Another parking structure for one of our hospitals

*We are putting in the tall boom and prepped to attach the long jib;
this is the crane that is shown in the children's hospital photo; it was
a lot easier to grease it before it was boomed up into position*

*Operating a tower crane is tricky when you're
working among other high booms the air*

I operated a big crane to erect the beige iron that was tied into the existing iron; you can see my little Broderson crane somewhat; I used that little crane to erect all the small iron struts underneath the big iron; that little crane was so cute!

I realized that I liked building structures a lot more than bridges because I stayed a lot busier erecting iron or driving pile. Bridges were too slow going for me, and I grew bored. I'm a bitch when I'm bored, so for the benefit and saving grace of my male coworkers, I gave up building bridges and stuck with the structural erection of buildings. I honestly can't say where these bridges are. One ran into the next. This is a good lesson to learn.

You spend such a huge portion of your life at your job that you better enjoy your time there; otherwise, it is time wasted. Life is too short to waste, so do something that makes you happy and proud of the time you've spent there, like completing giant buildings.

We ended up with the plastic chairs we used on our deck as our dining room table chairs. We also used plastic crates to sit on when he destroyed the last of our actual chairs that came with our table. He was like an overgrown child having overgrown temper tantrums. I figured that maybe I could embarrass the alcoholism out of him if he had to see with his own eyes all the damage he'd done while in a drunken blackout. It didn't work; rehab stints didn't work; nothing f—king worked.

We had an unusual visit one afternoon from an ironworker buddy of ours we'd known for many years and his much younger wife. They had odd looks on their faces as they sat in our plastic patio chairs around our table to visit with us. My husband looked embarrassed at our plastic furniture, and I gave him a look that said, "That's too bad, this is our new reality when you behave like an asshole."

We had a good laugh, however, when the young wife said, "You guys have the same furniture we do!"

I thought, *Poor girl, that's no doubt because he sits on the barstool next to my husband every day!*

I chose the plastic chairs because I laughed my ass off one night when he came home blitzed out of his mind and decided to become enraged and break one of our chairs, like he'd done with all our original wooden chairs. The chair bounced up like a rubber ball every time he smashed it to the floor. Every time he struck the floor with the chair, it came up so fast that it almost hit him in the face. Instead of realizing that he would not be able to break it, he swung it against the floor faster and harder. It was comical like watching a cartoon. He must have kept up the pounding of the chair for at least ten minutes until he actually wore himself out. He walked over to his recliner, sat down, and passed out. WTF! It was one of the funniest things I've ever witnessed to this day, and it makes me laugh just writing about it!

The same contractor I'd worked on two separate jobsites each day had me operate a crane on the island, just outside the sewage treatment plant. I was to set and pour concrete walls for a new terminal being built on one of the loading docks. The lake was on either side of our jobsite, making it a very cold environment for us to work in. There was a rhythm to pouring concrete when we created the walls. One day is spent setting and securing the forms that will contain the pour and shape the walls. The next day, the concrete trucks drove in one after another as I swung my bucket to the men who were standing on top of the forms. They would hold onto the bucket, guiding it and releasing the concrete into the forms. I would lower the bucket as the weight of the concrete inside became less so that the bucket remained in the hands of the men. I would swing back around to the concrete truck, allowing the bucket to drift under the concrete chute before setting it solidly on the ground. I had to move the crane as rapidly as possible while being safe so I would not touch anyone or anything while that heavy bucket was in motion.

I was next sent by that same contractor to another site that was designated to become a new phone company. The basement had already been dug out, and a ramp had been excavated for me to drive the hydraulic crane down that I would be operating. I was to set up in the center and once more set forms and pour concrete for the walls. I would be able to have enough room for the concrete trucks to drive down the ramp and set up next to me. It was the beginning of winter, and they wanted the basement portion of the building completed before the snow really stared to fly. They would proceed with the job in the spring as far as the structural portion of the building was concerned.

The air was so frigid that inhaling air through my nose hurt. I had already figured out to wrap a wide soft scarf around my face and to breathe through my mouth so that the hairs inside my nose didn't freeze. I had to breathe through my scarf to keep my lungs from freezing as well.

You don't think about what the winter air does to your body until you have no choice but to be outside *all day long* and have to deal with the consequences.

The film on your eyes freezes also so that at the end of the day, your eyes are red, and it feels as if someone threw sand in them.

That same feeling in your eyes also occurs if you catch someone welding anywhere in your peripheral vision. You cannot look at someone welding at all without it causing harm to your eyes. That is hard to do when you're sitting in a crane seat and cannot look away. That type of eye discomfort is referred to as "welding flash," and eye drops don't do enough to bring a noticeable amount of relief. I would usually feel better after a good night's sleep. Welding flash was more easily incurred on a cloudy day when the glare of welding is brighter in contrast to the sky.

I was lucky that the crane I was operating on that jobsite was one of the more modern hydraulic cranes I ever ran. That meant that it had a heater, a defroster, and windshield wipers that were all in working order. It was so cold on some days that I told the crew that if I didn't have to get out of that crane other than to use the port-apotty that I was going to stay inside of it with the heater. I told them not to take offense if I did not join them to eat in the jobsite trailer. I just didn't want to take the long walk over to it in the freezing air. They understood perfectly.

That jobsite was a far distance from where I was living at the time. I had moved even farther up north to an extremely small farming community. I was thinking about purchasing a farm of my own and growing sunflowers for birdseed. A well-known brand of birdseed was made not far from the farm I was I interested in. I could also have horses there as well as board them and raise potbellied pigs there too.

The drive from the property I was residing on to the jobsite was one and a half hours in one direction, so roughly three hours round trip each workday. I had to get up between three and four in the morning to prepare for the day and drive there. There was a really young couple who had their own dairy farm. The husband took care of the cows, and the wife watched the children in the community while their parents went to work each day. Her day care was reasonably priced, and they had two little daughters who enjoyed the company of other children during the weekdays. I could drop my young daughter off on my early commute to work, and she could go back to sleep on their couch that they had made up for her. It was so early that their girls were still asleep.

The husband would be milking their cows as I left for work, and my daughter enjoyed the freshest milk possible each morning for breakfast. I seriously believe that my daughter didn't succumb to any illnesses during that time period due to her drinking that milk that came directly from the cows each day.

The winter arrived "colder than a witch's tit," as the men would say (I know! Where the f——k did they come up with *that* analogy?) It snowed like crazy that year as well. I had to shovel the snow off of my crane because my broom wasn't cutting it.

Speaking of brooms, I'm going to pause here for a moment to tell you about a running joke regarding brooms and myself. Upon being spotted with a broom in my hand, it never failed that a guy on whatever jobsite I was working on would say, "Hey, where are you going on your broom? HA-HA!" meaning that I was a witch. That comment always brought him the laughter from the other guys that he was seeking. It was at my expense, but whatever.

I had a sense of humor, so I'd reply something like, "Well, WTF! You must be our comedian for the day." That would generate some laughter as well. I quickly learned to turn the tables by bringing my broom to the forefront. If I saw a guy using it to sweep off his semitrailer, I'd say, "Hey! Where are you going with my ride?" That provided us with a good break in the day for all of us to laugh, and regardless if I knew the men well or not that I was working with, it broke the tension and showed them that I had a sense of humor. Laughter is a powerful bonding tool.

All right, back to the wintry frozen tundra of the jobsite I was in the process of writing about. Cell phones were just coming out, and although they were a lot larger and bulkier than the ones we now use, it brought a sense of security to know that if I needed help during my drive to and from my jobsite that it was just a phone call away. I awoke to blizzard conditions one morning and dreaded making the stressful and dangerous drive into work. As with most jobsites, no work can be carried out without a crane and an operator to run it.

As I drove into work, it was scary. The plows hadn't been out yet, so I was slowly following in the path of the car in front of me. There was only one lane, and I could barely see the taillights belonging to the car ahead of me. The snow was coming down so hard and fast that I would lose sight of those taillights from time to time. I kept thinking that maybe it wasn't snowing so hard where our jobsite was located.

I arose so early in my house that all the others were still asleep, so I never turned the television on to check the weather before I left. I knew that driving so slowly in only one lane of traffic on the freeway was going to cause me to be late for work. I thought, *WTF! They'll be lucky that I chose to show up in all this shitty weather.*

It took me forty minutes longer than usual for me to make it to the jobsite. At that point, I was afraid I was going to get an ass-chewing. I hadn't called to say I'd be late because I couldn't pull off to the side of the freeway anywhere to make the call. I had huge piles of snow on either side of me. I didn't dare take one hand off of my steering wheel to make the call because the roadway was slippery than hell. I had to be able to steer clear of whatever happened in front of me so that I didn't collide with any vehicles, even if that meant ending up in a snow pile.

I was saying prayers of thanks as I pulled into the jobsite. I was preparing to get an earful at my tardiness when I was getting out of my car. It was snowing hard there as well. I noticed the foreman's truck parked directly next to the jobsite trailer but no one else's vehicle. "WTF, where is everyone else?" I said to myself.

I walked into the trailer, and the foreman said, "What the hell are you doing here in this snowstorm?"

I said, "Well, no one called to tell me not to come in." I told him that I was late due to the road conditions.

He told me how sorry he was that he forgot to call me after he'd called the rest of the crew to stay home. He also apologized that I'd made the trip all the way in from out of town. He told me to drive back home, and we'd try to work the next day. "WTF!"

I made the scary drive once more back up north, using only one lane of traffic. It was so icy by that point that people were driving really slow. I noticed multiple vehicles down in the ditch and lodged into snowdrifts. I wasted my entire day stressed out at the wheel of my car. It took longer to drive to the jobsite and back home than it took me to not only drive back and forth but to work an eight-hour day also. I usually got a lot of things done and taken care of when the weather interfered with a workday, but not on that particular one. I had spent the entire day in my car—that day sucked! WTF!

Another challenging day due to weather on that jobsite involved the wind. Back in the days I worked, we had a cutoff point concerning high winds in which we would shut down the crane. That was due to safety factors involving the structural capacities of the crane, the swaying it caused the suspended loads, and the detriment of the crew's health and safety. When working with ironworkers, they had a hell of a time maintaining their balance on the iron in high winds. Once again, back then, there were no safety harnesses. Connectors stood on the top sections of iron that they had bolted together. There was nothing above them to tie off to if they did have them. They would physically climb up to the next level of iron as it was put in place in whatever means necessary to do so. No one had heard of safety harnesses yet, and it would be quite a few years before we did. Those Ironworkers were high up in the air due to their sheer will, experience, and incredible balance.

I showed up for work, thinking that I would get paid my two-hour show-up time, and once those two hours were up, I'd make the long drive back home. I was surprised, however, when the foreman and jobsite superintendent asked me if I would consider trying to work that day. I thought that I should at least give it a shot because I'd driven all that way and I could use the money. We were working down inside that large excavated hole, so the winds would not be as bad as they would be if we were working up on top. Also, if I made one pick, I was paid for the entire day according to my contract. If we tried to work and decided that the winds proved to be too much, I received eight hours of pay.

I told them that I'd be willing to try, but if the forms we would be transferring to our next wall section began to spin or get away from the men handling them in any way, I would quickly lower them to the ground to stop their motion. In that way, the men wouldn't be hurt by them. I told the men to use their taglines attached to the forms in order to keep their distance so that if they began to spin, they wouldn't be struck by them. I wouldn't even have attempted to operate a friction crane in those conditions. As it was, I was going to be arm wrestling with the hydraulic crane's levers, especially the swing lever.

They were ecstatic that I was willing to try. I don't know if they expected me to be frightened to operate the crane in the high winds or if they thought I'd hair out because I was a *GIRL,* but they seemed surprised that I didn't put up a fuss about it.

It was a long and weary day, fighting against the winds all day long. At times, the forms we were stripping off of the previously poured section of wall were lifting the men, holding on to them with taglines clear off the ground. The men were flying! At lunch-time, I told them, "You guys were airborne!" as I laughed (so they didn't think I was bitching at them). "Just let go of the tagline, and I'll set them on the ground for you so that you don't get hurt." I even swung to the side after setting them on the ground, lowering them on top of each other to stack them. All the men had to do was put lumber underneath each piece to keep them separated. Then they could unhook them from my headache ball.

It was too windy to set the forms in place for the next section of wall to be poured, but at least we stripped the forms off of the wall section we'd poured the previous day. The men were able to clean and prep the forms we'd placed on the ground to be set in place the next morning. It had been a rough day, and we were all worn-out from dealing with the wind and the forms for the men. My arms were sore from flying giant "kites" all day long.

When I walked into the jobsite trailer at the end of the day, after closing up my crane, I was greeted with a lot of thank-yous from the guys. The foreman and superintendent told me that I'd done a fantastic job operating the crane in those windy conditions, and more importantly, I had made sure that no one was injured. It was very rare to hear the words "thank you" in that business, so I made sure to relish it when I did. That made me feel even more motivated to do a great job. It also taught me to make others feel that way about their contributions on the job, and from that day forward, I made sure to commend a job well done when I saw it. It makes a big difference to people who receive acknowledgment for their good deeds both on and off the jobsite.

That job went well, we stayed on schedule, and there were no injuries. It was almost Christmas time, and our jobsite was a slushy icy mess with mounds of snow piled up everywhere. It was also extremely cold. One day, an unusual vehicle pulled up to our jobsite trailer. It was a car and not one of the pickup trucks that would arrive every so often to bring us parts or supplies that we needed. After a while, I saw a man in a business suit and a long trench coat, and he was walking toward me. He had on a nice pair of men's shoes and not work boots or the winter footwear most of us had on.

He came up to my crane, so I got out and climbed down so that he could speak to me. He said, "I want to shake your hand and tell you what a great job you've been doing for our company (at that point, I was in shock). I want to wish you happy holidays and give you this ham for your family's Christmas dinner. I'm the vice president of the company, and I'm here to tell you that you can finish your career working with our company until the day you retire. We would love to have you join us!" That was one of my "greatest of all time" WTF moments!

I ended up sticking with my main company that I did the most work for, but I still worked for a lot of different contractors operating a lot of different cranes. I did that mostly because I'd worked with the men there for so long that most of them accepted me as part of the crew. They made me feel like I was one of them. I felt like I was working with a bunch of brothers who looked out for me.

When I worked for other contractors, there were usually a lot of men I was working with for the first time. That meant I had to prove myself worthy of my job title over and over again. I had to also deal with the chauvinist attitudes or the various come-ons and sexual advances that I did not invite or want to have to deal with. I worked with too many men who flat-out told me that I should be home taking care of it and my daughter. They told me on too many occasions that I was "taking food off of a man's table"; I was taking a man's job that he needed in order to provide for his family. *HELLO!* I needed to provide for *my* family too! WTF!

One of those men were one of the religious zealots that I wrote about who covered up the topless lady posters in our jobsite trailer when we were working to expand our sewage treatment plant. He would remove his flannel shirt and cover a poster with it so my virgin eyes *(really?)* wouldn't be forced to look at it. He took over the foreman's position on a jobsite I was working on. We were expanding our children's hospital. The building being constructed would be a combination of offices and a parking structure.

Up until our original foreman was removed to go run another jobsite, our crew of three along with myself on the forklift were working well together. We were all pitching in to do whatever was necessary to get the job done. I never minded getting out of whatever seat I was sitting in to lend my help with another pair of hands. Besides, it was good exercise, and for me, bored and not busy equaled *bitch!*

Once that religious fanatic became foreman, there was Bible study happening during both our coffee and lunch breaks. I believe everyone has the right to worship as they please and to be part of whatever religion they choose to partake in. I *don't* believe that any one religion is better than the rest. It was for that reason that I was appalled when he began teaching our crew members that all other religions other than his own were blasphemous. He specifically stated that Buddhist monks were murderers. WTF! Did he know somehow that I was a Buddhist? Was that why he was bringing up that "lie" to the crew members? He also carried on about his opinion about abortion being a sin. According to him, all pro-choice supporters were sinners and would be avenged by going to hell when they died. WTF! I am pro-choice. His checklist about me was beginning to stack up in favor of his reasons for disliking me—I didn't stand a chance with that guy.

When I got out of my forklift seat in order to hold a cable tight so the pile driver could attach a clip to it, the foreman charged over to me and, yelling in an angry voice, said, "I may have to put up with a woman on this jobsite, but I do not have to work with one! Get your butt back in that seat and don't leave it unless you have to use the port-a-potty. If I see you out of that seat, I'll call the office and tell them to remove you from this jobsite!"

What an asshole! I thought to myself. Then I thought, *WTF! Who the hell does he think he is?* I felt like storming off the jobsite and making my own complaints, but I didn't. I was more professional than that. I also wasn't about to get run off my job because of some asshole!

I stayed on that job until it was finished. The foreman didn't speak to me unless it was absolutely necessary. I stayed to myself and did the best job that I could for the crew. I stayed in my seat and brought along some wire work to be done on a big project I was working on at home. That kept me from being bored while staying in my seat. It also allowed me to feel as though I was accomplishing something instead of sitting there with my thumb up my ass, doing nothing. Truth be told, I couldn't wait until the end of each day so that I could put some distance between myself and that prick. He wasn't the first asshole I'd worked with, and I knew that he would not be my last.

The other operators in my union voted to name me "Apprentice of the Year." I was astounded and extremely proud to receive it. That was for my work as a union steward on the huge sewage treatment plant project, the speaking engagements I made on behalf of our union to gain more minority participants, and all the hours of my own time that I put in to learn how to operate a tower crane and to drive pile and sheeting. I was the first woman to receive that honor and wore a nice outfit and looked as "female" as I could to represent our gender in a large crowd of men at the awards ceremony. Our union's newsletter that's mailed to all of our members monthly had sent a representative to take my photograph as I received my plaque. Our union president at that time was to shake my hand as he handed the plaque to me. We posed briefly while shaking hands for the photographer.

As he took my hand, in a low voice that no one else could hear, he had this message for me. "I've been told that I have to accept the fact that you're here, but I don't believe women have a place in our union or in any branch of construction, and I never will."

Under my breath I stated clearly, "You're entitled to your opinion, but I'm here to stay, and I'm just one of the many to come, so perhaps you'd better brace yourself." I wanted to add, "You dinosaur mother f——king asshole!" but I remained ladylike, taking the high road and remaining professional. Stealing my thunder when I was rewarded for busting my ass was a big NO-NO! MEN—WTF!

After I became a journeyman *(woman)* in my union, I was voted in as Operator of the Year. I was once again the first woman to receive that honor in our state and was proud as ever to receive it. To me, that was a proclamation to all the male members that women had a lot to contribute on a jobsite. That time around, the president stayed in his seat and had another member in office hand me my certificate and shake my hand. In the photograph that was taken, the president is behind me in the background.

I was trying not to laugh as I accepted my award because not only was he still stuck with me being a member of his union, but I was getting another award for my work as well! I had plenty to say to him but kept my dignity and my opinions to myself. Nowadays, everyone thinks they're entitled to judge you on every element of your life. Being respectful of others may be hard to do at times, but it's absolutely necessary.

Sometime later, a different union member was voted into office as our president. He was looking for any member of our union who would be interested in becoming a new business agent for the area of Milwaukee. When I passed that information on to my ironworker husband, he was adamant that I sign up for the position. I think he just wanted me off the jobsites and away from all the men I was working with. The reasons I thought about doing it were that I'd be clean, out of the elements brought forth by the weather (for the most part), and that I'd be away from all the men on the jobsites.

The negative aspects of being a business agent were that I'd be driving all over the required area constantly in order to check on all the various jobsites. The hours would be longer, and I'd be needed at a lot of meetings, and many of those were in the evening. I knew that if I were to be hired as a business agent that it would open even more doors for women who would join in the future. I would miss time with my daughter, which was already minimal due to my working unknown hours on any given day. I would be sent out to work an eight-hour day but could easily find myself working ten to twelve hours depending on what took place during my shift. The time I could spend with my daughter was always my main focus.

I thought I would assess the situation with the newly appointed president to see if the idea of our unions first female business agent was even a possibility in his mind. When I told him that I was thinking about throwing my hat in the ring for the position, this is what he said to me: "Suzanne, the men are pressuring me to hire our first African American operator as a business agent. That's their vote for another minority to join with our Indian members presently holding office. I don't think they're ready as of yet to have a *woman* as our minority selection for our business agent, for Christ's sake. Maybe sometime down the road in our future, we can see what a woman can do as a business agent, but now is not that time. Hell, there are some men who are still trying to wrap their heads around the fact that you're still here. They thought your career as an operator was a *flash in the pan*."

WTF! There you have it; I remained a crane operator.

Keep in mind that the neanderthal thoughts and actions (not to mention words spoken) of the men I'm writing about happened a few decades ago. Since I've retired, we've had the "MeToo" movement, and women's rights and equal pay have been brought to the forefront of our present society. I know there are women's groups who would have had a field day with those clowns I had to endure working with. Working on jobsites these days is a much better environment for everyone working on them. Everyone is there for the same reasons: to earn a decent wage, for their health insurance, and to ensure their futures by earning pensions. Sexual harassment is not tolerated any longer—anywhere.

Our minority business agent was successfully voted into his position by all the male members of our union. In my opinion that "boobs are bigger than balls," I was correct in the assumption that he either didn't have a pair of balls or they just weren't big enough to wield the necessary power that a business agent requires. This was proven to me when I'd finally been called back to work by my main company after a very long and bank account draining layoff.

I'd been out of work for so long that whatever money I had left had to go toward paying for my health insurance coverage. I had a hell of a nice antique bottle collection that I'd gathered from the various jobsites I'd worked on. I had plans to decorate with them, but due to my financial distress, they were sold to an antiques dealer in order to pay some bills and feed my daughter and myself.

I was to operate a crane directly on the lakefront. I was going to drive a sheeting wall deep into the ground. It was to be for our now existing art museum. It was to have underground parking so the sheeting wall would allow the site to be excavated accordingly. The next phase of that job would be to drive in a lot of piling. Those pile would hold the erected iron in place.

When I pulled up to the jobsite, it was clear that they had already been working there for a while. All of the equipment, materials, and tools were there. The jobsite trailers were in place. In fact, there was already a crew working with a crane driving in sheeting at one end of the project. The crew assembled to work with my crane joined me at the opposite end of the jobsite away from the existing crew. I noticed that the two of us crane operators were the only operating engineers on the entire jobsite. That meant that the pile drivers had been operating the large air compressors that supplied air to drive the hammers to pound the sheeting into the ground. They had also been operating the forklift that brought the pipe pile and the sheeting to the cranes.

I was so pissed! WTF! I'd been sitting at home, waiting to be called back to work, when I could have been operating equipment on that jobsite from the first day it began. I asked the other crane operator why the hell he hadn't reported that fiasco to the union hall. He told me that he had come off of a long layoff also and needed the job so badly that he didn't want to rock the boat and risk the chance that he would lose his job. "WTF! That's why we belong to a union in the first place!" I reminded him.

I told him that I was going for a walk to find a pay phone at lunchtime. I would report that the pile drivers were operating equipment designated as our work under our contract. We could put a couple of operators to work on our jobsite. Back then, cell phones were not yet in the picture (it makes me feel *old* to have to keep writing about pre-technology times), so I had to walk a few city blocks in order to find a pay phone. I called the hall and spoke with our new minority business agent and told him to come down to our jobsite to see for himself what I was talking about. I told him to wait an hour or so before he showed up so that they didn't think that I was the person who alerted the union. He said that he'd wait until later in the afternoon and then he'd see me on the jobsite.

I felt better on my walk back to the jobsite about doing the right thing. I couldn't believe my eyes when the business agent showed up just as I was walking back onto the jobsite! What the f——k was wrong with him? I thought as one minority in the business to another that he would have my back, but that was so not the case! To make matters worse, shortly after the business agent showed up, our head superintendent arrived also. The two had a conversation, and after a while, the business agent drove off the jobsite and went on his merry way.

I had a feeling of "UH-OH!" in my gut. Soon after, a truck pulled in and parked right next to my vehicle. I recognized the crane operator who stepped out of it. He came over to the crane and set his lunch box on the catwalk next to the cab door. He then took *my* lunch box OFF the catwalk and set it off to the side of the jobsite on top of our toolbox. "WTF is going on?" I asked him.

"I was called to come and operate this crane," he replied.

"*I'm* operating this crane. That's why my lunch box was by the door!" I told him.

"Well, that's news to me," was all he said.

The head superintendent who had been speaking with my business agent was still inside the jobsite trailer. I went in to tell him that a mistake had been made; another crane operator had shown up to operate the crane I was already assigned to. He told me that since I seemed so concerned that a pile driver was running the air compressor that I could go run it instead of the crane. WTF! That business agent had thrown me under the bus, and it had cost me my crane pay! Back then, there was about an eight-dollar per hour difference between operating a crane compared to running an air compressor.

It was a much filthier job for me to do because the entire jobsite was covered by almost twelve-inch-deep mud. I had to wear my giant rubber rain boots and had to lug around the large heavy air hoses that joined the air compressor to the hammer as it was rigged to ride within the leads. I was so pissed off and wished I had never spoken to that business agent. There I was, covered in mud, and had taken a significant loss in pay, and the day wasn't even over yet! At the end of our shift, the head superintendent came over to my car where I was peeling off my muddy rubber boots and preparing to drive home. He had this to say to me, "We only needed you here for this one day so you can go back on the out of work list at the hall (my union hall). We will call you in the future when more work presents itself."

I was truly f——ked. I had already notified unemployment that I was returning to work, therefore I wouldn't receive any money from them until I signed up for it again. It would take two weeks before I would receive a check from them. I wouldn't be paid for my "one" day of work for two weeks either. All that day had done for me was to screw me out of getting any money at all for the next two weeks when I was already broke. Apparently, I was getting a *slap on the wrist* for calling the hall on the company. WTF!

A short period of time passed before I was called back to work. I was told to come into the office, and they would tell me where I was being sent to work. I thought that was odd because I was usually told to be on a jobsite before the crew so that I could perform the maintenance routine on the crane or whatever piece of equipment I'd be responsible for. When I arrived at the office, I was told by the receptionist that the vice president of the company wanted to have a word with me. I wondered what he had to see me about as I made my way through the maze of our office.

He told me that he knew I was the one who had called the business agent down to the art museum jobsite. He said that he was upset with me for my actions. Work had been slow, and they were trying to start the spring season off by keeping their employees with the most seniority working so that they didn't seek employment elsewhere. He reminded me that since HE was the one who signed my paychecks that I should direct my loyalty in HIS direction and that of the company's.

I told him my position was to do whatever necessary to provide for my daughter. I explained that I was proving my loyalty to his company by mainly working for them. I told him that there were

only about three women at that time in our union that could operate a crane. I was the only one who could drive pile, sheeting, and
use a clam bucket, and I was *his* employee. I told him since I was the
only minority female to do so that I was surprised and perplexed to
find myself laid off at all.

The minority business agent did a real number on one of the
few women we had in our union at that time. She usually operated
equipment in our excavating division. Since work was slow and she
had been on the out of work book for a long time, she thought she
would find some work in our building division. A call went into the
hall for an operator to run a small Bobcat skid-steer loader on the
arena project I was working on.

She showed up to work on my jobsite and was nervous because
she'd never worked on a jobsite where there were so many pieces of
equipment and materials in such close proximity to each other; in
other words, it was a cluster f——k. We had already set the outer
shell of the arena's iron structure and were now setting the very large
and expansive beams that would become the roof.

I told her I would assist her in any way that I could and if she
had any questions to feel free to come to me with them. Everything
went well for several days, and it was nice to see another woman
working on the project. Previously, the only other woman I would
see from time to time was the safety lady who worked for our city
government. When she popped in on the project, she only spent
a few minutes speaking with the superintendents of the various
unions employed there. Even though she got on my ass on the few
occasions my earplugs weren't in or if my safety glasses weren't in
position, it was still nice to see another set of boobs walking around,
wearing a hard hat.

One day before lunchtime, I heard a loud *SMACK* followed by
a bunch of yelling. My girlfriend came walking over to me, almost

in tears. She had been the one getting a loud ass-chewing from the foreman. She told me that she was operating the Bobcat loader in reverse when she hit something. As she was climbing out of the machine to see what she had hit, the foreman came flying over to her and began screaming. She had hit the sample cylinders of concrete from each truck that had delivered concrete to the project that morning.

There was always a concrete engineer that took a sample from each truck in order to test it to make sure its standards to hold the weights involved in the project were met. It was always important to know the materials used on any project would last for many years into the future. The concrete engineer had thought that he'd placed the cylinders out of harm's way. The jobsite was extremely crowded, and he should have placed them up off of the ground and not where they could be knocked over by accident. The cylinders were only about a foot tall and so low to the ground that my girlfriend couldn't see them as she backed up.

Although she had made an honest mistake, it was an expensive one. The concrete samples were irreplaceable; now there were no records to be had involving the integrity of the concrete poured on portions of the project. I never found out how they chose to rectify that situation. In a fit of anger, the jobsite superintendent had fired her on the spot. Someone must have notified the hall because soon after the incident occurred, the minority business agent appeared on the jobsite. I went over to him and pleaded for his help in retaining her job for her. I explained to him that because of the position the cylinders had been set on the ground, anyone could have easily knocked them over. They needed to be stored in a safer location and in a more visible manner. I also pointed out to him that it was her first job in the building sector of our trade, that she was usually involved in excavation. I stated that he needed to go to bat for her as she and I were the only female minorities working on the project that employed well over a hundred men.

I may as well had been talking to a brick wall. The man just didn't have the stones to go up against the people with any authority on the project. He was too concerned with having everyone like him and accept him (men, that is). She lost her job and would never be employed by that contractor again. WTF! I remembered how our past business agent came to my defense and kept my job for me if I had wanted it, and I broke a crane! My mistake was far more costly than hers had been.

I became so unenthused with that particular business agent that I refused to work with him further. I just took it upon myself to handle my own problems—*in one way or another.* That's where the saying comes in handy that there are "more than one way to skin a cat" (or deal with an *asshole).* WTF!

The first time I went to work on the site that was to become our present-day casino, I was working on one of the many jobsites with the foreman who was to become my second husband far in the future.

It just goes to show you that you never know what life is going to bring you. We were driving pile to hold up the iron that was to be erected. The excavators were working alongside us. They were digging the holes we were to drive pile in and then fill them back in so that we could track the crane over them. We also had a bulldozer at our service to level the ground the crane had to crawl on. We were in a somewhat confined area due to the fact that we were working alongside a very busy meat packing company.

That was disturbing to me because trucks would pull up in full view of us workers. They unloaded the cattle and promptly marched them into "the doors of death" that awaited them. They must have smelled fear or even death from those cattle that had entered before them because they would halt midway on their path to the doors. There were demons sent from hell, vicious men armed with electric prods, and nasty bad attitudes who would force the cattle forward. They would over use their electric prods and even drive a Bobcat skid-steer loader behind the cattle to force them into the building.

I was operating a Bobcat loader myself on our jobsite. I was the oiler on the crane and used the skid-steer loader to drag the pipe pile over to the crane from the area they were stacked in. I also brought other materials and tools over to the crew as needed.

Those were two of the biggest assholes that burned their demonic ways into my memory for all eternity. One of them carried the electric prod in his hand and constantly zapped the cattle as they continued on their death march past him. He doled out electric shocks to all, and it was clear that it made his day to do so. The other demon from hell was ramming the Bobcat's bucket edge into the hind legs of the cattle as they were attempting to walk; OVER AND OVER he rammed into them. I didn't know how either of those evil young men could live with themselves. I knew that I couldn't watch their disturbing behavior without taking karmic action against them for their evil deeds. If they were like that in their early twenties, who knew what kind of men those two asshole idiots were going to turn into as they aged? Who would feel their sadistic wrath in the future? The men I was working with were totally oblivious to the annihilation of the innocent creatures before them. They didn't give a shit, but *I* sure as f——k did! Unfortunately, I had a cyclone fence between the two assholes and myself. As we were driving pile directly to that fence, one of the assholes on the other side of it thought he'd come over and flirt with me as he waited for his next truckload of cattle to be brought in. "Well, hello, there, what's your name?" he asked me with his SNAKE tongue out of his demon mouth.

"VENGEANCE!" I barked at him. Then I spoke real low so that no one around me could hear what I had to say, except for the asshole. "What I would LOVE to do to you with that electric prod!" Then I added, "I'm operating a Bobcat loader, too, and I'm professionally trained to operate it. I could make it buck like a bronco all over your ass!"

Needless to say, he wasn't expecting those words to be said to him, and off he went to climb back into his demonic machine. Later on in that day, I saw him bash into the hind legs of a cow with the Bobcat to the point of causing it's legs to break and collapse. Then the motherf——ker *pushed* the dying cow with the Bobcat bucket up the ramp and into the butcher's chambers.

There are two points to make at this juncture. Number one is that "vengeance" would be a really cool name for a girl in my opinion, or at least a female superhero. Number two is that I was still fairly new to that line of work when I was on that jobsite and was still learning to focus on the job itself instead of the assholes surrounding me. If that had occurred later on in my career and I was in the crane seat, I would have shut down my crane. I would have climbed down and told whoever I was working with that I could not concentrate while blasphemous behavior was carrying on before my eyes. I would have made someone put a stop to it before work would resume.

Now I could have used my "girl card" and forced out some tears in which the superintendent on the job would be my knight in shining armor and drive to the company next door and report the two devils working for them in back or I could have come unglued over it and demanded action to be taken. I could have threatened to go over there myself. The last remedy would have brought to every man's attention on the job that I was a bitch; but hey, it wasn't the first or last time they'd deal with one, so WTF!

Since the crane operator's ability to focus is of the utmost importance, those two men's "assholeness" was a raging safety violation, and they needed to be terminated for those reasons first and foremost.

Also on the jobsite, working alongside us, was a gung ho overachiever bulldozer operator whose coffee cup resembled the java urn itself; WTF! It was enormous! He flew back and forth on his caffeine-fueled machine so fast that you had to keep an eye out for him at all times to keep from being run over. We were working on one of our city's oldest dumpsites from decades long ago. As the backhoe was digging up layers of history and loading it into awaiting dump trucks, you could see all the beautiful bottles, china, silverware, and other antiques along with the soil that held it hostage underneath the Earth's surface. I would grab up all the artifacts that I could on my lunch break. It was a full-on treasure hunt!

That jobsite was my first introduction to our city's bottle association. This was a club made up of people who shared their love of collecting and trading antique bottles among themselves. A lot of those people even took time off from their jobs to show up at jobsites where antique bottles were being brought to the surface. As the members of our crew and other workers walked to our vehicles at the end of our shift, those collectors would be lined up just off the jobsite property. They would offer cash to anyone who had bottles they were interested in purchasing. Those people would wait for us for hours on end just to have the opportunity to get their collections filled with our newfound treasures. I kept mine and still have some to this day. To take time off from their jobs proved them to be truly dedicated to their hobby.

That crazed bulldozer operator could give a f——k about antique anything! Historical value meant bullshit to him. "Get a life!" he would holler time and time again. "Hey, I'm looking for treasures here too! Take a lunch break like the rest of your crew. If you bump me with that dozer, I'll have your ass, dickhead!" I stated matter-offactly. The f——ker just went back and forth at an even faster pace. I cringed every time I heard the crunching sound that was made from the demolition of all the china layered underneath his tracks as he sped along like some freak at the fun house. Stop? He did not! WTF!

It had been a cloud of darkness on that particular job. I asked my foreman (who is my "now" husband) if he was all right one day because he wasn't his usual self. He seemed withdrawn and sullen. He told me that no, he was *not* all right because he was going through a divorce. I told him that I understood how he felt because I was going through a divorce also.

Just before that time of separation from my husband, I had been dealt a hell of a shock. The coal dumper had broken down at our power plant in a county to the south of us. The *dumper* was a train car that could be clamped in place. When turned on its side, the coal spilled out and fell into the hopper. They could not use the train to deliver the coal until the proper repairs had been made. Our company was hired to have equipment load barges with coal and then have our tugboats push those barges down the lake to the power plant.

The barges would be tied up directly to the dock wall, and then our crane equipped with a clam bucket would grab the coal and cast it onto their coal pile. The power plant bulldozer operator would push the coal up its hill and into their conveyor belt system. The belts would carry the coal into the plant.

I was assigned to be the oiler on the crane and also as the coal diminished from the barge being unloaded, I was to operate the Bobcat loader. With the loader, I would push the remaining coal into a pile in the center of the barge for the clam bucket to pick it up. We had rigging to attach the Bobcat to the crane so that the operator could swing the machine onto and then off of the barge once it was empty of coal. The tugboat then returned the empty barge back to our yard three and switched it for the loaded barge waiting there for transport. We were not able to leave the premises until four or five barges were unloaded each day.

When we began that process of coal delivery, it was taking us sixteen hours a day to complete. The ironworkers were working and welding nonstop, pulling two shifts around the clock to get the coal dumper up and running. The expense of paying for the tugboat's fuel, its crew, the overtime costs for the ironworkers, and us two operators was extremely expensive.

We were getting into a routine that dropped our hours each day down from sixteen to fourteen due to becoming more proficient in the duties involved. Near the end of the project, we were down to twelve hours on a good day where everything went according to plan. It also took me an hour each way to get to the power plant and then back home again. If I didn't take along enough food and water to last me for the entire day, I was screwed. The lack of sleep added up quickly over time as well; it was a tough job to complete, but I was making a lot of overtime pay. We had time to ourselves to work on the crane in between barge deliveries. We just had to be ready to unload them as fast as possible in order to get that tug boat underway for the next delivery. It was dark during the last barge or two, and the boom of the crane had been equipped with a string of powerful lights that were latched to it in order for us to be able to see the black coal on the barge. The darker it became, the more challenging it was for me to see all of the black coal I was pushing to the center of the barge at night.

The bright lights created a glare as the crane swung back in my direction to drop the clam bucket, and then it swung back toward the coal pile. My eyes had to readjust to the blackness of the night and the blackness of the coal on the barge. The crane is in constant motion when the operator is clamming. The operator falls into a rhythm of swinging over to the pile while constantly dropping the open clam bucket as he approaches his target. He spends a brief moment closing the clam bucket around the material before he hoists up the bucket as he begins to swing toward the pile and opens the bucket, releasing the material. The faster the operator can complete that cycle, the more productive the process.

Since the barge and tugboat crews were waiting for us to clear the barge before they could return it to our yard and trade it for a full one to make the return trip, it was a very expensive and time consuming project. We were all being paid time and a half pay after eight hours and double time after ten hours. We made time and a half for eight hours on Saturdays and then double time pay until Monday when a new pay week began.

I felt like I was working on a giant pinball machine when I was clearing the barges with the Bobcat. I was darting in and out, dodging the clam bucket as it kept swinging over my pile I pushed the coal toward. The operator gave me fair warning to MOVE MY ASS as he would be moving fluently and would NOT stop. It was up to me to be out from under his bucket as it slammed down on the barge, free falling from high above me. It was scary, exhilarating, and exciting; it was also a hell of a wakeup call at the end of each very long day. I narrowly escaped that bucket each night. After I had been relocated from that job toward the end of it to go operate a crane elsewhere, a guy was brought in to do my job. The clam bucket crushed the Bobcat when he was pushing the coal to the center of the barge. He proved to be too slow to get out of its way.

My training with the clam bucket with the crane was going very well. Every day, as we waited for the next full barge to arrive to be unloaded, I was practicing for as long as possible. I was getting into the rhythm of swinging, casting, hoisting, and dropping the bucket as I opened and closed it. My crane operator who was training me had to take a few days off to travel for a wedding in his family. Another crane operator who knew how to clam was coming in to replace him while he was gone.

I recognized his replacement operator when he showed up because I had worked several jobs with him before. He had always treated me well and he was willing to share his knowledge with me. I was unaware, however, with his ongoing feud with the operator I'd been working with so far on that project. The first thing he said to me was, "Go into the back of my truck and bring me my crane seat." "WHAT? What operator brings their own crane seat to the jobsite?" I thought, *HE DID.* That damn seat was heavy as I carried it to the best of my ability the far distance from his truck bed down to the dock wall where the crane sat (I felt like dragging that heavy piece of shit—WTF!).

As I approached the crane, I could see the operator using a wrench on the iron pedestal that the crane seat sat on. The next thing I knew, he was throwing the crane seat down onto the ground and asking me to hand him up his own *personal* crane seat. WTF, *really?* "What am I supposed to do with *this* crane seat?" I asked him.

"I don't give a f——k *what* you do with that assholes crane seat!" he said.

"You are aware that this seat on the ground here stays in that crane no matter who is sitting on it? My own ass sits in that seat. I'm learning to use the clam bucket in that seat on this job," I added.

"That's another thing—forget everything that asshole taught you. Now you're going to learn the RIGHT way to clam!" he firmly stated.

Oh, WTF, mother f——ker! I thought to myself.

Sure enough, his way of clamming was completely different than the way I had been instructed over the last several weeks, and now I had become *confused* as to what lever to grab to make what happen! It was like learning to speak Japanese for weeks and then someone saying, "Okay, today we will be speaking Spanish!"

When the regular operator came back from his trip, he was pissed off to find the replacement operator's "throne" installed in the crane instead of its usual seat. "Why, that motherf——ker!" the operator roared at the sight of the "throne."

"Get me the wrench!" he hollered down to me from the catwalk of the crane. I went to the toolbox to retrieve it as I heard him cursing behind me. The "throne" *CRASHED* to the ground as he threw it from the cab. "Now bring me the seat that belongs in this crane," he demanded. Off I went to our jobsite trailer to carry the heavy seat back to the crane.

After the exchange of crane seats, we were finally able to begin unloading the barge that had been tied up to the dock wall as the tugboat and crew raced back up the lake to fetch the next load. Things were back to running smoothly until I saw the replacement operator returning to the crane. Either no one had told him that he didn't need to make the long drive down to the power plant or he made the trip with the sole intent on fetching his "throne."

This wasn't good. As I looked over at the two *"grown up men"* (acting like they were *seven*), I saw a lot of arms waving and hand gestures happening. I heard a lot of swearing being spewed from their red angry faces. The two diva operators were at each other's throats! WTF kind of bad behavior szus that I was witnessing? I saw the regular operator jump down from the catwalk to the ground. He stomped over to the "throne" where he'd thrown it and kicked it! Then the red-faced angry replacement operator rushed over to the crane and kicked dirt onto its track (I'd seen my two hunting dogs behave in that similar fashion when they were having a tiff over a bone; each of them would kick dirt up at each other with their hind legs as if they'd just taken a shit). The replacement operator then stormed off to his truck, dragging his "throne" behind him.

WOW. WTF! Those two operators were BOTH two of the best crane operators in our union, yet each one thought that he was the *only* great crane operator. I learned from their DIVA behavior that we "all" have great attributes to bring to the job as operators—hell, as people in life generally. We all do our jobs (or anything else for that matter) in unique ways that no one else does. We each add our own little nuances. We are like snowflakes in that we are all different.

After the fiasco between the two men who were training me to clam with the crane, I combined some lessons I retained from each operator. I took the best tricks that each had up their sleeves and used those in my own repertoire. I was able to eliminate the unnecessary movements and utilize the quickest methods I'd been taught to operate the clam bucket even smoother, faster, and in a much less exhausting manner than before.

From that point on, whenever it was time for me to hop into the crane seat to train with the clam bucket, I was criticized for my method of clamming. I would simply point out that I was combining what I'd learned not only from him but his replacement operator as well. I explained further that the manner in which I was clamming was the easiest and more beneficial way for *ME* to do it. Then I reminded him that he, as well as the replacement operator, were two of the best crane operators out there, even though the techniques they each used were different from each other. One way of clamming was not better than the other way. Both methods worked, were efficient, and got the job done. I felt as though I were a cheerleader for both of those operators egos! *Go, team! Rah, rah, rah! WTF! Go, team, go!*

Two things bothered me about that marathon hours long job. One was that I had extremely little time to spend with my daughter, husband, or our dogs. My ironworker husband and I had a rule that because we did work such long hours and the fact that he boomed out (worked out of town or outside our state) that if one of us got laid off or finished a job, we would take off two weeks to decompress and spend quality time with our daughter. That usually involved taking her up north to the Wisconsin and Michigan border. There was a small town there that my husband's brother lived in at the time. We enjoyed spending time up there fishing, enjoying Mother Nature, and the nearby lakes.

I had told my husband that since I was working enough hours for the both of us that he should take the entire summer off from ironwork and spend it with our daughter. I felt that it was something special I could do for him since he had to work far from home for quite a while when she was born. There had been a long period of time in our area where there was no one putting any money up for new construction.

The second thing that upset me and kept recurring week after week was that we were scheduled to work every day. If there was one day out of the week we all wanted to work, it was Sunday because you were paid *double* your hourly rate. I got up every Sunday morning at three-thirty and got prepared to go to work when just before leaving my house, I'd receive a phone call, telling me that the lake was too choppy for the tugboats to push the barges down to the power plant. WTF! How did that happen every Sunday morning? It happened because our company didn't want to pay us double time— choppy water my ass!

Instead of just telling us that we had Sundays off so that we could sleep in for a change and make plans to spend time with our families or take care of personal business, they had us get up early and prepare to work Sundays. To me, that was just rude, piss-poor planning, and not giving a shit about anyone other than the man holding the purse strings; that was a major WTF behavior that kept repeating itself.

I dragged myself home after a long Saturday working on that job with the purpose of just climbing into bed and attempting to catch up on some sleep.

Working at our power plant

Receiving the apprentice of the year award for our district

Bridges and more bridges

Where?

EVERYWHERE!

Carole Casamento
Managing Editor

Building the stadium

WHEN I met Suzanne Traczyk she was operating a crane at Miller Park, the future home of the Milwaukee Brewers.

Traczyk has been an Operating Engineer for 12 years and is a member of OEIU Local 139 and she is working for the Edward E. Gillen Co.

The noise is deafening, it's a constant boom, boom, boom as the 81 foot steel pile is driven into the ground.

The crane shakes. Boom, boom, boom in a steady rhythm until 75 to 80 feet of it is underground.

"It's like creating your own little earthquake, it's like a 5.6 on the Richter scale," said Traczyk who lived in California, and is familiar with earthquakes.

Each pile takes 35 to 45 minutes to sink and when one is sunk, she turned the crane to pick up the next, then hoists it upright as the 81 foot pole swings and sways in the air.

All the while Traczyk was talking to the pile drivers on the ground who are members of the Carpenters union. They guide the pole into place. Between them, they talk with their hands in the secret language of the construction trades. The piles are placed into position just as the engineers ordered. It's like a bizarre ballet as it gracefully moves into place.

The crane operator then lowers the hammer a few times to set the pile. At this point if the position is wrong, the operator can lift it out and re-position it. After a few more hits, it's too late.

The first hit sent down a shower of rust pieces and I was glad to have safety goggles and a hard hat on. Once the piles are driven into the bedrock, they are filled with rebar and concrete. Then everything ties into them and the structure begins to take shape.

As an operating engineer, Traczyk said she prefers to drive pile or set iron. To set iron means to lift and place the skeletal structural — the high steel — of a building into place. She says, "It's like putting together a puzzle."

Training's required

The apprenticeship to become an operating engineer takes 6,000 hours. Unlike other trades they use hours instead of years, because the weather is such an unpredictable factor in their work and that affects the training schedules.

Traczyk started out working as a laborer and learned to operate some of the construction equipment. Then after moving to Milwaukee she got hired on as an oiler.

Oilers do the maintenance on the cranes and other heavy equipment that covers their jurisdiction.

Why heavy equipment?

Why did you go into construction in the first place? It's hard, dirty, sweaty and you either work long hours or you're laid off. It's not real steady work.

"It's the most money I can make without a college degree, that's why I do it. I couldn't afford to finish college, and I ended up doing this to pay off some of those bills. Now I have a pension

(Continued on Page 7)

(Continued from Page 4) and good insurance so I just keep going."

Sometimes it's hard, you have to deal with the weather. It's like sitting in a hot oven with the hot air blowing on you. There is no air conditioning on construction sites.

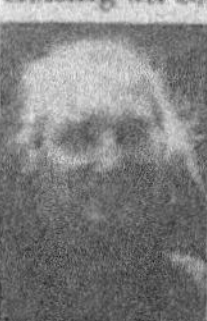

Wages are great, but on Miller Park, a high priority job, they are working 12 to 13 hours a day, six days a
Traczyk week.

"Winters are hell," she said, even though she has never operated the crane in winter but works outside on maintenance. You just keep moving. Operators work year round. "This is the sub structure, the underground structure that holds everything else. In order to build in the spring, the piles must be in the ground beforehand," said Traczyk.

The new Miller Park is projected to be up and ready on opening day 2000.

(See pictures on Page 12)

Happy to fill a tall order

"We're trying to pioneer here."

Suzanne Traczyk was fed up with a co-worker's sexual come-ons.

"I'd like to lick you all over like a Popsicle," was one of his more elegant remarks.

Traczyk, a crane operator, customarily ignores such talk. But the man persisted, never mind that he was married. Once he tried to follow her into a portable toilet.

She complained to her husband, an ironworker. His advice?

"Do what a man would do — and hit him. Wait 'til you get to the parking lot, and let him have it."

So not long after, the 35-year-old woman slugged the offender smack in the face.

"After that," she remembers, "the man understood 'no' better."

Working now at a construction site at the University of Wisconsin-Milwaukee, Traczyk is plain about her ambitions.

"We're trying to pioneer here," she says, warmed by gritty bibs, a jacket and hard hat. As she speaks, a new, four-story business school is sprouting.

Hers is one of the most male-dominated fields in Wisconsin. There were an estimated 1,158 grader, dozer and scraper operators in the state in the 1990 US census. Women were said to number 14, or just over 1%.

Says Traczyk,

"All I want to do is work. Work hard and do it better than anybody

e appreciate that and call
o work for them."

's specialty is operating
ugh with an abundance of
more often she's the No. 2
at makes her the "oiler,"
the yellow giants lubricated
the operator.

re paid $16.02 an hour, less
a crane operator earns.
ne can hoist and move
to 150 tons. Traczyk, too,
e a bulldozer, backhoe,
oader and other equip-

ornia native, she had an un-
nal girlhood, inspired by her
her-father, who took her
ping in the mountains,
hing and hunting wild boar.
a crane in my sandbox, be-
not," she says.

y job: a concrete plant la-
hammering cement-choked
nd tunnels. The plant need-
; she needed money. "My
stretch in hell," she says
back-breaking labor.
k met her husband, from
e, while in California. She
re, married him and had a
now 8. Mother and daugh-
nsited his construction job

ces her curiosity about his
er childhood. Because her
ked for a military contrac-
of his film and footage was
"I didn't see what he did,"
ays.

nere for Marshall Field's, in
ooms, left small rewards.
y the day care and have $20
says. "My husband told me,
going to work, you better get
— or stay home with the

k phoned unions and began
ticeship with the operating
Six years later, the Milwau-
in has her sights on operat-
er crane, the T-shaped equip-
d to erect high-rises. Tower
rators can earn as much as
hour. "It's like an office in

I was extremely exhausted after working such long hours for weeks. My plans were blown to smithereens soon after I pulled into my driveway. As I approached my house, I noticed my ironworker husband standing next to the driveway as if he was waiting for my arrival. That job occurred long before there were cell phones or pagers. I opened my car door and was reaching beside me to grab my lunch box when he said in a frantic voice, "I have to tell you something! I have to tell you *now!*"

He went on to explain to me that he'd been dropping our daughter off at her gramma's house (his mother) each day while he was having an affair with a woman he had been dating during the last period of time we were separated. The reason he was coming clean to me about the affair was because she had become pregnant with his kid! WTF! The curtain of dark depression SLAMMED down on me once again. WHAT THE HELL HAD I BEEN WORKING ALL THOSE HOURS FOR?

He told me that it happened because I was gone "too much" of the time and he felt *lonely*. He also said that the days he wasn't seeing *(screwing)* his girlfriend, he was seated at his union's day hall, playing poker with his union brothers. Of course, that meant that most of the money that I was busting my ass to make was going to pay OTHER ironworkers bills instead of our own due to his gambling. Screw going to bed—I wanted to climb under a rock.

I couldn't believe it. That relationship of ours had always seemed to be "one step forward, then two steps backward." That situation, however, was a GIGANTIC leap backward! I was done in by the news and retreated into our bedroom, threw his belongings out on the couch where he would begin sleeping. I told my daughter that she was welcome to enter MY room whenever she wanted, but he, however, was not.

Other than getting up and going to work, I was in bed. I was so depressed that I could barely drag myself out of bed to go to work or do anything else, for that matter. After that rude awakening and upon completion of that job, I declined all offers to work overtime if I could for a very long time.

As I'm writing these tales of work woes, it is winter and unusually cold. The main temperature is two degrees below zero, and with the windchill, which is what it actually feels like, it is between twenty and thirty degrees below zero. These frigid temperatures have called to mind some extremely difficult days I had due to working in frozen temperatures.

Now I've already written about how challenging it was to find urinary relief in areas where there just wasn't any bathroom facilities. That was especially true in our pipe yard where we stored all our various sizes of pipe pile and our collection of pipe sections we used as casing when drilling caissons. Those pipe came in many sizes from small to extremely large in circumference. I had those large pipe to duck in and out of in a hurry to pee. I was *quick* so as to not "flash" the freeway traffic that drove on the overpass above a portion of our yard. I'd discreetly peed behind the giant tires of our frontend loaders if I was operating one at the time. I'd also crouched below the body of my crane although a headache would ensue if I happened to bump my head while arising from my crouched position. I'd also been known to squat down in the tall grass and then jump up as quickly as possible, "HELLO!" like a Jack-in-the-Box, hoping that no one noticed that I'd disappeared for a moment or two.

In the frozen winter months, however, it was not advisable to disrobe to near nakedness due to the possibility of obtaining frostbite in the nether regions. Even if I was lucky to find a port-a-potty, such as the rare appearance of one in our Gran Trunk yard where all our crane booms, barges, and boulders were stored, it was like peeing in a refrigerator or freezer. It was not advisable and definitely NOT FUN.

I was moving and stacking pipe pile in our yard four. That was the yard that was located across from the frontage road that existed as an access point to the Port of Milwaukee and the sewage treatment plant on Jones Island. That yard was directly across from Lake Michigan, and a portion was covered by the overpass above it. I was operating a neanderthal forklift of sorts called a Pettibone. That piece of equipment was so old that I couldn't recall the year in which it was manufactured. The Pettibone could lift like a beast! It was the King Kong of forklifts.

I'd been amazed by the weights of pipe or sheeting that I'd carried with it. It had giant hydraulic clamps on its forks that allowed me to tip my load and control how many pipe pile I wanted to release at a time if indeed those were the materials I was carrying. I had to keep my eye on its tires whenever I lifted massive weights with it because the tires would blow out before an item was too heavy for it to lift. I had my ass chewed out whenever I did end up with a flat tire, usually due to picking up a nail, railroad spike, or a piece of wire puncturing it. The tires at that time were seven hundred dollars apiece when I began my career and cost eleven hundred a piece when I retired. Lord only knows how expensive they are these days. I was constantly picking up sharp objects off of the grounds of all of our yards and jobsites. I even had a large magnet attached to a wand so that I could use it to sweep the ground free of bits of iron debris.

Whenever I climbed up into the Pettibone, I felt like Fred Flintstone on his dinosaur at the rock quarry where he worked in the *Flintstones* cartoon. I also felt like Fred in his car at the drive in restaurant when the waitress brings out his gargantuan rack of ribs and sets it on top of his tray mounted to his car. Then his entire car flips over due to the weight of the ribs—ha-ha! I've picked up too heavy or too large of a piece of pipe with the Pettibone and tipped forward with the rear tires up off of the ground because the load was too heavy for it. Hey, an operator has got to know exactly what their machine they're operating is capable or *not* capable of doing.

It was freezing ass cold outside one morning, and I had the heater on inside the Pettibone as I moved pipe across the yards length to set it in its proper area. The Pettibone may have been old, but at least it had a working heater inside. The cab was getting a little smoky and stinky. I looked toward the heater and saw small flames flickering on a greasy rag left there by a previous operator. I had to pee really bad, and now a fire was starting directly to the right of me. I grabbed the fire extinguisher that was located behind my seat only to see that it was empty, and no one had bothered to replace it! F—k! Now I needed to pee, and I needed to get the fire put out. I hightailed it to our boat shop that was located a few blocks away from the yard I was working in.

Was it absurd that the Pettibone's cab had a fire in it? No. Was it absurd that the fire extinguisher in the cab was empty when I needed to use it to put the fire out? No, nothing was surprising to me about any of that. Was it absurd that I had to drive to the boat shop to use the bathroom? YES! I just pulled into the driveway of the boat shop with gray smoke billowing out of the door's window as I leapt down to the ground from the cab.

I ran inside and yelled at the men working there to go put out the fire inside the cab of the Pettibone and that I had to pee! The guys looked at me with panic-stricken expressions on their faces as I heard a few of them say, "What the f——k! That crazy bitch!" as they ran outside to the Pettibone.

Ladies, when wearing any sort of coveralls or overalls and all the other layers the weather requires you to wear, you must think ahead of time when it comes to peeing. Therefore, as I hoofed it to the bathroom in triple time, I was leaving a trail of clothing on the floor behind me on my path to the bathroom. It was like a critical striptease—gloves, scarf, hat, outer jacket, what the hell, threw off the hard hat, shed the dark safety glasses so I could see where the hell I was going, unhooked my overall straps and unbuttoned their sides, began to unbuckle my belt, and hopefully make it in time to drop my drawers at the toilet! It was always such an ordeal compared to men who just unzipped their pants and whipped their dick out! I was jealous that it was so much easier and far less time-consuming. Usually, if I was lucky enough to have any bathroom at all, it was an extremely smelly port-a-potty and I felt like I was getting nearly naked in a refrigerator or a stand-up freezer. I should have just given in and worn those adult diapers, but my precious princess ego wouldn't allow it (damn it!).

I heard a story about a previous female employee who ended up peeing in her coveralls because she couldn't undress fast enough to use the port-a-potty on a jobsite one winter. It was a big joke to the guys, and they brought it to my attention throughout all the winters I worked with them. That occurred way before I became an operator, and they were *still* bringing it up. I was NOT going to be a representative in their joke repertoire as far as peeing in my pants went! "Why did you drive that thing with a fire lit next to you?" the boat shop's foreman asked me.

"If I bailed out and ran to the boat shop to get you guys, by the time we got back to the Bone, the cab would have been burnt to shit! WTF! I tried to put out the fire, but the extinguisher was empty. No one told you that it needed to be replaced?"

"No, but I'll find out who was operating it last and chew them a new asshole!" he said in an angry voice. He knew better than to ask me why I didn't just pee behind one of our giant pipes if I had to go so badly because it was f——king freezing outside! He not only found the culprit who left the empty fire extinguisher in the cab and indeed chewed him a new asshole, but he must have figured that since I risked catching on fire myself so that I could use the bathroom in his building that he better order a port-a-potty for the yard I spent a lot of time working in. Hell yeah! It was cold as hell to drop my drawers in a port-a-potty during wintertimes, but at least it cut the wind, and it was far better than exposing my naked ass in the frigid winter air.

Since I'm writing about working in the frigid Wisconsin winters, I'll continue with a few tales of other *freezing* jobs as well. One winter in particular, there were a few days that we worked in below zero temperatures. The rule back then was if the actual reading on the thermometer was five below zero that we could stay home and not have to drive in for our two hour show up pay. That temperature reading would not reveal the "windchill"; that would register what the air outside "felt" like. If we did drive into work and the temperature rose above zero, we were most likely expected to work. In those cases, which were many, we were not happy campers at work on those days.

The big pain in the ass when working in freezing temperatures was trying to get your equipment started and to keep running. The crane I operated regularly in our main yard had big issues with the cold winter temperatures. I had to jump its batteries nearly every day throughout the winter months. First, I had to thaw the frozen locks on all its crane doors just to get inside it. I kept a small torch hidden beneath the crane just for that purpose. Then I'd have to get the forklift started and warmed up in order to place a battery charger on top of a piece of plywood that rode on the forks. I would drive with it to the crane and scope the forks out close to the crane's side door. I'd climb up on the crane and connect the cables from the charger to the batteries in the crane and hope for the best.

That process could take anywhere from thirty minutes or longer, depending on if the batteries would take a charge. It became such a pain in the ass that I finally ordered a battery charger specifically for that crane and mounted it behind the truck portion of the crane. I tied it down with bungee cords after covering it up with a tarp. That eliminated all the time it took me to get the forklift up and running, find the plywood, and then retrieve the battery charger, returning it to the mechanic's shop when I was finished using it.

One day, we had shown up at the yard office, expecting to be sent home after two hours. It was simply too damn cold to work. I always felt that if it was too cold for machines to run in the air outside, then it was too cold for the human body as well! Everyone got to go back home and return to the warmth of their houses, except for me. WTF! I had to stick around until a semitrailer making its way across state lines was unloaded. As the yard's crane operator, it was my job to do so. I was to get him on his way as soon as possible, and then I could return to my home also.

The big problem for me was that the crane had turned into a giant block of ice overnight, and I couldn't for the life of me get the frozen engine to turn over. When I would jump the battery of the crane, car, or any machine or vehicle and I could hear it start to drag, it was time to stop cranking the ignition and let the batteries charge longer (there were two batteries connected to each other in the cranes that I usually operated). I wanted to hear the cranking sound revving up and then the engine itself to turn over and run.

I kept attempting to turn over the engine every half an hour. Within that time, the battery would charge enough to sound as if the engine would turn over, and then it would peter out. I was told that the semitruck driver had called to let us know that his estimated time of arrival was around two o'clock that afternoon. I worked in our yard shop organizing tools and materials, all the while wishing that I was home instead, like everyone else.

I was finally successful in getting the engine to turn over at about one o'clock. That gave me an entire hour to warm up the engine and dry out my brake drums. To dry out the drums in any wet weather situation, I had to connect my hoist lines to anything of substantial weight. I would hoist up the load and ride the brakes as I lowered it. That removed any frost and icy areas along the brake bands of the cable drums. It also warms up the brake bands so that they expand from their cold, contracted position, and will grip upon applying the brakes. If the drying out and warming up of the brakes is not performed, the load could cause the drum to slip through the brakes. The load would then free fall until the brakes are able to catch it or it smashes onto the destination you're attempting to land it on or the ground. I've had that happen to me, and it's very scary because it could cause damage to the surface I was intending on landing my load on, and worse yet, it could cause bodily harm or even death to the workers handling the load.

On one such occasion during an extremely wet day with bouts of torrential rain passing through at times, everyone had gone home. The foreman insisted I stay and load an extremely heavy air hammer that his crew needed in order to work the next day. His job was across our state's southern border, and his crew's air hammer they were driving pile with had broken down. If the hammer was not replaced, they would lose two days of work rather than one due to the weather. I warned him to stand clear of the hammer in case it slipped.

Sure enough, after drying and warming up my hoist drum and brake to the best of my ability in those conditions, the hammer slipped. I was able to catch it just as it hit the trailers deck, but it still broke a few of the boards. It was expensive and a loss of time to deck the trailer. The head superintendent (who had never operated anything other than driving his car) didn't believe in "wet" brakes until that incident. I had hoped that he learned a lesson that operators weren't talking through their asses when bringing those safety hazards to his attention. But as we all knew, money spoke louder than words. WTF!

The semi finally showed up in our yard carrying a very large piece of equipment. He thanked me for sticking around to unload him as he had to make other stops on his way home. He apologized for taking so long to show up, but the road conditions were horrendous with all the ice and snow he had been driving through.

I rigged up the piece of equipment and told him that I'd hoist it up high enough to the point at which he could drive out from under it and he could be on his way. I was going to remain connected to the piece as I set it on dunnage I'd laid out on the ground. I wasn't sure if I was loading it on to one of our semitrailers the next morning or not yet. I made sure the dunnage was placed squarely underneath the load so that it wouldn't freeze to the ground and could stay reasonably clean to set it upon another trailer. When I finally was able to go home, it was only one hour earlier than my usual quitting time when I was working in our main yard.

It was frustrating to not be able to use the bad weather day to take care of personal business, run errands, or catch up on chores at home, but in the same token, I made money on days like that when no one else did. It was all how I chose to perceive those events.

On another extremely cold winter day, I was elected to stay in the yard office and wait for my assignment while everyone else was sent home to the warmth of their domestic interiors. I was told that to our south in another county far from our own, we had a crane awaiting transport to another jobsite. They had finished using it at that location, and now it was blocking the surveyors on the project where it was parked. I was to drive down south to where the crane was parked and move it to the other end of the jobsite.

I figured that it would be easy money for me. I would drive down there, check it's fluid levels, start up the crane, and get it running. I could stay warm in my car while I gave the crane's engine time to run for a bit before moving it. As soon as I parked it in its new location, I could drive home and get paid for the entire day; simple, right? WRONG!

When I arrived on the jobsite the crane had a sheen of ice crystals encapsulating its entire exterior. I had no idea how long that crane had been sitting there. That jobsite was located way out in the boondocks. It was on the edge of a forest of trees that in no way allowed the sun to penetrate the frozen iron crane. My first chore was thawing the frozen locks that secured its doors. I had thought ahead and brought along my trusty torch and lighter in case I needed it, which I surely did. I had to keep running back to my car with the heater blasting away the numbness in my hands and fingers in between each lock I was attempting to thaw. It was below zero in the sunlight; I had no idea how cold it was in the crane's shaded location. Once I finally got all of the doors unlocked and open so that I could get a little light inside the back area of the crane, I was ready to give her a go. I had plenty of vents to allow the fumes of the starting fluid I was about to use to escape out the back door. I didn't have any success and figured that it would take a while, but with each try, the engine would warm up a bit.

Back and forth I went from the frozen crane into my running car with the heater blasting. WTF! That was one of the coldest days I'd ever had to work in! It was rare for my feet and hands to go numb from the cold with all of the heavy duty cold weather gear I had on. I had a car pull up onto the jobsite with two men dressed similar to myself. They were looking at me with suspicious expressions. I announced to them that I was the crane operator sent out to relocate it so that it was out of everyone's way but that I was having a hard time getting it to start in the present conditions.

The men thanked me for doing so and told me that they were there to pick up some tools so that they could work elsewhere that day indoors. We said our goodbyes, and by that time, I was leery of losing whatever juice was in those batteries completely. I checked the fluid levels in the batteries cells and found them to be low. I called the mechanic's shop and apologized for making one of them drive to my location in the frigid temperatures, but I needed fluid brought out for the batteries and, more importantly, a battery charger. That baby was just not going to turn over on its own.

Once he drove out and I assisted him, I had him hang out while I moved the crane in case it conked out on me. So what had started out as an easy-sounding job that had promises of me having a short work day had turned into anything but. I can't mention how many days that happened to me where I'd think I'd get to head home for the day or be able to run some necessary errands, only to be let down and made to work anyway—regardless of what the weather brought to the day. WTF!

One winter, we had showed up in our yard, fully expecting to be allowed to return home after our two-hour show-up time because there was a *BLIZZARD* raging outside. We could barely see a few feet in front of us because the snow was coming down so fast. I had to follow behind a car's faint taillights in order to drive very slowly into work. Once again, most everyone was sent home, except for myself and two men to help me load a semitrailer with drill tools. Those in charge of a job south of our state border were hoping the roadways would be cleared by the next morning so the semi load of drill tools could be delivered there.

Reluctantly, we went to the "back forty" of our yard to clear away anything that would be in the way of the crane as I drove it back there. Also, the men could shovel the accumulated snow off the deck of the trailer while I got the crane running, warmed up, and moved. I had told the yard foreman that I was willing to try to load the trailer in the heavy snowfall, but if it became too dangerous, I was going to call it a day, and we would be going home. I told him that it was very slippery and we could always come in a little early the next morning to load the trailer for transport.

It took me a while to get all the snow swept off my crane and for me to move it into the area we needed it set up in. All that time, the blizzard raged on, and the wind had begun to pick up. It was as if we were trying to work in a giant snow globe with the snow swirling everywhere around us. My old American friction all-terrain crane had no heater or defroster of any kind; also, the windshield wipers didn't work. I had only the engine behind me to warm me up, and I used my "Swedish windshield wiper," which was my handheld squeegee, just like the ones at the gas station.

I had to keep my door open and lean my head out of it to see what was going on, and I found myself spending more of my time out of the seat, removing snow from my windshield, than I was sitting in it to operate the crane—it was ridiculous. There were too many factors that could go wrong: the man on the trailer could slip off of it, someone's fingers could be pinched within the rigging, the load could bump into one of the men. I simply couldn't see well enough to call it a safe working environment. I was also worried that my load could slip at any time due to the snow covering my cable drums causing wet brakes bands.

I finally said, "F——k it, we tried and gave it our best shot in these horrendous conditions. We're going to go home like everyone else did. These conditions are too dangerous, and I don't want anything to happen to you guys." I had the guys warm up in the mechanic's shop while I went in to talk to our yard foreman about shutting it down for the day.

As I approached his office, I noticed a truck running outside his door with no driver inside. It turned out that the truck belonged to a young operator who had recently been employed by our company. He was the son of one of our well-known and seasoned crane operators who had worked on and off for our company in past years. He was in his early twenties, rambunctious, gung ho, and a hell of a nice guy. He had stopped in the office to pick up some items his crew needed on their jobsite the next morning.

When he heard me say that it was snowing too hard for me to see the men clearly and in my opinion to operate the crane safely, he chimed in, saying that he'd be willing to finish loading the trailer with the crane if I wanted to leave. I explained to him that there was no heater, defroster, or windshield wiper other than my squeegee. I told the yard foreman that he could run the crane only if the men who were warming up in the mechanics shop wanted to work in the terrible weather longer than they already had.

The three men worked into the afternoon and finished loading the trailer without incident after I went home. Sometimes you need to stick to your guns. It's the crane operator's call as far as safety measures go, and that includes weather conditions. Does that make you more money and popular? NO. Does that keep people safe because you put people's welfare before money? YES! WTF! You can't please everyone all of the time, so you need to do what you think is best and f——k the rest!

Here's yet another jobsite that we worked in freezing ass weather. Condominiums were going to be erected along the river just a short distance from where the river feeds into our Lake Michigan. Those condos would be erected close to our city's festival grounds. Our company was hired to drive in all the pile that would be their base. Each pile would take a while to pound deep into bedrock. I was the crane operator on the job and had to show up before the crew to get the equipment checked out and running to warm up.

The pits had been excavated to where we were to drive pile. It was very tricky for me to straddle those holes. I had to be careful that my extremely heavy crane didn't tip over into one of them or cause the sides of the holes to collapse due to the weight of the crane. It was winter, and we froze our asses off each day because the wind would whip across the frozen river that wrapped around two sides of our jobsite. It not only blew frigid air our way but also the disgusting stench of the sewage treatment plant which was located directly across the river from us.

It shocked me when I found out that most of the expensive condominiums that were to be built upon the pile we would drive were already sold. The people who had purchased them only had the architect's drawings to view their future homes from. Every morning, when I showed up to the jobsite, I noticed a small station wagon with an older man sitting inside it. He would usually be parked near another pickup or two. I could see him reading his newspaper, and there were fishing rods and tackle visible in all of the vehicles.

The men were waiting for the darkness to turn into dawn so that they could start fishing during the morning hours; the salmon were running. By coffee break, a lot of men were leaving their fishing posts along the river for the day to go home. The older man in the station wagon would stop by me if I happened to be near the road and ask me if I wanted his catch that day. I would say, "Sure, I'll take them," and then I would thank him before returning to work. It was so cold that the fish would be frozen solid by the time I was finished working for the day. Our river was so polluted that the only safe way to eat the salmon that were caught was to smoke them first.

I had a good idea to keep the raccoons out of my garbage can at home during the night. I would toss the frozen fish down the gully at the end of the alley where I lived. I'd place the fish the man gave me in plastic bags and put them in my trunk while I drove pile for the day. By the time I tossed them for the raccoons, they were frozen fish popsicles!

I would notice the older gentleman traveling back and forth next to our jobsite throughout each day, even on the coldest days with the wind whipping across the frozen water, causing the wind-chill temperatures to plunge below zero. One day, I asked him why he spent so much time in his car instead of spending the frigid days inside his warm house. I've never forgotten the reasons he explained to me.

He had worked at his job for decades until he reached his retirement date. All the while he worked, he supported his stay-at-home wife who did her part by raising their children and keeping up their home. After their children grew into adults and moved out of their home, the wife had the house all to herself all day while he worked. When he retired, she told him that he better find something to do with himself all day because he wasn't going to hang out there at home! WTF! The poor guy worked hard for all those years, and he still couldn't relax and enjoy the comfort of his own home. His hard work paid for the house in the first place!

I couldn't believe it. I told him he should go home and tell his bossy wife that he'd worked every day, all day, and now that he was retired, it was HER turn to go out and earn a paycheck! What I actually felt like saying to the older man was this: "Grow a pair! Put your big boy pants on and go be the MAN of the house for a change." I could already tell just who wore the pants in his family, but I felt that he needed a cheerleader in his court anyway.

I would rather be in a knockdown, drag out fight with my husband before I'd live in my car all day! WHOOPS! I forgot, I *did* have to live in my car for a bit (and in jobsite trailers) when I'd lost one of our knockdown, drag out fights with my husband, and IT WASN'T FUN. Speaking of the ironworker husband, I'd imagine putting pieces of his body down inside each long pipe pile I'd driven into the ground. I could have gotten away with it scot free because the rebar would be inserted into the concrete poured into each pile. It would have been impossible to pull those pile out of bedrock I'd pounded them into. The rebar would have to be torched out of it, and all the concrete inside would need a jackhammer to clear it. It would be both costly and time-consuming to resume any contents found within each pile. *What the hell,* I would think, *Out of sight, out of mind!* Ha-ha!

It was so cold one day that our equipment couldn't handle it. We lost the batteries in our welders, and I had a hell of a time getting the crane's engine to turn over. The foreman called the day too cold to continue, and we were closing up the jobsite to go home. I walked over to the area we stashed our pipe pile that were to be driven as the job progressed. We had a pile driver who was trimming off the collapsed bottoms of pipe in order for us to use them. That would happen to the pipe pile every so often as I attempted to punch them into the bedrock.

There he was, toughing it out in the freezing cold air, wearing his "F——k you, you f——king f——k" T-shirt that was sleeveless. He came to work without a jacket or coveralls and was sitting on frozen pipe pile as he used his torch to trim the pipe. I told him that we were all leaving and that he could put his torch away for the day. He told me that he wanted to stay and keep working. WTF! Here the macho *(maniac)* stubborn asshole was, sitting on frozen iron, in freezing air without a jacket, just begging to get frostbite! Machismo or just plain *stupid?* I think we all know the answer to that question! I'm going to take you back now to the second phase of the casino as it grew to become a bigger structure. I was told that I'd be driving in a lot of extra pile that time around. The pile I'd be driving in was not only going to hold up the large addition being spliced into the already established building but also for a future parking structure as well. They had big plans for the future of that facility.

As they grew financially, they would invest in enlarging their money making property.

I operated a crane that was so close in proximity to another crane that we were each assigned a signal man to let us know when it was safe to swing our crane. We would each alternately swing around to grab on to our next pipe pile we needed to drive. Our two cranes were driving pile for twelve hours five days a week, and we drove pile for ten hours on Saturdays. By the end of each shift, I could hardly climb down from the crane. My knees were shot from holding the leads brake with my left foot and holding the heavy hammer with the brake under my right foot. Plus, as the hammer pounds, I had to pump the brake to keep the cable from spooling off of the drum uncontrollably as the hammer descended with each blow to the pipe. I felt like I was at the gym, doing leg lifts on a weight machine all day. It was a lot of work and very hard on my body, but WTF! The paychecks were enormous.

I had worked with the foreman on several jobs. He had worked for the company longer than most of the other foremen. Since he was getting "long in the tooth," he'd push people to their limits that were working under his direction. I believed he did that to show the company that he was more valuable of an employee than the young bucks that were beginning their careers as his was coming to its end. His knowledge was valuable, but his ways of thinking were old school. Our lunchtimes were always a little shorter than everyone else's, and he always made us stay later than the second pile driving crew so that he could pound in one or two more pile than they had gotten in each day. He was a nice guy, but he was a pain in the ass due to those practices that he alone pursued.

There were no such things as "rain out days" when you worked with him either. He would put on a raincoat and head out to work in a downpour if that's what Mother Nature was dishing out. I'd caution him about the wet brakes on the crane and the dangers of working with them, but it wasn't anything he did not already know. He was an ass-kisser to the authorities in the office.

One particular day, I saw lightning in the distance, and we just happened to be working on the side of the jobsite where I'd been cautiously working alongside the live high wires that provided juice to the local businesses. I had learned in my training that if you can see lightning as I had that it could use my crane's boom as a lightning rod. I was also taught that if you could hear thunder, the lightning was too close for comfort.

"F——k it," I said. "I won't take a chance on anyone getting struck by lightning because they're working next to this crane. Hell! *I* don't want to get electrocuted sitting in this giant metal machine reaching high into the sky!" WTF! If he wasn't going to call it, I was. It was always the operator's decision when it came down to a safety factor. I told him we'd wait in the trailer until the electrical portion of the storm passed, and then we'd go back to work in the rain and finish the day. I made sure to remind him that it was a rare occasion that I would push my luck and those of the crew as well by working in the rain at all. I'd seen too many injuries to men because they had slipped, fallen, or the crane's brakes had slipped, causing a load to drop abruptly. I was willing to do it on that day because the foreman had expressed to us that we were on a tight time schedule to get the pile driven into the ground on that project.

We went back out after the storm had passed and finished the day. I had made sure that I spoke to him about going into the trailer to wait out the storm as professionally as possible so that I didn't sound like I was being a bitch. I did not agree with him whatsoever about working outside in wet weather. Standing my ground about those safety issues that day must have earned me a bit of respect with him because he asked for me on many jobs after that to join his crew as his crane operator.

Beautiful old bottles and antique glassware were glinting in the sun when it shone. They beckoned, *"Come and get me,* and I'd go out on my coffee and lunch breaks with a plastic bag and haul my treasures to the trunk of my car before resuming my *ping-ping-ping-ing* of driving pile. The men only picked up a bottle or two every so often. One guy showed me an old perfume bottle he'd found and asked me if I thought his wife would like it if he took it home for her. To promote good behavior, I said to him, "Of course she would! How thoughtful of you." Then, to be cheeky, I added, "Who knows? After giving her that beautiful antique bottle, you might get lucky tonight! HA-HA!" to which he grinned as his face turned red.

We had a female blow counter who grew bored rather quickly when counting each blow my hammer made hitting the pile. She kept wandering off to search for bottles while I was swinging around to draw up my next pile I'd be driving and then swung back into position with it. We would be waiting for her to return from her treasure hunting in order for me to open the air valve to the hammer. That waiting around was enraging my foreman, so he had to count the blows himself. As enthusiastic about bottles as I was, I already knew to only look for them on my own time. It was sad for me to see so many of them demolished, crushed, and lost down the holes that were excavated for me to drive the pile in.

One day, the foreman complained to me about the two or three minutes it took for me to walk over to the port-a-potty and walk back to the crane. He had already had the female blow counter removed from the jobsite for making us wait for her presence. It was apparent that his patience was wearing thin due to the long hours we were working on that jobsite. I always move with purpose and I don't lollygag as I'm walking. I wanted those pile into the ground more than anyone else there because it was *my* painful knees and hips holding those brakes and pumping constantly on the hammer brake. It was *my* aching shoulders and back thrusting the big plow handle levers forward and then holding them back to hoist those heavy loads. It was *my* neck forced all the way back with *my* face looking up at the sun to keep *my* eyes on the hammer. It was *my* overworked brain keeping track of where each of my three cables were at all times and the three separate functions I was using them to perform. I also ran the air to the hammer as well. Pile driving was difficult because I was constantly multitasking, and it was extremely dangerous work.

One day, after lunch, as I was exiting our jobsite trailer, I thought to myself, "What is wrong with this picture?" Something was off and out of place. WTF! "Oh, HELL NO!" I hollered, "Who the hell put the port-a-potty right next to my crane?" The men behind me were in agreement as I heard many "WTFs" uttered behind me. "I need a word with our foreman. I'll be with you men shortly. Could one of you please hop into the forklift and return that port-a-potty back to where it was? Either that or just chill out and I'll move it myself after my conversation, thanks."

I already knew that the only person who would have had it moved was our gung ho foreman. He had it moved directly beside my crane so that I would have no need to walk far to use it. I calmed myself down, realizing that it was his personality to push me hard to always drive "one more pile" in whenever possible. It wasn't about me personally because we were moving along really well and we were ahead of schedule. I knew, however, that he never would have tried his newfound technique of narrowing down the crane operator's urination time on any male operator. He thought that as a female, I'd fold under his constant pressure, but *no.* If I cowered or bowed down at any time in my personal or professional life, maybe my life would have been easier, but I just wasn't designed that way; it's not in my DNA.

In a calm and "charming" voice, I said, "Now, honey, you know that's the only time I get to stretch my legs, and I really need to keep the blood circulation going. I promise you that I'm moving as swiftly as possible." Then I added a little joke so that he knew I was understanding of the meaning behind his actions but that I needed him to understand mine as well. Then, to make sure he didn't try that sneaky shit again, I said, "Oh crap, I could have driven five or six pile by now if all of this didn't happen."

We exited the trailer, smiling as I'd moved our conversation on to something else entirely. For an old guy, a young lady's smile and gentle demeanor can make his day better instead of saying, "Look, motherf———ker! Blah, blah, blah" in front of everyone and thus ruining the rest of the day for everybody. It's when a negative eruption occurs that causes a day to stand out in your memory.

Some jobs would seem to drag on for an eternity, and that particular job was one of them. When you work long hours every day for six days out of the week with only one day off to allow your body to rest, you can become quite exhausted as the weeks pass on. My knees, hips, shoulders, and neck would finally get more of a break when our job finally wound down to working every *other* Saturday. Our crew was to alternate Saturdays with our second pile driving crew, as well as reducing our ten hour Saturdays down to eight hours. Our weekdays would be lowered down to ten hours instead of twelve.

At that point in time, I was hobbling and limping along to the parking area at the end of my shifts. My knees and hips were like burning hot coals; I hurt. The good news was that our hours were reduced because our crew had become a well-oiled machine due to us working so long together. Everyone knew what had to be done each day. We all knew our specific jobs that each of us needed to perform, and we were well ahead of the production schedule. We were also just too worn-out to argue and disagree. We helped each other get through the day and did what was necessary to make each other's workload easier. Every once in a while, I would work with a crew like that one where everyone got along and worked well together. It was a rare occasion, but it did happen.

Usually, when I was on a pile driving job, where there were two cranes and two crews, a third crane and operator were brought on-site. That would be our "service crane." I'd been a service crane operator myself on many jobs. The service crane is there to unload all the pipe pile that is trucked in to the jobsite. It's there to load up or unload all of the necessary equipment needed. It switches out broken equipment for repairs with replacement equipment, such as welders or air compressors. It also moves equipment, tools, and pipe pile alongside the crane, utilizing those items as it progresses across the jobsite.

The service crane is kept very busy, providing service to both cranes driving in pile. Our service operator had been a seasoned operator within our union. He was a new member of our company and he was *LAZY.* I can't abide laziness to this day in my life, and I believe it's because I've had to work for too many assholes like that one.

First off, he was a diva. He kept stepping out of the crane seat and cab, barking orders at everyone around him. An operator makes the machine she (or he) is running do what the *foreman* is signaling her (or him) to do. The foreman makes the decision what, where, and when he (or she?) wants something done; it's that simple. That's what we're trained at our school to do. We are proficient in the knowledge of what our machine is capable of, and we are professionals at making the machine do whatever is asked of it; nothing more. An operator's concerned with the safety factor, not the course of how the job's progression is going to go, unless you were that clown—I mean, *guy.*

That diva eventually became the crane operator driving pile with the second crew. On the Saturdays that his crew worked and ours was off, he developed a really nasty habit of not showing up for work. It almost never failed that I'd be catching up on some wellneeded sleep when my phone would ring. It would either be his foreman or the superintendent in charge of that jobsite calling me. My presence would be requested to drive pile during his absence. I would be so irritated by his selfish actions. He had made it well known to everyone on the jobsite that he was going through a divorce. He felt like shit every morning due to drowning his miseries in alcohol at the tavern each night as soon as his shift was over. WTF! He would apologize to me on the Mondays after I had to work his Saturday shifts for him. He just kept pulling the same shit on the Saturdays he was scheduled to work; on and on it went.

To make the scenario worse was the fact that the old friction crane he was driving pile with was the old Linkbelt that had a quick release button on each brake pedal. If you were to accidentally touch that button, your load dropped instantly. I'd had it happen to me and had seen it happen to other operators also. I avoided operating that crane whenever possible because it was too dangerous. To make matters worse, there was a metal cover that resembled a desktop that you rested your arms on while activating the levers. That cover blocked the vision of your feet and where they were positioned on the brake pedals. I always had to lean back and look underneath that cover to make absolutely certain I was not near that quick release button. Honestly, after putting in the long hours on that job each week, I was not about to deal with that old piece of shit crane. Also, everything about the design of that crane was opposite of how most other cranes were constructed.

The cab was located on the opposite side of the crane, and the drums of cable had covers on them so you couldn't see if your cable was "bird nesting" or not. Bird nesting is when your cable spools off of the drum so fast that it becomes free from the rest of the cable on your drum. If that situation occurs and you don't fix it immediately, when you hoisted the load, the cable would crisscross over itself and cause crimping and crushing of the cable underneath it. The cable itself is actually wire rope that consists of intricately woven smaller wires that are layered over each other. There are restrictions as to how many broken wires, gapping within the layers of the cable, and stretching are allowed in using your existing cable. When those restrictions are breached, the crane must be taken out of rotation for use until new cable can be installed. It is the crane operator's duty to check and monitor the cable in use on the crane regularly. In fact, there are daily, weekly, and monthly checklists for the crane operator to abide by.

After working at a stressful job such as driving pile all week, I felt it was a safer option for me to move his crane off to the side of the jobsite and walk my crane into position to drive the pile for his crew. I wasn't about to have an accident because I was so used to operating my own crane. I wasn't about to take a chance on accidentally touching that quick release button on the brake pedals. The men didn't mind waiting for me to switch the cranes. They were happy that I showed up so that they could make their time and a half hourly rate. After about two thirds of the pile allocated for that project were driven, the *"diva"* operator up and quit our company to go and work for a competitor contractor on the same jobsite. All he needed to do for them was to make a pick now and then with a hydraulic crane. He just up and burned a bridge in order to down-size his energy expenditure. He went from being very busy to visibly napping in his crane in between the couple of picks he had to make each day; lazy, lazy, and oh yeah—*LAZY (WTF!).*

One of the first lessons my ironworker husband taught me about construction work was that you never "burn bridges." That meant that I was to finish the job I was hired for. I could move on to a new project once I completed the one I was already working on. That would show the employer that I could be counted on. He told me that in that manner, I would gain their respect and that of the men I was working with. Also, he told me to work hard and give them *eight hours of work for eight hours of pay.* If I were to adhere to his advice, I would most likely be hired for future projects by those employers.

That was a tough job to work on, and I learned a lot of lessons from working on it. One of the most important lessons I learned was from that lazy ass operator. He taught me how NOT to represent myself on the jobsite and to NOT BE A DIVA, DRAMA QUEEN, or even worse, a LAZY ASS! WTF!

Another clown/diva I worked with on several occasions was the result of my own doing. In my beginning years, I would work with my union to bring other women and minorities in to join us in order to extend our training and benefits we offered to everyone. They set up meetings for me to speak to the audience about what duties were required from me on a daily basis on the jobsite. I would answer all the questions at the end of each meeting. On the days I was expected to speak, a business agent would pick me up at my jobsite and return me once I finished. A temporary replacement would work in my place for the duration of time I was to be absent.

The clown/diva I will write about was one of the minority men that came into our union as a result of one of my speaking engagements. He later told me he thought, "If a broad could do it, so could he." However, he came to the jobsites he was sent to work on with a sense of entitlement, like he should be moving up faster and training less than others due to his minority status. The main company I worked for sent their employees to jobsites based on their seniority within their company. In other words, the last hired was usually the first laid off when work became slow. The main issue I had with that man was that he wasn't listening to anyone who was trying to teach him something—least of all, a woman.

I was out of work over the course of a long winter during one of the years I was living up north; I was far from the city I usually worked in. The company had kept him working during my layoff. They had him drive far north to the town I was living in at that time. They had work inside a huge company there. It was a publishing company progressing through an expansion.

There were huge holes excavated for the pile to be driven into. Those pile were to hold the extremely heavy machinery that was going to be brought in. He was operating a brand-new Bobcat skid-steer loader that the company had just purchased. He drove that new skid-steer loader directly into one of those large and deep excavated holes. He was okay due to the interior roll bar, but the machine was trashed.

After his accident, the company decided to call me to replace him on that jobsite. I was pissed off that I wasn't hired on that job in the first place! I lived a lot closer to that jobsite, and I'd worked for the company many more years than the diva. I had to decline their request as I was working as a crane operator for another contractor at that time. I did mention, however, that they should have put me on that jobsite in the first place for the reasons I've just mentioned. They told me to call them for employment once my job ended.

The next jobsite tale I'm going to write about involves that same clown/diva. It was the last time I worked with him because I told the company that I refused to work with him in the future. Those reasons will be made clear by the end of this story.

I was given a nice easy job; challenging, but compared to my usual work, easier. I was to operate a barge-mounted crane to clear out the remnants of the city's old wooden marina that the public used to moor their boats in the warm weather months. I would have an empty barge attached to the forefront of the one my crane was mounted on. I was tucked inside the marina, tied up to the sheeting wall that lined the lake.

I had one man sent to assist me by unhooking the wood sections the workers would attach my rigging to. I had to be careful not to knock one of the workers who were hooking me up into the water, and also, I was told not to come in contact with the humungous tree behind me because it belonged to the adjacent park. All my assistant would have to do was unhook my load once I swung it over to the barge and landed it.

Once all of the wood was removed, the wooden pile would be vibrated out, and new iron pipe pile would be driven in. A new con-figuration was designed to accommodate more boats in the future. New metal decking and docks were to be put in also. That was to be a long-lasting job. I was happy that it was a short drive from my home and that it was only the two of us working there. The pace of the job was relaxed, and the view of the lake was spectacular. The air was fresh and clean because we had the park next to us filled with green trees.

The real challenge on that job proved to be dealing with the clown/diva. He did not like having to take orders from a woman and felt it was beneath him to do so. He had it made on that job. All he had to do was unhook my load and every so often, walk beyond the tree line to unhook my load there. We were not rushed on that job at all. We would have to wait for the two workers dismantling the docks to hook me up to the sections they cut loose. The men we were working with were nice, and it was one of the better jobs I worked on throughout my career—except for *him*.

For the majority of time during the day, I'd have to dog off my brakes (securely set them), get out of my seat, and climb down from my crane, walk over to the refuse barge, and unhook my load. I'd walk back to my crane, climb back into my seat, and resume operating. I was a one-woman show. The two men would have to wait for me as they perched precariously on the dock remnants. That took far too long in comparison to having the clown/diva do the job he was hired for and unhook my load so that I could immediately swing back over to await the two men's next pick.

I got sick and tired of climbing down out of my crane to go do the clown/diva's job, only to climb back up into my seat and do *my* job. Every time I looked over along the dock wall, I'd see him casually bullshitting the day away with the head superintendent on that jobsite. I'd finally had enough. The next time I had to unhook my load, I walked to the edge of barge and hollered over to him, "I need you over here to do your job. I can't keep climbing out of this crane to do it for you. Come to the barge and help me!"

He said his goodbyes to his newfound buddy whose ass he'd been busy kissing and marched angrily over to the refuse barge. He sulked like a child for the rest of the day. The company should have just sent me by myself to do that job because he began working at the pace of a snail. The job was progressing much better when I was doing both of our jobs, and then he refused to speak to me at all.

That evening, I received a phone call from our company's head superintendent—another member of the "I Hate Suzanne" non-fan club, a leading member, I should say. He told me that he'd received a phone call from the head superintendent on the jobsite I was working on. He requested that I be replaced. He stated that he thought I was rude and acted out of place when I yelled over to "my foreman" from the barge I was on that afternoon.

"What?" I yelled into the phone. Now that was the man who always laughed as he laid me off from work, finding humor in the misery he caused me. He was laughing then as he said, "I know, he thought [so and so] was your foreman. So tomorrow you can come into the yard to work, and we'll have someone replace you on the barge crane."

Instead of replacing the lazy asshole clown/diva that had been sent to work with me, I was to lose my position. He never bothered to correct that misinformed superintendent on that jobsite. I was pissed off once again with having to deal with that male ego bullshit. I told my superintendent that I had to retrieve my tools and belongings from the barge crane before I could make it into the yard. I also added that I'd prefer to never work with the crybaby clown/ diva again. I told him what *really* happened on that jobsite, how he'd spend the day bullshitting with the superintendent instead if doing his damn job. He had cost me a lot of money that I would have made on that long-term project. I was done with that asshole!

I went to the jobsite the following morning to get all my tools and personal belongings out of the crane on the barge. I saw no sign of my "helper," so he must have planned on coming to work a little late in order to avoid me. The men removing the marina had pulled into the parking lot while I was out on the barge. They were putting on their work clothes and gear while I was putting my belongings into my trunk. "Hey, where are you going?" one of the crew asked me.

"I've been removed from the jobsite," I answered.

"We don't want you to go. you're doing such a good job. You're so careful when you're around us with the crane and the rigging. We trust you not to knock us into the water."

"You should tell your superintendent that. He thinks the man who was supposed to be unhooking my loads I swung over to the barge is my foreman. He's not. He was sent here to help me. Your boss thinks I was out of line hollering at him to come do his job. All he was doing for the majority of the time was bullshitting with your boss. That was the reason you had to wait so long so long for me to return the rigging to you so that you could hook up the next piece. That was why you saw me getting in and out of the crane so much. Anyway, it was nice working with all of you, and I wish you luck with the rest of the project," I explained to them.

That experience taught me that it was okay for a man to raise his voice and speak his opinion to another man, but if a WOMAN raises her voice to a man, all HELL freezes over. WTF! There were two brothers who worked for our company because their father had been a foreman there for many years. All three were pile drivers. I'd worked on a few jobs with their dad, and he was a decent foreman and always treated me well. The two brothers were another story, however. They both were the type of men who always thought they were right and it was *their way or hit the highway.* All of us women have had to deal with men like those two, no matter what occupation you've worked in. They had to be kept separated due to their constant bickering with each other so they would usually work on separate jobsites.

When the dad retired, the older brother was made a foreman. That title went straight to his head. He was very bossy and doled out orders while standing around, watching his crew work. He drove me crazy because his ideas were generally the hardest and slowest ways of getting anything accomplished. He'd been in construction years longer than myself, and yet there I was, a woman, new to the industry, and I could figure out how to do most anything better than he could. I could do everything faster than he could, except for peeing (only because I was expected to go pee in a port-a-potty if our jobsite was so blessed to have one). I did NOT like working with that guy at all, and it pissed me off whenever I was stuck putting up with his incompetence on a jobsite. *WTF!* ran through my mind on an endless loop the days I was assigned to work as his operator. I was surprised he and his brother could wipe their own asses without help!

I had noticed that whenever I had to work in our main yard that there was hardly any organization to it. I hated the fact that anytime I needed to load a drill tool or a piece of equipment like a welder, I had to move four things that were in my way to get to it. That made no sense to me that I was wasting so much time and screwing myself in the future by putting those items back to where they were. So in every spare moment of my time, I rearranged the entire yard so that every item had an area, a specific place. I made sure there was a clear path for me to grab it with the forklift if I or anyone else needed it. I created the yard to resemble my own personal "Menards" yard area. That was my objective. Keeping the yard looking like that was a whole other ball game. I was a BUSY, BUSY gal!

We had a portion of our yard that was a field with many trees and shrubs along with tall grass and weeds. We also had two barges that had been tied up to the sheeting wall that lined two sides of our yard. The barges had been there for so long that they also had trees growing on them. Since I needed all the room I could get my hands on in order to spread out the equipment more, I decided to clear those unused areas—all in my precious spare time.

I learned just how much I could accomplish within five minutes time. Even if I managed to take down only one tree with my chainsaw, it made room where before there wasn't. It took me a long time to clear the shrubs and trees from the land and the barges. I used our bulldozer to rid the area of the tall grasses and weeds. I also used it to level out the newly vacant property. My yard foreman was so grateful that I had taken it upon myself to voluntarily organize our yard that he had dump trucks of gravel brought in so that I could spread it over the newly cleared property with my bulldozer.

The men had many jokes to tell me when I walked into the yard one morning to find a riding vibratory roller machine so that I could compress the graveled area. I would hear over and over statements such as, "Once she gets on her vibratory roller, we won't be able to get her off of it" or "You better not let Suzanne see you using her vibrator" and so on and so forth.

I compacted the ground to the point that I could run the forklift over it and even set up my crane on it without either machine sinking down into the soil. We had long sections of leads that we used when driving pile, taking up an enormous amount of space. I took our telescoping forklift and my crane to set the lead sections out on the barges in the river. I bet I doubled or tripled the usable amount of property that was our yard.

Everything finally had a place of its own, and it was so much faster to find the items we ended to load up for jobs. The one brother that annoyed me so much to work with would make a point of coming into the yard to make himself busy in between his jobs. By being busy, I mean he'd spend his days in the yard, bossing me around when I was already working for my yard foreman. My foreman told me to just work together with him because the company had nowhere to send him at that time.

I was busy loading and unloading trucks, going to and coming in from jobsites. I also had many deliveries I needed to unload on most days. I would also hop into the forklift or my own vehicle and travel to our Gran Trunk, yard four, or our boat shop to load or unload something. On some days, I'd be back and forth from our main yard to those other yards I just listed, many times each day. With that foreman tagging along, it was taking me twice as long to get anything done. I got to the point where I dreaded having to work with him.

As it turned out, he was difficult for anyone to work with. I heard stories from many of the men as to why they didn't want to work with him. He was an oddball and stuck in his ways; he was not about to change. It seemed to become a game between my yard foreman and the truck drivers I worked with there. When I heard, "Guess who's coming into the yard to work with you today?" from my foreman, he'd be wearing a wicked cheeky grin on his face as he said it. Immediately, I'd state with disdain, "WTF!" to which I'd hear snickering from the truck drivers. I'd also hear them utter, "Better you than us!" under their breath. I didn't know for sure, but I think the truck drivers had running bets going with the yard foreman as to how long it would take until I blew my stack and hollered at the dumbass—I mean *guy* I was forced to work with each time he showed up in the yard.

After years of that nonsense dealing with that *"slow as a sloth,"* every idea that popped into his feeble mind being the one and only right way to do something, I came to an understanding with myself. I'd dealt with that attitude in the majority of the men I'd had to work with on an everyday basis. That attitude reared its ugly head more so in that guy than in others.

I was tired of allowing men I worked with, or anyone else for that matter, ruining my day for me. I realized it was NOT them but *"my own PERCEPTION of them"* that I was allowing to dictate my days as being stressful instead of happy. How ridiculous was it that I was sabotaging my own self and flipping the switch on my days from light to darkness? It was all *me!*

I wish I had learned that lesson many years earlier, but I'm glad that I had that enlightenment at all and have put it to good use ever since. That aligns with the first rule of my "dojo kun" which is to *"seek perfection of character."* The second rule is *"respect others."* I had been failing miserably at that one. Just because I was thinking those poisonous thoughts in my head instead of shouting them out loud to the world didn't mean a thing as far as how it was poisoning my spirit to do so. I thought, "What did I have to lose by letting him shine?" What was the big deal about having to do things *my* way? Who really gives a shit about how a task is completed or a job gets done, just so it gets done! Everyone has something to offer; maybe organizing that area (or whatever we were doing at that time) was his forte. How would I know unless I gave him and his ideas a chance and provided a supportive and positive attitude about it?

In a calm and professional manner, I said to him, "Let's give your idea a shot. If it doesn't work out the way we need it to, I have an idea also." Then I added, "We'll put our minds together and figure something out." The key word I used was *we,* not me. That new perspective paid off in spades for me. In reality, if we were working on a jobsite and not in the yard, my job would have been to pull levers according to the hand signals I was being given. I was not paid to think about how to run the job; that was up to the foreman.

After that, things went smoothly between us. I no longer felt dread when he was assigned to work with me in the yard. Once we began working well together instead of butting heads, I learned to understand the way he looked at things and why. His perspective was different than mine, but I learned to respect that. We had conversations during our hours of work together, and I learned that he had been going through a difficult time in his life. Due to the hours he'd put on at work, his wife had felt neglected and found solace in the company of another man. She had moved out of their home and took their children with her.

I heard that scenario from many men I worked with. They put in a lot of overtime hours to pay for their family expenses when what the family required was more participation and presence from their father, husband, or boyfriend. Hell, I wrote a little bit before about my own situation from not being home enough due to working long overtime hours.

His sharing with me where he was coming from helped to reinforce the reasons he could be so disagreeable with me at times.

On too many occasions, the situations in some men's lives was being brought to the jobsite with them and reflected onto me. A good example of that was that I worked alongside a guy in the yard who ran the tool shop there. His shop contained all the tools, materials, and hardware required on our jobsites. He was in charge of loading and unloading toolboxes heading out to or returning from jobsites. I would usually be the person to load the toolboxes he'd prepared or take to him the ones I unloaded returning from a jobsite.

One day, I noticed that he was coming unglued on me with a short temper and a bad attitude. We'd worked together for many years, and I knew that I personally hadn't done anything wrong to piss him off and cause his behavior issues. I just let it go and gave him some space. His attitude toward me continued for the next couple of days until I was thoroughly fed up with it. I had asked the truck drivers if they knew what was upsetting him so much, and they told me he was being shitty with them as well. They told me that the guy's wife was giving him a lot of grief at home, and apparently, he was unknowingly bringing his personal life to work with him. He was angry at women in general at that point in time. Since I had a pair of tits, I qualified to be included. I'd finally had to snap back at him after one of his tirades against me for reasons I've long forgotten, "I'm not your wife!"

That seemed to snap him out of it. His attitude and behavior returned to normal almost immediately. I never knew if he was acting subconsciously and not realizing how brusque he was behaving with me or if he just, in fact, had it with women. After all my years of dealing with *only* men on a day-to-day basis, I understood that phenomenon further because I'd reached my limits dealing with them. I noticed similarities between them and, without meaning to, they naturally slipped into various categories in my mind: lazy; okay to work with; *not* okay to work with; a funny person who brightened the day; an asshole; a hard worker; someone who should keep their big mouth shut or thinks with his little head instead of his big one, my worst nightmare, and so on. I could go on and on with the categories.

In a lot of those cases, the women those men belonged to wore the pants in the family. The men went home after work or hit the tavern after work, in preparation to return to their homes only to be bossed around by their women. I heard a lot about the countless "honey do" lists that were handed to them on the eves of their long awaited weekends. Instead of catching up on some well-needed rest, they worked even harder on their days off.

That was the reason I figured out that when they showed up on Mondays, they were only too happy to boss the one pair of boobs around for the week—me. The *worst* man I had to deal with for many years flat out told me one day, "I don't know what it is about you that rubs me the wrong way. Maybe it's because you have the same name as my wife." WTF! From what some of the men told me, his wife most definitely wore the pants in that family. What surprised me, though, was the fact that he had three teenage daughters at that time. I personally call that karma for his bad behavior.

I may not have been "one of the guys," but my communication skills I'd taken on through the years allowed me to speak their language as one of them. For example, when I became to bogged down by a guy's belligerent behavior, I'd say, "With an attitude like that, there's no way you're going to get lucky tonight when you get home" or "Are your blue balls affecting your brain right now?"

Another appropriate quip would be "Let's try thinking with the *big* head rather than the *small* one, shall we?" or a nastier note, "You need to have your wife suck some of the poison out when you get home."

Since men seem to have sex on their minds for the majority of the time they're awake, they understood entirely the message I was conveying, even though it sounds like I was joking or attacking. Either way, it got their attention and also got my point across.

Dealing with inane behaviors and clashes between genders was causing daily stress to myself. The stress was compounded by concentrating on the physical dangers of the jobsites, and we worked beyond the limits of our physical and mental capabilities. I thought to myself, "Why am I busting my ass every day?" I felt as though I was working myself to death at a very young age.

Every day that I worked in our main yard, I had to walk past the owner of the company's white Lincoln Continental. It had custom red pinstriping and *Gold* spoked rims on its wheels. I thought, *I should be driving a car like that! I deserve a great car to make sense of how hard I work and to make up for all the long hours I work, WTF!* I had worked on and off for a contractor that used their "daughter" to go and expedite jobs for them. She would walk onto a site that had other *male* contractors there to bid on it also, only to have the job immediately awarded to her because she was the one female there to put in a bid. The state government had regulations pertaining to the percentage of jobs they wanted issued to minority contractors. She also ordered the iron needed for the bridges they built and got the best monetary deal due to her being a minority. That was a smart business decision on their part because they build new bridges and reconstruct old ones to this day. I know those facts to be true because I was one of their many crane operators who constructed a good number of them. I will write more about my bridge-building experiences in the chapter "Challenging and Just Plain Scary."

I sat down one day and drafted a letter to the owner of our company. I specifically told him that I was growing weary as I passed his Lincoln Continental every morning as I made my way into our main yard. I told him that I wanted a car like that too! Actually, I was thinking of a gold 1957 Corvette.

I told him about the bridge contractor's daughter walking onto sites and winning bids to get their jobs because the state government supported female endeavors. Her bid was usually not the lowest bid offered either.

I told him that for a percentage of the profits earned on each job, he could use me as his minority expediter. He was already aware of the fact that the contractor was winning the bids on a lot of jobs right out from under us was because they drove pile as well and offered to do the work for less money than our company had bid. I reminded him of all the pile that needed to be driven on either side of the bridges as they required substantial support for their on and off ramps. I wrote also that I would be willing to attend any schooling necessary to learn how to expedite if he wished. I was already aware of the costs of most of the equipment and materials we needed to do our work from all my years of experience in driving pile, sheeting, and drilling chance anchors.

I wrote my rather long letter as professionally as I could and took it in to our main office. I asked our receptionist to place my letter in the owners mail slot. A few days passed before I received a letter of response in the mail. He wrote me that he thought I had a good idea.

Unfortunately, he had his daughter, who was a lawyer, research the possibilities of making my offer a reality. It wasn't meant to be, however, because I was not a relative of his family. The results of going forward with my idea would be illegal under the accusation of fraud. He then thanked me for doing a good job out on our jobsites and wished me good luck in the future. As an afterthought, he wrote that he wished me good luck also on obtaining the car of my dreams (WTF!). It was a very nicely written letter and signed by him. I was happy that he had taken me seriously enough to investigate my theory, but I was unhappy knowing that I'd still be out in the field, busting my ass, WTF (I guess my corvette would just have to wait).

I tried to oust that matter out of my mind, but I kept trying to come up with ideas to improve my work situation anyway. One day, I had a "light bulb" moment. I'm sure we've all had a day every so often when your brain screams, "A-HA! Eureka! I've got it!." I've read and believe that our minds operate like a computer in that if you're struggling with a problem, your subconscious will keep mulling through different equations until it comes up with a solution to the problem. An example of this is when you're thinking, *What was the name of that actor who played in such and such movie? I've seen him a million times but I can't think of his name right now.*

Two or three days later (or even the middle of the night!), the name suddenly pops into your head. That was how it was with my idea to improve my monetary environment as well as my working situation.

I like—oops, *LOVE* WRECKING STUFF! Some of the most fun I've had on jobs were when I was "demolishing" something! One of my favorite *SMASHING* techniques was when I used a backhoe to pull apart a building. I used it's boom as if it were my own arm and "punched" down the walls with the bucket curled underneath. I then used it as a big hammer to flatten all the walls and window frames so that it would fit into a dump truck: SO FUN! I felt like the female version of the Incredible Hulk (minus the green color). Harnessing the power of a big machine was playtime for me.

Swinging the wrecking ball into a concrete wall was every bit of fun and made a big thud as it struck the concrete. It also felt like a small earthquake because the vibrations would shoot through the surrounding soil. The rhythm of swinging the wrecking ball with the crane proved to be an extreme form of meditation for me. I noticed the same rhythm whenever I used a clam bucket to grab material from one place and sling it to another. I could pound all my worries away with my demolition pendulum. I would float out of the crane seat at the end of the day as if I had sprouted angel's wings.

As I thought about how much more fun I could have taking apart a structure in comparison to the stress of making increment movements of mere inches ever so slowly with a gargantuan machine in the act of pile driving or setting and "treeing" iron in place, the duties that were involved were worlds apart from each other. When driving pile, I had to seat the top pipe ever so gently into the ring welded to the bottom pipe so as not to crush it. I had to hold that hammer brake firmly as I held it above the Piledrivers who had welded the ring. That hammer was like a guillotine; one slip of that brake, and a man was dead. Talk about utilizing your full power of concentration!

In setting precast so that no one's fingers were crushed as they spun the nuts onto the bolts to hold the piece in place, I'd seen a man's finger crushed completely flat from two pieces of precast, colliding as a crane operator swung it into place. I've always remembered that disastrous afternoon as if it happened yesterday. It ended that ironworker's career as he lost the use of the majority of his hand, even after many surgeries to not only rebuild his finger but mend the extensive nerve damage. In setting structural iron pieces, I had to be extremely careful not to knock an ironworker connector off his precarious perch as I swung one end of the next piece of iron in the required sequence and then drift the other end toward his connecting partner.

As I've mentioned, the ironworker connectors had no nets to catch them if they fell and they were not tied off to anything. The demolition crew that came in before us on many jobsites were brought in from the state to the south of ours. They removed whatever structure stood before our future reconstruction of the new project. There did not exist a demolition contractor in our state at that time. That was a male minority outfit, not a *female* minority one. Therefore, I thought that I should become a female minority owner and operator of "my own" demolition company. Hell, I had already worked with a demolitions expert during the three years I had spent as a laborer at the cement plant in California.

I planned on buying a crane that worked well but didn't have to look pretty for what I intended to put it through. I would also need to purchase a dump truck, a frontend loader with interchangeable buckets, and forks for lifting debris and iron rod segments. I would use a backhoe for those jobs small enough to not require a crane. You can do practically anything with a backhoe. In fact, if I were more knowledgeable about the workforce I was entering when I first began in the construction trade, I would have been a backhoe operator instead of a crane operator. You do work a lot more hours in comparison, but more hours equal more money. The machine sits closer to the ground instead of reaching eighty feet (and a lot farther) up into the sky. Although backhoe pay scale is a few dollars less than a crane's per hour, it's a lot less dangerous. Less danger equals less stress in my book.

I would have only needed minimal equipment and tools to work as a demolition company compared to a pile driving company. The equipment was costly to acquire for pile driving, and it would all break down frequently due to the punishment it would take, so I would've had to hire full-time mechanics to keep it up and running. As a demolition company, I would only need an employee or two to use a torch to cut apart the iron that would be enmeshed in the structure I would be demolishing. I was familiar with using a torch so I could be helpful with that also. I needed to be able to acquire the business aspect of owning and operating my own company, so I enrolled in night classes offered to minorities.

They were specially designed to bring minorities, particularly females, into the realm of business ownership. Those classes were state-funded and offered at low rates and were condensed for those who were interested in taking them. It was going to be tough to endure night classes after working long hours on a jobsite every day, but if I could make a lot more money in the future and not continue working my ass off in the manner I was, then why not go for it?

When I began my classes, I learned that I was the only woman looking to start a construction company. One woman was beginning a photography business, and the remaining thirteen or so attendees were intending on opening up day care centers for children out of their homes. When we had to go before the class and interpret our business plans as an assignment that was given to us, my audience had no idea what I was talking about as I was explaining my insights into the future jobs that I wished to obtain.

Fortunately for me, the woman in charge of the class was impressed with where I wanted to take my business in the future. As a representative of the state, she was happy that not only would a void be filled in the construction workforce but that it would be owned and operated by a woman. The one item she was not content with, however, was the idea I had for my business cards. I had drawn a she-devil complete with horns and a forked tail. She was cracking a long whip with a headache ball attached to one end of it. The headache ball had demolished a small building. Down in the bottom corner of the card, it said, "S & M Demolition." The caption read "If you have an obstruction, we will whip it into shape for you." Did I mention that the she-devil was wearing a miniskirt, cone bra, fishnet stockings, and stiletto-heeled boots?

The woman in charge was not impressed as I stood before the class once again, holding my poster of the intended business card design. My audience looked aghast with their mouths open like a school of carp fish. I explained that my T-shirts and baseball caps would have the same she-devil design and that I'd hand them out to the contractors who employed me. The woman in charge approached me and said, "That is just not tasteful and professional looking. In fact, it's fairly obscene for a business card that you're going to be handing out to promote your business."

WTF? Whose business was that going to be anyway?

I told her that it was meant to be rather humorous and would be unforgettable in the men's minds. I told her that I knew how they thought, and they'd get a kick out of my idea and they would appreciate the sense of humor involved. If I wanted to pass that class, I was expected to change my idea because she wasn't having it.

I came up with a "conservative" concept for a business card model and vowed to myself that I would be selective as to which clientele my more humorous business cards would be handed out to. I would reward repeat clients with the hats and T-shirts I originally proposed in the classroom. At the end of our class schedule, we were studying our projected costs we each required to operate our individual businesses. My construction costs far outweighed the money needed to operate a day care center. In fact, my fellow classmates grew bored rather easily whenever I stood before them discussing my various plans, requirements, and costs for my business because they had no idea what I was talking about.

We were given forms to fill out in pursuit of grants available to minority businesses new to the state. I ended up being one of the very few to qualify because I was the only female interested in starting a business in construction. I would need a lot more money than the grants were offering since the equipment I needed was costly. The woman representing the state said that there was more money available to get me started if I did my research to find it. At the time I was going through that process, there was no Internet, cell phones, or any of the devices we have at our expense presently that would have provided great assistance to me.

As I was taking those classes in the evening and working long hours each day, I really didn't have any extra time to do the research she spoke of. I wanted to pursue the use of explosives to bring down major structures in the future eventually and needed to seek out training for that as well. I didn't know when I would have the time for all the research necessary to find the funding for my business.

The final straw that put a damper on my plans came after one of my final classes when I was asked "why" I wanted to start my own business. When I explained that I was working too many hours to have any time left over to enjoy my life, and I felt like I was working way too hard with the result being that I was making other people very rich, I was surprised with my mentors resounding statement. She said, "Honey, if you think you're working hard now, just wait until you begin your journey as the owner-operator of your own business."

She explained to me that most people spend up to sixteen hours a day starting their own companies. I wouldn't have any extra time until my business was up and running. She also told me to be prepared to not even make a profit my first year in business, and whatever money I did make would most likely have to be put back into my business.

I was done. I was already a member of the strongest union in the construction business. I was making the highest wages possible by being a crane operator. We had the best health insurance and pension plans in place. I was also offered the option of retiring at the age of fifty-five or twenty-five years of service, whichever came first. I decided to remain where I was. I wanted less time and more money at work, not the *opposite!*

When I was living in the northern county, far from Milwaukee, I was called for a job in Manitowoc. I had been laid off awhile and was anxious to make some money. Even though that city was quite a long distance from my residence, I was excited because I'd be operating a small hydraulic crane *inside* the Manitowoc Crane Plant. Since I'd operated the older models of Manitowoc cranes, I was very familiar with them and I'd even operated their new giant Manitowoc cranes to set iron and precast. They were expanding their operations and needed to beef up the areas where heavy new machinery was going to be brought in to accommodate the new equipment. They were building a whole new assembly line to create a newer design of crane. Needless to say, I was a huge fan of those cranes.

I was working with a new contractor. I had never worked with the men before, which always created a strange and weird atmosphere for myself until the men saw for themselves that not only did I know what the hell I was doing, but I was damn good at it as well. I met up with the foreman and told him that I'd been sent out of the union hall. First I had to drive the crane inside the building through the huge overhead door. I had to drive in some sheeting which was extremely hard to do with a hydraulic crane. It just doesn't perform fast enough for that particular task. We managed to get the sheets into the ground enough to pour concrete behind them. The men became a lot more comfortable with me in the seat of the crane when I figured out how to reach the fully loaded concrete bucket into previously unreachable areas.

The largest challenge presented to me on that job were all the overhead power lines that were fully energized as I worked carefully beneath them. They didn't want to have to turn off the electrical power because they wanted to keep their other assembly lines that surrounded us up and running. It was scary because I didn't want to fry myself or anyone else for that matter. I made sure that every move I made with that crane I knew where my boom was in relation to the high wires above me. I was proud of myself walking out of that building every night, knowing that I never touched even one of those many high wires.

People were working in the plant all around me, and I had to be hyper aware of where they each were. The only barrier between my crane and the people working at their stations was a ring of caution tape tied to orange barrels set up around my crane. The plant employees would stand near my crane and watch me work while they were on their coffee and lunch breaks. Number one—I get it; who doesn't enjoy watching a construction project from start to finish? I know I did and still do. Number two: it was quite an oddity to see a woman operating a crane back then. It always kept me on my A-game to prove to all the men surrounding me, whether they were working with me or observing me in action to prove that, definitely, women could do that job just as well, if not better than a man could. Unless I was working alone for the day, it was a part of my job to prove myself over and over again to the men surrounding me. That concept alone could be stressful and fatiguing.

I was surprised one morning as I walked on to that jobsite to find that the Laborer's Union had sent out a woman to join us for the duration of the job. She told me that she had just begun working construction. She had safety training but hadn't worked on a jobsite before. I was overjoyed at seeing another female other than myself each day. I helped her whenever possible. I answered her many questions of, "Why are we doing this?" many times over. I taught her how to use proper hand signals when addressing the crane. She would occasionally hook me up to the various materials I was using, so I taught her proper rigging skills. I had fun discussing "girl stuff" during our half-hour lunch periods.

I warned her about the drug testing arrangements they used there at the plant because they were quite unusual. Everyone hired on that job was drug tested whenever their office officials could schedule it. All the men would enter the men's restroom with a security guard there to collect the urine specimens as the men provided them. Since I was the only woman in the beginning of the job, it shocked me when a female security guard escorted me to the ladies room and stood directly in front of me as I peed into the specimen cup! I thought, *WTF!* Where exactly did they think we would hide drugs for them to have to watch us pee like that?

All jobsites do drug testing, and they are NOT done in that fashion, period. Personally, I was just happy to use an actual bathroom, so I didn't give a shit, but I could see how issues could arise with other women. When my new laborer friend went in for her drug test, she came out of there, saying, "You're right, I couldn't believe the female guard stood before my stall and watched me pee!" That plant must have had incidents where their employees were adding ingredients to their urine specimens in an attempt to pass their drug tests—WTF!

I was so excited to be inside a plant that created my most favorite cranes that I went inside of their gift shop they had for the people who came to participate in the tours of their plant. I loaded up on T-shirts, hats, decals, and a Manitowoc crane duffel bag to carry it all home in. I also brought my camera to work along with an extra roll of film. I was taking photographs of the various crane sections as they moved along the assembly line. It was cool to watch a small piece begin at the assembly line's starting point and end up a major crane piece at the end of the line.

Thou shalt never irritate a woman, who can operate a backhoe.

Thus endeth today's lesson. Women are angels, and when someone breaks their wings, they simply continue to fly…on a broomstick. They are flexible like that.

Once again, I found this so funny I wanted to include it. I don't think the owner of that pickup truck thought it to be so hilarious.

Even though they got out names mixed up, it was still
nice to be recognized for what we were doing

Various jobsites I worked and trained

An advantage of my daughter seeing me at work was that she realized that the noise, the DIRT, and the GOD-AWFUL WARDROBE were *not* for her.

She completed years of college and now makes more money than I ever could have.

*I don't remember where or when I found this, but
I loved it so much that I had to include it*

As I was taking photographs during my lunchtime one day, a security guard came up to me, demanding the film inside of my camera. He told me that they did not allow photographs to be taken inside the plant. They did not want their patented plans on the manufacturing of their outstanding cranes to fall into their crane building competitor company's hands. There were several different crane manufacturers in existence, and their cranes all operated very differently from each other. They all had their own individual quirks, and it was hard to remember their differences when you hopped into their crane seats. It was not like driving a car in that you could drive any one of them and their operating sequences were alike. I often commented on how much easier it would be to operate the various series of crane if they had universal capabilities as far as the levers, brakes, and drums. Then again, the patents on different components are what allowed more than one company to manufacture them.

My response to the guard's request for the film in my camera caused me to hit the rewind button on my camera, pull out the film canister, and quickly drop it down the front on my shirt where it lodged on my bra. "The film belongs to me," I simply stated. He wore a shocked facial expression (there was that gaping O-shaped mouth and large round-eyed look again) as I explained that as a crane operator and *not* an espionage spy, I was simply a fan of the crane itself, and I'd always enjoyed learning how things were built. I told him that I'd operated many different Manitowoc cranes, even the old plow-handled variety.

I had operated the several old (ancient) Manitowoc cranes that my usual employer owned. Some were mounted on barges because you could lift an elephant or a tank with those cranes. In fact, I'll explain some of the heaviest picks I made throughout my career while in the seat of those cranes in the chapter "Challenging and

Just Plain Scary." The security guard looked at me like "I was one of *those* girls"—*WHACKO!*

I took my camera outside as the security guard instructed me to and photographed the variety of Manitowoc cranes they had already completed. There were rows and rows of them—I was in crane heaven! Then the dumpster outside caught my eye. Inside it were huge bundles of computer tape. The tape was silver on one side and turquoise blue on the other. My mind quickly calculated all of the windsocks I could weave together using those tapes. My brain has always worked in that way in that when I see something, I could turn it into an artwork, whether it was jewelry, clothing, or some decorative item. I took garbage bags filled with that computer tape out to my car and placed it into my trunk. I thought it rather obscure that I wasn't allowed to take photographs there, but they abandoned all of their computer tapes that built their cranes into a dumpster. "HELLO!" Where was their security then? WTF!

As the job wound down and was reaching its conclusion, they had my laborer girlfriend help me load out all of the equipment we were no longer using. Both of us used a bander and steel strapping to secure the excess materials we had bundled together. I was using the frontend loader combination backhoe to haul the equipment and materials outside to the area where we would eventually load them onto a semitrailer for transport back to the contractor's yard.

I was coming out of the building with all the small tools loaded into my bucket, waiting for my laborer girlfriend to push the button that opened the big door for me to exit through. I moved forward with my machine through the doorway when she signaled me to. I was almost entirely across the door's threshold when I heard a loud cracking and squealing of steel on steel sound. I immediately stopped and looked above as I leaned out of my seat to locate the sound I'd heard. She had only raised the door high enough to allow the frontend loader portion of my machine to exit but didn't raise it all the way up to allow for the backhoe portions boom that was sticking straight up in the rear of my machine. The backhoe had ripped through the lower third area of the expensive overhead door.

My girlfriend said that she hadn't considered the rear portion of my machine when she stopped raising the door. I felt so stupid for trusting her to look out for my machine and taking her signal for me to drive through the doorway. I assumed she knew enough by then to always open the door all the way as we had been doing all along. I was marched immediately to the women's restroom by their female security guard, and she handed me a specimen cup for me to pee in and be drug tested. As I've mentioned previously, it is always considered the operator's fault. I learned a very valuable lesson that no matter how well I knew someone, I trusted *only myself* to check everything out in regard to my equipment, machine, and surroundings from that day forward. I didn't care if I hurt someone's feelings because they didn't feel that I trusted them or their knowledge.

She and I were canned right away. They told me that we only had to finish loading out, and we were to be laid off anyway. No one was happy about the damage to the expensive overhead door that would have to be replaced. I was very upset that it overshadowed the good work that I'd done with the crane inside of the building. I had been proud of the fact that I hadn't come in contact with anything including the power lines overhead, inside of the building. By taking a hand signal I was given, I damaged their door. I thought that a woman would have my back far more than a man, but she was not very aware of her surroundings for working on a jobsite. I explained to her to always make sure that doors were opened up all the way in her future ventures and that if she ever had any questions about work, whether we were on the same jobsite or not, that she could call me for information. She was moving up north to Michigan to live, and she helped me relocate my potbellied pig when she did. I'll write more about my unique and very intelligent pet in the next chapter, "Critters."

I'm going to sidestep my tales of jobsites (like *Tales from the Crypt*—remember that scary show?) to tell you about the jobsite thievery I encountered on various jobsites. My clothing would disappear! I know you're thinking. *What in the hell are you talking about, Suzanne?* I'm telling you that I could never, *never, NEVER* leave any of my shirts, hats, boots, coveralls, overalls or rain gear, tools, and safety gear overnight in a machine I was operating. I couldn't leave anything in a toolbox on a jobsite or in a jobsite trailer. I'd left my clothes inside a jobsite trailer after being on a jobsite for a long period of time, thinking that I didn't want to haul all of my belongings back and forth from my vehicle each day. I had gotten too many phone calls late at night, redirecting me to a different jobsite the next morning. WTF! I found myself having to wake up extra early in order to go and get my gear out of the trailer or machine from the jobsite I'd been working on for quite a while.

Sometimes I was f——ed because my new jobsite would be a far distance away or in the opposite direction from where I'd left my belongings. No matter what, I could never leave my lunch box, water container, or thermos there either because I would save time and money by preparing my own food the evening beforehand. I'd seen too many men have to go without food or water because we ended up having to work through lunch or work later than usual, and they couldn't drive off-site somewhere to look for food or something to drink.

Sometimes I would show up to work in the morning to find that our jobsite trailer had been switched with another one or taken away to someone else's jobsite. When I worked in the yard, and the semitrailers were bringing back equipment, materials, and jobsite trailers from jobs that had finished, I would find all kinds of men's shirts, lunch boxes, hats, gloves, and gear that the men hadn't been able to remove.

One job I had been on for months, I'd left my brand-new insulated flannel shirt hanging in the jobsite trailer. The next day, I ended up having surgery in the hospital and lost time from that job while I was recovering. When I finally got back to that same jobsite, I expected to be able to wear my new warm shirt that I'd left there. Instead, it was not hanging from the hook I'd left it on, and I couldn't find it anywhere. I asked the guys who were in the trailer with me about its whereabouts. They had no clue where my shirt had disappeared to.

Lunchtime came along, and all the men who were spread out over the whole jobsite came into the trailer to eat their lunch. I saw a buddy of mine who I hadn't seen in a while. He told me that he was torching the ends off of the pile so they were even, and then welding boots (round plates) on them. The bottom pipe pile driven into the ground first is closed by welding a round steel plate on them called a "boot." That kept all water and foreign material out of the pipe pile so that the concrete could be poured into it and iron rods placed inside, once the pile was finished being driven. I said, "Well, that explains why your shirt is all burnt up. Wait a minute—is that *MY* shirt?"

He told me that he didn't know. He found a shirt hanging in the trailer to wear so that he didn't burn up HIS shirt. "WTF! I've been looking all over for my shirt. That was brand-new!" I loudly explained.

"You know better than to leave any clothing in here. Someone will wear it!" he said.

"Yeah, and that f——ker is YOU!" I said as all the men witnessing our rousing discussion started busting up, laughing. "Mother f——kers!" I grumbled; then we ALL started laughing (heaven forbid any of them would take my lunch box because that would've been like taking raw meat out of the jaws of a lioness!).

What was I going to do? There was no crying in construction. Even when I whined too much, I'd hear, "WA, WA, WA" from the guys. One guy rubbed his forefinger back and forth with his thumb, saying my whining was the sound his miniature violin was making. WTF! I never found any sympathy on a jobsite. I thought that I would deter the men from wearing my clothing by using a big black permanent marker to write my name on the labels inside of my shirts and jackets. I thought that maybe they would be too embarrassed to wear them, knowing it was a *"girl's"* shirt or jacket. I was proven wrong, however, when the yard foreman ordered me a special trench raincoat. I needed as much protection from the weather that I could get because rain, snow, hail, or otherwise, I had to be outside in the yard, unloading all the deliveries that arrived each day that I worked there and in each of our three other yards as well.

The raincoat covered me clear down to my ankles so that I wouldn't be forced to wear wet clothing all day. I loved my new raincoat! I wrote "SUZY" in bold black letters all the way down the back of it. Now who in the hell would wear that if you happened to be a big masculine man? One of them did because it disappeared on me overnight! I searched everywhere for it, and according to any man I asked, no one had seen it. So not only did a guy take my one-of-akind trench raincoat, he must have taken it home. WTF! Those guys were capable of anything; they had no shame.

Boots for work were very expensive. We had to have steel-toed boots to work on any construction project. I used to complain to the men that I could have bought three pairs of beautiful *girl* boots with the money I had to pay for a pair of work boots, especially the insulated winter work boots. I wasn't about to have to worry about my boots disappearing from a jobsite trailer or work vehicle, so when I saw a pair of winter ones on sale, I jumped at the opportunity to purchase them. They were WHITE, and because of their color, men weren't buying them. They were purchasing the brown color of the same exact boot for full price. WTF kind of thinking was that? At the end of the day, walking around and working on a jobsite, your boots were guaranteed to have dirt and grease on them by the end of the shift.

So I showed up to work the next morning, wearing my stark white boots to the jeers, sneers, and jokes referring to how *illuminating* my boots were. They joked that I needed to be working in Antarctica to be wearing those boots to work and blah, blah, blah. I told them they could laugh at me all they wanted, but I only paid half price for them because they were white. I also explained that they were EXACTLY the same as my previous boots as well as the ones they also had on their own feet! I explained that due to the conditions we were about to spend the day walking in that my boots would no longer look stark white by the end of the day.

As each hour passed by, the dirt and grease were attracted to my boots as if they were magnetic. At the end of the day, there were no more insolent remarks made about my chosen footwear because they blended right in with the dirt I was walking on. I felt good about saving the sixty dollars by buying them and felt lucky to have found them on sale to begin with. As I was walking to my vehicle at the end of our shift to go home, I was approached by one of the men I'd worked with that day.

He was a good family man raising several children with his wife. I knew that he could use every dollar he earned because his wife homeschooled their kids all day while he was at work. Therefore, I was not surprised when he asked me exactly which store I'd bought my white boots at for such a remarkable price.

The next morning, when I arrived at work, he was one of several men who had gone after work the previous day to purchase the white boots. It was alarming and eye-catching in the way it is when you're wearing new white tennis shoes for the first time, except there were about four pairs of them walking beside me. I said, "Look at us, we're the White Boot Brigade!" I just had to say something. I couldn't help myself, ha-ha. Of course, on that morning, there were no jokes, and no one was ridiculed for their foot attire.

I'd learned a lot from other's mistakes. For instance, as I was crossing over our bridge that spans the mouth of our Milwaukee River where it exits into Lake Michigan, I was looking down to see our boat shop. If the large overhead door was open that signified that employees were inside working. I always noticed the big electrical crane the Port of Milwaukee had down there as well. It rolled along railroad tracks that were laid into the ground along the dock wall. It was used to lift the heavy tugboats and other vessels from the river. It also placed boats into the river. On that particular day, it registered in my mind that there was something very wrong about what I was looking at. WTF! The boom of the crane was wrapped BACKWARD over and around the crane!

I realized that what I was looking at was the result of an operator leaving the boom lever engaged. Someone had been fired for sure for that mistake. That boom had just been replaced in that crane, and it had come at a very high price. Also, nothing moved in or out of the water the entire time they were replacing the boom, and now the Port of Milwaukee would be at a standstill once again.

I had the displeasure of operating that crane to remove one of our tugboats from the river and set it up on blocking along the dock wall. It was to be repaired and receive a new coat of marine paint. At first I was excited to operate a different kind of crane than the ones I usually ran; that was until I got into the seat of it. It was the height of a two-story building, so I had to climb up into it. I wondered if it would be like operating the tower cranes I'd run before because it was electric; it was *not.* It was SO *SLOW* that I could have taken a NAP in the time it took me to hoist up its block—-UGH! WTF! That *wasn't* fun!

To make matters worse and even less fun, that crane took not one operator to run it but *two.* That meant that I had an elderly (OLD!) operator who was employed by the Port of Milwaukee sitting so close in his seat behind my own that I could feel his breath on my neck! YUCK! The cab was small, and the boom lever was located on the wall behind me. That was the lever he was to engage or release upon my command. I felt like a dubious maniacal puppeteer as I loudly gave commands to the old geezer operator sitting so closely behind me. I knew that whoever sat at an engineering desk designing the crane had never operated one before because the location of the levers and the seating arrangement didn't make any sense to a seasoned operator whatsoever.

It took so *LONG* for that crane to lift the tugboat from the river that I was there ALL DAY. It didn't help my boredom that I could hear a soft snoring sound coming from the old f——ker operator sitting behind me. I kept chanting to myself, *"It's a paycheck, it's a paycheck, it's a paycheck."* It was a hell of a bizarre way to make one, but it was indeed a paycheck.

I did see another crane with its boom butt (the bottom piece of boom that's attached to the house of the crane with big pins that usually stays in place) bent over in our yard for one summer. I saw it and thought, *Holy f——k! Someone left the boom lever in place and has failed to throw out the master clutch.* They must have walked away from the crane, not realizing that it was booming up ever so slowly until it pulled its own boom butt up tight to the boom's hoist drums. They were lucky that a boom wasn't attached or they would have had a bigger disaster occur. That was someone else's WTF moment and not mine for a change.

The next jobsite recital I could have written in the chapter "Challenging and Just Plain Scary," but I said WTF too many times that I will just write about it here in this chapter. We were to drive a lot of pile with three different cranes and crews working at the same time. Each crane began driving pile at the farthest end of that jobsite. We drove pile in front of the cranes and on both sides. They would back us up as they finished piles in those vicinities. The plan was that the cranes would track in reverse through the jobsite and exit out the front, completing their pile driving repertoire.

The humungous problem with that jobsite was the thick clay mud that hindered us with any movement that we made. It was very dangerous working around those constantly swinging cranes because we could not move fast enough to get out of their way. I was hired to be an oiler for one of those cranes in that giant mud pit. Part of an oiler's duty was to keep the crane clean, but that proved impossible on that jobsite; there was mud flying everywhere. All our equipment and materials were covered with it. I had no choice but to stay up on the catwalk and hold on for dear life as the crane swung back and forth.

I had to join the men in the mud every time we needed to move our very long air hose that ran from our big air compressor to the rear of the crane driving pile. The mud was so thick that if we weren't careful, our feet would pull up out of the big rubber rain boots we were wearing every time we took a step. Having to constantly walk through that mud was extremely fatiguing. The mud was so thick that whenever I turned to walk in the opposite direction, my foot would turn inside of the boot. We had to place long timbers down on top of the mud each morning so that the operators could "walk the plank" to their machines without getting slick mud on the bottom of their boots. We would have to repeat the process of laying the timbers down and then removing them from the mud after the operators shut down their cranes at the end of the day and left the jobsite. They were taking coffee cans to the cranes each day to pee in and were on their own maneuvering their way to the port-a-potty if necessary.

I saw a scary incident occur when a crew of men attempted to move a long section of air hose. After they managed to hoist the air hoses up out of the mud, the foreman began to pull ahead. The men followed behind him, trying to pull the hose along as they trudged through the thick sludge when all of a sudden, the foreman was unable to pull his boot up to take his next step. *SPLAT!* He did a face-plant. I couldn't believe what I was seeing when the men behind him fell like dominoes, one after the other, and face-planted as well! I slogged through the mud over to try and help them up. Those poor guys had to work the rest of the day covered in thick nasty mud. I tried very hard *not* to follow in their footsteps.

I was always the last to leave the jobsite because I had to carefully climb all over that crane when our shift was done to do some greasing and put the window covers in place. The area of our jobsite was not the safest at that time, and therefore, it was surrounded by a ten-foot-high cyclone fence. When I left the jobsite, I could barely trudge along, carrying my water cooler and lunch box. It was cold during that time, and we were all wearing our insulated winter coveralls. When my coveralls, which were heavy in the first place, had mud all over them, it felt like I was covered in weight belts.

As I made my way slowly up the sloping tiers of the parking structure where my car was located, I became more exhausted with every step. I had to sit down on the concrete surface to unzip the legs of my coveralls. It was difficult because the zippers were encased in mud from the jobsite. I noticed that some of the men on the jobsite had broken zippers, most likely incurred by all of the mud coating them. They just wrapped good old duct tape around their waists and their ankles (I swear I can fix anything with duct tape and tie wire). They would just cut themselves free from the tape at the end of the day or if they needed to use the port-a-potty.

I felt vulnerable in that prone position on the concrete floor of the parking structure. I thought to myself, *Now I know what a turtle feels like when it's stuck topsy-turvy on its back and can't right itself.* I also thought that I was asking for trouble. There I was, in a notso-great area of our city, a lone woman in a parking garage with no one around, and it was at nighttime. The only light available to see my surroundings was within the parking garage. Anyone could have been waiting in the shadows, and I'd have a hell of a time defending myself. Doing karate in mud-covered coveralls would be quite a challenge.

I'd never requested to be removed from a job before, but I was about to after thinking about how I was rolling the dice with danger just to get to my vehicle each night. I told the jobsite superintendent of my request to be relocated to another jobsite and why. I also informed my union of the same ideas I'd given to my usual company. Upon placing women on a jobsite, I recommended that there was a safe, well-lit environment for them to park. Also, they needed to make sure that they were not in an isolated area that invited unwanted attention. I explained that it was simply a matter of safety for us women. I was thanked for bringing those matters to their attention since it was a new initiative to place women on jobsites back then. I was sent to the main yard to work, and in the late afternoon each weekday, I drove our frontend loader combination backhoe across the city to the jobsite.

The cement deliveries among other trucks were casting mud from their tires when they left the jobsite. It was fun watching the driver's shocked expressions whenever I pulled up alongside them or passed them in my frontend loader backhoe. It wasn't an everyday sight to be seen, especially with a female at the wheel. After being laid off for quite a while one year, I was called to go operate cranes for a bridge-building contractor. Back then, it was written in our union contract that the contractor an operator was working for was required to provide parking for them. Of course, the contractors usually balked at that expectation.

That contractor dealt with the matter by placing us in a paid parking lot about five city blocks away from our jobsite. The good news was that the person who worked there watched over our vehicles during the day. The bad news was that I had to haul all of my tools, lubes, oils, lunch box, water, and clothing those five blocks to get to the jobsite and the crane I was to be operating. I began pulling up in my car before work so that I could grease and lube the crane, lock the jobsite back up, and then go and park my car for the day. That job began late in the fall and went through the winter. Once snow was on the ground, I could pull all of my gear to the jobsite on a sled.

On my first day of walking onto a new jobsite and working with a new crew of men I'd never met before, I felt the usual uneasiness of preparing to prove I belonged there yet again. A young man approached me immediately and, in his cocky manner, asked me, "What the hell are *YOU* doing here?" laughing as he spoke. I ignored him and proceeded to enter into the jobsite trailer. When he came in, he spoke in a loud enough voice for everyone to hear, "Don't think we're going to babysit you or come to your aid every moment of the day. You're gonna have to carry your own weight around here, just like the rest of us."

The superintendent on that job used to be an expeditor for the usual company I worked for. I'd known him for several years, and he greeted me, shook my hand, and welcomed me to the jobsite. He told the men in the trailer my name, my background with my usual company, and listed some of the larger projects I'd worked on. He then introduced me as their service crane operator. I would be providing pile, equipment, and materials to the two cranes and their crews who would be driving the piling on the jobsite. I would also be loading and unloading the semitrailers pulling onto the jobsite. He added that if anyone needed a pick (anything needing lifting with my crane), they were to talk to me about it.

I said hello to my new crewmates and said that there would be one exception to his statement. I looked over at the young punk who had greeted me so rudely when I first stepped onto that jobsite. I said, "Except for you! If you need something moved, you better go find yourself a wheelbarrow because I won't move a goddamn thing for you. If your mother could have heard how you spoke to me, she would whip your ass."

The superintendent looked at me in surprise and asked, "Really?"

"Really," I replied as I gathered my lunch box and water jug before heading to my crane.

I heard him say, "Well, let's get to work then."

It only took two weeks after everyone there saw that I knew what I was doing, that I was a hard worker, and that I was willing to help out, that the young man approached me to apologize. I accepted his apology and told him that he needed to think whether he would want his girlfriend, wife, daughter, or mother being spoken to or treated in the way he had treated me. He said, "No, of course not." I won't say that we became "buddies" after our conversation, but we did finish that job being civil to each other.

That jobsite was the most "eye-opening" lesson for me on what NOT to do. It was the most unsafe outfit that I ever worked with. They absolutely tortured their equipment. I ended up working for that outfit for a lot of years on and off before I found it not worth my time or safety. I came to a point where I told myself I was done with their "merry men of mistakes" for good. I'd use my layoff time from my usual company to work on my own personal projects rather than continue to work for a contractor that I deemed unsafe.

Back to the unsafe jobsite. There was an old man crane opera-tor from the dinosaur era who was very threatened by having not only a *much younger* new crane operator aboard but a *female* one as well (oh my!). He only got out of his crane seat (throne) to use the porta-potty (throne); otherwise, he was GLUED to the crane seat. I had never seen an operator driving pile and getting the pipe pile stuck in the leads as much as he did. He kept sending a pile driver over to get me and my crane to come and pull the pile back out of the leads. Every time he requested the crane, I brought the extend-ing forklift instead. I kept explaining to him that I was not going to induce side pull on the crane's boom because it would destroy its integrity. I showed him time and time again that it was a much safer process to extend the forks of the forklift, chain the pipe pile to the fork's frame, and then hydraulically pull the pile from the leads—no harm, no foul. In his case, however, the saying "You can't teach an old dog new tricks" applied.

Although he had been driving pile for decades, he continually f——ked up by hoisting his pile up and lodging it once again in the leads. The foreman would always shake his head in disbelief, and all the crew members would moan about it. They were taking an unbe-lievable amount of time on each pile cluster they were driving with that *old* man in the seat (throne). One day, I was annoyed at being taken away from what I was trying to accomplish doing my own job, only to help him do his job that I said loud enough for his foreman to hear, "I've been driving pile for a lot of years. You should switch seats with me, and *I'll* drive the damn pile. You can go operate the service crane!" *That* got his attention.

Here's a concept that you wouldn't think of as "a thing," but it is—old men's egos! WTF! I was respectful of the men who were there before me in the construction world, but it took me quite a while to realize that some of the older operators considered me a threat that could "put them out to pasture," so to speak. I had seen some of that behavior doled out to some of the up and coming male operators too. I was perceived as a double threat being a younger operator and also a FEMALE operator deemed a necessary asset on a jobsite at that time.

I learned that lesson more so when I began having difficulties with my American friction crane. I was having a hard time getting it to turn over in the mornings and couldn't figure out why. I had to jump my batteries before work for over a two-week period of time. I had no previous problems with my batteries draining before that. I reported the problem to my foreman and began to start work even earlier in the morning in order to deal with the timely task of taking the forklift to get the battery charger and driving it over to the crane. I then had to extend the forks holding the charger up to the crane and hooking up the cables. That whole process took twenty to thirty minutes and was a total pain in my ass—WTF! It was not a positive way for me to begin my workday.

I showed up extra early one morning for one reason or another, I can't remember why. As I pulled into the jobsite, I noticed a glow of light emanating from the rear door of my crane. The back door had been slid open, and I could see the silhouette of a man in the back of my crane. We'd been having an issue with people tagging our equipment in the nighttime hours (placing graffiti on our equipment with spray paint) or else they were putting sugar in our fuel tanks and other such f——kery. My gut shouted, "Sleever bar time!"

I charged up to the crane with my sleever bar in hand, ready to crack some skulls. I shouted, "What the f——k are you doing in my crane?"

The man turned sheepishly around to face me, and it was the old man (ancient f——k) operator. "I thought I saw a light on in here, you must have left a light on."

"Bullshit! I check everything before I go home at night. There was no light left on in my crane. It's still light out when I leave for home. I'd have no need to turn on a light at all. Go and deal with your own crane. And why would you be here this early anyway?" He had no answer for me; he'd been busted.

I reported his f——king around in my crane to my foreman. He had a talk with him later in the day. It turned out that he'd been turning on my interior lights after our shift ended and I'd left for the day. He would then return early the following morning and turn the lights off before we were to begin our grease time. He did that intentionally with the hopes that the foreman would fire me for being incompetent as an operator. He hoped that the company would terminate my employment. The old fart operator didn't want me there, plain and simple. He spilled his guts to the foreman because they'd been friends for many years and had worked on many jobs together. He thought that the foreman had shared his views of working on a totally male employed jobsite. It was lucky for me that he didn't; either that or I had changed his views with my work ethic.

At lunchtime, the foreman was bold enough to tell the men what the old (jackass) operator had been doing to my crane to make me look inferior in the eyes of the men. He told them that the next man who f——ked with my crane or any other piece of equipment, for that matter, would be fired immediately. Everyone needed to be professional and keep their head in the game.

I told the foreman that I had something to say also. I said, "I'm married to the biggest asshole I know. You're all amateurs in comparison. You may as well save yourself the time and energy in plotting to make life difficult for me or in trying to get me out of here. This is a party for me here compared with what I deal with when I walk through my door at home. I'm a hard worker, I'm part of your team, so let me help you because that's what I'm here for."

After that, things went well for a while until a "demon" stepped onto the jobsite. WTF! He wasn't quite the devil like my ironworker husband was, but he was in close competition. That guy looked like a pit bull, but he was more like a yipping ankle biter chihuahua in a pit bull body (a fat one!)

He barked orders at everybody and wore a sneer on his face for the majority of the day. Rather than get a forklift to move his smaller equipment and materials, he made me move the hydraulic crane all over the jobsite. My crawler crane was needed on another jobsite, so they had traded it with the hydraulic crane. I was worn-out at the end of each day due to lifting the heavy iron pads from their brackets and then returning them after I was done setting up the crane for the pick. I then had to suck all of the hydraulic components of the crane back in to prepare for the next position and pick. He would bark at me the entire time I was getting the crane set up. We were not in a hurry at that stage of the project and were merely picking up the cut off sections of pipe pile left behind from the pile driving crew.

We were also moving loads of rebar and pipe to future areas the pile driving crew were to advance to. I don't know if the company just didn't have another job to put him on at the time. I just knew that we had been progressing along nicely until *he* showed up. In other words, he was a real pain in everyone's ass—WTF!

One Monday, when he showed up at work, he drove one of the superintendents work trucks up to my crane. He told me that he was tired of waiting for me to set up the crane, so he had his brother-in-law make me some wooden pads to put under my outrigger rams instead of lifting the heavy iron ones. At first I thought it was nice of him to do that until I tried to pick one up. He had four-by-four-inch hardwoods cut into four-foot lengths. Each four-by-four was nailed to the next one. I can't remember if there were seven or eight of those boards nailed together, but the pad was solid with no space between the boards. Then he had three quarter-inch plywood squares nailed to the tops and bottoms of each pad. Two pieces of rope were nailed to each side to be used as handles. Hell, there were so many nails holding those square pads together that the weight of them alone was heavy. Honestly, I don't remember which pads were the heaviest, the iron ones or the wooden ones. I only knew that I was the one who had to lug them all over the jobsite. WTF!

I got the message that whenever I had to work with that guy, it was going to be "his way or no way at all." What was new? He had the power, he was the *big shot,* he was the foreman, goddamn it, his word was gold; and the whole world better bow down and kiss his feet! He was the closest asshole I had come across that matched the yard foreman dickhead I worked for as a laborer in California.

I was already knowledgeable in dealing with his personality disorder, so I had him pegged. He had the audacity to abuse his power at work because he had none at home. I mentioned this ass earlier in the book. He told me that I pissed him off simply by sharing the same name as his wife; whatever the f——k *that* meant!

I came up with the idea to avoid injury by carrying his heavyas-f——k outrigger pads by running a chain through all the handles and then chaining them to the rear end of my crane. Whenever I had to move my crane, I dragged those damn pads around with me.

On occasion, I'd grab the forklift, scoop them up, and drive them into place. They were indestructible after all, and I couldn't give a f——k if I messed them up. If he was hoping to injure me in order to get me off of that jobsite, he was dead wrong. He was not yet aware of my tenacity, tolerance of bullshit, and just what a stubborn Swede I was. WTF! He was going to go before I was; the war was on!

One morning, during the winter, I arrived to a very unusual sight. It was dark and quiet; most everyone was still sleeping. The streets were covered with the snow that had fallen during the night. I had placed all of my tools, lunch box, water, and equipment on my sled and began towing it behind me to the jobsite. I knew enough to walk down the middle of the empty street so that I could see anyone moving toward me from the dark recesses of the buildings I was passing by. As I turned onto a main city street, there was still no traffic at all. That was good because to my amazement, there were flames coming up out of each manhole. The covers had been blown off of them and ended up God knew where. WTF! It looked like something out of the movie *Apocalypse Now,* where they bombed everything with napalm.

An explosion must have occurred down in the sewer system somewhere; it looked scary as hell! I didn't know how anyone was supposed to drive on those city streets to get to their jobs in the coming hours. I made it into work and prepared for the day, only to be shut down the minute the foreman showed up for work. He informed me that we were to evacuate the jobsite as soon as possible because the sewer tunnels ran directly below us, and a fire was raging throughout them. If we had driven a pile into the ground, we would have been blown sky high.

It was a few days before we were allowed to go back to work. We were met with another surprise when we moved on to another section of our jobsite to drive more pile. When the first pile punched through the preexisting concrete floor, it zipped through as if free-falling through air. There was no substantial material for the pile to seat itself. Something was drastically wrong with our new location.

A backhoe operator was brought in with his machine to excavate the area we were to drive pile. As he broke through the concrete floor, his entire backhoe pitched to the side, and he was on the collapsed edge of a caved-in room. No one had any idea that there was an abandoned room or chamber below the surface of our jobsite. The maps of the city, in its previous years, had been destroyed in a fire.

Once again, we had to leave our jobsite until that section was excavated, the concrete removed, and fill brought in by dump trucks to bring the soil up to ground level. It was then all compacted in order to withstand the heavy weights of the cranes. We were lucky a crane hadn't tipped over from crushing through the concrete slab and sliding into the vacant area below.

The hydraulic crane I was operating on that jobsite was very old and had seen much better days. The boom was bent so that when it was completely extended out, I could see a visible curve to one side. The curve was due to side pulling, and that was a big NO-NO, WTF! We were all taught as apprentice crane operators how to avoid damaging a crane's boom in that manner. When I sucked that boom in at the end of our shift, it would chug-chug-chug along as it struggled to retract. That crane also leaked hydraulic fluid from just about every seal that it had; its gaskets were shot! I kept adding oil to it daily and put engine diapers (just as it sounds but for a crane) both on and under it. I did not want the oil leaking into the soil on the jobsite. I reported the leaks daily to my foreman. After a time, it became a waste of oil because it was constantly draining out.

The superintendent finally scheduled the company's mechanic to come into the jobsite and replace the gaskets on the crane. The sucky thing about it would be that I'd be off from work while the crane was down. That meant no income for me until it was up and operational. We had to wait a bit for the ordered gaskets to show up, and when they finally did, the mechanic arrived on the site with them.

I was anxious to return to work and pursue paychecks, so I checked in periodically for a progress report. I even drove in one day to talk to the mechanic and see how far along he was toward completion.

Finally, I was able to return to work and enjoy a crane that wasn't a slick mess of oil everywhere I touched it. That all changed rather rapidly when a winter blizzard hit us. I made the treacherous drive into work one morning with barely any visibility. To make matters much worse, the temperature was five below zero, and that was *not* including the windchill. I fully expected to be sent home and was, in fact, pissed off that no one had called me to stay home so that I didn't have to make the unnecessary drive into work. It was an extremely dangerous commute due to the low visibility and the slick icy road conditions. It wasn't just my own driving I had to worry about but everyone else's also. It was an extreme version of "bumper cars" out there!

We were all dismissed to go home because the wind was blowing even harder, causing the snow to permeate everything. Then as I was grabbing my belongings and heading for the door, the guy opened his mouth and volunteered me to operate my newly repaired crane to unload a truckload of pile. He also grabbed an unwilling apprentice pile driver who had no choice but to comply. That egomaniac was so eager to brownnose and kiss ass with the superintendent that he was willing to risk our necks and the integrity of my crane to do it. I told the superintendent how hard it was to get my crane warmed up in those temperatures to run properly. I informed him that the new gaskets they had purchased and had paid to be installed would not expand to contain the oil in the hydraulic hoses, and the crane's leaks would reappear.

"Blah, blah, blah, let's go to work!" Those words spewed from the demon foreman's mouth. Then he added, "You just don't want to work in the cold. It's winter, goddamnit!" as he headed for the door. "What are YOU waiting for?" he demanded of the apprentice who was looking at me like a hare in a snare.

"Hey, I don't believe we should go out there either. That foreman's a f——king moron!" I stated to the apprentice, who followed me out the door like a sad, sad puppy. I told him my philosophy as we trudged through the snow toward my crane: "If it's too cold for the equipment to start, it's too cold for the human body."

It took me quite a while to get my engine to turn over. As I was waiting for the oils and fuel to warm up, I realized that I had a broken windshield wiper, so I'd have to resort to periodically leaving my seat and manually scraping the snow off my windshield so that I could see the foreman and the apprentice balancing on top of the icy semitrailer load of pipe pile. I had no working heater and no defroster, so I had to scrape the ice from the inside of the windshield as well. I had to operate the crane with the cab door open so that I could lean my head outside in order to see what the hell I was doing. I found it totally absurd that we were outside in that shit at all, and I was shocked that, number one, the superintendent allowed us to remain on the jobsite at all due to safety factors; and, number two, "WHY?" What was that clown foreman's motive? To me, it was grandstanding on his part, saying, "I'm so macho weather doesn't effect me."

"Stupid" is what *I* called it. I had originally declared it too slippery to have men standing high above the ground on icy iron. I had warned them about the gaskets that had just been replaced not being able to expand to contain the oil in the hydraulic lines due to the frozen temperatures. All my rational statements were ignored. The men knew I was correct and chose to do things *their* way. That trailer had been parked on the jobsite and did *not* have to be unloaded in that storm.

I had no idea that I was doomed to work with that asshole foreman many times in my future. I will write more on those most unfavorable circumstances in the pages ahead. As soon as that semitrailer was unloaded, I was out of there. The next day was a degree or two above zero, and the sun was shining, so it was expected to warm up a little more by lunchtime. We had a lot of work to do just removing the snow that had fallen during the storm from our equipment and materials.

Sure enough, when my crane's engine was running and warmed up, I could see oil leaking from where my new gaskets had been installed. Later in the day, the mechanic had been working on a piece of equipment and came up to me, chewing me out for operating the crane in those previous debilitating temperatures. He told me that I had wasted his time to repair my crane and the money it had cost the company for the new gaskets. He also told me that if I needed help in the future *"not"* to call him. Surprisingly enough, that mechanic and the malfunctioning foreman would both come and work for my usual company—*unlucky me.*

Why didn't the men bring those weather and safety issues up to each other? I think that one man didn't want to look less "macho" than another one or that they didn't want the other men to tease them mercilessly. They didn't realize that to an outsider, me, of another gender, it just looked like dumb and dumber! WTF! They couldn't get over themselves or get the hell out of their own way. They didn't realize that if one man slipped and incurred an injury that it would cause the contractor's insurance to go up, and their safety record would be compromised.

Those numbers would affect their bids for new construction projects. They were not looking at the "big picture." They were not interested in hearing about it on that day or on the many other weather-challenged days I was forced to work on. The weather played out as the main factor in one of the most traumatic, disastrous, if not the worst construction accident ever involving the crane called Big Blue. I will write about it in the chapter titled, "Challenging and Just Plain Scary."

I'd witnessed a pile driver foreman sliding off of a slippery semi-trailer deck while unloading it in a downpour of rain that resulted in him requiring immediate knee surgery, and he was unable to work for months. He lost out on making a paycheck for the duration of that time, and it ended up costing him a lot of money to pay for the remaining charges left over after his union's insurance covered what they were designated to. He also had to go through a lot of physical therapy so that he'd be able to resume working after he was healed. I can tell you that after any surgery, you can predict the weather sooner than any weatherman can report on it. The weather affects the degrees of my pain levels throughout each day.

I've fallen off of my catwalk while trying to climb into the seat of the friction crane I operated in our yard because it had a sheet of ice on it one morning. Unfortunately for me, the fall was about eight feet down to the frozen ice and snow-covered ground where I landed on my kneecap. To this day, I cannot kneel on my left knee because if I do, I feel like an ice pick is being jammed into it. Once I knew that I hadn't broken any bones from my fall, I had to climb back up the crane and get in that seat. I had to be tough as nails out there.

That company was known for building bridges, so after that long-term project in the heart of our city, I set off to build quite a few with them. I traveled outside our county to the middle of nowhere to build a bridge that was to cross over a fast-moving river. That area was located near a small town. The juvenile delinquents who lived there must have been bored with themselves and therefore found amusement in breaking the windows of our crane and other heavy equipment each night by throwing large rocks through them. That SUCKED! WTF! It took us so long in the mornings to clean up all the broken glass and to get it out of the crane's cab. It was a costly expense because our windows were customized for each piece of equipment we were using. They repeatedly broke the windows on our jobsite trailer as well. We were accumulating serious downtime whenever the windows had to be replaced.

Each of us operators took the measurements of our windows and gave them to the jobsite superintendent. He took the measurements back to the company's yard and had laborers cut window covers out of sheets of metal.

When they were brought out to the jobsite, they arrived with a big box of bungee cords for us to secure the heavy window covers with. It was extremely hard to hold on to those heavy covers while trying to maintain my balance as I placed them over the windows. One thing was certain in the construction business, and that was that everything was HEAVY! For that reason, I worked out at the gym, lifting weights daily during the periods of time that I was laid off and on weekends when I was back working. I had to keep up my muscle capacity. It seemed that each year, the restrictions that OSHA put out for chain-link size increased. The chains that were rigging for my cranes grew longer, larger, and heavier. At the end of my career, I was walking the lengths of chain one end at a time until I couldn't drag them anymore and then going back to retrieve the opposite ends. If I had a forklift on site, I'd have to haul them to my crane with that. I just couldn't carry them over my shoulder any longer.

I struggled at covering the windshield of my crane with its metal cover because it was difficult for me to find placement for the bungee cord hooks. Also, I barely had any catwalk in front of it for me to stand on. My balancing act ended abruptly after work one afternoon when the metal window cover slipped from my gloved hands and landed like a guillotine onto my foot! If I wasn't wearing steel-toed work boots, it could have chopped off my toes. As it was, I ended up with a deep purple stripe of a bruise across my foot from the edge of the steel toe as it bent downward from the heavy cover. After that, every time I pushed down on my main brake pedal, my foot was aflame with pain.

The next situation I had with the extremely heavy windshield cover occurred when it slipped yet again on a different day, and it knocked me off my balancing act, taking me to the ground with it. WTF! I was done with that shit! I told the superintendent that while the other crane was working on the opposite side of the river had a good-sized piece of catwalk in front of it, mine did not. I told him that in both of the incidents I'd reported, I could have been seriously injured. I either needed a piece of catwalk welded to the front of my crane or I needed to operate a different crane.

He decided to take the less expensive and timely route by having a pile driver come out to the jobsite and weld a piece of catwalk on for me. When I eventually returned to work for my regular employer, they were switching from the lighter wood window covers to metal ones also.

When I told them about the two incidents that could have proved disastrous when the covers slipped from the bungees, they came up with a better idea in which to secure them. They welded bolts to the corners of each window frame and drilled holes appropriately in the window covers. They were then held in place by spinning nuts onto the bolts. That way, no one would be missing a foot due to any guillotine action.

When I resumed work with my usual company, I noticed the behavior of stupidity was prevailing time and time again. It was the common sense among the crew members and myself that the office personnel should remain in the office. The superintendents each had their own individual workspaces within our main office building. From there, they would dole out pertinent information over the phone to each of their foremen concerning the daily operations on their jobsites. When any of us were assigned to working in the yard, we knew what had to be done there.

The many tasks that kept the yard in operation rarely changed; they were just ongoing. They included the loading and unloading of semitrailers that traveled to and from jobsites, the unloading of deliveries, and keeping the yard organized throughout each day. The organizing of that yard was an enormous job in itself since every foreman who entered there deemed themselves to be the most important person on the planet and had zero time available to put away any item in the space it was assigned to. They pretty much pulled into the yard and dumped whatever it was that they were returning onto the ground from wherever they had parked their vehicle. They expected whoever was working in the yard to put it away for them. The person who did not enjoy working in a messy environment was me. I ended up working in the yard for a few years after having a life-changing brain surgery which I will write about in the chapter "Challenging and Just Plain Scary."

It sucked when one day, our more aggressive (to put it as nicely as I can; f——k it, who am I kidding? ASININE) superintendent came out of the back door to the office and informed us employees working in the yard that a steam cleaning outfit was coming into the yard at his request. He wanted all of the heavy equipment to be power washed to get rid of the grease and dirt that had accumulated on the exterior of our equipment. It was easy for him to be an armchair heavy equipment operator when the only seat he was sitting in was an office chair. WTF! I explained to him that while a pressure washer would work on the exterior of the crane, it would not be advisable to use it on the boom butt and cable drum areas and especially not on the tracks. An operator spends a great deal of time pumping grease into a large array of zerk fittings that are located throughout the machine for lubrication of its many parts. A high-pressure stream of water would rinse free the grease needed there for maintenance. There's a placard placed on most heavy equipment that reads "I need grease to live."

All of my explanations went in one of his ears and out the other. I think it was more a matter of "that is going to happen because I SAY IT IS" rather than using common sense in his case (as was the case with many other men as well). I was very disappointed when I walked into the yard one morning to find the outfit that was hired pressure washing the entirety of my crane. I asked them to please be careful in the engine area to keep from dislodging any wires, zerk fittings, or small engine parts. I also pleaded with them to keep from getting my brake pads wet on my cable drums so that my brakes wouldn't slip when I operated the crane later in the day.

Our city's main marina makeover, I was removing all the old wood docks; it was like a giant video game: don't knock the men into the water and don't connect with the trees behind me

Bridges: I remember these two were far away.

Top photo: my daughter visited my jobsite, and I was explaining the progression of the structure; between her father, uncle, myself, and her stepdad, my daughter has witnessed nearly every significant structure coming to fruition in all their stages of construction; she can see a building and tell you which one, two, or three of us worked on it

LORRAINE REYNOLDS: See that guy grinning with Lorrie? He does that all the time when he has her as his helper. She likes her work here, she likes the crew, the job, the company. She likes the world, and we like Lorrie.

SUZAN UPPSTROM: "The kid" is only 19, and her hair is so long she can almost sit on it. A very warm, goodlooking woman. She works in the dust-collecting division.

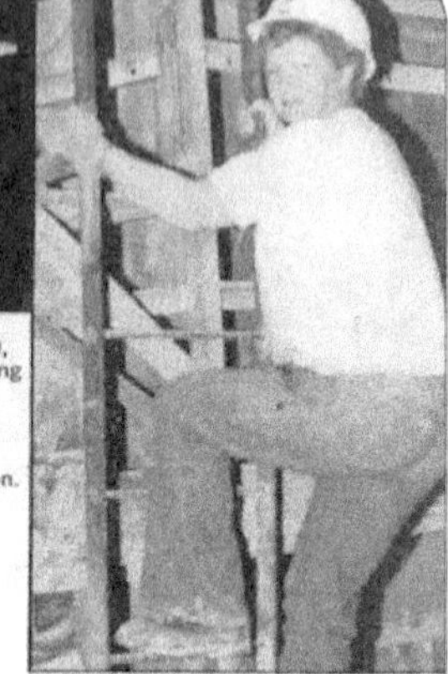

JOYCE REYES: Joyce grabs people and hugs them. Soon (after the first blush), people grab Joyce and hug her. It's a universal language. Joyce is a very hard worker, an extraordinary human being.

DIANE TAYLOR: Petite Diane rides a 650 Yamaha motorcycle almost 50 miles to work and back. She's a kiln-room employee, and it's hard to get her to smile for the camera. Diane is a strawberry blonde who wants to work in forestry.

FAYE JOHANSON: Faye's a dryer-helper, here in the dryer control room. She's small and very pretty, if you take away the hardhat and dust. A nice, intelligent person.

SANDRA WIKE (right): Sandy is full of mischief, and constantly teases the gang. They love it, and her. She's a lot of fun, but she still does her work. She took off her glasses when I took her picture; she probably couldn't see me.

Photos and captions by Author Hurley

One word tells why women are working in cement plant

By TOM HURLEY
Member, Local 46, Voice cartoonist and correspondent

SANTA CRUZ, CALIF.—If you were one of those who waited for the influx of women into the cement industry with some trepidation, take heart.

They didn't come—at least, to the Davenport plant of Lone Star Industries, Inc., in Santa Cruz—as a screaming hoard of "women's libbers," or as out-of-work truckdrivers in pin curls.

They came as just plain women, goodlooking and female. They wear lipstick, for the most part, and they, hate to have their pictures taken without combing their hair. They bring lunches that look a heckuva lot more tasty than our own.

Why they came to work in such an environment is simplicity itself.

I can spell it all out in one word: MONEY!

It might be a disappointment to someone, but that's the fact. At least, it is here.

No one seems to have been seeking adventure, no one is striking a crushing blow to male chauvinism, no "proving" anything, just money. That sums up the total motivation, male or female, for those who happen to be working here in the dust and noise.

When asked if they would still work in a cement plant if they could achieve the same wages elsewhere, more than half said they thought that working with men and doing physical labor in a plant such as this was more satisfying and "less stressful" than some other jobs they have done in the past.

All agreed they've been treated well by their coworkers and by management.

No one indicated any special problems.

I might note here that separate and adequate facilities have been provided for the women by the company.

Only one woman interviewed showed any hesitation when asked if she thought she might be able to handle all the jobs available to her at the plant. In all fairness, there are certain jobs that must be done that simply cannot be handled by all the men working there. In that respect, being male or female is not significant.

Do these new workers at the plant want to stay?

Most say they do, most certainly. Only two indicated they might have other plans.

As an old-timer who knows what the union has meant to us, I wondered if our women workers also understood. They did. They agreed that the pay and benefits were superior and that this would not have come about without union effort. For the most part, these women were without other union experience and new to the concept of unions. They were well aware of the sometimes unhappy press and image of unionism, and they had some thoughts about the matter. Actual experience seemed to them an important and positive declaration of the value of organized labor.

What would these women do if they could get the same pay and benefits working elsewhere?

Most I talked to said they'd rather stay put. They liked the "free" feeling (Continued on page 23)

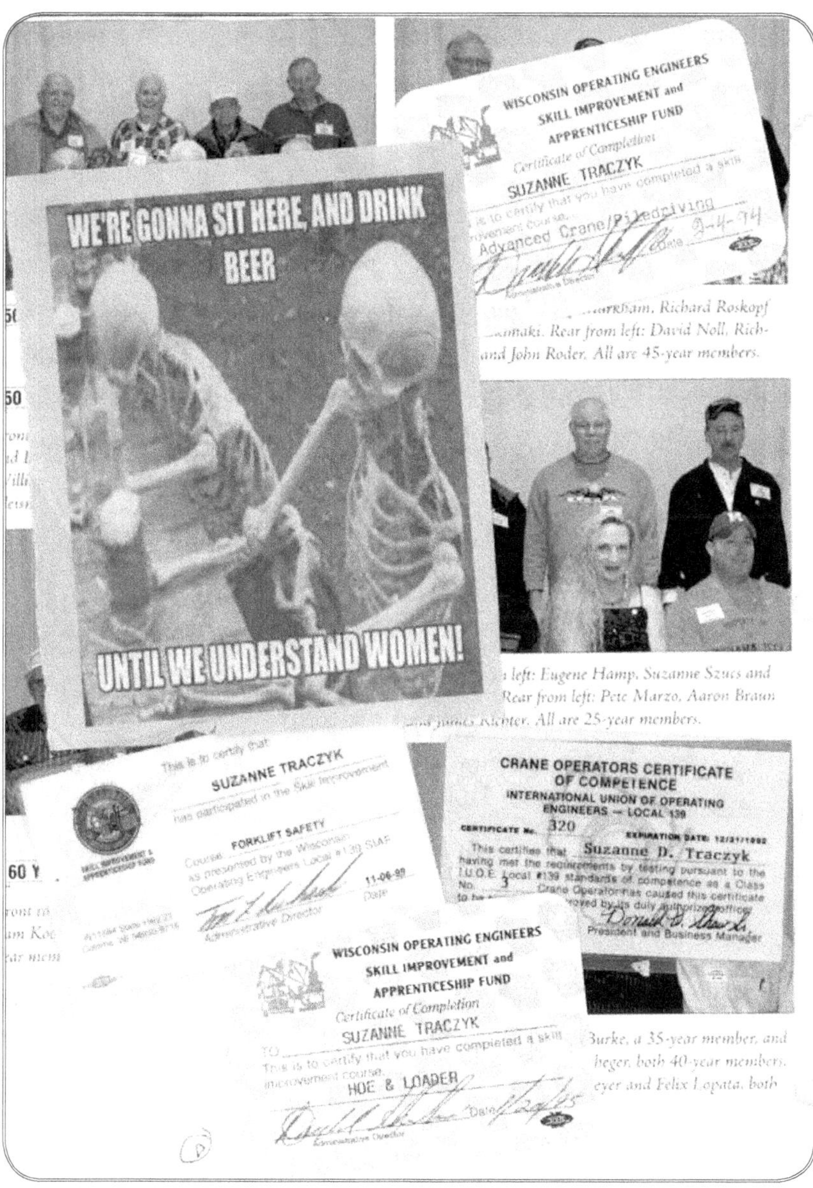
WE'RE GONNA SIT HERE, AND DRINK BEER
UNTIL WE UNDERSTAND WOMEN!

WISCONSIN OPERATING ENGINEERS
SKILL IMPROVEMENT and
APPRENTICESHIP FUND
Certificate of Completion
SUZANNE TRACZYK
Advanced Crane/Piledriving

SUZANNE TRACZYK
FORKLIFT SAFETY

WISCONSIN OPERATING ENGINEERS
SKILL IMPROVEMENT and
APPRENTICESHIP FUND
Certificate of Completion
SUZANNE TRACZYK
HOE & LOADER

CRANE OPERATORS CERTIFICATE
OF COMPETENCE
INTERNATIONAL UNION OF OPERATING
ENGINEERS — LOCAL 139
CERTIFICATE No. 320
Suzanne D. Traczyk
President and Business Manager

The mechanics had rolled out their power grease gun that ran off of electricity. They told me that I would have to replace the grease throughout the entire machine due to the pressure washing. It took me hours climbing all over that crane like a spider to thoroughly grease it. I was pissed off. WTF! All of that nonsense so that my crane's exterior could look clean until the wind picked up and blew dirt all over it again. All that because some asshole walked outside the office into the yard and opened his mouth!

The real surprise came when I entered the crane to dry out its brakes before operating it. I HAD NO FLOOR! I had parts of a floor, but when I looked down at my brake pedals, I could see the linkage that made them work and I had a clear view of the ground; then I was really pissed off! I marched into the office and told the obstinate superintendent that my worst scenarios about them using their pressure washer inside the cab of my crane had become a reality. He said, "Well, can't you put a piece of carpet or plywood down on the floor to cover the hole?"

"Uh, NO, my brake pedals are in the way." I then reminded him that there were three brakes rising from the floor of that crane because it was set up to drive pile (three drums of cable were required to drive piling, sometimes four; therefore there were three or four brakes to contend with; that was a main reason it was a difficult job to do).

He came out into the yard with me, and I showed him the huge hole in the floor of the crane's cab as we stood below it on the ground. "Wow!" he said. He looked at me and apologized, stating that he had no idea how fragile the old iron on that crane was, and then he just sauntered back into his office where he belonged. WTF, motherf——er! Needless to say, I froze my ass off every winter after that happened to that crane.

When the mechanics saw the hole in the crane's floor, they just shook their heads in disbelief that someone from the office could step into our world and wreak havoc on all the equipment the company owned. The poor mechanics were busy for days greasing and lubricating all the equipment that had been power washed. That included the heavy equipment that was located in the three yards, the boat shop, and all the jobsites within our area.

Another bridge I helped to build with the contractor known to do so was in a county outside our city. It was in an area where there were nothing but cornfields surrounding it. We were working directly next to the farmhouse whose occupants were responsible for those acres of corn. It was to be a small sturdy bridge to accommodate all of the heavy farm equipment that would be driving over it constantly during the growing and harvesting seasons. I was also surrounded by tall trees that lined the country road along with a power line that supplied electricity to both the farmhouse and the neighbors in that area.

We had to work from the center of the narrow country road. The traffic had been rerouted to accommodate us until the bridge was finished. The bridge was small, so I would be operating the sole crane on the project. I met with my crew members for the first time and was informed that they were not bringing out a port-a-potty to the project because I would be the only one using it (WTF?). The foreman told me that the men were fine with urinating behind a tree and usually brought their own rolls of toilet paper to the jobsite in case they had to take a dump (first, EW, and second, gross). WTF! I told him I was fine with walking out into the cornfield to pee, but if, in fact, no one dared to follow me out there. I said that if anyone entered that cornfield and caught me with my pants down, peeing, that I could promise that I would be the only person exiting that cornfield. If anyone needed me to operate the crane and I wasn't in the seat, they would have to engage a little patience, and I'd be with them as soon as possible.

As for the "taking a dump" portion of the human body's elimination process, I'd notify him when I'd be driving to the gas station located at the beginning of the country road we were working on. If anyone didn't like it, tough shit. He should've reminded himself how lucky he was that I was willing to go and pee in a cornfield! He looked at me and chuckled. Then he said, "All right then! Let's get to work." Apparently, I had passed his mental gymnastics portion of his field test.

It was a cool little job because everyone there worked together to unload all of the forms and set them into place. I swung in the concrete, and while it cured, I was out of the crane, stacking all of our materials we no longer needed, and banded them together for transport back to the yard. We all got along extremely well, and the job moved along smoothly. While the entire bridge was curing after our last pour of concrete, our crew was dispersed to other jobsites until it was time to go back and strip the forms from the bridge. I was sent to their yard to operate the crane and forklift there. I will write about that after I explain the WTF moment on this jobsite tale.

We were reassembled to strip the bridge free of its forms, clean them up for future use, stack and band them. The second day I showed up on the jobsite to finish the process of stripping the bridge, the only other person to show up was the foreman. He told me that he and his crew had been sent to work on another jobsite and that I could either work there alone or go to their yard and work until further notice. "WTF! What about finishing the stripping and loading out this job?" He told me that it was up to me what I chose to do that day. He explained that he'd already shown me everything that needed to be done there. The only problem was that I'd have no one else to help me do it (WTF! That was the "physical" portion of his field test!). I thought that for sure I could do that by myself. In fact, I was learning from working in my usual company's yard that I accomplished the most when I worked alone. I became my own solution to my problem by deciding to stay and strip the rest of the bridge myself. I would be climbing up and down from my crane many times throughout the day, but I chose to look at it like a giant StairMaster, like the one I used at the gym. I would be paid to work out! That was actually how I viewed every day in construction from the beginning—paid to work out. In that case, however, I would be my own boss and I'd have peace and quiet while I worked.

The WTF moment was who in the hell had one person working on a jobsite out in the middle of nowhere? If an accident were to happen, no one would have realized it unless someone happened to drive out to the jobsite to check on its progression, but it was a long drive and hard to find at that. That was before there were cell phones or pagers, and I would've had to drive myself all the way back to the nearest gas station in order to get any help from someone, and that was a good twenty-minute drive. Presently, one person left alone to work on a jobsite is not permitted for safety reasons. Men back then enjoyed antagonizing. To leave a woman alone on a solitary country road out in the woods is putting a target on her back. With all the martial arts training I had been through, an intruder onto that jobsite would have been wearing the target. I had numerous weapons to wield in all the tools I had surrounding me (everything is a weapon). I always carried my trusty screwdriver in my pocket anyway.

I succeeded in grouping together the materials to be loaded out and banded them. The bridge was ready for soil to be brought in and compacted around it once the crane was removed from the jobsite. I had only seen those stacking and banding requirements for that sole contractor. Each item had specifications on how many across and how high they were to be stacked. That allowed the entire area of the semitrailer to be utilized. It was like stacking big "cubes" onto the deck of the trailer, and it was easier and sturdier when it came to lashing everything down for transport.

The foreman who ran their yard came up with a printed diagram for each item or *items* entering his yard to be stacked into storage. Those pages were distributed to each foreman in the company. If a jobsite didn't comply with the measurements that he'd laid out in detail and a messy load of materials were trucked into his yard, he sent it back to be reloaded properly. That mistake was rarely made by a foreman because the excessive transportation costs reflected negatively toward that jobsite's foreman; it also detracted from the job's profit margin.

I loved his yard because it was the most organized one I'd ever worked in. I tried my damndest to make my usual company's yard an organized and clean area for everyone.

Unfortunately for me, I was the only one there interested in keeping a presentable work area. I always thought of the yard as my own personal "Menard's" lumberyard.

The head honchos of the company with the beautifully structured yard would cut bonuses usually provided to the foreman on a jobsite completion unless they failed to honor the code of the yard foreman; yep, money talks! I worked in their yard, learning where everything went with the assistance of his helper who happened to be a woman. I learned that both the foreman and his helper were in the laborer's union. When I was brought in to operate the crane for them, I was upset to find my hourly pay rate lowered as their "yard" crane operator compared to when I worked out on a jobsite. It was for that reason that when I was offered a full-time permanent position by the foreman to be his crane operator, I declined. As much as I enjoyed the more peaceful and relaxed work environment there, I was in it for the money and therefore asked to be placed back on a jobsite or release me to work for another contractor.

I explained to the woman that she could make a hell of a lot more money by becoming an operating engineer and that I could teach her how to operate the equipment they had in their yard so that she could take the test up at the operator's school to become an apprentice. I was surprised when she told me that she would be too intimidated to work on an actual jobsite and that she preferred to keep her position in the yard at her current pay rate. WTF! I was *floored!*

This next job could also go in the chapter "Challenging and Just Plain Scary." I've written that last sentence so many times that I will take a pause here to let you know that there's a challenging and scary context to any situation on any jobsite. You get so used to what it is that you do professionally out on a jobsite that you could become complacent. It's hard not to take the safety of your work for granted because your circumstances could change in an instant. I know that for each time the voice inside my head said, "I'm crushing this pile driving today (or setting iron, etc., you get the picture)," the shit hit the fan. WTF! Always remember that there is someone better at what you do. There is also someone who is not as good at what you do, if that's any consolation. This piece of advice goes along with anyone's path in life. Keep your head in the game and practice the art of "Satori"; that's Japanese for "live in the moment."

Onward to an intense bridge job with the same bridge building outfit. I had already made up my mind that they were the most unsafe contractor that I'd ever worked with, and I was considering terminating my future work endeavors with them. The practices they used out on a jobsite were theirs alone and not up to the safety standards I was trained to work by.

The bridge reconstruction was in a county far to the north. I parked my vehicle in the ride share area offered for public use at one end of the bridge and walked across it to the crane I could see on the other side. There was a mechanic going over the boom that had been lowered down to a horizontal position to the ground. I assumed that he was greasing it's lubrication points in anticipation of my operating it. I grabbed my grease gun and went over to assist in its maintenance. I introduced myself and was extremely surprised when he informed me that not only the crane was I to operate but the crane on the opposite side of the bridge had been toppled by high winds. It had happened because neither crane had been tied off to a "dead man" and had swung through their brakes. I was there to tear the crane down and load it out so that another crane could be brought in for me to operate.

After nearly a week of exchanging cranes, we were finally ready to finish the reconstruction of that bridge. I set precast along the off-ramp to look nice while at the same time holding the soil of the hillside back. I was ever mindful of the transformers behind me and the powerlines connecting to them. Things went smoothly until they told me that it was time to strip the wooden concrete forms from our side of the overpass. Those forms had been used to pour the cement for the walls and pedestrian walkways on the bridge. I had noticed a crane parked in the center of the freeway when I first started on the job. The crane had barriers around it to keep the traffic from hitting it. That was the crane they had used to set the forms and pour the concrete that made up the bridge. I thought, *WTF! I would have four lanes of traffic whipping by me in both directions.* Was it going to be a stressful event? You bet your sweet ass it was!

The worse part of that scenario was that even though they attached a tagline to the form so that the man in front of my crane could grab onto it in order to land the piece, it was spinning in the air and flying about like a failed kite. In the meantime, the traffic kept speeding along underneath where we were working! Any form removed from the bridge could have easily gone through a windshield if the men on the bridge above me didn't properly secure it's rigging. Every pick presented itself as a potential disaster. I was alarmed that they didn't at least shut down one lane of the freeway until we had the bridge stripped. At break time, I brought up my concerns to the foreman, and he said that if I was "afraid to do it," he'd ask the operator of the other crane on the opposite side of the bridge to do it.

I told him that I would continue to do it, but I wanted to complete the task as soon as possible and be done with it. I also wanted him to record in writing the fact that I'd expressed my concerns about the safety factor in the work we were doing. In that way, if a form did break free and was damaged or caused any property damage, my ass would be covered somewhat. WTF! Heaven forbid if I didn't have the *cajones* to do a job that one of the male operators was willing to do! Boobs are, after all, bigger than balls!

It was a huge relief for me to remove all the forms from the bridge and have them safely secured on the ground before me. We stacked and banded them so that they were ready to load out. My next harrowing task was simply to walk (RUN!) back across two lanes of speeding traffic so that I could get to my car and leave for the day. No one would slow down enough for me to get off of the expressway! WTF! Everyone had already gone home by the time I finally crossed through the traffic to go home. I did not EVER want to operate a crane from the center of an open highway EVER again—and I didn't! You have to draw your own line in the sand. That procedure was just too unsafe in my book. Nowadays, they HAVE to shut down the lane or lanes they're working above—WTF!

I was off to operate a crane for that same contractor refurbishing yet another bridge. That one spanned a wide, deep, and fast-moving river. It was also high above the river by about sixty feet. It was a hell of a drive for me to get there. It was far to the southwest of where I lived. The hours were long ones. I was operating an older large hydraulic crane. It was big enough to lift a work platform full of men and their equipment over the side of the crane. I had to carefully hoist the men on the platform over the side wall of the bridge, lower it below the bridge deck, and then boom up as I lowered the load of men so that they fit snuggly below and underneath the bridge. It was very tricky because any sharp movements could cause one or more of the men to fall off of the platform. That was before there were mandatory man baskets and hoists that are used today. They did have harnesses they wore by then and attached themselves by lanyards to the platform.

That was before there were cell phones, and on that jobsite, there were no radios or walkie-talkies. They would either keep a signalman in front of my crane to let me know when they wanted me to move ahead or else they would just yell up to me to do so. That was extremely unsafe, but that was how that outfit worked back then. I was shocked that I had no way of communicating with the men to know that they were all right working essentially underneath me! I'd worked in the blind plenty of times, and if you just make the necessary movements you are signaled to make, you'll be fine. My signalman had to lean over the side of the bridge all day in order to get instructions from the foreman down below.

It was when they needed my signalman's help down on the platform that caused me to ponder, *WTF!* The foreman told me that when he whistled loudly for me to lift my outrigger stabilizers just enough to allow me to drive slowly ahead with the crane until he whistled again. I was then to set down the stabilizers and level up the crane so that they could continue working in the next area.

That procedure saved us a lot of time compared with me hoisting that big platform out from underneath the bridge and hoisting them up and over the wall so that I could then drive the crane ahead. Yes, that saved us a lot of time, but if I happened to bounce at all as I was slowly driving ahead, the men below me could bounce their heads against the concrete bridge above them. Worse yet, a man could have become dislodged from the platform and be hanging from it, holding on for dear life, or if they weren't tied off, plunge to their death far below. I would've had no way of knowing what was going on with them because I simply couldn't see them! I found it hard to believe that they had been hanging men over and underneath bridges like that, but they assured me that it was their usual procedure and that many crane operators before me had done it in the manner we were doing it.

WTF! I would say a prayer every time I had to lift them on that platform up and over the bridge wall—"Will they make it or will they drop into the river below?" Once again, that job could have been written in the chapter "Challenging and Just Plain Scary," but I said "WTF!" so many times on that job each day that it ended up in this chapter.

If there was such a thing as doing *"TOO GOOD OF A JOB,"* this one was it for me. I was my usual company's yard crane operator at that time. As I've written before, the yard list of tasks to be accomplished throughout each day was unending. There were just not enough hours in the workday, and there were constant interruptions that included unannounced deliveries that would show up to be unloaded. There was the loading and unloading of semitrailers that were coming or going to various jobsites. All of those interruptions were a priority and an emergency which required my immediate attention. WTF! Everyone I came in contact with was more important than anyone else (in THEIR OWN MINDS, that is).

If I was laid off for any amount of time or sent out to operate a crane on a jobsite, whatever was unloaded off the semitrailers during my absence was left off to the sides of the yard. They would leave all of it for me to deal with when I returned. It was as if I were a mom picking up after too many messy sons, WTF!

It was during a very busy time for me in the yard that a crane operator had to be replaced so that he could attend a funeral for a family member. He needed to travel out of the state immediately. I was sent to his jobsite to drive pile with his crane. The job had only begun a few weeks beforehand.

A new stage was to be built on our city's festival grounds that were located adjacent to our Lake Michigan. The atmosphere was nice with a beautiful view of the lake. It was nice to be on the secluded festival grounds in the off season. There were hardly any people who worked full-time there in comparison to the huge crowds of people who attended all the concerts and events whenever a festival was in operation. The grounds are home to one of our country's largest celebrations of music; it's called "Summerfest." We were driving pile so that a new comedy stage could be built upon it. We were also driving pile to hold up decorative precast walls which would be flower planters that divided the stage area from the majority of the public walkway.

The project manager came out of his office to meet with me. He told me that there was only one restriction that I needed to adhere to. I was not to track my friction crane over the manhole that was centrally located in *the middle of our jobsite!* In that instance, it was actually a large grate to allow rainwater to run off into the sewer system. Any manhole of any kind presented a weak area in the ground's surface. The weight of the crane could very easily have collapsed the manhole and its surrounding area. I told him that I would have a spotter to make sure the manhole remained clear of my tracks whenever I had to move my crane.

He had a doubtful and troubling expression on his face that I'd seen on almost every superintendent or foreman's face the first time I walked onto a jobsite. It never got old, my feelings of disdain for the lack of encouragement or exuberance that a female crane operator could walk onto a jobsite and *CRUSH IT!* Thank God, I usually changed their minds upon the jobs completion. WTF! Why did I have to deal with that same crap every time I walked onto a new jobsite?

I told my crew that I had A LOT of work to do in the yard. While I was helping them during their crane operator's absence, my own work was piling up even more. I wanted to put as many pile into the ground as possible and knock that job out so that I could return to my own area and catch up on my work there. They understood my situation, having seen it all for themselves every time they had entered our yard. It was a good thing my hardworking pile driver buddy was there. He would be marking out the pile we'd be driving and rigging it up for me. Every time I would swing the crane around to pick up another pile to drive, he'd have it ready to go. All he had to do was put the pile chain around the pipe pile so that I could hoist it up, swing around with it, and pound it down into the ground. We worked together like a well-oiled machine. "Pound, swing, pick up, swing, pound"—we kept that rhythm up all day long, putting the most pile into ground in one day than they'd been taking three days to pound in.

We finished the entire area required to build the comedy stage and then needed to cross over to the other side of the grounds and drive pile to hold concession stands and bleachers on for the Miller Brewery Stage. It was one of the larger stage areas where some of the widely known bands would play. Our problem was that there was a "sky glider" overhead that carried passengers down the main pedestrian road that we needed to travel under.

They expected to have to break the crane down in order to track under the glider. We would have had to drop the hammer out of the leads and disconnect it, drop the leads (that the hammer rides inside of when driving pile), and disconnect those, take the boom out of the crane, and truck all those items to our new jobsite destination. That would have taken us one to two days to complete. Once on the opposite side of the sky glider, we'd have to put our equipment all back together again, taking the same amount of time.

I told them that I'd been in a similar situation before when I had to walk a crane underneath powerlines and didn't have the time or space to remove those powerlines. The pile driver foreman rode on top of my crane's roof, holding a long, wooden two-by-four. As we approached the high wires, he lifted them up with the wooden piece of lumber just enough for the high points of my crane to travel under them free and clear of touching them.

We would do the same thing to crawl underneath the sky glider. I lowered the leads and hammer at the same time. We disconnected them, and I told the forklift operator to slowly and carefully pull them along the pavement to the other side where we were to work. I then lowered my boom all the way to the ground, placing my boom's tip on a piece of plywood to keep it from scraping along the ground as I tracked. I slowly tracked under the glider with my buddy up on the roof, lifting the sky glider's cables as we passed underneath. As soon as my boom tip traveled beyond the glider, I began booming up. By the time the crane had cleared the glider completely, I was already boomed all the way back up into place. We quickly attached our cables to the hammer and leads and, at the same time, hoisted them up together. We were back in business that same day. We even drove in a couple of pile before our shift ended.

Before I continue, let me just tell you that back in my days as an operator, a time-saving trick like that was considered awesome; it never happens in present time. The rules have changed. OSHA has tightened the regulations for what you can do and can't do anymore. To go against *the powers that be* will get you a warning or cost you your job. That was a big reason I was glad to have been trained "old school." We thought out of the box and did what we needed to do to get the job done safely; just not always according to the candy-ass rules that govern jobsites today.

After that time-saving maneuver, the superintendent came up to me and treated me like I was his long-lost buddy, boobs be damned! He could not believe that I came up with that idea that saved us so much time. He was so impressed by the amount of pile we'd driven since I was in the crane seat that he called the head superintendent back at my company's office and requested that I remain the crane operator until the job was completed.

I f——ked myself! I was in such a hurry to work through that job so that I could return to my own that I was then stuck there working even longer than originally planned. As I write this as a much older and wiser woman, I will tell you the great lesson I learned from that jobsite. I was an asshole to think and behave that way. Whether it's your work at home, your job (whatever that may be), or your day-to-day requirements, there will ALWAYS be work.

At whatever area in your life, the list of chores both big and small is endless. You'll no sooner finish one task when another one appears on your radar. There are no free moments until you close your eyes each night. For myself, back during my work years, I even dreamt I was driving pile in my sleep or setting iron. There was a constant pinging of the iron hammer as it struck the iron pipe pile.

I thought it would drive me to insanity, and maybe it did at times. I would wake up thinking I had finished my shift at work (in my dreams) only to be dumbfounded to realize my alarm was going off, arise, and go to work for real! Some mornings, it took me a few moments to realize if I was at work or home!

That's why it's so important to appreciate each day. Cut yourself some slack. There is only so much you can do in one day, no matter what it is you are doing. There I was at a clean jobsite with fresh air that permitted me a beautiful view of the lake as I worked. Rather than fully enjoy my surroundings and the fact that I was working alongside decent men for a change, all I could think about was hurrying back to a super hectic and stressful dusty as f——k yard where I was expected to do everyone else's jobs as well as my own. I was eagerly willing to leave a job where I was fully appreciated to go to one where I was not and instead felt taken for granted. That was really f——ked up!

After walking away from that job, upon its completion, I learned to notice something beautiful throughout the day (such as my view of the lake) because it is that one beautiful vision that will hold your sanity and dignity close to you. Now I know as you've been reading about my trials and tribulations in this chapter, you've been thinking to yourselves, "Why all the swearing, Suzanne? WTF is up with that bullshit?" To your question, I will offer you this explanation: *"Swearing is the native tongue spoken in construction."* I found that to be true early in my career after my first layoff.

I was raising my young impressionable daughter when I was working in the construction world as a union crane operator. At home, I tried very hard to choose my words carefully around her so that she had a fighting chance of growing up free from inheriting a "sailor's mouth" from either myself or her ironworker father. Although I could control myself, I had zero control over my husband's vocabulary. Instead, I used the words that were my go-tos as I grew up. Those words were *shoot, heck,* and *darn!* If I found myself really perturbed, I'd go a little farther by saying, *"Darn it!"* I learned those words because my mom said them then as well as now.

I used to get a lot of crap about it from all of my surfer buddies in high school. I'd hear them try to rattle me by saying over and over again in their sing-song voices, *"Shoot, heck, darn, shoot, heck, darn"* over and over. They'd sing it like it was a Martian language they'd never heard before. It drove me nuts and embarrassed the hell out of me which, of course, was their objective.

When I would come back to work and be thrust into the lion's den of men cursing, farting, and blowing snot out of their noses, it was a culture shock for me. I'd been so diligent about refraining from swearing in front of my daughter that my clean untarnished vocabulary was what I brought back to work with me. That was usually met with the sing-song voices and again taunting me with, *"Shoot, heck, darn. Shoot, heck, darn."*

Oh no, not again, would be my first thoughts. It would inevitably wake the beast within myself until I burst out with, "All right, you candy-ass motherf——kers, want me to f——king swear? Goddamn it, I will! Now get your goddamn f——king asses back to f——king work and cut the shit and shut your f——king mouths! Let's go, you f——king f——ks!" That would generally cause the carved pumpkin faces to appear. The ones I've described before with the gaping O-shaped mouths and the wide awake open eyes. That was one way to silence a group of juvenile delinquents! It really is true what they say men will never grow up; they're just larger boys. Then there's the other saying, "Can't live with them, can't live with them." Amen to that, sisters!

As far as the swearing goes, you are a product of your environment, so to speak. Hell, I even heard my devout Christian crew members drop the "F-bomb" on occasion out of frustration. What you experience on a jobsite in the field of construction is like walking on Jupiter or Mars compared to a job in retail, the food industry, or, for example, a secretary. I know this to be true because I *was* a secretary for a period of time, and I was bored out of my goddamned mind. Filing papers and answering phones all day was just not my cup of tea.

There were no words to use on those situations, such as "I can't believe my own ears and eyes. Is this really happening right now?"

"Did he really just say (or do) that to me?" Or my personal favorite, "Oh no you didn't!" or "NOT happening here!" or "GET OUT OF THE GODDAMNED WAY!" Those reasons were what the expression "What the f——k!" was made for. Turns out the guys were right; "shoot," "heck," or "darn" just didn't cut it!

So that is my explanation for all the swearing in this chapter. It is what it is. What more can I say? As for the shocker pregnancy I mentioned and didn't elaborate on, some things in life should remain private. For those of us who live with or have lived with anyone struggling with one addiction or another or who lived in or are living in an abusive situation: "No one's stories are worse than anyone else's. They are all shitty, and none of us deserve to live like that." The only people we can enhance toward the positive are ourselves. The lessons for those we've attempted to help or fix are theirs alone to learn, not ours to teach. I figured that out after sixteen years in my first marriage. I also learned that mental abuse is just as bad if not worse than physical abuse. We each as human beings need to work on our own issues and learn our own lessons in life.

Now, as promised, your reward for enduring all the WTFs you've read and other obnoxious curse words: Here's "CRITTERS."

CRITTERS

You can't work outside and not come across critters of some sort: winged ones or four-legged ones, furry ones, or feathered ones, the world of construction and Mother Nature are bound to collide. They fall victim to their environments being disrupted. I had no clue that I'd be playing a part in the dismantling and destroying of so many tiny worlds. It just never occurred to me that critters would come into the picture, but they most certainly did. I did my best to redeem my good karma by coming to their assistance whenever I could to make up for my uninvited presence.

Remember that television advertisement many years ago that said, "You can't fool Mother Nature"? Well, it's true. Mother Nature is not going to move out of your way so that you can roll on in anywhere you want with big heavy equipment like excavators, cranes, front-end loaders, and such. They won't compromise their freedom for all the two-legged forms of life marching through in their hard hats either.

Here are a few tales in which I tried to make up for my unexpected intrusions or those days I simply appreciated the enhancements they granted me by adding a little beauty to my day and putting a smile on my face.

When I was an apprentice, just starting my journey called a "career," the first big jobsite I was sent to was the Jones Island Sewage Treatment Plant. I've already written plenty of stories of my close encounters of the freaky kind, and this tale is no exception. As I walked through the security gates, the first thing I saw was a huge vat of human waste being churned by a giant steel wand. Seagulls were riding on that wand, around and around, oblivious to its tremendous stench. I remember thinking, *What the f——k kind of shit-churning bacteria-filled ride are those birds fighting each other to ride on? YUCK! and PEW!* That would prove to be a picture embossed on my brain that would be hard to erase during my coffee break and lunchtimes.

There were two big cranes, our crew, and another crane we would be putting together to drive in a lot of pile. All of the pile would be holding up a multistoried building that was to be put together with a lot of iron and covered with precast panels. An even larger crane was being brought in and put together to raise the iron and set the precast by the main contractor in charge of the project. To my happiness and surprise, the larger crane came with a female oiler apprentice. YEAH! another girl! I was so excited to meet one other woman in a sea of one to two hundred men working on the jobsite.

We became fast friends, and since we were both new at being union operators and oilers on the jobsite, we had to show up for grease time one half hour before the crews showed up for work. It was very dark out with only the building beside us illuminating our project with its security lights. We both had to bring in flashlights so that we could see our locks to insert our keys into in order to enter our cranes. We also needed the flashlights to spot all of our zerk fittings we needed to grease before starting up our cranes' engines.

Our cranes sat far down below ground level. That area was to become the basement of the new building to be erected. The cranes had carefully crawled down a ramp that the backhoe and bulldozer operators had created for them to get into place. That was the only way in or out of the project.

One morning, we had our insulated coveralls on due to the winter weather making it's swift arrival. We could hardly move with all the winter attire we were bundled up in. We also were bogged down by our lunch boxes, thermoses, tools, and materials we'd need for the day. I had just unloaded all of the items I'd carried and was concentrating on unlocking my crane's doors and removing it's window covers when I heard her scream out, "WTF!" I nearly jumped out of my skin! I spun around and she was already standing by my crane telling me in an alarmed voice, "There is the biggest rat walking around my crane!"

I've never been a gal who's afraid of rodents. I had a pair of rats, some mice, and various hamsters and guinea pigs for pets as a kid. Apparently, she didn't share my sentiments where rodents were concerned. In fact, she was beside herself, going into maniac mode.

"It's okay, it's a lot smaller than you are," I said, attempting to calm her down. Then to poke a little fun at her, I said, "Besides, you're a tough as nails construction bitch here!" I laughed, trying to diffuse the situation with some humor. "I'll go over there and shoo it away for you so that you can get your crane checked out," I added. I walked over to her crane, searching for the rat with my flashlight as I went. The beam of my flashlight caught some movement, so I shone the full beam of light on where I saw motion. *HELLO!* There it was, and it was the only "rat" I've ever seen that was as big as a cat and had a WHITE STRIPE running down it's back to boot!

"HOO, HAW, HEE!"

I took short sharp breaths to calm my startled self. I backed away ever so carefully, not to make any sudden movements or loud noises so that I didn't alarm (or more appropriately, ARM) the SKUNK! "Did you see it? Did you see it?" my still excited girlfriend asked.

"I don't know what rats look like where you live, but that is NOT a rat; it's a f——king SKUNK!" I no sooner said those words, and she turned around and hightailed it up the ramp and out of the hole. What the f——k was I standing there for? I grabbed my belongings and walked back up the ramp too. In the meantime, the skunk could enjoy his or her breakfast in peace.

The crane operators showed up and were surprised by the silence of the cranes and the sight of their oilers standing on top of the ramp, looking down into the massive hole that was our job-site. "What's up, ladies? We got to get to work," my crane operator asked. "Mother Nature has put a kibosh on our start-up time this morning," I answered. "A skunk is dining on the garbage you guys threw out of your crane cabs yesterday, and we're waiting for it to walk away from the rigs. If I get sprayed, I'm going home, so I took a position on top of the ramp so I'd be out of its range of attack."

"Well, it looks like we'll have our coffee break now instead of our usual time today until the stinky bastard gets the hell out of the hole," said my girlfriend's crane operator.

The third crane operator said that we'd better be ready to move out of the skunk's way if he exits the same way he entered, which was the ramp. Although we all laughed at his remark, we were indeed ready to haul ass out of there! That skunk didn't give a shit that he (or she) was dining in a sewage treatment plant because he/she could out stink all of the human waste processed on the island!

The skunk finally waddled his way up the ramp, taking his sweet time. He looked over at us stationed alongside the adjacent build-ing as we were waiting for his exit. His little beady eyes seemed to say, "HA, HA, HA! I have something you don't have, and it's not aromatherapy!"

That striped critter taught me to bring in garbage bags every day on the jobsites I worked on from that day forward. I did NOT want to work in a dump and I did NOT want to be greeted in the morning by an unexpected stinky surprise!

My garbage collection efforts did not deter a raccoon from raiding a dumpster now and then. Every so often, I would find one stuck in a dumpster, unable to climb out. They seemed to repeat that behavior, failing to recall that they were unable to escape from them in the past. I would go retrieve whatever piece of lumber I could find to angle down into the dumpster so that they could "walk the plank," freeing themselves of their captivity.

The guys thought I was nuts. They could've cared less about a captive raccoon or any other bird or animal, for that matter. They would say things like, "Why are you wasting your time? Just leave him in there. That's what he gets for dumpster diving in the first place." To that, I would always reply, "What the f——k is wrong with you, you mean motherf——kers! If I find you stuck somewhere, I'll leave *YOUR* ass there!"

They would shake their heads and walk away. The funny thing about saving a raccoon that's stuck in a dumpster is that they don't want anyone observing their escape. They would wait until they could not see, hear, or smell humans. I only saw a couple of them exit. I would want them out of the dumpsters because people were always throwing garbage into them throughout the day. It got to a point where if someone saw a plank of wood protruding in an angular fashion out of the dumpster, they knew I was on a raccoon rescue mission. They would leave their bundles of refuse on the ground beside the dumpster, knowing that I'd put it inside once its prisoner had escaped.

One morning, as I walked into the yard, passing by the dumpster, I checked inside to see if there were any captive critters who had decided to raid it the night before. There were two eyes peering up at me. It was the biggest gnarliest raccoon I'd ever seen trapped in a dumpster. I think he was so large that he felt insecure about waddling out on the plank of wood I stuck in the dumpster for him. I kept peeking periodically to see if he had departed yet. Every time I looked at him, he snarled as if to say, "What the f——k are you looking at, bitch? Haven't you ever been stuck somewhere before? WTF!" Thankfully, when I peered in at the end of my shift, the ornery furball had left the dumpster—WHEW!

Birds will make nests ANYWHERE. It's a good thing that one of the first pieces of business you're trained to address each morning before you start any piece of equipment is to check all your fluid levels in the machine. One crisp early spring morning, I was to drive one of the giant frontend loaders to our Gran Trunk yard to load big boulders onto one of our barges. Once loaded, the barge would then be pushed by one of our tugboats south on Lake Michigan, down to a jobsite along the shore of Illinois.

I lifted the huge and heavy cover off of the radiator, only to find myself looking into the gaping mouths of four tiny baby birds in a nest waiting for food to be flown in by their mother. The nest had been built right next to the radiator cap that I needed to twist open to check the antifreeze level. I looked around me and found the mom perched on the roof of one of our sheds that we used for storage. I had my gloves on and thought that if I moved the nest, she would not be offended by my human scent.

I moved the nest onto the roof where I'd seen her perched so that she could see it clearly. As I warmed up my machine, I kept my eye on her. She would fly from one point to another, surrounding the nest, but she would not fly to the nest directly. I drove off of the yard property and went on to complete my task at hand.

After a long day of loading boulders, I finally was able to return to the yard and check on the nest. Loud chirping sounds were emanating from the nest with no mother in sight at all. I became very worried for the hungry tiny baby tufts of feathers. I didn't spot the mother bird the entire time I was locking up my machine and placing the window covers on it. I took leave of all my safety gear I had on and took my daily whore's bath to wash away all the grease that had transferred to my body throughout the day and still there was no mother bird in sight. WTF! I couldn't take on four tiny baby birds! I didn't have time to squish worms and feed them constantly to baby birds, never mind finding the worms in the first place!

I could not go home with a clear conscience, knowing that those vulnerable babies were left defenseless and starving on the roof of the shed. They would have either frozen to death by the next morning or have been picked off by our resident hawk or our community of raccoons that lived beneath our trailers. That was when I became a well-known animal delivery service to our city's Humane Society.

I made a phone call from our yard office, using the phone on my foreman's desk. I explained my dilemma to the woman who had answered. She told me to bring the nest with the baby birds on in and that they had volunteers there who would take the time to feed the babies. Thank God, what a relief! Although it would cost me a lot of time driving the feathered orphans to their nonpermanent home, I proceeded to do it. Before I left with the nest of baby birds secured in a box with rags tucked around it, my boss looked at me like I was nuts. He shook his head in disbelief and said, "WTF Suzanne, are you nuts? It's just some baby birds. We have plenty of birds flying around here. They would have been food for some other hungry creature."

One bird insisted upon building a nest in the tip of my yard crane's boom. Every year, that silly bird would risk bouncing around 110 feet up in the air as I boomed up, down, and swung all around. I'd see that bird and think, "*Pleeeeezzze* don't build a nest up there!" I would envision either an egg plopping to the ground from way up there, or worse yet, a baby ball of feathers plunging to its death. Not only did I have to worry about the safety of the humans working around me, but I was then responsible for the lives of baby creatures. WTF! Oh, the added pressure and stress. Whenever I had to lay my boom down to the ground so that I could grease the boom tip sheaves and oil the rollers that ran along the top, I would pull out the incomplete nest to give the determined mother-to-be bird the idea that my boom tip was NOT an ideal nesting site.

She never could take the hint, however, and continued to try and build one up there year after year. She would always get tired of trying to keep up with the movement of the boom and eventually abandon her original nest site plans. Why on Earth did she have to try and build it there in the first place? Maybe her tiny bird brain couldn't remember the results she had the previous year.

One wet and muddy spring, we had a section of sheeting wall collapse into our main river. That section ran along our Gran Trunk yard, and we figured that the tons of large boulders we stored there to load onto barges caused the collapse. We first relocated all of those large boulders and then brought in heavy equipment and materials to repair the damage. We brought one of our cranes that was permanently mounted on a barge up the river. It was going to be driving in a new section of sheeting wall just outside the collapsed section. Once the sheets were driven in, long rods would be driven underneath about ten foot of ground and be welded to iron beams to help hold the new sheeting wall in place.

When it was all secure, it was backfilled and compacted to solidify the soil. That was a long project, and I was the operator of a large extending forklift that had outriggers on it to allow me to be able to not only lift heavy bundles of sheeting but also the iron beams we were using. I had quite a distance to scope loads of iron and timbers out from the land and onto the barge the crane was on.

The crane operator had his hands full and could rarely leave his seat, so I would walk over the ramp to the barge and put down blocking so that I could get back in my forklift and drop off the load I was delivering. The crane operator got my attention, and thinking that he needed me to get something for him, I walked over and stood near him next to his crane door. Instead of needing my assistance, he shared with me the fact that a bird had built a nest in an iron compartment located in the base of the boom butt.

He told me that the barge had been sidelined long enough for the mother bird to build her nest, and when the crew prepared the barge to move up the river to the jobsite, the eggs had hatched. He didn't want to disturb the nest by trying to relocate it. In spite of all the commotion and noise of the jobsite, the mother bird kept bringing food to her babies. She was a very determined mother bird! Those baby birds would have a nice surprise when they finally flew away, realizing their world would not be such a noisy place after all. The nests that we *were* used to finding on the barges were those built by mother ducks and geese. The barges were docked riverside in our Gran Trunk yard when they were not in use. That was also where they were parked in order for our huge frontend loaders to load them up with the various-sized boulders we stored in that yard. The men were annoyed by all the nests and would kick them off the barge and into the river. They especially didn't like the geese because they would shit all over the barge, and every so often, a crew member would slip in some of the shit and fall on their ass. You must always watch where you stepped on land or anywhere else in my book, so I think that was their own fault.

I always felt bad for the nesting mothers that I came across whenever I operated a crane on one of the barges because it would end up being too busy and too noisy. They would soon abandon their nests and fly elsewhere. One day, as I took my first steps onto one of our barges, I noticed that a mother duck had built her nest right inside one if my crane's track pads. I told her that I was sorry for the noise that I was about to make but that I'd stay out of her way the best that I could. I told her to hang in there because it was going to be a bumpy ride.

I told all the crew members and the foreman that if anyone disturbed the mother duck in the nest by trying to remove it from its position or by attempting to scare her off the nest on purpose that I'd make sure they would be taking an ice-cold dip in our polluted river! The mother duck managed to put up with us noisy loud humans for the entire day, but she was not there the next morning or for that following day. At that point, the eggs had been unprotected from the frigid temperatures for an extended period of time, and I knew that the eggs had frozen. The foreman working on another barge told me that a mother goose had made a nest, and as soon as she abandoned it, he put an egg in one of his inside pockets of his insulated winter coat. Between his jacket and his body heat, the egg made it through the workday. He told me that he kept it under a warm light in his trailer until he could take it to his property in the northern part of our state.

He and his wife kept ducks and chickens there for the eggs they provided them. Later on another jobsite, when I asked him if the egg had hatched, he told me that it did. He had one of his chickens hatch it with her own eggs and said it looked hilarious to see his chicken with her brood, and one of them was taller than any other bird they owned! His gosling probably thought himself (or herself) to be a chicken. Since his property was so far up north, it was impossible for him to drive back and forth to go home during the week. He stayed in his trailer that he'd parked in a campground. His wife was left on her own to care for all of their chickens, ducks, their new goose, their pig, and cow. She had kept one of their roosters for a pet and took him everywhere with her. She thought that it was fun to sew miniature costumes for her rooster to wear, and she would then photograph her dressed up bird.

It was fall when I was sent out on a job where he was my foreman. I was to be his crane operator, and we were to drive pile. One morning, before work, he showed me a picture his wife had given him of her rooster. She had hand-sewn him a tiny costume for Halloween. There was the rooster, dressed up like the devil! She was going to take her rooster along when she took their grandchildren trick-or-treating; it was hilarious! He did *not* share in my laughter at the photograph, however. He told me that he was worried that she was alone up in the woods for too long and was beginning to lose her marbles.

That made me laugh even harder, even though he was as serious as a heart attack. I told him that she should put together a calendar of her rooster in costumes for each month of the year. I told him that she could make a fortune; hell, I would have bought one for myself. That was before there were cell phones or the Internet and before we had heard of "Grumpy Cat" or any of the other celebrity animals that we see today.

I told him that she could sell her calendars at Farm and Fleet, which is a store that sells everything from work clothes to farm equipment and supplies for animals and livestock. He told me that I was not being helpful to his situation with my suggestions. Even though I was being serious, he thought that I was just busting his balls about it. I never found out if any of my suggestions made it to fruition. After all *"a bird in the hand is worth two in the bush"* as they say, ha! ha!

I was sent out on a job to drive pile for a huge building to be built upon. It was an unusual situation and a pleasant one because we were on a large vacant lot without interference of any kind. There were no high wires and no other structures. I had a clear field of vision in all directions. We were the only contractor working on the project at that time, so there was no foot traffic near or around the crane that I needed to be aware of. There was also no traffic on the road we were working off of because it was seldom used.

I was working with a foreman who was a very chill guy. He was never in a hurry and was not prone to making any loud outbursts or chewing anyone a new ass. Since we were in a remote area, we did not have to take the precautions each night of hanging our rigging and welders from the headache ball of my crane so that it was out of reach from anyone with thievery in their hearts. I would place the forks of our forklift on top of our toolbox each night so that no one could open it in our absence.

All the other crew members had left the jobsite, and I was running through my lockdown procedures when I noticed a seagull hopping around the back forty of our jobsite. There was a forest that ran along the back perimeter, and we'd seen more than one coyote on several occasions coming and going from the forest area. I noticed that the seagull had a broken wing and was no longer able to fly. That, of course, meant it was unable to fly to safety, and it seemed to be scrounging for food. It had found some nourishment in the scraps my crew members had thrown to the ground from their lunches. I knew immediately that the seagull would end up being a meal for one of the coyotes before morning if I left it there to fend for itself.

I thought, "How hard can it be for me to grab that seagull?" Well, first off, when you get up close to a seagull, it is a *big* bird!

It had a very sharp beak as well! Even though I wore my leather work gloves, my hands still ended up a bloody mess. Just trying to corner that bird was more of a workout than I had predicted. I had a huge box that I was going to put the seagull in. It had been full of rags for us to use on the job, so I put almost all of them into a garbage bag and kept a few in the box as a cushion for the seagull. When I finally had the bird in my grip, I had to keep it far from my face because it had gone into warrior mode, pecking and biting any portion of my body it could reach.

I somehow managed to get it into the box, and I worried that it would injure its wing further, bashing around inside of it. I was committed to driving the seagull to the Humane Society, so off we went. The ladies working there greeted me and my big box when we entered the lobby of their facility. It was nice for me to be among other animal lovers because when I handed over the box to them and told them that the seagull needed it's broken wing repaired, they said, "Thank you for taking the time to bring the bird in, we'll take good care of it. We'll fix its wing, and when it's properly healed, we'll release it back into the wild. Until then, we'll keep it healthy and comfortable.

Not once did anyone I came across in that building say, "What are you, nuts? It's a seagull, for Christ's sake. It's going to die anyway!" For that reason, I ensured my ears from hearing that statement by not telling the guys about the seagull I'd rescued the afternoon before after they'd left for the day.

There were two bird sightings on different jobsites in two completely different areas that made my day just by seeing them. I had to get up particularly early in the morning to drive over an hour away to get to a jobsite located in a small town. I will write about that job in the chapter "Challenging and Just Plain Scary" because it was indeed challenging to say the least. What stood out for me was one evening after a very long and exhausting day, I was finally on my way home. I had gotten to the outreaches of the town I was working in and was driving along a country road when I spotted the beautiful colored feathers of a male ring neck pheasant. He was gorgeous! He was pecking at the sandy gravel along the roadside. He must have clambered out of the cornfield behind him. I actually pulled off to the side of the road slowly as to not frighten the bird. I sat, admiring his bold beauty, and felt rewarded to have come across him. I hold the vision of him clearly in my mind to this day.

I was looking forward to my annual fall pheasant hunt with my faithful forever furry friend (and my furry son), Jazz. He was a German Shorthaired Pointer and the best intuitive bird dog I'd ever seen. I had trained him from a pup to go in the direction I wanted him to go by using hand signals. If the brush was too dense or the corn was too high for him to see me, I had trained him to obey my whistles also. He loved pheasant hunting so much that I could not retrieve my shotgun until I was ready to jump in the car and leave because if he spotted my gun in its case, he'd start jumping up and down relentlessly and making loud yipping noises until we left. His behavior would drive me to insanity until he was riding shotgun (pardon the pun) next to me in my car.

We were known to spend a couple of hours hunting at our favorite public hunting grounds. I would let him carry the bird we'd harvested back to the car. I'd dress the bird once we were home, carefully stripping the feathers from the carcass to use them in my crafts and then cook the fresh bird for dinner. It was always a day filled with fresh air and exercise and provided us with a needed break away from the city. The companionship between me and my dog and the good meal we provided at the end of the day was an awesome experience. I don't know how many years we hunted together because there were so many. He was still a puppy when I began taking him with me so that he'd get used to walking through the thick cornfields and pastures we hunted in. I also didn't want him to be alarmed when he heard the gunshots from myself and other hunters. I had trained him to ignore the sights and smells of the rabbits we encountered so that he could focus on our grand prize—the elusive pheasant. Jazz lived to be seventeen years old, and I retired the both of us from hunting when I noticed that it was taking a toll on him; that was when he was around twelve years old. I tried to hunt without him once afterward but found myself feeling unenthusiastic about it and left for home after only an hour or so. It could never be the same without him, so I gave it up entirely.

After we had spent so many years together, it was more of a dual partnership when we hunted together, and he had grown to have opinions and ideas on the subject. To be honest, it became like hunting with an old man instead of a dog.

On one trip, we had just left the car and had to cross an alfalfa field in its early stages of growth. The plants were very low to the ground yet and were only about five inches tall. We had traveled about halfway through the field with him walking in the lead with his nose to the ground. He would stop now and then to get a really good whiff of a spot, and I would make a short whisp of a sound to regain his attention before he would trot back into his position ahead of me.

I had walked on ahead of him and noticed that he wasn't catching up to me. When I turned around to find him, I saw that he looked like a little doggy arrow pointing with one paw up and his tail straight out. I whispered, "Come, there is nothing there," thinking with the plants only a few inches tall that a bird would not be sitting there in front of my eyes. He stood like a statue, ignoring my commands. I called again without him easing up on his arrow stance. "Look, you son of a bitch, there is NO bird there! I'll prove it!" I had lost my patience with him and was eager to get out to the cornfield and hunt. I quickly walked back to where he was pointing and started moving the alfalfa back and forth with my foot when, *WHOOSH,* up came a pheasant from underneath the alfalfa, narrowly missing my shocked face as she flew across the field and into the corn!

It startled me to the point that I lost my balance and did a butt plant, grasping desperately to my shotgun. "WTF!" I was in shock with disbelief.

My dog looked at me like, "Yeah, WTF, bitch! I told you a bird was here. Hell, I even pointed it out for you! Just how long do you think I'm supposed to hold that pose, goddamn it? What do I look like to you, a f——king *ballerina?* I *don't THINK* so!" Then he stomped off in a huff like the hunting "diva" he was, heading toward the cornfield. To add insult to injury, he stopped dead in his tracks and turned to see if *I* was keeping up. I could hear his panting breath saying, *"I'm the pointer, you're the trigger. There's no trigger without the pointer! Get it? Got it? Good!"* as he resumed his trot toward the corn.

On another trip I took him on, we had just entered the corn after crossing the alfalfa field. I don't think we were even in the drying overhead corn when I heard a brisk rustling of commotion coming from his direction. The rows of corn were planted tightly together, so I was struggling a bit as I tried to walk among them while carrying my shotgun at the ready to take an immediate shot if a bird were to kick up. I was lagging behind Jazz at a farther distance than usual, so I was making brief whisping sounds to draw him back nearer to me. He didn't come, and then I heard him take off like a rocket but in the opposite direction from myself. "WTF! Now what the hell is going on?" I said to myself.

He was gone for a few minutes, and then my temper started to flare up. "What the hell, that dog thinks he knows everything, god damn it!" I was angry at his irresponsible behavior and dismissive attitude.

As it turned out, on that particular day, he DID know everything there was to know about hunting because he came up to me with a live pheasant in his mouth! I couldn't believe my eyes. He had brought me another hunter's bird. The birds wing had been shot, and it could no longer fly. Apparently, it could not outrun my four-legged hairy hunting partner with its two tiny legs and would become the primary course on my dinner table that evening. Wow! What a dog! My dog then appeared to develop a humongous doggy ego; he would not relinquish his prize. I managed to get it from him so that I could put it out of its misery, but then I handed right back as he sat staring yearningly at it while wagging his tail profusely. He was so proud of himself he kept that bird in his mouth for the entire ride home in the car. Rather than looking out his side window like he usually did, he kept staring at me as I drove all the while, gently holding our dinner in his mouth. He looked up at me as if to say, "This one is all me. I didn't need your gun at all! In fact, you could just drop me off from now on and wait in the car while I run out there and retrieve our dinner." Then I imagined him adding, "WTF! You humans are just too slow for me, and not just in the physical department either—*be-OTCH!*"

On that day, I knew what it felt like to be a mom who dropped her teenage son off at the movie theater and returned to pick him up when the movie was over with. I was just his ride. WTF!

Jazz was becoming older (like a grumpy old man) and couldn't be bothered any longer by the ignorance of human behavior. It was as if he was sticking up his middle toe in his paw to the world as if to say, "I'm too old for this shit!" On one of our last hunting trips, that newfound attitude of his (or I should say "old" found attitude) was clearly prominent in his behavior.

We had spent two or three hours out among the rows of corn without kicking up any pheasants at all. I figured that since it was nearing the end of the hunting season that they were not stocking the public hunting grounds any further. It was cold after all, and I was trudging through a thick slippery frost as I made my way through the corn that morning. I was thinking that Jazz's paws must have been cold by then with all the trotting around he was doing. I told him that we were calling it a day, that it was time to head for home. He however, had "other" ideas. He was not following me to the car. I had to keep whistling for him to come, and I was still being ignored. I understood that he was used to being successful during our hunts and had usually returned to the car triumphant and with a bird in his mouth to prove it. The time we were wasting while standing out in the cold was causing me great frustration, so I flat-out called him to come.

He trotted reluctantly toward my direction, zigzagging along like he was still hopeful that a bird would rise. He seemed to be hemming and hawing as if his actions were telling me, "But, Mom, I don't want to go home!" When he was finally about ten feet from me, I opened the car door for him to jump inside, and he froze in his tracks. I said, "Let's go!" in an angered voice as I was fed up with his unruly behavior by then.

He looked up at me with his nose in the air, and instead of leaping up into the back seat, he began pacing rapidly back and forth as if we had just shown up for the hunt. He kept his gaze on me, and I could sense his doggy thoughts as he pronounced, "It is *I,* Jazz the dog, who is the hero in the day of our hunts! It is *I* who brings you the pheasant! I don't see you crawling around on all fours with your nose to the ground like a Hoover vacuum cleaner! You are not the one with your nose millimeters above the ground with the unpleasant whiffs of manure and pheasant shit. No siree, it is I. I am the important one here, the one who suffers to put food on your table. You only provide the wheels and the bullet. I am the one who shines, NOT YOU. Now you expect me to up and leave without first fulfilling my destiny? Well, I say FUCK YOU! I'm not leaving without a bird!"

I'd had it with his shit. I told him, "Get your diva ass in the car now! I'm ready to shoot YOU, stuff you, and set you in the corner for a decoration (I decorated with the dead, taxidermy at the time; the interior of our house looked like a cabin from the north woods)." I heard a low growl under his breath, and he slowly slinked up into his seat. I interpreted his growl as, "All right, goddamn it!" He chose to look out his side window all the way home without glancing over at me once. We didn't have too many hunting trips after that. My dog could be a real asshole at times, but so could we all. He was right, though, I gave up pheasant hunting because without HE, Jazz the dog, it was no longer fun for me at all.

As for the other bird sightings, I had to get up at three in the morning to get on the road as soon as possible to arrive on time at a jobsite on the southwest border of our state. It was a long and boring drive there and then back at the end of the day. To add insult to injury, we were working twelve hours a day to complete the project as soon as possible. I had zero personal time during the duration of that project. It was just drive, work, drive, sleep, and eat when I could. There was only a ten-minute break in the morning and one in the afternoon; other than that, it was just go, go, go.

Although the money I was making working twelve-hour days was good, I quickly tired of the toll it was taking on my body. I had to forget about having a personal life because there simply wasn't time for one. I had to focus and keep my eye on the prize—those big dollar signs. I could not catch up on my sleep until the job was over, so the fatigue quickly added up, and I felt a little more depleted each day.

That was a hard job to do, but there was one morning when I witnessed a sight so extraordinary that I couldn't believe my eyes. It was just dawn when I finally drove into the town that my jobsite was located on the outskirts of. It was so quiet, and all the businesses were closed, and all the citizens of the town were still asleep. I only noticed a handful of homes showing any lights illuminating within.

One creature was already up and out on the town. I saw a wild tom turkey marching right down the middle of the sidewalk like he was the mayor of the town or owned it entirely! I thought to myself, *Am I dreaming? Did I fall asleep as I'm driving? Is that a real turkey I see walking in the middle of this town?*

I blinked my eyes a few times and shook my head to wake myself up. Nope, he was real; he was still there. I was halted at a stoplight and was staring momentarily in his direction, yet the bird remained calm, walking as nonchalantly as he pleased. I swear he nodded his head at me as if to say, "Good morning to you, madam! Have a pleasant day."

Okay, maybe I did doze off at the light and dream that part, I'm not sure. I do know that I was so excited to see a wild turkey that it made my whole day. I smiled when I thought about him because who the hell sees a turkey in the middle of a town?

When I arrived on the jobsite, I told the guys what I had seen on my way into work. My foreman looked at me with a serious expression on his face and said, "It's a little early in the morning to be drinking, Suzanne!" It was so shocking to hear him say those words in such a serious manner that we all busted out laughing.

After a few moments, I came back with, "Okay, all you assholes, let's get to work!" We all laughed some more as we made our way out of the jobsite trailer to begin a long and grueling day. Laughter is the best way to begin your day, no matter how you choose to make your money.

I was on a huge project as a crane operator putting together a big Manitowoc crane with the ironworkers. I would become the oiler on that big crane and also operate our extending forklift, bringing in the iron that was to be hoisted each day. We were building a six-story parking structure for one of our main hospitals. I'd already operated a crane to build a parking structure for that certain facility, but we were continually adding on to the hospital and had run out of parking options.

The parking structure we were putting up was across the river from the hospital. That portion of river ran through an aqueduct that had been built to provide an area for the water to run through its course and also provide room required for rain run-off in the area to prevent flooding.

A park had been maintained on both sides of the waterway for the neighborhood, hospital employees, and people visiting patients to enjoy. Since we were short on space due to the big crane sitting in the lot we were erecting iron in, we used the parkway across the street from our lot to stock all of our iron. As I was across the street in the parkway one afternoon, searching for the iron we needed next, I heard a loud snorting sound. When I turned in the direction of the water where the sound had come from, I saw a big buck standing there. I was shocked at the sight of the magnificent animal with a huge rack of antlers branching out from the top of his head.

We stared at each other for a few seconds when he shook his head, turned on his back hooves, and shot back down toward the water. I could just imagine him saying, "What the f——k! Every time I emerge from this aqueduct, there are always humans everywhere!" Then, as he turned and headed back down in the same way he had come up, I imagined him saying, "Where the hell is the forest? And how did I come to be in this godforsaken city in the first place? WTF!"

I couldn't believe that I'd just seen a big buck! I was so excited that I began telling every guy I came across about my special vision. The word traveled fast up the five floors of iron we had erected by that time. We were setting iron on the very top floor when a booming voice of one connectors yelled out, "Goldie"—that was the name given my husband by his union brother ironworkers—"what's your wife been smoking? We want some too! HA-HA!"

Jokes all around the jobsite came in rapid-fire succession. Although I tried not to be embarrassed by the loud announcement to the entire jobsite, I could feel my cheeks reddening *Sheesh, men!*

We had a coyote living in our yard four of my usual company. Most all of us had seen it. I saw a soft side of a dump truck driver one lunchtime that was so moving to me that I'll always remember it. The salt used by our city during snowfalls in the winter months was stored on our Jones Island which was where our yard four and our boat shop were also located. In the summertime, you'd see dump trucks hauling salt to various locations to stockpile for winter. During the winter months, the dump trucks would be delivering salt locally.

I saw a dump truck driver open a can of tuna and set it on the side of the road in a protected area from traffic. I was operating a crane in yard four and was awaiting the semitrailer that I was going to load some pipe pile onto. I walked over to the dump truck driver and asked him if he was leaving the tuna for one of the many feral cats that roamed the island. He told me no, that he was leaving it for the female coyote that lived down there because she was so skinny the last time he'd seen her. I told him that I was so proud of him for being so thoughtful and that he inspired me to be helpful too. I told him that I would start leaving some food for her also.

I had to meet with the foreman of the boat shop in yard four after a period of time had passed since my conversation with the dump truck driver about the coyote. The boat shop foreman and I were standing on top of a stack of pallets in yard four to get a better view of all the pipe in various locations around the yard. I would be digging out a specific pipe he chose and carrying it back to the boat shop with the forklift I was operating as well as the crane.

He screamed and jumped high into the air, tumbling to the ground from the stack of pallets "What the f——k happened? Are you okay?" I asked him as he gathered himself to stand.

"Did you see that?" he asked me in an alarmed voice.

"I didn't see anything, I was looking in the direction you were pointing," I answered.

"There was a dark flash underneath the pallets we were standing on. I think something ran underneath us," he explained.

I laughed so hard at the shocked expression he wore on his face. I told him about the coyote that lived on the island and must have been napping underneath our mountain of pallets we were standing on. I told him that the poor coyote was far more afraid than he was. The guys working at the boat shop that day laughed when I told them what had happened in yard four. Some of them were aware of the coyote living there, and a couple of the guys told us that they'd seen her before.

It was not too long after the boat shop foreman's introduction to the coyote that he had gone back to yard four to find a piece of iron he needed to complete a project. He saw a sight that he couldn't wait to tell me about. During my next trip to the boat shop, he came up to me, very excited to tell me what he had seen in yard four. He said that he had been standing just outside his truck near a pyramid of stacked pipe pile. When he shut his truck door, five little puppy heads poked out of the ends of five of the stacked pipe pile all at the same time. They were curious to see where the noise had come from. He told me that it was so cute to see a chubby coyote face peering out of each pipe, one puppy to a pipe. He told me that it couldn't have been timed any better. All of their faces appeared at exactly the same time. He had thought of me right away, knowing that I would have loved to have seen them for myself.

Now we knew that she must have had many more litters of puppies, especially after another foreman and his fellow worker told us this story. The worker needed to change the brake pads on his vehicle and had asked his pile driver foreman buddy to help him do it after work one afternoon. They went to do it in yard four because there was plenty of room there in which to do it, and there were also tools available that they could use.

My crane flooded out, driving pile for our present stadium

One of the three parking structures I worked on for one of our hospitals using the Manitowoc crane we put together in the photo below

Dual crane pick unloading the house of the crane we put together to build the parking structure above

Worked fourteen- to sixteen-hour days unloading coal brought in to the power plant south of our city when their coal dumper broke down

Casting coal from barge on water to coal pile on land

I operated cranes in the construction of at least twenty bridges. I worked on so many of them that I can't remember all of their locations.

Hundreds of piles are needed to support the new stadium; after they are driven into the ground, they are filled with rebar and concrete to hold the superstructure

Congratulations to these recently retired operators:

James P. Braun—April 1, 2013
Dennis W. Brown
James Carey
Stephen Carlin
Glen Colligan
Brian Differt
James D. Elliott
Kenneth G. Funk
Jose F. Garza
Loretta J. Goin—one other woman
David F. Guden
Bruce Hagedorn
Harry H. Hepp
Ronald Herbst
Glenn D. Hill
Daniel L. Jensen
Steven M. Johnson
Bernard Kirschbaum
Steven Kvammen
Michael Labarber
Alan J. Lese
Richard J. Maerzke
Howard Market
Michael Mastic
Eugene Matthews Jr

Duane Mittelstaedt

Ronald Moehring

Matthew Nelson

Jon A. Pagel

Alan B. Plahetka

David C. Porter

Kim C. Reinhardt

Jeffrey B. Roehl

Danny R. Saari

Michael Schwarm

Donald Shaw Jr.

John Shepherd

Peter Shirley

Suzanne D. Szucs

Harold Tucker

Kenneth A. Ven Rooy

Jeffrey J. Verheyen

Dennis C. Vick

Gary Voss

Charles Warner

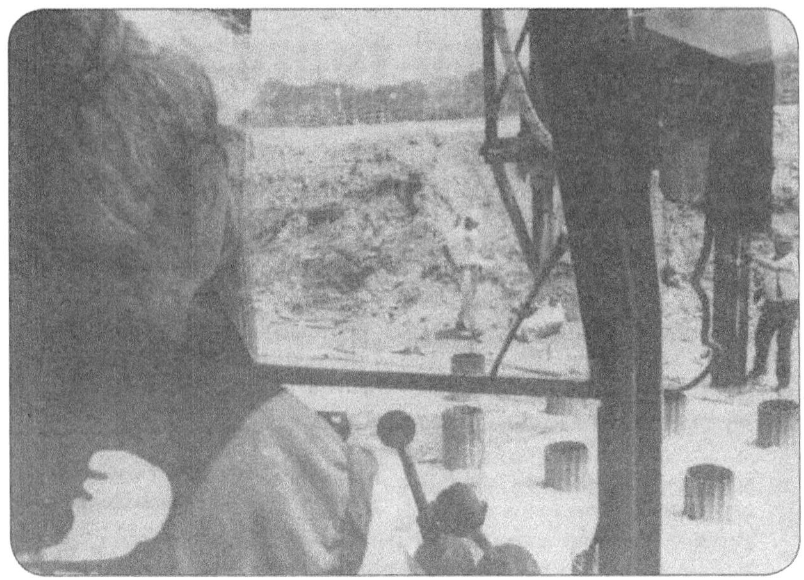

Suzanne Traczyk, a member of Operating Engineer Local 139, is shown driving a pile at Miller Park, the future home of the Milwaukee Brewers

They were working on the car underneath the overpass that runs from the island up and over our main river and then drops down into our city and also veers off to the west. It got to be dusk, and they were finishing up installing the new brake pads when they heard a siren. It was some sort of rescue vehicle or police car, and all the howling from the coyotes broke out upon hearing the vehicles siren. The men told us that the howling came from all directions around them. They were completely surrounded by them, even though they hadn't seen any of them; they were totally caught off guard. There were so many coyotes that the two men grew uncomfortable enough to leave the island as quickly as possible. They were scared! They told us that we would be shocked by how many of them they had heard.

We had a few buildings in my main company's yard that were so old and decrepit that it had been decided by the powers that be to remove them. I was excited to find out that I would get to tear down the buildings since I loved demolishing buildings with heavy equipment so much. I would be pulling down the buildings using a big backhoe, and then I would hoist the sections of wall with the crane, depositing them in a dumpster or loading them onto a semi-trailer to be driven out. I first had to pull off all the wild grapevines that had permeated each building.

As I was cutting apart the thick old grapevines from in between the buildings, I was surprised to find an ornate iron arbor underneath them. Back in the day, the blacksmith had apparently constructed it, and then I knew where all those wild grapes had originated. It had always remained a huge mystery as to why grapes were growing throughout our yard.

The ornate arbor was so beautiful that I felt bad having to dismantle it. The foreman of our boat shop loved welding unusual iron pieces together to make yard art. I picked up the occasional railroad spike I randomly came across because I didn't want one to puncture my tire or anyone else's, for that matter. Rather than toss the railroad spikes into our metal recycling bin, I gave them to the boat shop foreman. He would weld them into beautiful flowers or mailbox stands. I thought that he would love the ornate iron arbor. I called him about the arbor I had found, and he told me that he'd bring a torch to the yard after work and cut it apart to take home.

As I finished pulling the grape vines from the arbor, I found a nest. There were two baby doves sitting in it with no sign of their mother anywhere in the vicinity. The two birds were of good size and looked as if they were ready to fledge soon (fly). She may have abandoned the baby birds, but I certainly could not. I went to retrieve an empty box and placed the nest gently inside. I carefully tucked some rags around it's perimeter to keep the nest from sliding around inside while I drove it to the Humane Society once again after work. I was going to wear a path in their entryway carpet, but what else was I going to do otherwise?

A lot of work came up and interrupted my dismantling of our then vacant buildings. It was a few months before I could put any time into making any progress on that project. In the meantime, the boat shop foreman thanked me profusely for informing him of the antique arbor. He had made a beautiful gazebo out of it and erected it on the rear deck of he and his wife's home. He proudly showed me photographs of it, and it was, indeed, beautiful. He knew that I loved to make things also and shared a bunch of his shark teeth with me so that I could make some jewelry with them. He and his wife made annual trips to Florida, and he would search for shark teeth on the beach where they visited.

As I was preparing to disassemble the old buildings, I noticed a pair of young doves hanging around the exact area in which I'd located the baby doves in a nest. Could it have been possible that those were the same two birds? I knew that some birds such as hummingbirds return to the same site they were born and live each warm season in the same area. The two young doves showed no fear as I walked around them. In fact, I found myself going out of my way not to step on them.

I got down on my hands and knees to pick up the remnants of glass from the windows that I'd removed from one of the buildings. I was crawling around on the ground with the two doves so close to me that I thought, *What the hell, I'll see if one or both of them hop onto my arm.* So there I was, crawling around on the ground while making little cooing sounds to try to imitate them when I heard these words from above and behind me, "What are you doing down there, Suzanne?"

I looked back up over my shoulder, and there it was, the cocked angle of the head and the quirky expression on his face that said, "What are you, nuts?"

It was the head superintendent of our company. Oh, boy, it was an embarrassing moment for me to say the least. I could feel my cheeks turning red. It was a good thing I was wearing my mirrored sunglasses to hide my wide-eyed stare. I looked back at him and said, "I'm picking up shards of glass off the ground so that no one gets a punctured foot or a flat tire once these buildings are gone." He wore a sneaky knowing grin on his face as he turned to walk back into his office. There was no doubt in my mind that I'd been "busted" in my absolutely female moment. After all, I'd never seen a man down on all fours attempting to communicate with Mother Nature—*ever,* ha-ha! Every year, during the early months of spring, pairs of snow geese returned to their annual nesting sites. They were in fairly short distances from one another along the sheeting wall that bordered our main yard. Even though the river could be between a twenty and thirty drop below them, they seemed to like the idea of their goslings following them over the sheeting wall and into the freezing cold river as soon as they hatched from their eggs. The sheeting wall offered some protection for the nests from the harsh winds blowing off the icy river. I was always surprised that they returned to our very busy yard because of all the noise going on around them and the men walking around so closely to their nests.

I felt bad for the mother geese because most of them refused to leave their nests for any reason. The males were usually close by, aiding in their protection, and they could usually be found swimming in the river in close proximity to the nesting moms. The moms soldiered on through any storm that were thrown at them; many times, I'd find them covered in snow. They didn't get up and look for sustenance, so I began bringing bread with me to work to feed them on my coffee and lunch breaks. I knew I was being helpful in my endeavors because they wolfed down the bread as they were sitting there, starving. It would kind of piss me off, however, when the food I was feeding to the devout nesting mom would be devoured on occasion by their goose husband who was merrily swimming "free as a bird" in the river below. Upon seeing me approach the nesting area, he would fly up to steal the meals I provided her if I wasn't sneaky about it. That just goes to show you that the male population in ALL species can be very selfish, and *it's ALWAYS about THEM*—go figure! On one afternoon, that proved to be detrimental to one male goose. I tried to keep myself out of sight from the male goose swimming below as I tossed bread to the females. After all, if they couldn't see me as I tossed the nourishment to their wives, they wouldn't fly up to take it from them (bastards!). One afternoon, I thought that I was in the clear, out of sight of one male goose who was very aggressive, I might add. I had placed huge stacks of lumber in front of his wife's nest so that the men I worked with couldn't see it. I had strung up lines of caution tape in front of the nests that I was unable to hide. The men didn't like the geese nesting and thus creating more geese. They didn't like all the slippery goose shit everywhere. To all their complaints about the geese, I'd simply say, "Tough shit! If you stomp on those eggs, I'll stomp on you!" I'd shown up to work too many times with a black eye or a fat lip so they knew I was a scrapper and left the nests alone.

I was both shocked and startled when the aggressive male goose flew up from the river and was coming over the top of the lumber bundle. His wings were flared open, and it made me realize, "Holy f——k! Geese are HUGE birds!"

I'd never been so close to a flying goose and never thought that one would be flying directly at me! I didn't mean to, but my reflexes reacted before I could stop myself and I punched him! I felt so bad as he flew back down to the river. "WHEW!" That scared the shit out of me! Two good things did happen because of my accidental punch. First, the mom goose got to eat her entire meal in uninterrupted peace, and second, that male goose never attacked me again!

I don't know how many years I fed those returning pairs of geese, but it was enough time that they would look for me throughout the yard as they began to build their nests. Geese not only return to their same nesting sites year after year, but they also mate for life. I have great respect for that aspect about them; talk about commitment! They were also territorial when it came to their nesting sites. The guys would occasionally complain to me, "Hey, one of your geese attacks me whenever I go to (blah, blah) area!"

To which I would add, "Well, then, stay out of its area (DUH!). You can call for me and I'll go over and get you what you need since they don't attack me. Also, it's not *my* geese, it's *OUR* geese."

I would usually get this response: "Yeah right, what are you, NUTS?"

We had a particularly slow work season one year. I had been laid off for the winter, which ended up lasting even longer than normal. The bad news was for the newly returned pairs of geese roaming the yard in search of building materials for their nests. When I called in to the yard office to check on the work situation, I reminded the guys to watch out for the geese walking around the yard so that they didn't accidently run one over. The geese liked to follow me around as I drove the forklift or the skid-steer loader. They were kind of like big dogs and had become my wild pets.

Out of the blue one day, I received a phone call from one of our three semitruck drivers in the yard. He said, "When are you coming back?"

I told him, "As soon as possible—tell someone that you need me back in the yard to work."

He said, "Your geese are looking for you. They walk all over the yard every day. They're in our way when we're driving our trucks and the forklift too."

"Who am I, your mom? Are you seven? Feed them! They're hungry. You guys are always throwing away the crusts from your sandwiches or excess bread on the ground (yes, *seven!*). Throw the bread in their direction, and they will probably leave you alone."

"All right," he said. Then he added, "Hurry back!"

"It wasn't up to me to be off in the first place. I need the money." There were a lot of noisy geese greeting me when I got called back to work.

The cutest goose tale of all was when the eggs hatched from the nest I'd blocked with the stacks of lumber. When the goslings emerge from their eggs, they are a greenish hue in color. They are so adorable with their tiny featherless wings, and they are fuzzy all over. Those goslings were fearless! They would follow their parents immediately over the sheeting wall upon hatching. The drop to the river below was an average of thirty feet. The parents swam alongside them, toward a shady grassy property located across the river from our yard. Lots of geese families chose to reside there with their broods.

I was busy working when one of the baby gosling charged me, flapping his tiny featherless wings and making a big ruckus with his little goose sounds. He was obviously alarmed about something, so I walked over to his nest to see what the problem was. His family left him behind! They were in the river, swiftly swimming across to join the other geese families camped out on the grassy shore of a quiet and peaceful oasis of a business located there. The poor little guy didn't want to jump over the sheeting wall on blind faith and drop thirty plus feet into the icy river below. That's a lot to ask of a baby goose! He had just hatched from an egg and only drawn his first breaths of life, and then he was expected to take an unexpected leap into the water—*what's that?* Oh yeah, and then he had to swim— wait! What is *that? Swim?* I suppose he may have been missing the incarnate gene that told him instinctively to blindly follow his parents over the wall.

Maybe he was the black sheep—I mean *goose*— of his family and was defiant. Maybe he was a rebel without—no, with a cause— of self-preservation. All I knew was who in the hell would want to go through the biggest challenges of your life the very moment that you've just managed to escape from your egg? Not me! Not you! If you ask me, that fuzzy little green guy was the smartest one of the bunch! He was smarter than all the nest dwellers along our sheeting wall putting their newly hatched goslings through those Olympic escapades!

I felt so bad for my newly orphaned buddy that I picked him up with my gloved hands and, you guessed it, put him in a nice cozy box among some soft rags. I added a little bowl of water and some lettuce from my sandwich. I tucked him into a nice quiet spot in my personal cargo container that I had turned into "my shop" and told him that I'd check on him from time to time throughout the rest of my workday.

There was a foreman who had been working in the yard that day and had been a witness to my gosling rescue project. He asked me what my intentions were regarding the baby goose. I told him that I had planned on reuniting him with his family after work had concluded for the day. I was going to drive him in my car over to the geese "compound" located in the rear of the business across the river. He volunteered to come with me and distract the male geese so that they wouldn't attack me. That way, I could get close enough to the moms with their babies and return the gosling to them.

It was so nice of him to take a few minutes of his personal time to help me reunite the baby goose that I was taken back by his offer to assist me. It was unusual for a guy to give a crap about the future existence of a baby goose, but hey, I'd take all the help I could get so that I could return the gosling to his family.

As we drove across the bridge to reach the property on the other side of the river, I kept the box on my lap containing the baby goose. During the short ride, the baby goose was stretching up to me, covering my neck with little tiny goose kisses. He was so affectionate that I was astonished. I took that as gratitude for my help. I later found out that baby geese bond with the first creature they see and think that creature is their mother. It was a good thing that I didn't know those facts at the time or I would have been tempted to keep the baby goose as a pet! Lord only knows what would have been in store for either of our futures if I had chosen to do so. Bringing a goose along to work with me on a daily basis was not an option— that I knew for sure.

As I walked behind the building with my baby goose in his box, I could see all the geese families congregated there. The males began protesting my presence with loud honking. My buddy walked behind me, and as we approached, the male geese stormed us. They were honking and running at us with their outstretched wings flapping wildly; they were intimidating! I said, "Fuck this!" and quickly retreated to my car, baby goose in tow.

"I wasn't expecting *that* to happen!" my buddy walking in a fast pace behind me proclaimed.

"Shit! Now I have to drive clear across the city to the Humane Society!" I complained.

That was when he informed me that any goose family at all would adopt my orphaned gosling. He told me to drive through my neighborhood park on my way home and stop at the pond there. If I let the baby goose go on the ponds edge, a goose family would claim it for themselves.

I didn't know about how the goose society maneuvered its way through life, so I was open to try anything to reunite the baby goose with his life among Mother Nature. My foreman buddy wished me good luck and was off to reward himself for his good deed with an ice-cold beer.

I drove through the park he had mentioned and pulled off to the side of the road near the pond they had there. As soon as I began to approach the shoreline I noticed a male goose swimming aggressively in my direction. His wife was swimming with their brood behind him far from harm's way. Now I didn't know if he felt that my presence posed a threat to his family or if he saw the head of the baby goose poking out above the box that I was holding onto like a goose Jack-in-the-Box. Perhaps he heard the little peeping sounds emanating from the baby goose.

Whatever the reasons were, that adult male goose did not like my human self holding the baby goose and came up out of the pond with his wings stretched wide and began hissing at me.

I thought to myself, *Holy shit! I have to get out of here before he full on attacks me!* I set the box with the baby goose on the ground and backed away slowly. I watched from a safe distance as the father goose nuzzled the box, pushed the baby goose out of it, and immediately nudged him toward the pond. As I retrieved my box, I happily watched the baby goose being accepted into their growing goose family. Altogether, there were a dozen goslings! I knew the mom goose didn't hatch eleven eggs in her nest, so I learned that geese have big welcoming hearts when it comes to baby goslings who need to learn the ways of the goose society and to be protected from predators by the fearless goose daddies! That adult male goose was my hero that day.

One of the coolest things I've seen happened when I was staying on our property we have that's centrally located in our state. I was working very long hours in a town that was closer to our northern property than it was to the city we resided in at that time. I was driving home late one afternoon after a long day of work. I had to keep my eyes peeled for the deer that sporadically ran across the country highway in front of me from time to time. The sun was just beginning to set, and as I crossed over a tributary, I happened to glance up the creek. I saw a huge osprey with its wings flared out. It was soaring low to the water, following the length of the creek as it searched for fish swimming below the water's surface.

That bird of prey was so gigantic and magnificent with its wingspan that took up the entire space over the narrow stretch of water; it's wing tips covered the water from shoreline to shoreline. It looked like a prehistoric pterodactyl dinosaur. It sounded like how I imagined a pterodactyl would when I heard it's loud shriek. Taking in the vision of that majestic bird made my entire day a good one!

I must also mention that in our main yard from time to time, I would see our grumpy old man opossum who lived there. He was so raggedy looking that the first time I saw him, I thought he was a piece of old gray shag carpeting! His fur was matted and knotted in places, and of course, he moved along very slowly as opossums do.

Every once in a while, I would move a piece of pipe, and I'd see a gray furry face poke out the end of it. He'd have a mean grizzled expression, looking at me in disgust. His peering eyes seemed to say to me, "What the f——k, Suzanne! Can't you see I'm trying to catch some shut-eye here?"

If I happened to make a loud noise while working anywhere in the yard, for instance, moving our welders to fuel them before loading them for a jobsite, I would see his grizzled face pop out from wherever he had chosen to sleep the night before. He always looked fed up with us noisy humans and gave me a sneer that said, "Really?

Must you be so goddamned noisy!" He'd duck back into his hiding spot and resume his daytime napping.

I hopped on my forklift one morning and drove into the back forty off our main yard in search of a drill tool that needed to be loaded immediately to send out to a jobsite. I was walking among our drill tools searching for the correct size required for the job. I was super surprised to see the eyes of a brand-new baby fawn following my every move. I had been in that area the day before, and it had been fawn-free, so it must have been born during the night before. I had never come across a baby fawn on any jobsite that I'd ever been on. The mom must have walked up onto our property along the riverbank; the water level was extremely low at the time. Our yard was enclosed by a twelve-foot-high cyclone fence with rounds of razor wire at its top and enforced with an alarm system. It was only possible for a pregnant doe to enter by way of the riverbank.

The noise of the constant daily yard activity must have driven the doe elsewhere to seek asylum. In the meantime, I set a container filled with water near the fawn and let it be. I hadn't seen it until I was directly upon it, so I hoped that the men wouldn't go back there and disturb it. I also hoped that the mother would return to the poor baby she had left all alone.

I checked several times from a distance to see if the mother had returned and was becoming increasingly alarmed when she still hadn't shown up to feed it. Nearly all the men I worked with were deer hunters and had no qualms about killing them, so I worried about their reactions if they learned of the fawn's existence also. It was funny in a way that I used to be a deer hunter myself, but after working for many years along so many men who were flat-out assholes, I quit hunting deer and wished that I could have hunted some of them! Some men I'd crossed paths with were such douchebags that it wouldn't have bothered me one bit to waste a bullet on them.

I finally told my yard foreman in private at the end of that work-day about the spotted treasure I'd discovered that morning in our back forty. He told me that if the mom wanted to return to her fawn that she would find a way to do so. He told me to wait until the next day to see if she would return. Day two came and went, and there was still no sight of the fawn's mother—what the f——k! Where the hell was she? The little guy needed nourishment, goddamn it! I was getting stressed out, worrying about the welfare of the baby fawn. It occupied a space in my mind as I went through my workday. I preferred to keep all my attention focused on the task at hand, but I knew that the little guy had to be starving for his mother's milk.

At the end of the day, as I was getting ready to walk out to my car and go home, my foreman asked me if the fawn's mother had returned yet. I told him no and that I was really worried about the little guy. I told him that if I found a gnarled dead fawn that had been eaten by coyotes during the night that I would no doubt become a crying blubbery female mess and would not be able to operate ANYTHING, never mind a crane! Good guys could not take the sight of a woman crying. They don't know what to do about it but want it to stop. Somewhere in their upbringing, the knight in shining armor theory was instilled in them. Now it's the bad boys who witness a woman crying and truly don't give a shit, and they're usually the reason you're crying in the first place.

I happened to know that my yard foreman was a good guy because he always spoke highly of his wife and was the father of three daughters. I knew he'd seen them shed a few tears, and he did not want to see mine. I had planted the seed in his head to contemplate throughout the evening how to put my worries at ease by the morning of the next day.

When I showed up at work, after everyone left the yard office to begin work for the day, he told me that he would call the DNR

(Department of Natural Resources) to see what they thought we should do about the abandoned fawn. Their answer was that unless the fawn approached us or was crying out for help to leave it be with the hopes that the mom would return. As I was searching for a drill tool in the middle of the day, I was startled when out of the blue, the fawn ran up to me. He was bleating, sounding just like a baby lamb. That was it for me! He was skin and bones and starving to death. I knew that he needed nourishment pronto! I quickly loaded the drill tool and went in search of a big enough box to place the fawn in. I placed some cushioning rags in the bottom for his comfort and went into the back forty to try and capture him. It was time to take another trip to the Humane Society. The little devil was *FAST!* He may have been skin and bones, but he was as fast as a four-legged rocket! Rocket became his name from that moment forward. I was getting more worn-out than he was as I tried to corner him. He'd even slipped between my legs like we were in a cartoon.

I was wasting too much time away from my duties, so I went to enlist the help of one of my men, but who in the hell would be willing to help me save the baby fawn? Of all the people around, only one man said he'd help me. After I told my foreman that I'd waited long enough and couldn't take it anymore, I had to get some relief for the baby fawn. The man who volunteered was the one man who I thought was my least likely candidate. He was the "dead deer collector" for a county northwest of our city. He was hired to remove all the deer hit by cars from the roads and freeway system throughout his county. He kept a dumpster filled with bloody mangled dead deer carcasses in our Gran Trunk yard that was not only unsightly but stank to high heaven. He was also an avid deer hunter. The only deer he liked were dead on his dinner plate or stuffed into a sausage casing.

I told him no, that I didn't want him to help me. I told him that he didn't give a shit about deer in general, so why would he want to help me? In a nice calm voice, he told me that he wanted to help *ME*. Then he added in true hunter fashion that the fawn could grow up to be a really nice buck someday, and *that* he would like to hunt. Until then, he was willing to help me catch it and get it to food and safety. That was an honest answer if ever I heard one. I was just glad that I found someone to help me corral the little rascal.

He told me to fetch him a long rope as we walked into the back forty of our property. We both approached slow as I went to the right, and he went to the left with the little fawn in between us. As I looked at the little guy standing between us, I could see his tiny ribs protruding from his sides. He was so narrow that there was no mass to his body; he looked so fragile. He might have looked fragile, but that little bastard was quick! Whenever we managed to get close to him, he squeezed past us. It was like trying to get a grip on a watermelon seed between your fingers; it inevitably popped out! We'd been at that game for a while: grab (us), dodge (him), repeat. I thought that perhaps we'd wear him down by tiring him out but the only beings getting tired were us.

He finally got behind us and bolted down the road that we'd walked back there on. The noises from the yard coming from around the turn at the end of the road must have startled him because he leaped over the sheeting wall and was standing on the narrow strip of shoreline beside the river. I was scared that if he ran into the river, it would carry him away, and in his weak state, he would drown. That was when the truck driver jumped into action. "Throw me the rope," he told me.

After I tossed it to him, he began fashioning a knot at the end and forming a lariat. He told me to be ready to grab the fawn as soon as possible so that it wouldn't be strangled to death. WHAT? I could only watch in horror as the truck driver circled the lariat above his head like he was in a western movie, and he threw it far and outward toward the fawn's head. He got him! As he pulled the fawn toward him, the noose portion of the lariat was quickly tightening around the little guy's neck.

At that point, the fawn was in panic mode and resisted being pulled toward the truck driver. I was ready to grab the fawn as soon as it was within my reach. I had kneeled down on the edge of the sheeting wall and was leaning over it as far as I dared to; it was about an eightfoot drop to the shore. The truck driver was directly next to me, and as soon as the fawn was below me, he lifted him up to where I could grab him. As I hugged the fawn tight with one arm, I used my other hand to loosen the noose from his neck enough for him to breath comfortably. I knew not to remove the rope completely, however, because we were lucky to have captured him in the first place. Who knew if we'd be lucky enough to succeed a second time. The truck driver, myself, and the little fawn were all soaking wet with the stinky river water. I didn't care. I was so happy to know that he was safe and would be FED.

I held on to his skinny little body while the truck driver went to use the phone and find out where to take him. As the truck driver used the phone, he also put in a call to his wife and had her find some information on what to feed the fawn. He made arrangements to meet with a deer rescue unit. He would drive the little fawn halfway from where their deer reserve was located, and they would travel halfway to meet him.

We placed the fawn in a huge box, and the truck driver left work early on that Friday in order to stop at his house to feed the fawn before traveling on their long journey. His wife had bought *a lot* of milk, so they fed him until he was finally full. They put him inside their dog's kennel where he surprised them by playing like a big puppy with their two dogs. Not only did the truck driver and his wife take the time to feed the little fawn and drive him to meet with the deer rescue unit, but they donated fifty dollars toward the cost they would incur by feeding him. We captured the fawn on a Friday because I could not leave him alone in that yard starving and fending for his helpless self through the weekend.

That following Monday, the truck driver showed me a photograph they'd taken of the fawn inside their dog kennel playing with their dogs. He told me that the little fawn seemed so happy and he was so personable. The cutest part of the photo was seeing his face all covered with milk! He told me that the little guy drank a lot of it, and then he was filled with energy. I told him that he and his wife were my heroes.

Who doesn't love the zoo? I know I do. The best job that I ever did was when I was the operator involved in revamping the big cathouse at our local zoo. I was sent to drill chance anchors into the ground, using our mini excavator after removing it's cab. I also used a Bobcat skid-steer loader to bring the chance anchors inside the building. The rods I drilled deep into the ground allowed the ironworkers to come in after I completed drilling. They placed rebar and steel mesh in shapes to resemble a natural habitat into each enclosure. Laborers would follow next and coat the mesh with cement. The painters would provide the finishing touches.

Some of the leopards, jaguars, and tigers were relocated while we worked, but at the farther ends of the building, there were cats who remained in their enclosures. Some would follow me back and forth as I entered and exited the building. They seemed curious as to "what" we were and "what" we were doing. I had a very curious peacock who became my feathered shadow. He was fearless, taking it upon himself to be my personal zoo mascot. He would usually perch on the top of my skid-steer loader as I drove it around; otherwise, he would sit up in a nearby tree as our constant spectator.

I would arrive extra early so that I could stop and admire the animals as I passed by them, walking into work. Every morning, I passed by the elephants, rhinos, and the mom hippo and her baby standing on the bottom of their pool. On the way to my car at the end of the day, I'd walk through the Australian House and see the kangaroos with their joeys, the emus, and koalas. It was a unique, pressure-free jobsite where my only worry was not to accidentally back up over my newfound peacock buddy since he seemed to enjoy following me everywhere.

As I'm going through the second half of my life, I'm finding that animals bring me more joy than most people. They don't break your heart, make rude comments, say they'll do one thing and then do another. They don't blow you off when you're waiting for them. They're not selfish in their habits. You don't have to worry about them not returning your calls or your texts. Instead, you can enjoy their beauty, craftiness, and madcap antics or just simply their cuteness.

You can be having a very boring, run-of-the-mill, blah-blah day, but if you seek out a simple beauty such as flowers, birds, or an animal sighting, it's those things that can brighten your day. The fun critter memories I've shared with you are what I chose to take away from the mundane jobs I worked on. It was the "blood, sweat, and tears" jobs that, although hard to ignore, I put in the back seat of these healthier memories. Remember this: you can *make or break* each day by how *you choose* to perceive it.

Now, to end this chapter, I will tell you about one of the most interesting and intelligent pets I've ever had the pleasure of living with for some time: *Frederick Von Schnicklefritz* or Vonschnick, Vonnie, or simply Freddy. He was such a character that he was deserving of ALL his nicknames (which included some not-so-nice ones when he was *naughty!*).

I was driving home after a long days' work where I was the crane operator building one of our bridges. I was stuck in the crane holding onto rebar forms for long periods of time while the ironworkers were wiring them together. I was checking out a local newspaper handed to me by one of my crew because I was bored. I read about potbelly piglets for sale. I thought to myself, "How cute!" I was living up north on a farm that was surrounded by cornfields. I had plans of purchasing my own farm and growing sunflowers on the property to sell to a birdseed company in our area. I had dogs and cats and thought, *Why not add a potbellied pig to the family?*

The piglets were residing in a farm not far off the freeway that I'd be traveling home on, so I decided to make a little detour. When I arrived at the farm, the owner walked me to a barn. There were six tiny piglets left that they were selling. They were all huddled into a corner, and they were all SO *CUTE!* They were white with black spots, except for one who was all black. I thought that I would take one of the spotted ones because they were pretty. As I tried to catch one, however, I found them to be unexpectedly quick! I ran here and there, trying to catch one before they hid under various obstacles making it impossible to catch one. I heard a tiny grunting sound and turned to see where it was coming from.

There in the corner the piglets originated from, I saw the little black piglet. He was the runt of the litter, but he had the most bravery in his heart out of the entire bunch. He stood his ground fearlessly, letting me know exactly how he felt about my intrusion into his premises. The closer I approached him walking ever so softly, the more little grunts I heard emanating from his opinioned snout. His little upturned nose was twitching away, sizing up his opponent by my aroma.

He was the one for me! I just had to have him in my life; he was adorable. I paid the farmer lady and reached down to lift my prize piglet from the barn floor. I stuffed him into my jacket, holding him close to my chest with one hand while I drove the rest of the way home with the other.

When I pulled into the driveway, my daughter came out to greet me, and she was so excited when she saw Frederick that she was squealing herself. Startled by her reaction, my new piglet peed all over the front of me before I could release him from the confines of my work jacket. I didn't care—I had a pig! What an addition he'd make to my farm family.

He was my faithful companion for several years before a wrench was thrown into the plans I had for owning my own farm and growing sunflowers for birdseed. Those reasons for my farm dreams dissipation are meaningless to me now, so I won't go into details.

I had to move back to the city since all my work was there once I concluded making bridges and made the decision to work exclusively for my usual company. The city had an ordinance that didn't allow me to keep Freddy living with me, so I had to find him a new home. A girlfriend of mine was moving back to Michigan and knew of an older lady there who owned a llama farm. My girlfriend drove Freddy up to the llama farm where the lady fell in love with him. Fred didn't like the llamas, so the lady brought him inside her home to live with her; he had it made. I will always remember my beloved piggy and how he would leap straight up into the air (as high a hop as a potbellied pig could make!) with his short stubby legs at the sound of corn popping. That was his favorite snack along with licorice and watermelon. Although my dogs and cats would seem to get into tiffs with Freddy, at nighttime, they all cuddled together, either sleeping piled on top of my pig or using his massive belly for a pillow. I will never forget all the joy he brought to me.

The stories I could tell you about that pig are endless, so I will move on back to work. I'm going to end this chapter by telling you about some of the "fake" critters I learned to use wisely on the jobsite. When I climbed up my first tower crane, I observed an owl perched on a railing just behind the cab. He remained perched there, even though I finished my climb upward and was about to enter the cab through a door in the floor. When I told my instructor about it, he told me that it was a fake owl and that he had wired it to the railing. He told me that it was there to keep other birds from landing anywhere on the tower crane. It kept the crane free from bird shit and guarded against any nest building activity.

I thought, "Well, hell, if it works on a tower crane, it will work on ANY crane!" Since I worked on a lot of various cranes, I took that idea further by purchasing a lot of rubber snakes. Since snakes were also a predator of birds, I could just lay a fake snake on top of the roof of my crane to keep it clear of bird shit. If I happened to forget to retrieve my fake snake at the end of a job or was sent to a different crane before I could get it, there was no big expense lost to me. I would just grab another snake out of the trunk of my car to use on my next crane. The funny thing (to *me*, at least) was that more than one operator had been scared by the snake he unexpectedly encountered when climbing upon the roof of his crane to grease the boom hoist when I'd had to leave or forgot one behind—haha!

The other "fake" critter I came across was at our Harley Museum we have within our city of Milwaukee. Our company had driven the pile holding up the existing building there and had to shore up the sheeting wall lining the river beside it. I was assigned to operate the big air compressor on land close to the sheeting wall and to also operate the extending forklift. I would use the forklift to bring iron beams and sheeting to the crew working on the barge in the river. As I drove down the entrance road onto the jobsite, I was startled to see a good-sized coyote standing on the lawn in front of the building being erected.

He stood in place, frozen as if he were contemplating pouncing upon a rodent or a rabbit laying within the grass. When I asked the guys in the crew if they had also noticed the coyote, they laughed at me. They told me it was a "fake" decoy to keep the geese from landing on the lawn and crapping everywhere. "What the hell?" I responded. I had never seen that tactic to deter birds. That could have proven helpful on jobsites to keep the raccoons, opossums, and *skunks* away. Hell, a fake coyote could have provided a spectacle to behold on the mornings the men showed up to work; it would have separated the men from the boys—ha-ha!

During a very snowy winter, as I was making my way through the drifts of snow in our alley to go to work, I saw the cutest thing. There was a little baby bunny attempting to cross the road to make its way into the wooded area there. He was so chubby that his tummy had bottomed out in the snow. His little legs were moving, but he was going nowhere. I put on my winter gloves so that my human scent would not linger on him, put my car in park, and set out to rescue him before he was either devoured by a predator or run over by a car. When I picked him up, he was so small that he fit in the palm of my hand. He was the cutest little chubby "Buddha" bunny!

I placed him in a safe place far off the side of the road so that he could scamper off to safety. I would have lingered with him a little longer, but I didn't want to be late for work and have to explain my tardiness to my crew. I didn't want to see them rolling their eyes when I told them I was late due to saving a baby bunny from the snowdrifts. I could just hear them saying, "Suzanne! What are you, NUTS?"

"No way, not today—not happening," I told myself because I got to hold the cutest baby bunny to begin my morning. I took that fun memory with me to work another long-ass day in the frigid cold elements while forcing my frozen freezer of a crane to maneuver whether it or I wanted to or not.

FUNNY AND ABSURD

Although this chapter is titled "Funny and Absurd," they consist of totally different components. *Funny* is self-explanatory while *absurd* is made up of ridiculous, ludicrous, and bizarre; I'll let you be the judge. To me, a lot of what "absurd" encompasses is borderline WTF! Anyway, I will now indulge you into the lunacy of some situations I encountered within my career, working on male-dominant jobsites (I should say *all male* jobsites, plus me). Keep in mind that all the valuable lessons I learned have assisted me in my personal life also. Hopefully, many lessons I've described in this book will be beneficial to you as well.

I'm going to begin this chapter with an episode involving a raccoon since I just wrote about critters. We had a delivery driver guy hired to use our yard pickup truck to run small items, equipment, and materials out to jobsites as the requests were called into the yard. He was hired on because he was the brother of a woman who worked in our main office. She was doing a good job and had been an employee of the company for a while and asked that he be hired on as a favor to her.

He always seemed a little rough around the edges each morning as work began, and he was slow to catch on as to how we needed things to be done and what was expected of him. We pretty much had to spell everything out for him and reminded him repeatedly of his job requirements. He was quiet and seemed like a nice enough guy.

One morning, as I passed the dumpster at the entranceway to our main yard, I noticed an extra-large raccoon huddled in its corner He looked pissed off that he couldn't get out of there and didn't appreciate being looked down upon as he sat there. I put a wide plank of lumber down into the dumpster to make a ramp to allow him to escape his confinement. Instead of being appreciative and climbing out, he growled at me as if to say, "Fuck off! Can't you see I'm having a rotten morning here, bitch?"

I said, "Okay, buddy, good luck!" and made my way to start up the crane for the day.

I would check from time to time to see if the grumpy raccoon had found his way out of the dumpster; nope—he was still sulking in his corner. Every time I peeked in, he growled at me (the ungrateful furry bastard!). He was the biggest and fattest raccoon that had ever been stuck in one of our dumpsters. Because of his size, I had put an extra-wide piece of lumber into the dumpster for him to use as a ramp. It should have been no problem for one of Mother Nature's acrobats to "walk the plank" out of the dumpster.

As time moved on through the course of the day, I worried that the garbageman would drive into the yard, place his forks under the dumpster, lift it up and over his cab, and deposit its contents into the garbage container that made up the majority of his truck. The raccoon would be stuck inside and crushed by the rest of the garbage deposited during the remainder of the day.

At the end of our shift, as I was walking toward our yard office to grab my lunch box and head home, I looked into the dumpster one last time. The grouchy raccoon sat stubbornly in his corner. The pickup truck driver walked up to the dumpster and stood beside me. He said, "Is this the raccoon you want to get out of the dumpster?"

I told him that indeed it was, and all of a sudden, the pickup driver reached down into the dumpster, grabbed the big raccoon by the scruff of the neck, and pulled him out of there!

I stood shocked and dumbfounded as he asked me where I wanted him to deposit the then snarling raccoon. "Into those bushes, please," I answered, still in shock.

He set the raccoon down at the base of the shrubs I had pointed out and then nonchalantly walked toward the yard office.

"Thank you!" I called out. I looked over at the large raccoon, and he was still sitting where he had been set down. I think he was as shocked by what had just happened as I was. Then the both of us went our merry ways. The semitruck drivers had gathered together to get their items to take home. They were laughing at the expression I wore on my face during the dramatic raccoon rescue. I said to the pickup driver, "What the f——k! You could have been bitten! A raccoon could have rabies!"

"Hey, you wanted him out of there, so I pulled him out, it was no big deal," he replied.

The guys in the room thought that the whole situation was funny, and then one of them said to me, "So what if you lose a raccoon here and there? There are many more to replace them. We have too many of them around here anyway."

"Who the f——k made you the raccoon police?" I snapped at him. WTF!

One more story I will tell about the short-lived career of our pickup truck driver. One afternoon, he was at the gas station we used on a regular basis and was located near our main office. The driver was not only getting gas but putting air in a tire also. The yard foreman received a phone call from the gas station attendant asking him to call the pickup driver and alert him to the fact that he'd driven off the premises, towing the air compressor machine alongside his truck. The air hose was still attached to his tire, and the air compressor machine had been ripped from its post at the gas station. The company then owed them a new air compressor, and their truck driver was driving down the road with a compressor bouncing alongside it! What the hell? How could someone not notice a big silver box made of metal bouncing alongside of their truck?

When I asked that question out loud to the yard foreman and the semitruck drivers, they told me that the pickup truck driver had a bad habit of sniffing the permanent ink pens and was probably higher than a kite. What? Who in the f——k does that? Apparently, he did. I always wondered why he had grease on his face when all he had to do was check the oil in his pickup truck.

"That wasn't grease, that was ink. He's a stoner, and he just lost his job because of it," was the last thing the foreman had to say about it upon hearing my remark about the driver's dirty face.

"Good, now I'll have felt pens to send out to jobsites where they belong," our man in charge of supplies stated.

So I learned to be wary of men wearing mustaches that were not grown by them or were not made of hair at all.

Speaking of ink on the skin, I'm going to write about inked skin of the permanent kind. Every year, for my birthday, I do something special for myself as we all do. I was an apprentice at the time and was married to the ironworker husband who had "insisted" I began a career in the trades in the first place. I was really proud of myself for being able to do such a difficult and strenuous job. I enjoyed the fact that nothing of any stature was built without using a crane so that I would be a necessity on a jobsite.

For my birthday, to mark that important time in my life and to celebrate my bold career choice, I decided to get a new tattoo. I was going to get a crane. A crane is a symbol of good luck and longevity. I also chose it due to my martial arts training and as a symbol of the cranes I operated. Way back then, there were no legal tattoo parlors in our county, so I had to drive a few hours to a farther county to get my tattoo.

It took about an hour to get the crane I described to the artist on one of my legs. It's on the outside of my right leg above the ankle. The crane is standing on one leg in water, and there's a water lily blooming, floating on the water's surface. It's a pretty and feminine tattoo.

When I pulled my car into our driveway, my ironworker husband was working on one of the Harley Davidson motorcycles in our garage. He came up to me and asked me where I had been all that time. I told him that I'd gotten a tattoo for my birthday. Upon hearing that, he threw his arms up in the air and said, "What the f——k! You get a new tattoo like other women get a new hairstyle!" and marched back to the garage to resume work on the motorcycle. "So?" I said. I could not comprehend what the big deal was. It was MY birthday, MY body. The next day, we went to our separate jobsites where he must have complained to anyone who would listen about his crazy wife who had gotten yet another tattoo. When he told them that I got a "crane" tattoo on my leg, he hadn't been specific about the crane being a bird. Shortly thereafter, I attended one of my union meetings in the evening hours after work.

I had countless union brothers approach me throughout the course of the evening. They each had told me that they heard I had tattooed a crane on the lower portion of my leg and that the boom of the crane was inked up the entire side of my leg!

"Ewww, ugly!" was my response, and then it was *my* turn to say, "What are you, NUTS?" I informed them that NO, a crane such as the ones I operated was NOT on my leg for all eternity. I had a crane—the bird—tattooed on my leg. I told them that work on their jobsites must have been pretty boring for them to be speculating about a tattoo I'd gotten on my leg. "GET A LIFE!" I told each of the men who had inquired about my tattoo. Sheesh, those guys weren't even working on my jobsite, WTF!

The men who had gone through the apprenticeship program with me had a front row seat during our classroom time one winter to the sight of a much larger tattoo. I had always tried to get my tattoos around the times that I would not be out in the field, working, so that they wouldn't be subjected to the dirt and exhaust in the atmosphere or the layers of clothes that I had to wear. It caused me great discomfort if the material of my shirt stuck to the freshly inked area, and I also didn't want the color of the ink pulled out from my skin as I peeled off my shirt. It was for that reason that I had the great idea of cutting a giant hole in the back of one of my flannel shirts so that the inked skin on my back could heal easier in the fresh air. After all, we were expected to spend two weeks in classroom instruction before we were released to go back to our jobsites that we had been working on. The men had to look at my tattoo almost the entire two weeks, but I didn't care. I just wanted it to heal properly before I returned to work. I would be piling on all those winter clothes, including my Carhart coveralls.

I was very surprised to learn that our union was striking the Jones Island Sewage Treatment Plant. That would be the jobsite I would be returning to in order to drive pile for a new building there. They had been informed that the different unions working on that project were taking the liberty of hopping onto pieces of heavy equipment instead if using an operating engineer to do so. Until the matter was straightened out, a picket line would go up, and the jobsite's progress would grind to a halt. Shame on them, they all knew better. I wasn't walking around on the iron or welding and cutting with a torch, even though I knew how!

The instructor we had in our classroom sessions thought that it would be an excellent example of how a picket line can shut down a jobsite and get the people in charge of a project to sit up and take notice of the situation at hand. He thought that by us apprentices joining the picket line each day, it would teach us to unite as a brotherhood (and *sisterhood*) and would bond us as such throughout our careers. (1) We were stronger together working as a unit; and (2) there was strength in numbers.

Since we had below zero windchills at that time with the winds blowing off the frozen lake directly upon us, we had to layer up in clothing and then encase ourselves in our insulated coveralls in order to stand outside all day. That just figured that I had gotten a rather large tattoo covering one of my shoulder blades when a picket line suddenly went up! I tried the best I could to put a thick layer of moisturizer between my skin and all the material I was wearing, but at the end of each day, I still had to peel off my thermal shirt from my skin it was stuck to. Damn—I was not about to sit through another long session at the tattoo parlor.

On one of the mornings when we showed up to the picket line area, I could hear pile being driven down at the end of the sewage treatment plant. That was exactly what I was doing before I had to take two weeks off from my job to attend my schooling. Since my crane was the only one down on the island driving pile, I figured that the company had replaced me while I was at school. Crane operators showed up for work before anyone else. Grease time was included in our pay, and it started a half hour before work would begin. I mentioned earlier that it equaled to two and a half hours of overtime pay each week. Whoever the crane operator was, he must have been oblivious to the strike we were on because he'd walked into work before the picket line was in operation.

The men who had showed up to picket were growing increasingly angry with each ping they heard of the hammer striking the pipe pile. They were not receiving their usual paychecks and had created friction between them and their employers by picketing and going on strike. I was hearing disgruntled statements such as, "That crane operator is taking food from my families table" and "I'm going to kick his ass when he dares to walk out of that sewage treatment plant!"

Just a pause to acknowledge and let you know that the idea of someone acting as a barrier to supporting a man's family was one of the main reasons that men told me they did not like me working in the trades. They told me more times than not that I should have been home, raising my daughter, since I had a husband (the ironworker) who made good money to provide for my daughter and myself. They felt it wasn't fair that two good incomes such as ours were sustaining one household. Basically, they thought that I was greedy. Since my personal life was *none of their business,* I refrained from telling them that my husband did not share his money with me. I did not state that he had a gambling, drug, and alcohol addiction that absorbed a great deal of his finances. You will have to keep in mind that these memories that I'm sharing with you come from many years ago.

As the growing consensus was that they were going to kick the ass of their fellow union operator as he walked off the jobsite, it occurred to me that perhaps the operators on the jobsite were unaware of the picket line. I told the men to at least let me walk onto the jobsite since I worked there myself and that the crane they heard driving pile was indeed my own. I could inform the operators of the picket line being enforced and, in honoring the strike, bring them back out with me. I had the clearance to enter the jobsite because I would be returning to drive the remainder of the pile there as soon as our classroom schooling was finished. I told them that whoever was in that crane seat was my temporary replacement. I also mentioned what good union men I worked with in our company and that I was sure there was a reasonable explanation to be had.

The men gave me a short window of time to go into the jobsite and inquire as to why brother operating engineers were working when a strike was on and a picket line was enforced to promote it. When I climbed up onto the catwalk of my crane, the operator looked puzzled at my presence since he was my replacement in the seat. I informed him as to why I was there, and he looked horrified. He had no idea we were striking the project because he had begun work so early. I told him to gather his oiler and the forklift operator quickly because we had to get out of there; angry men were awaiting his explanation. When we walked out, he profusely stated his apologies for his ignorance of the situation at hand. He even offered to join us in the picket line along with his two other operators. Once that hammer quit pounding, progress on the job came to a halt, and our demands were met. It was a great lesson for us apprentices to learn. There was definitely power in our numbers as all the workers in the various unions on the project joined together. The necessities for our union came to fruition.

In later years, during another layoff, I had a tribal tattoo inked down one entire side of my back, and yes, I was called back to work as it was healing. A tribal design is done in all black ink. It goes deeper into more layers of skin than the colored portion of tattoos go. The black ink is usually the outline of other tattoos.

To fill in all the space on my tribal tattoo was exceedingly painful I swear I was levitating at times! I had to really Zen out for that one. The tattoo artist's final words to me once he had finished were to not scratch the tattoo when it itched or some of the black ink could come out, and he would have to fill it in with fresh ink. "NO THANK YOU, I will NOT scratch it," I told him. Well "famous last words" is what my mom would have said because as it healed, it itched like hell! I held in there and didn't scratch it, but I felt like an army of ants were crawling all over my back. I was operating the crane in our yard one afternoon, and it happened to be fall time. All of us were wearing our flannel shirts over our T-shirts. I couldn't take the creepy-crawly itchy feeling on my back for one more minute. The men were rigging up pieces of equipment for me to move elsewhere because we were organizing the yard.

I came out of the crane and said, "Fuck it!" as I peeled off my flannel shirt. I climbed down from the crane and started rubbing my back from side to side across the front of my crane. I just needed some relief; I didn't care any longer if some of the color came out of my tattoo! I just wanted the itchy feeling to subside because it felt like my skin was trying to crawl off of my back.

"What in the f——k are you doing?" one of the guys asked me. "My tattoo feels like ants are crawling all over my back," I answered as I kept rubbing against my crane. I must have looked like one of the polar bears at our zoo when they rub their backs up against a rock.

"You got another tattoo?" I heard one of the other guys ask. "Jesus Christ, how many is that now?" another guy chimed in. "Seven, it's so nice you're interested enough to keep count," I added, laughing.

"How many do you have?" I inquired in a cheeky voice. "Uh, I don't have any," he said.

"Guys, no guts no glory!" I stated matter-of-factly, all the while smiling. We all started laughing at the expense of the guy naked of tattoos. It made the afternoon more enjoyable to joke around for that short while. When they dish it out, you have to be able to take it and throw it right back in their faces. It's humor that bonds and forms comradeship. It's not every day that a guy sees a woman rubbing her back against a crane because she has an itch to scratch. Hell, it's not every day that you see a woman in a crane in the first place, ha-ha!

I was sent out with a crew to pound in a sheeting wall alongside an excavated hole in order to hold the soil back so men could walk down into the hole safely. The tricky part of that job was that it was inside a company, and the hole was put in to hold a new machine being brought in for their manufacturing process. I was going to have a forklift with a hammer rigged to stay on its forks and drive sections of sheeting down into the soil. It was scary because the hammer weighed so much that it was a challenge to keep the forklift from flipping over forward and falling into the hole.

We were moving along nicely on the project, and since we were working inside, there was no time lost due to whatever the weather conditions were outside. The only main issue I had on that job while working was that a woman was hitting on me every time I left my forklift to use the ladies restroom. Now I understood that by doing a man's job and by wearing men's clothing, it could be misconstrued that I was a lesbian. After all, my ironworker husband at the time had never gotten me a wedding ring (or an engagement ring either). I would notice her passing by me several times during each day that I worked there.

Whenever I had to use the women's bathroom, there would be a note to me hanging on the hook inside the solitary bathroom stall door. The notes would go on and on about how much we had in common by doing a man's job and that we should get together at the nearby tavern that was within walking distance after work some day in our near future. I would ignore the notes and get back to work as quickly as possible. Her fascination with me was becoming rather obvious to my crewmates. She was hanging on the outskirts of our job a little too much and for longer periods of time.

One afternoon, I went to use the bathroom, and when I came out of the stall, she was seated on a bench directly in front of me! "Why don't you answer any of my notes?" she flat-out asked me.

I told her that I was married and had a daughter. I also told her that I needed to get back to my job as soon as possible because I had a crew standing around, waiting for me to get back into my machine before work could resume. I didn't have time to be writing notes.

She stared at me and said that she didn't see a wedding ring on my finger and therefore didn't believe that I was married (I heard that a lot through the years from men who would ask me out; others asked me anyway and didn't give a shit if I was married or not). Then after all that, she asked me to dinner that night. I told her that my answer to her advances was no but that I was sure she was a wonderful woman and good luck to her in the future. I just wanted to move past the situation and get back to the reason I was in that building in the first place. As I left the bathroom and was descending the stairway to the ground floor I was working on, she was following behind me, trying to convince me to go to dinner with her or at least accompany her to the tavern for a further discussion after work. It was obvious to me that men weren't the only gender that didn't take no for an answer. I didn't care for drama on a jobsite and wanted to avoid any further issues with the woman, so I inquired of my crew the location of the men's restroom. I was so used to having to pee outside that I didn't care what bathroom situation I used; I was just happy I had an alternative to *"au naturelle."* Big mistake!

"Why would you want to use *our* bathroom?" they inquired, among snickers and giggles like little schoolgirls who knew a private secret. The men had already assumed that I was dealing with relationship woes with that woman.

They broke into loud laughter after I complained of her following me to the bathroom and cornering me there. The foreman himself walked me over to where the men's bathroom was located. As I left the crew behind, I said to them, "I have to use your bathroom all the time anyway, so what the f——k!" as if to say, "What is YOUR problem!" Same shit, different day. I used their bathroom until that job was finished. I made sure that no regular employees saw me go in before I used it, and the woman finally took the hint.

The other obscurity of that particular job was the fascination I developed for the skinny long brown cigarettes called More that my foreman chain-smoked as he stood before me to give me my hand signals. At that time, I'd been smoking cigars from as far back as a teenager in California. I tried to smoke ladylike cigars like Hav-A-Tampas that had a birchwood tip or Corona Whiffs which were little delicate cigars that had a tip. Sherman's I liked to smoke because they came in colors, and I could match them to whatever outfit I was wearing when off a construction site ("diva-ish," I know). I also loved the raw rolled leaves of the Backwoods brand of cigars that were berry-flavored but was reluctant to smoke them because I didn't want tobacco stuck in my teeth (Yuck! Not pretty.). Those were special to me because they looked like the ones smoked by one of my heroes Clint Eastwood, in his spaghetti westerns. I thought that my foreman's brown cigarettes looked like cigars, and they must have been good or he wouldn't smoke so many of them. My curiosity got the best of me, and when I got around to trying them, I liked them. That started a whole new bad habit that I would struggle to break later on in my life. I always stuck with my motto, "Never let them see you sweat." Therefore, I refused to smoke at work, home, or in my car. The last two places were because I didn't want the stench wafting through either of them. I learned to not smoke at work because one of my mentors would not make a heavy pick with his crane until he lit a cigarette. Watching the correlation between his habit of smoking and his anxiety over lifting a heavy load made *me* even nervous! People working around a crane need to feel confidence radiating from its operator, *not* uncertainty.

There was a period of time when I decided to mentor a new girl that had been hired by my usual company. She wanted to learn how to operate a crane, so I got permission to teach her using the company's cranes after work, a couple days a week. Since it was after hours, and all the men had left the yards in which our training sessions were held, she had seen me smoking now and then. I had a small pipe made of bone that had a lion's head carved out of it. Once in a while, I liked smoking a tobacco mixture that had dried cherries and vanilla incorporated into it. She seemed somewhat obsessed with my cigars and pipe. One afternoon, she drove up to the crane we were to use that day, and when she approached me, I noticed a pipe of her own! It freaked me out that she was imitating my smoking habits, and that was all the incentive I needed to permanently retire my pipe. I was looking at a younger version of myself as I watched her puffing on her pipe, and that was *not* what I was there to teach her.

This next tale from a jobsite includes two excerpts from a story I will tell in the chapter "Challenging and Just Plain Scary." That job was jinxed right from the get-go. Unfortunately, every once in a while, I would work on a jobsite where if something could go wrong, it would. However, these two items I will write about are the fun and funny memories I've chosen to take away from that jobsite.

As a crane operator, you watch your headache ball go up and down before your vision a gazillion times each day (yes, I exaggerate—many, many, many times) as you raise and lower loads throughout your workday. I was bored one day and wanted to pick up the morale on that formidable jobsite. It was fall, and we'd had gray skies for a number of days. The temperature was steadily dropping with winter fast approaching. We were all wearing our drab Carhart coveralls, so everything around us as well as *on* us were various shades of gray and brown. YAWN—*boring!* I was setting iron with the crane, and we were working on a structure that was to be the architectural building for a university in our city.

It was the month of October at that time and I had the brilliant idea of painting my headache ball to look like a pumpkin. I sprayed the entire headache ball bright orange using our safety paint and then with permanent black markers (nothing is "permanent" when applied to a headache ball; it's worn off sooner or later) to draw it's face. When I sent up the next load of iron, I heard shouts of glee. "What the f——k?" I heard laughing and clapping. We were the only crew ever to have a Halloween headache ball! It lifted everyone's spirits, and it turned a boring morning into a fun afternoon.

Everyone began talking about what costumes they'd be wearing to various Halloween parties and what their kids would be wearing to trick-or-treat. It's the little things that can turn any situation in either direction (*"Good or bad, happy or sad,"*—Tina Turner's song lyrics) negative or positive; choose positive, happy, and good every time. Doing so makes your life a lot easier; trust me on this one. Not only did it improve our day, but it lit up the university campus and the entire neighborhood. You could see my headache ball for miles in all directions. The guys would come across other ironworkers, and when asked what jobsite they were working on, they'd tell them, "The architectural building going up with the crane that has the pumpkin headache ball." They'd reply how they had heard about it. It made the job memorable in a good way compared to all the bad things that happened on it.

After Halloween passed, I thought that it would be too obvious a choice for me to paint my headache ball to look like a turkey for our next approaching holiday, so I went in another direction. I had the use of our safety paints, so I chose our hot pink safety aerosol paint. After covering the headache ball, I used black marker to make a face with a "winking" eye as in, "I can see you all and you're doing a great job!" Also, the *pink* headache ball screamed out to anyone who could see it that a woman was operating that crane.

Once again, I heard laughter coming from the floors above; included were the occasional, "What the f——ks!" I eventually was called away for a short time to operate a crane elsewhere in order to drive pile. I was a commodity on a jobsite because I filled the need for a female, and I was the only female who could drive pile and sheeting at that time; there were so few women in the trades back then. There are many more women now, I'm proud to say; yet compared to the number of men, we pale in comparison. We could use a lot more women out there.

As soon as a man sat in the seat of my crane during my absence, the first thing he did was to paint over my winking hot pink headache ball. He was probably too "macho" to operate a crane in the manner that I'd left it in. Now where's the fun in that, I ask you?

On that same site, there were two ironworker brothers that joined our crew as connecting partners. One was loud and boisterous, and the other was the exact opposite. He was very shy and had quite a stutter when he spoke, but he was the nicest guy you'd ever want to meet. The outgoing brother brought a camcorder to work one day and asked me to film him and his brother walking the iron and connecting the beams as they were flown in by the crane.

I forgot to mention that when I was able to return to that jobsite after having been pulled away to drive pile on another jobsite, I had been demoted from the crane's operator to its oiler instead. The man in the crane seat during my absence wasn't about to relinquish it to a girl—*heaven forbid!* He was fat and sassy and planned on staying that way. WTF!

One afternoon, after fulfilling my duties as an oiler, I managed to climb several floors of our iron skeleton building so that I could film the brothers at work. Back then, as I've previously mentioned, they were not tied off to anything. It was like going to the circus and watching tightrope walkers. Those men may not have been walking on ropes, but they were walking high above the ground without nets below, on iron beams with widths between six to twelve inches. It was really something to watch those guys work. I felt in awe watching them scrambling up the iron to get to their posts, standing only on their spud wrenches that they would stick into a bolt hole.

The outgoing brother was excited to see me using his camcorder to record him. He began walking like an old man, shaking and weaving a bit, using his spud wrench as a cane to walk across the iron beam in my direction. He began speaking to me in an old man's voice, and although I don't recall what he said, I do remember laughing because it was something funny. In the chapter "Challenging and Just Plain Scary," I'll write about what prompted me to give the tape I recorded to his wife who is a friend of mine.

Now on to the "shy" brother. We decided to try working on a brutally cold day of five below zero. I was the oiler, so it was not up to me whether we worked or not. If I had still been sitting in that crane seat, I would have called it too cold to work, and we would've all gone home. The contractor was from the state to our south and drove up to our jobsite every day with a couple of his men to work. They didn't want to waste their several hours of drive time to and from the jobsite due to the weather (it was my personal opinion that you should stay in the warmth of your own home on days like that and call your entire crew to tell them to stay home and be warm as well). One of my main views I spoke freely out loud about from winter to winter was that if it was too cold for the heavy equipment to run (in my case, cranes), then it was too cold for human bodies to be out working in that atmosphere. Usually, my words fell on deaf ears unless I was in that crane seat and called the day due to various weather conditions. That view of mine all came down to SAFETY.

It was up to the two connectors if we were to work in the frozen conditions since it was the two of them who had to perch themselves high above the ground, stoic amongst the frozen winds. They had to walk the ice-coated slick iron also. I was surprised that they decided to try working on that day. The macho crane operator was all in, even though the boom functions on the crane kept freezing up. He'd be swinging in a piece of iron, and as he went to boom it down toward the connectors, the boom would freeze up and no longer move at all. He had me kneel down in the snow under the front of the crane, below the cab. I had what we called a "weed burner," which was a propane tank with a torch attached to it. I'd light that baby up, and while keeping it far enough away so as not to melt any of the lines, the heat would dissolve the ice, and the boom would function for a little while longer. I'd had to perform that ice-melting procedure about five times before I told the operator that I'd had enough of kneeling on my knees in the snow. My coveralls were soaking wet at the knees by then, and my frozen knees were aching.

I told him I'd had enough of trying to keep warm in the subzero weather and voted to call it a day. I reminded him that if a crane operator made one pick, he was to be paid for the entire day. He was on board with the idea of going home. Now it was up to the ironworkers to make their decision to complete the day or go home early.

We would have to wait until they came back from lunch. They had all gone to the bar on the university campus for their lunchtime. During my early years in construction, it was common for all construction workers to go for a beer or two, chased perhaps by a shot (or shots?) of alcohol. Most bars they frequented for lunch they also spent hours in at the end of each work day. Their presence guaranteed a profit to the bars proprietors. Those bars usually had a lunch menu of some sort, and some bars that previously didn't provide one came up with one for the workers of the nearby construction sites. It was good business for them to do so. That was how I met my ironworker husband when I lived in California.

At lunchtime, the ironworkers were so frozen that they practically ran to the tavern in order to feel some heat. I put away the weed burner and vowed to go home if the damn boom hoist froze up again. Lunchtime had come and gone without the return appearances of the ironworkers. "Suzanne, do you know where they go during lunchtime?" the foreman asked me.

I replied that I did because I'd taken my obligatory classes there when my dream was to become a chiropractor, so I remembered where the tavern was located. "Well, go and see if they plan on joining us out here. I'm tired of freezing my ass off, waiting around for them," the foreman added.

Off I went in search of our missing crew. As I entered the small tavern that the university provided for its students on campus, I heard loud singing, clapping, and laughter. The room was packed with people devoted to avoiding the subzero temperatures outside. I about peed my pants with shock and laughter when I got an eyeful of their early afternoon entertainment. There was our "shy," stuttering ironworker connector dancing seductively on top of a table surrounded by young attentive female university students! He was singing (in a good voice, I might add) loudly while making the faces of an enticing Casanova, and he wasn't stuttering at all! I asked his outgoing brother who was obviously amused by his brother's performance, "What's up with your shy brother all of a sudden?

And where's his stutter?" He told me that whenever his brother got drunk, his stutter and shyness disappeared.

He looked as if he thought that he was the reincarnation of Elvis Presley, but he reminded me of Eddie Murphy in the movie *The Nutty Professor.* In that movie, the nerdy professor drinks a potion and turns into a vain suave ladies' man. It was obvious to me that if the shy ironworker was now dancing and singing stutter free on a table top that he wasn't fit to climb several floors of icy iron to perch high above the ground in ANY temperatures.

His brother asked me if the foreman expected them to return to the frozen jobsite, and I told him that I'd been sent to find out. He told me that they were done freezing for the day and that he'd buy me a drink if I wanted to join them. I told him thanks, but I was intent on heading home as soon as possible to get out of my wet coveralls and stay warm for the remainder of the day. I went back to the foreman and the crane operator to tell them we were going home and that the ironworkers said that they would see us in the morning. For most people, it was "add alcohol—instant asshole," but for our shy ironworker, it was Casanova all the way, baby! Ha-ha!

Although I began my days by joining the crew in the jobsite trailer in order to get the low down on our plan of progression each day, I did not choose to habituate the trailer for coffee break or lunch. Back then, we were allowed to smoke inside the trailer, and it was so crowded in there that when you walked in, you walked through a cloud of nasty cigarette stench. Also, working with all men day in and day out, I needed to seek refuge for a little "me" time. I needed to be away from all the burping, farting, bullshitting, and bad jokes— usually at my own expense. I would instead retreat to my vehicle to blast my heater and work on a beading or crochet project.

The guys kept inviting me to come into the trailer for coffee break, so one day, I took them up on it. Unfortunately, I chose to accept their invitation on a Thursday morning; our coffee break was at nine-thirty. Most of the guys were struggling to stay awake from little or no sleep the night before, and almost all of them were suffering from hangovers.

It was payday on Wednesdays on that job, and it was a wellknown fact that every Wednesday and Saturday nights, a poker game went on at one of the ironworkers' homes. His wife was so happy that her ironworker husband was guaranteed to be home those two nights a week in order to host his poker game that she would prepare food for all the guys who showed up hungry.

I'd been on jobsites where there were several Thursdays when some ironworkers didn't show up for work depending on how well they had done at the previous evening's poker game. It was an unfortunate decision I had made on that Thursday morning because all the guys LOOKED LIKE HELL! They were green around the gills, and when I opened up my sandwich to take a bite, I heard a round of *"UGH!"*

"You're not going to eat that stinky tuna fish sandwich in front of us, *are* you?" one weak voice sniveled.

"Oh no! Are those green things *pickles* in there?" another ironworker asked in a shaky voice.

"Why, yes, they are!" I exclaimed exuberantly. I was proud of my tuna salad recipe after all. We made some small talk as the men were a faded version of their usual selves, devoid of any deeper conversations. They all had a bad case of "bottle flu," something I was bored living with in my personal daily life as the wife of my own ironworker.

Coffee break came to an end, and as we were about to exit the trailer, I reminded the men that it was going to be Valentine's Day on Sunday and that they only had two days left to find special gifts for their women. Just as we opened the door in order to exit the trailer, one ironworker bolted for the door. He just made it past the door frame to puke next to the steps into the snow. It caused a catastrophe of events as each ironworker exited behind the one who puked in front of him, each vomiting into the snow. Unfortunately, I was the last one out. Thanks to my garbage can of a stomach, not to mention my sobriety, I was unaffected by the pungent disgusting mess the entire crew left in the snowbank next to the stairway. My last refrain to the men as we trudged through the snow to go back to work was, "What the f——k! Now you know why I don't eat lunch or have coffee break with you clowns!"

A few of them just waved me off as if in a "F——k you" fashion while the rest of them ignored me. I told the crane operator what had happened once I made it to the crane, and he had a good laugh, acknowledging how happy he was that he chose to sit in the crane for coffee break, warmed by its engine behind him.

The following Monday, when I walked into the jobsite trailer for our safety meeting during which time the crane's engine was warming up, I saw a roomful of glum faces. It even looked like a couple of the men had slept inside the trailer during the night. I asked them what was wrong. "We're getting a divorce," one of them stated with a forlorn expression on his face.

"What? It was Valentine's Day yesterday," I pointed out. It was bad enough that instead of going home after their tavern stop the previous Wednesday after work, they had gone straight to their poker game. They had cashed their checks at the tavern before the game and then proceeded to lose a lot of the money required to keep their households running until the following payday once they started playing poker. That had happened in my house on more than one occasion, and it was maddening. Naturally, they were not a welcome sight in their homes by the time they showed up there.

Twice in one week, the disappearance of the men in their lives had proven to be too much for their women when they pulled that crap on Valentine's Day. They were too hungover, broke, and not present, even though their bodies were snoring away in their recliners.

Let me tell you, it is NOT a "romantic" gesture or sight to see your husband laying back in his recliner with his flytrap of a mouth wide open for a landing site for airborne insects. Occasionally, a loud snort could be heard as the landing strip was cleared due to loud obnoxious snoring. Either way, whatever was in the air around his head was either sucked in or blown out—maybe both. The dark puffy eyes and the disheveled hair that stuck out in all directions reminded me of Gene Wilder in the movie *Young Frankenstein;* that was who my ironworker husband looked like after an all-night bender. Or was that Bozo the Clown? I'd have to say both.

Since I lived that scenario in my own home on too many occasions to count—and it PISSED ME OFF—I had no sympathy for the trailer full of crybaby men. As I was told by my parents when I was growing up and had screwed up, "You made your bed, you lay in it." Sarcastically, I brought it to their attention that since they weren't welcome in their homes any longer that they had better start seriously "kissing some ass" and make up for their horrendous behavior or get ready to settle in for the night in our jobsite trailer. I mentioned also that they'd have to sleep in their coveralls because our small electric heater wouldn't provide enough heat during the nighttime hours in our below freezing temperatures. *"See ya, wouldn't want to be ya,"* I sang as I exited the trailer.

On another job, I found an amazing present one day. I was throwing some garbage into a dumpster when I spotted a pink fabric that sparkled. As I moved closer to it, I noticed that it was stapled to a sign that someone had made for an office presentation.

We were expanding a potato chip factory by drilling huge caissons so that iron beams and rebar could be attached later in order for the structure to be built upon. We were working just outside their office headquarters. That fabric was a gauzy chiffon with sequins throughout it in the form of dots. It had been unwrapped off the bolt of fabric from where it was bought and therefore very long and about three feet wide. I couldn't believe my luck! I found something so beautiful amongst the objects in a dumpster!

I pulled it out of there and removed the staples in order to free it from the homemade sign the employee had made. I rolled it up and figured that if I didn't use it to sew into something, I could use it as a long scarf to wear.

I knew that the men were going to give me a hard time about my pink girlie treasure, so I was attempting to shove it inside my jacket before any of them noticed, but it only made me look ridiculously fat, and it was showing below the hemline of my jacket. When I heard them laughing loudly in the distance, I knew they had observed the comical sight of me trying to hide all of that material on my person.

"Whatcha got there, HB?" I heard one of the guys yell to me. (Heartless Bitch—one of the *nicer* nicknames the guys liked to use. That particular nickname I earned in high school by my surfing buddies. If the waves were cranking, I wouldn't quit surfing, no matter if I'd be standing up a date. My karate classes and training were first, surfing was second, and my horse was third. If I had a boyfriend, they were fourth in line for my attention, thus the nickname. My ironworker husband blabbed that information to his connecting partner on a jobsite, and the rumor mill ran wild with the information.)

I fessed up and said, "I found some really pretty material laying in the dumpster."

The entire crew started laughing loudly, except for the foreman. He looked away from me as if embarrassed and said, "Jesus Christ, Suzanne, what the f——k!" He started walking in the other direction, and I could hear him add, "Goddamn women!"

I keep pressing upon you to take the good things that you notice during the day home with you and leave the rest at work. On that particular day, it was my new pink chiffon scarf with sparkles!

The cars I drove to work throughout my career were "runners." That meant that they were not necessarily pleasant to look at, but they got good gas mileage and had a heater and defroster that worked, and they ran well. Jobsites were either dusty or muddy, and if I were driving pile, there was shit flying around in the air with every blow my hammer made, striking the pile. The car I'm going to write about now I called my "ski boot" car. It was actually a Le Car, but the shape of it looked just like my downhill ski boots which was where my analogy came from.

After work one late afternoon, I had an appointment to get my hair colored. That process allowed me to work in my chosen profession by using my two rules to success when being a lone female working in a male-dominated career. Rule number one was "Never let them see you sweat"; and number two was "Never let them know that they're giving you gray hair!" My list of rules for that categorization went on and on, by the way; after all, I had twenty-eight years of making them.

I parked my work car in front of our house and hopped into our truck and drove out of our driveway, and on to my appointment I went. When I returned about three hours later with my newly refreshed blonde hair, I thought to myself, *What's wrong with this picture?*

Puzzled, I walked into my house when my young daughter ran up to me, filled with exuberance, and announced, "Mom, you should have seen your car—it *FLEW* through the air!"

I looked over at my ironworker husband who was chuckling away in his recliner and said, "What the f——k is she talking about? And where the hell *is* my car?"

Apparently, a drunk driver had been speeding up our street and plowed directly into my car and caused it to "jump" from the curb as it was crushed. The drunk driver reversed, dislodging from my car, only to hit the neighbors car across the street from us. He proceeded up the block, hitting two more vehicles before his car finally came to a halt, unable to run at all anymore. He had careened back and forth, zigzagging in his progression up the street, all the while hitting those cars on either side of the road. He was a drunken pinball machine on wheels.

By the time I had arrived at my house, my car had been towed away, and all of the glass had been swept up by the cops who were finally able to arrest the drunk driver responsible for all of the damage he'd done in our neighborhood. I told my husband that I needed to get my tools, hard hat, and gear for my job out of my car to take into work with me.

He drove me to the scrapyard where my car had been towed. He warned me about what my car now looked like and also told me that it was totaled. I could not believe that the accordioned chunk of metal I was looking at was the car I'd driven that very day. The front seat was shoved back into the trunk so that my rear seat was barely visible. There sat my hard hat on the floor behind the crushed driver's seat. I twisted my hard hat in every direction, but I just couldn't pull it out of the small opening it was trapped in. I was unable to retrieve any of my gear, clothing, or tools that were sandwiched in my trunk. I had no choice but to write off all my belongings and arrive early at my usual company in order to replace all of my safety gear, hard hat, and materials needed for my crane before going to my jobsite—what a pain in the ass!

I also needed to find a replacement vehicle in my sparse free time that I wasn't working. I went to the police station to see the accident report because I intended on suing the drunk driver responsible for the loss of my assets. When I spoke to the arresting officer about the drunk driver, this is what he had to say to me: "Just be thankful you were not in your car when he plowed into it, and as far as getting any reimbursement, it would be like getting *blood out of a stone.*" WTF! He added that the drunk driver was unemployed and had no insurance.

That was the absurdity of this story; "words of wisdom" provided by that officer were sorely lacking of any comfort for me. I was f——ked! The funny aspect of the situation was that my daughter was so excited that she saw a "flying car" as if it was magic. We hadn't taken her along to the tow yard with us since she was at her gramma's house at the time, so she didn't see the aftermath caused by the crash. For quite a while, I had to explain what she meant when she told people that she'd seen my car fly.

I may as well tell you about the many "fans" I gained while standing out as the only female on most of my jobsites. The first time I realized that I had a fan, I was setting iron for a huge arena we were erecting in the heart of our downtime area in our city. If it weren't for the fact that almost all our jobsites were enclosed with cyclone fencing, I could have even called a lot of my fans *stalkers.*

As we were working each morning, I noticed a man, maybe ten years older than I was at the time, at the same position and at the same fence. Every time that I noticed him, he seemed to be staring at me. I was somewhat used to catching people's eyes who looked upon our jobsite because I stood out like a sore thumb, a "stranger in a strange land," so to speak. I remember thinking, *Doesn't he have job to go to?* Apparently, he did not because every morning when I walked to our jobsite trailer for coffee break, there he was, staring intently in my direction.

One day, I noticed him waving wildly in order to get my attention. When I looked directly at him, I was waved over to join him at the fence. "Hi, is there something I can help you with?" I shouldn't have asked. Whenever I asked a man at work that question, it almost always led to a lot of snide comments, sexist or bad come-ons. He told me that if I agreed to have dinner with him that I could choose any restaurant in the city that I would like to dine in.

I told him that I was married and therefore declined his generous offer. He told me that it was of no consequence to him if I was married or not and that the offer still stood. I returned to my job and chose to ignore him after that incident.

I would go through those uncomfortable and awkward situations every so often throughout my career; they really DON'T care if you're married or not. Sometimes that just intrigued their competitive nature and became a game to persuade you to change your mind and give them a chance to impress you. You must be faithful to your integrity, honesty, and heart as well as soul. In other words, "no means no," but there's no reason to be a bitch about it. You just have to politely retain your boundaries.

I had to put up with a lot of jokes and comments from my crew concerning my "fan at the fence," but it brought a lot of hilarity during our coffee breaks, and we all usually returned to work, laughing or smiling. My "fan" continued to holler out his invitation to dinner so that I couldn't help but hear him until, one day, I walked over to him at his post at the fence and said in a joking way, "I don't think your wife or girlfriend would like you asking me out, do you?" That question brought about a laugh from him. That was a good lesson in spinning an uncomfortable situation into a more jovial one.

I was driving pile in a very congested part of our city along a main street that cut through the heart of our entertainment district. They had huge plans to enlarge the growth in that area. We were driving pile so that a multilevel parking structure could be erected. Although those businesses and living quarters were being built, parking was at a minimum. I was sitting in my crane, driving down a pile when I saw a city bus pull up adjacent to our jobsite and pause at a bus stop there. Usually, during the day, I would see many incidents involving the bus pulling up to the bench at its regular stop for passengers to disembark and new passengers to climb aboard. Usually, the passengers disembarking would walk on toward their next destination with the exception of one woman. That woman arrived every day at the same time in the afternoon.

She would plant herself on the bench provided at the stop once she stepped off the bus. She would stare intently at me for the remainder of the day. Once I buttoned up my crane for the evening and walked toward my car with the rest of the crew, she would then rise and walk away. Obviously a "fan," she did not approach me but watched me with a calm expression on her face. The guys kept asking me if I knew the woman, and I always answered that I did not. Since I was working with a lot of men I'd never worked with before on that project, they spoke to me as if she were my secret girlfriend I was keeping from them. I figured she must have been coming from work because she showed up at the same time every afternoon.

As I've mentioned before, I never owned a wedding ring from my first husband, the ironworker. That coupled with my greasy filthy attire usually made the men I never worked with before to think that I was a lesbian and that I was not married to a man at all. I admit that I looked like them and did the same job as them. I had no control over my unappealing work attire and wardrobe options. I did make sure to put on makeup each morning, but that was mostly for myself so that I did not feel like I was transitioning into a man. Anyway, perhaps my "fan" was either taken herself or too shy to approach me because she never traveled far from the bench she watched me from. She did wear similar attire that I had to at work. Maybe she also worked in a male-dominated field and simply enjoyed seeing a reflection of herself in the workforce; I never found out. I was slowly getting used to the "fans" I came across.

Something absurd happened on that same jobsite. Springtime rolled around and was coming to an end. That seasonal transition brought about the beginning to our cultural festivals held every weekend at our lake shore park. The very first festival to start those weekends off was our Gay Pride Fest. It was shocking to me that we were told to evacuate our jobsite and put up a particular kind of fence along one side of our jobsite. That was because they were planning on marching their huge and popular parade through several blocks of the main street we were adjacent to. It was also planned for them to march down the street that was the entrance to our jobsite. That was a street that all the workers were directed to park on due to the special permits required for us to do so.

They did not want my crane visible along their parade route, so we cleaned up the street after I folded up my all terrain crane after removing its boom and drove it off-site and back to our yard. I would have been more than happy to fly one of their flags from my headache ball if I would have been asked to. I had never heard of a jobsite being shut down and its crane removed due to a parade route. The cost of the permits to shut down the use of a main city street and also an entire jobsite was unfathomable. It took us two days to tear down the crane for its departure and to put up the barricades and particular fencing that they required. After their festival weekend was complete, it took us another two days to remove and return the items they had requested and to also put the crane back together. That parade had cut into our building completion schedule by four days.

A FARM KID JOINS THE MARINES

Dear Ma and Pa,

I am well. Hope you are. Tell Brother Walt and Brother Elmer
the Marine Corps beats working for old man Minch by a
mile. Tell them to join up quick before all of the places are filled.
I was restless at first because you get to stay in bed till nearly 6
a.m. But I am getting so I like to sleep late.

Tell Walt and Elmer all you do before breakfast is smooth your
cot, and shine some things.
No hogs to slop, feed to pitch, mash to mix, wood to split, fire to
lay. Practically nothing.
Men got to shave but it is not so bad, there's warm water.

Breakfast is strong on trimmings like fruit juice, cereal, eggs,
bacon, etc., but
kind of weak on chops, potatoes, ham, steak, fried eggplant, pie
and other
regular food, but tell Walt and Elmer you can always sit by the
two city boys that live on
coffee. Their food, plus yours, holds you until noon when you
get fed again.

It's no wonder these city boys can't walk much. We go on "rou[te]
marches," which the platoon sergeant says are long walks to
harden
us. If he thinks so, it's not my place to tell him different. A
"route march" is about as far as to our mailbox at home. Then
the city guys get sore feet and we all ride back in trucks.

The sergeant is like a school teacher. He nags a lot.
The Captain is like the school board.
Majors and colonels just ride around and frown. They don't
bother you none.

This next will kill Walt and Elmer with laughing. I keep getting
medals for shooting. I don't know why. The
bulls-eye is near as big as a chipmunk head and don't move,
and it ain't shooting at you like the Higgett boys at home.
  All you got to do is lie there all comfortable and hit it. You
don't even load your own cartridges. They come in boxes.
Then we have what they call hand-to-hand combat training.
You get to wrestle with them city boys.
I have to be real careful though, they break real easy. It ain't
like fighting with that ole bull at home.
I'm about the best they got in this except for that Tug Jordan
from over in Silver Lake. I only beat him once. He joined up
the same time as me, but I'm only 5'6" and 130 pounds and he['s]
6'8" and near 300 pounds dry.

Be sure to tell Walt and Elmer to hurry and join before other fel-
lers get onto this setup and come stampeding in.

Your loving daughter,
Alice.

I found this too cute not to include

*This was after my first day of work as an apprentice operating engineer;
if I could tell my younger, smiling, naive self something insightful,
it would have been to "RUN, not walk back to college"), ha- ha; I
would have said, "Buckle up, girlfriend, you're in for a bumpy ride";
I drove in the pilings that are beneath these condominiums, the
riverwalk alongside them, and the parking garage for their tenants.*

*As well as the underground parking for the building on the right;
the river walk was built using a crane mounted on a barge*

It takes a lot of iron to construct an arena.

It's like putting together a "giant" puzzle—with A LOT of parts!

I would be smiling in the amazement of "WOW, I did that!" You never know what you're capable of until you do it.

These photos make me feel my age because this building has since been torn down and a new one erected. I never thought I'd outlast one of the buildings I helped piece together, HA!

This photo and the one below it show that just putting a big crane together is a harrowing and dangerous job. Back then, the ironworkers did not tie off or have any special or particular safety requirements. They were up there on their own free will and for a paycheck.

It took us several days to put that crane together. The part they are connecting is attached to the tower of the crane, and it allows me to reach far, far away.

You can see in the photo above how far from the crane I'm setting those beams of iron. That's what I meant above on a good day,
it was like "flying a kite." On a *good* day; otherwise, it was "WTF!"

```
June 28, 1990

Edward E. Gillen Co.
218 W. Becher Street
Milwaukee, WI 53207

Gentlemen:

Be advised effective immediately, Suzanne Traczyk, of the Operating
Engineers and employed by your company, has been appointed union steward
for Operating Engineer employees employed on all of your projects and
is also steward for all Operating Engineer employees employed by all
companies performing work on Jones Island.

                              Sincerely,

                              INTERNATIONAL UNION OF OPERATING
                              ENGINEERS, LOCAL NO. 139


                              Harry Badding
                              Business Representative
```

That went over like a lead balloon with *a lot* of guys and would
result in several of my worst WTF! moments of my career. I may
have been the first female union steward on a large construction
project, but I certainly won't be the last!

Due to its historical value, this building could not be demolished. It's a good example of blending new architecture with the old.
It was a bitch to clear that corner of the building when unloading
the pipe pile off a barge with a crane mounted on another barge;
there was a lot of rocking and rolling on the river!

Driving in a sheeting wall along our river

My fans came in all sizes. Two of my favorite fans were little girls that were with their dads who were holding them because they were indeed that small. The first little girl I noticed whose dad was holding her was when I was working in a parking structure for one of our hospitals. I was grabbing some rags to use in my crane from our toolbox when her dad said to me, "She insists that we come here so that she can watch the construction in progress."

Her eyes were watching me, enlarged with fascination. I said hello to her and was describing in detail what she was looking at as the men were working behind us. She watched them as I spoke to her about the results of their actions. She pointed with her tiny finger and spoke in the excited garble of a two-year-old that let me know she was engaged in our conversation.

It was then that I noticed her cute little pink cowgirl boots. "Uh-oh!" I said to her dad who was struggling to hold his then wriggling daughter. "If she has a fascination with boots and construction, you might have a little *me* on your hands," I told him. I continued with, "I started building construction in my sandbox with miniature heavy equipment when I was a little girl, and I still have a fever for collecting boots to this day. I wear them for work, and I make up for wearing men's work boots by wearing my collection of fancy *girl* boots during my off hours from work."

"Lord, help me!" he replied, and we both laughed at his future raising his daughter. From that day forth, I usually noticed the father and daughter duo at the same time almost every day for the duration of the job. If my hands were free from the controls of the crane, I stepped out onto my catwalk and waved at my two-year-old mini-me to make sure I acknowledged her visiting the jobsite. I'd get a big smile in return and an enthusiastic wave from my newfound friend.

The other little girl that stands out in my memory was also just two or three years old. I was the oiler for a huge Manitowoc crane, and we were erecting iron for another arena in our downtown area. Every day, just after lunch, I noticed a man holding his young daughter. They were observing us at work. Was she enjoying what looked like a giant puzzle slowly coming together. Or was it that it resembled giant blocks or monkey bars to her? I didn't know. Most kids were afraid of all the noise of the loud engines racing and all the clanking of iron as it was flipped and rigged to be flown up into the air to the ironworkers waiting for it. Then you had the loud banging of steel on steel as the "bolting up" crew of ironworkers slammed all the bolts into place at each connection point. They'd use five-and ten-pound hammers to seat the bolts through and then spin on the nuts using torque wrenches. All the noise I just described echoed in an extremely loud way the more the new building became encased by its precast shell.

That was too loud for youngsters whose ears were still developing. I did what I'd done for my daughter whenever she came to visit me or her dad at work. I walked over to the dad when I had a spare moment and handed him a bunch of earplugs. I told him that he should put them in her ears because the noise level was so loud that us workers were required to wear them. He told me that he was shocked that she would ask him to take her there to watch the construction. He said that he had a hard time explaining to her why we weren't working on Sundays when she wanted to go there. He told me that she seemed impressed to see someone like her mom working there.

I told him that they had made my day and added that he'd best be prepared because he very well could have a daughter that worked construction one day. I had another dynamic duo to wave to every day but Sunday.

On that same project, I was searching for certain rigging that we would need in the near future, when a woman next to our fence called me over to her. I figured that she was going to ask me what exactly it was that we were building. I was used to being asked that question on a lot of my jobsites I'd worked on. The woman was at a bus stop, clearly waiting for a ride to work because she was holding a lunch box as well as her purse draped over her shoulder. In her free hand, she held a big cup of coffee which she handed out to me in between the sections of fence. She said, "Here you are. You look like you can use this more than I can. It's nice to see a woman who works as hard as myself."

The kind gesture as well as the compliment was so meaningful to me that I recall it as if it only happened yesterday. I couldn't even recall what we did for the rest of the day because it did not mean much to me, but the kindness of that woman I will remember always. She taught me an important lesson that the small acts of kindness are the ones that deem themselves the most powerful. I tried taking that lesson I learned from that kind woman into my future from that day forward. That began my mission to amp up my compliments and helpfulness to those I worked with, whether I felt like it or not. I learned that you are responsible for the outcome of your day by the actions you choose to take. The smallest thing, such as a kind word or sharing your experience and training with someone else, can turn another person's day around along with your own.

I debated on whether to include this story or not because it will probably make me seem like a nutjob, which I can assure you I'm *not*. I'm going to include it because it will be instrumental in explaining how dire and volatile my first marriage actually was. There will be a story in the chapter, "Challenging and Just Plain Scary," that will shed an illuminating light on that fact. In keeping with the title of this chapter, I will finish by writing a tale that's "absurd" and then end with a tale that's "funny." Please keep in mind that we all have our moments.

I used to hunt deer every season as did a lot of members of my ironworker husband's family. A lot of men I worked with took time off from their jobs to go hunting, hoping to bring meat home to their families. The contractor who I built bridges for closed the entire company down for the ten days of gun hunting season. Too many men took time off to go hunting to make it feasible to remain open. My husband and I were far up north, deep in the woods to hunt. We were stationed upon a high ridge that overlooked a pond. He had placed me at a tree to use as support for my rifle while I aimed it toward the pond. We had seen a lot of hoofprints down by the water, so he placed himself out of sight on the other side of the pond. A long period of time had passed, and I was searching through the dense forest behind me when I heard a loud crunching sound emanating from the pond area. I turned carefully around, raising my gun so I could get in a position to take a shot at the deer walking through the dry and frosted grass.

I was aimed and ready to shoot when I saw a great rack of antlers rising up from the ground. I thought a deer was rising up from where it had bedded down for the night. A closer look proved to me that it was *my husband holding a rack of antlers on top of his head!* He had no doubt found them laying on the ground in the swampy area we were hunting in. My first thought was, *SHOOT HIM!* It was the perfect opportunity for me to finally be rid of his mean abusive ass once and for all!

Hunting accidents happened every year. Who would blame me? He looked like a deer! The little devil on top of my left shoulder was dancing a little jig while screaming, *Shoot him! Shoot him!* Ah, but then there was the little angel sitting on top of my right shoulder. With her halo all aglow, she calmly said into my ear, using her soothing voice, "Now that is your daughter's father you're aiming your rifle at. What are you going to tell her about how you 'accidentally' *shot her father?* As a Buddhist, you know that you can't look her in the eye and lie to her."

Then she took flight from my shoulder like some shimmering white moth and rose toward the light. As for the devil stomping a fit into my left shoulder; I had to flick him off to the ground like a piece of lint that was stuck to my shirt. I said to him, "Not this time, Bubba!"

I kicked myself in the ass (mentally) the entire time it took me to lower my rifle and aim it toward the ground while setting the safety to "on" before I changed my mind. My question to you is this: was it absurd of me NOT to take that shot and save myself years of further physical and mental pain and anguish? Or was it absurd of me to think of the idea of shooting him down in the first place? I have never been able to answer either of those two questions.

It turned out that my ironworker husband had come across the carcass of a buck that had been shot by an arrow during the bow hunting season. It must have eluded the bow hunter who had shot him by running down into the swamp at the base of the hill I was posted at. It had most likely bled out before dying there. The arrow was visible among the bones outlining the buck that had collapsed there. The entire skull was what my husband was holding on top of his head which was, I might add, one of the stupidest things that I ever saw him do. He was not only lucky that *I* didn't shoot him, but he was also lucky that he wasn't shot by another hunter in the immediate vicinity.

A skull of a buck that is devoid of both hide and matter is known as a "German mount" if displayed as a trophy like a traditional mount would be. As a fisherman and hunter myself at that time, I decorated in the dead, meaning I had taxidermy abundant in my home. My home, although located within city limits, was reminiscent of a cabin in the north woods. I placed the German mount on a wall in my living room as a daily reminder of the decision I chose. In that manner, I was able to turn a very negative obscure idea into a positive piece of art. Whenever I glanced at the skull, I realized that the outcome of that day could have been very different. Right or wrong? I'll never know, but very different, yes.

Now to end this chapter with a funny story that would have been very embarrassing if I would have known any of the drivers passing by that morning. I had (have) chronic pain as a lot of us do. I had been given a tube of capsaicin cream from my daughter's gramma to try on my wrists because I was dealing with a lot of pain there at that time. The cream had helped both Gramma and Grampa back then. My wrists were irritated because I was operating a newer model of hydraulic crane at that time that had joysticks instead of levers that operated it's functions. At the end of my shifts, my wrists felt the equivalent of playing video games all day. I could see that function set up as inciting carpal tunnel syndrome for operators in the future.

I thought, "What have I got to lose? I've tried everything else to no avail. I should give it a shot." I generously rubbed the cream all over my hands and wrists before leaving for my long one-and-a-half-hour drive to my jobsite I was working on at the time. As I pulled out of my driveway, I felt a warm, tingling sensation just as I had in the past using my Tiger Balm. That product contained a form of menthol that helped me somewhat with pain.

It was winter, and it had been a particularly snowy one. In fact, the snowdrifts on the side of the freeway were quite high from the snowplows having recently cleared the roads. I was about one-third of the way to my jobsite when the warmth from the cream I'd administered to my hands and wrists turned to a hot, steaming, fiery sensation, and it was not lessening in any way. In fact, the heat was increasing; I took off my winter driving gloves and pulled up my jacket sleeves in the hopes that the cold winter air would cool off the boiling hot sensation growing in my hands and wrists. It wasn't stopping! It was getting hot, HOT, *HOTTER*—I was on FIRE!

I pulled over as tightly as I could to the snowbank on the side of the freeway. I ran out my door sure that the drivers passing by could see the invisible flames shooting up from my arms! My car was running, my door remained open as I ran as fast as I could and plunged my arms into the snow. I was shocked that the entire snowbank didn't melt instantly upon my abrupt intrusion. I had noticed my arms were red in color in the areas I'd applied that cream before I had made a mad dash for the snow pile. Now as I pulled them from the soothing icy sensation of the snow, they were red from the opposite extreme in temperatures. What a rough start to my day, and as I looked up, emerging from my dive into the snowbank, my face became red as well. Rubberneckers! Drivers slowly passing me by, gawking at the sight of the crazy woman rocketing out of her car and diving into a snowbank.

I could just imagine the tales told in the offices that day of the sight they'd seen as they drove into work. It couldn't have equaled the hilarity of my crew with their endless wisecracking when they overheard my explanation of why I was late for work that morning. I don't know which was worse: the ever-encompassing heat I felt from that dastardly cream on my arms or the endless jeers from the court jesters I had to work with. WTF!

On a final note, if I had a dollar for every time I was told, "You don't want to go in there" as a man exited a toilet I was endlessly waiting to useI'd be rich! First off, it was a port-a-potty, and it already stank!

I felt like answering, "I know you're full of shit, but you give yourself too much credit." Jeez!

My favorite lunch, perfect for construction work, was a roasted turkey leg. You know those big giant turkey drumsticks that are sold at fairs and festivals? Those kind. We had a nearby grocery store that used to cook those the same way they cooked rotisserie chickens. I would have to order them ahead of time because they sold out so fast. I could take one turkey leg to work in my lunch box with an ice pack, and the thing was so big that it would take me two lunches to finish eating it. The guys thought it was the funniest thing ever to see a woman ravenously devouring a ginormous turkey leg, waving it as if it were a magic wand as she spoke with effervescence as I pointed out to my comedic comrades while staying true to my Viking heritage that it would make a good "club," and also as a martial artist, it would make a hell of a "throwing star." Either way, it would hurt like hell if I happened to hit them with it—ha-ha!

CHALLENGING AND JUST PLAIN SCARY

This is going to be a hard chapter for me to write. There, I said it. It took me two months just to jot down the memories and how I wanted to put them into words on scraps of paper. These memories are hard to live with. I'm hoping that once I write them out in full that they will quit appearing from time to time as nightmares. Even though these stories happened years ago, I can recall them easily in the present because some of them were that devastating.

In three of these stories, my life nearly ended, but rather than deal with something scary right off the bat, I will tell you about a jobsite under the "challenging" category.

The asshole I worked with as employees of the bridge building contractor had unfortunately come to work a couple of years later at the usual company that I worked for. He was the guy who made an apprentice pile driver and myself in five below zero temperatures (not factoring in the windchill, mind you) unload a semi load of pipe pile in blizzard conditions. He was the guy who insisted that I use the outrageously heavy outrigger pads he'd had made for my crane. He was also the man who didn't like me for no other reason when he first met me because his wife and I *had the same name.* Sometime later, I came to realize that she wore the pants in his family. a big, robust (FAT!) man, and her being a tiny, diminutive stature of a woman. I didn't care; I couldn't stand the motherf——r!

I ended up with him as my foreman on a jobsite in a more expensive area of town. We were driving pile in an excavated area to erect a new pump house. It would be supplying water to the nearby area. It turned out to be one of those *jinxed* jobsites where a lot of bad things happened. First off, the residents in that ritzy area were opposed to the noise we made driving pile. Although we began work at 7:00 a.m., we were not allowed to make our first strike on a pile until eight, and we were not permitted to work past four in the afternoon. The people in the area wanted the project magically completed without a whisper of a sound being made. It was a very large and congested jobsite with a large variety of different unions working on the project.

Our materials were stockpiled in a yard at the far end of the jobsite. It was quite a balancing act for me to navigate the long pipe pile from the yard over to the crane within reach for the operator to pick it up. I was operating a larger extending forklift to handle the heavier weight capacities of our materials.

The harder I worked and the more I got done, the more resentment was directed to me from the foreman. The man was a prick to anyone other than the crane operator, who he had ridden into work with. Not only did the foreman pick the operator up on his way into work, but he would make him drive once he reached the operator's home. They would reverse that scenario on their drive home from the job each day, making the crane operator an operator/chauffeur. One morning, when the foreman arrived, he looked at everyone except for me as he ran through our planning for the days goals in productivity. Later that morning, he spoke to my good buddy who assisted me in rigging up the materials I was to haul with my forklift. He said, "Tell *her* that I need a welder brought over to the crane" as I stood directly next to my buddy.

WHAT? I was standing right in front of the foreman, and yet he refused to acknowledge my presence. My buddy said, "You tell her, she's standing right in front of you!"

Not only would he not look at me or talk to me directly, he began sitting in front of me when we broke for coffee or lunch break. We normally sat on buckets in a circle as we ate so that we could see and talk to each other. I was surprised that we didn't have a job trailer on that large jobsite as all the other contractors did.

I felt like I was in third grade, for Christ's sake, as I was forced to look at my foreman's back when he sat on his bucket in front of me. The guys were asking me what was going on in private but not daring to say anything in front of the foreman. I'd tell them that he was just being a dick, as usual. I knew the foreman was just trying like hell to provoke me into quitting his jobsite, but I wouldn't give him the satisfaction. Living with the ironworker first husband had prepared me well for all the bullshit the assholes of the world could dish out. I remained my pleasant self and kept my laughter at his juvenile behavior on the inside and endured his adolescence.

I came upon a freaky science fiction sight when I walked to the side of the river that ran along one side of our jobsite. It was "neon green." I had never seen anything like it, except for when Chicago puts dye in their river so it's green for St. Patrick's Day. When I asked my buddy to go see it for himself, he confirmed that he saw a green river as well. We were alarmed; were the fish that came out of there going to be green too? And how about the birds that ate the fish? Would they then turn green? What the hell was going on?

It turned out that some slick city engineers wanted to note the exact flow of the waterway and had come up with their brilliant (not!) idea of turning our river water an ungodly shade of green to carry out their survey of the water flow.

A tragedy occurred while we were working on that jobsite. There was a train that ran a few times each day through the center of the town we were working in. A young boy was walking along the tracks to school one morning. He had headphones and the hood of his sweatshirt covering his head. He must have had the volume turned up extremely loud because he didn't hear the train behind him rapidly approaching. He didn't even hear the trains whistle blowing as its conductor tried like hell to warn the boy to get off the tracks. The train ran over the boy, and he was killed. The morale on that jobsite was as low as it could have possibly become, and the train that ran through that town was a daily reminder of the accident.

The last trauma I endured on that jobsite was when the foreman had to come down from his high horse and talk to me face-toface. Our hammer had broken as it was driving a pile down into the ground. It sat high up in the air in its broken state. It was so high that the foreman had a superintendent come out on our jobsite and come up with a game plan on how to fix it. The superintendent himself told me that he wanted me to put a sheet of plywood onto my forks, and then I'd drive my forklift as close to the leads the pile sat in as I could. I was to scope him up and out as he stood on the platform so that he could closely examine the broken hammer.

I scoped him up and out, back to the ground, back and forth as he required. I knew that he wasn't tied off while on the plywood I held, and his excuse was that he needed to be mobile when climbing onto the hammer. I figured that he and the foreman were in charge, and as the operator, I was to take their signals. That night, I received a phone call at home, telling me that as an operator with many years of service and experience under my belt, I knew better. I should have refused to allow the superintendent or the foreman access to ride on the forks of my machine unless they were tied off and wore the appropriate safety harnesses. I was given a verbal warning that would be recorded in my employee record. I was given one more chance to comply with all of my company's safety rules. Otherwise, I would be given a written warning. After that, if I had another safety violation, I would be let go from the company. All of that grief because I followed the direct requests of my foreman.

The next morning, at our safety meeting, the foreman told the crew that he and I had both been reprimanded. He told me specifically that if I didn't agree to what he was asking of me that I should speak up and say no. That was short-lived, however, when he suggested that I ride him once again on the forks of my forklift. When I told him no, he began giving me the silent treatment again, which I was grateful for. I didn't want to see him, hear him, nor work for him anymore—*ever.*

The first accident that I witnessed on a jobsite was my introduction to working with a contractor that specialized in building hospitals. It was already underway when I showed up as the oiler on a large crane assembled to set the iron for a new hospital building. It was a congested and very active jobsite. Laborers were pouring concrete into forms around us nearly every day. This was before workers had to use proper scaffolding and follow the rules of use for scaffolding that is in place today. Back then, they were standing on whatever they could put together.

The ironworker rod busters were racing ahead of the laborers, setting tie-wired rebar forms inside of the wooden ones the carpenters had put together. We were setting iron in close proximity to the forms being set and poured with concrete. On the day of the accident, I was watching the two laborers setting up planks of wood across the top of two barrels. They were standing on top of the long planks of wood, waiting for the concrete truck to arrive so that they could pour that column. One of the men made his way over to his partner, and by doing so, it caused the weightless end of the planks to kick up into the air. The men were dumped off to the side, and as they fell to the ground, they landed upon the rebar that was sticking up into the air. Both men were punctured and lay there, screaming in agony. Men ran over to help them, and one man ran for the nearest phone to call for an ambulance.

As soon as the men were lifted from the rebar that had pierced them, they were taken to the nearest hospital entrance. Thank God we were directly next to the hospital that we were adding onto. We never heard if the two men were going to be okay or not. What shocked me was that everyone jumped into action to clear up that jobsite because OSHA safety inspectors were on their way to the jobsite. I'm sure that accident wasn't the only one that brought about new safety regulations involving covering open rebar with caps to place on the ends. There became a whole slew of rules and regulations regarding the use of proper scaffolding and anchoring it so that it's incapable of tipping once it's put in place.

I met an ironworker who began his career as a crane operator. He was lowering down a bundle of rebar from the roof of a building when the load shifted and toppled sideways. All the rebar fell from high above, crashing through his glass ceiling and front windows. The rebar drove through his body and pinned him to his seat. They had to take him in his crane seat out of the crane as one unit and take him to the hospital that way. He was lucky to have survived. He told me that he'd rather be high in the air after that accident so that he was never underneath the rebar in that manner ever again. That was his reason for deciding to becoming an ironworker.

My first "jinxed" jobsite was when we set iron for the university's architectural building. That was the same jobsite that I wrote about in the "Funny and Absurd" chapter. It was the one where we were attempting to work in five below zero temperatures, and the ironworkers got lit at lunchtime and called it a day. It was the same jobsite where all the ironworkers were getting a divorce after forgetting their women on Valentine's Day.

The job started off rough immediately. The very first day, we began putting the boom into the crane after both had been delivered to the jobsite. We worked long hours that day. As we were connecting the heavy pendant cables that lift the boom up into the air, one cable slid off the top of the boom section we were connecting. The large knuckle that the pin ran through to join the two sections of pendant cable together hit me directly in the kneecap, taking me down to the ground. As I lay there on the ground, looking up at the stars in great agony, I thought, "Why in the f——k are we doing this in the dark with only the headlights of the foreman's truck to work by?" I could have sworn my kneecap has shattered, but as time went on, some of the pain became less intense, so I went back to work. I didn't want to lose my job, so I made it into work the following day with heavy bruising and lingering pain in and around my knee.

Things went along smoothly for a time on that jobsite until we began decking the lower floors below the ironworkers connecting the iron for the higher floors above. A semitruck pulled up to the jobsite with pallets of bricks that needed to be unloaded. The bricks would make up the outer walls of the building once its skeleton of iron was completed. Since the bricks arrived way earlier than anticipated, we were at a loss as to where to store them. We had minimal room as it was on that jobsite, so the ironworkers suggested that we hoist up a couple of pallets of bricks to each floor they had previously decked. In that way, the masons would have some bricks on hand when they began their work.

The truck driver was hooking up the crane to the pallets one at a time as he rigged them. One pallet was being hoisted up to the third floor when the rigging began to fail. The pallet was about up to the second floor when it began to rain bricks. The straps used to wrap underneath the pallet and up to the headache ball had ripped under their weight. One strap had severed entirely, and the pallet tilted.

Everyone scattered out of the way of the falling bricks, and we were lucky that no one was struck by them; someone could have been killed. The decking that some of the bricks hit was heavily dented, and a couple of holes had been punched through by the bricks also. It took a lot of extra time to cut loose the damaged pieces of decking. It was difficult to swing out those pieces and then swing in new ones because iron was already erected above the damaged floors.

The worst thing to happen on that jobsite involved an ironworker apprentice. He had been a semitruck driver for many years. In fact, he had made deliveries to ironworkers on construction sites on many occasions. He decided that he was tired of driving for a living and wanted to make the kind of wages and benefits that the ironworkers did. He quit his job as a semitruck driver and became the oldest ironworker apprentice that I had ever heard of. He was in his late-thirties and had a harder time hustling around the jobsite in comparison to the younger apprentices. I gave him a lot of credit for not allowing his age to factor into him chasing his dreams.

One afternoon, he was assigned to work with the decking crew. Decking is corrugated sheets of steel. The bundles they arrive in are extremely heavy. There is a sheen of oil in between each sheet to keep them from sticking together. The ironworkers would use their sleever bars to wedge between the sheets to separate them in order for two men to pick up one sheet. They would carefully walk the iron beams to place the sheets beside each other. The edge of each sheet sat over the edge of the sheet put down before it. A welder would then tack the two sheets together by spot welding along the adjoining seam. Once the sheets were in place and tacked together, the men were able to safely walk across the floor. It was slippery due to the coating of oil, so only ironworkers that did not have to connect iron would walk on those decked floors.

The apprentice was crossing a decked floor but did not look closely to see if it had been tack welded yet. It wasn't, and when the apprentice stepped on the seam of two sheets of decking, they separated. He fell between the open sheets but quickly threw his elbows up, catching them on the sheets. He was dangling dangerously up on the fourth floor, screaming in pain. He could have slipped through those slippery iron sheets and fallen to his death at any moment.

The rest of us managed to finish that job in one piece, but not long afterward, devastation would hit. The ironworker that had given me the camcorder to film him and his shy (right?) brother connecting was working demolishing a structure. He was up on a manlift high in the air, cutting loose a large steel plate. To get a better angle, he climbed outside the man basket (which is now a safety violation), and he had detached his lanyard in order to reach the area he needed to cut with a torch. Back then, the safety lanyard was an eight or ten-foot section of a certain type of rope. The rope was of a high quality, but the present lanyards are far different and much improved upon (it was and is illegal in safety regulations to detach your safety lanyard when you are up off the ground and working as he was). When he cut through the remainder of the steel plate, it swiftly fell to the ground, taking the ironworker down with it. It was a Friday right after lunch break that he lay on the ground, smashed flat by the heavy iron plate.

He had been an ironworker for as long as my first husband, who began working at seventeen years old. He was one of my first husband's "partners in crime" as they got in a lot of trouble together. I was and am friends with his wife, and it was a very difficult time for her and her two daughters that he was a stepdad to. A funny memory (now, *not* then) was when I was throwing rocks at his car after he dropped off my first husband *long* after bar closing one early morning, thinking that he was a woman as he sped away. I wrote about that incident in the chapter "What the Fuck!"

At the funeral, I gave a copy of the tape we made that day at work with his camcorder to his wife so that she could see her husband and hear him speaking whenever she wanted to. The ironworkers, friends, and family filled the church where his service was held, and you couldn't find a parking space for many city blocks because he knew so many people.

One very hot summer, we began a pile driving job across the street from our casino that I worked on all phases to build. We were to drive pile on which spectators bleachers were to be erected on a newly landscaped soccer field. We were also driving pile to hold up a huge electric scoreboard. I had my fourth surgery scheduled to remove the endometriosis that had once again bound up the insides of my abdomen. It caused me agonizing pain to push down on any brake pedals, so instead of operating the crane, I was running the extending forklift on that jobsite because it was safer for me to do so. We were limited on space, so our material yard was located down the road a bit from where the crane was driving pile. I had to drive down there to fetch the pipe pile we would need as we moved along. We had an old-timer who had been with the company his entire career, stationed in the material yard so that he could weld the boots (steel plate bottoms) onto the first piles to be driven in each location. It was superhot outside, and the old-timer had to wear welding sleeves to do his job. Welding safety gear was a cropped long sleeved suede jacket and was worn to keep the sparks from burning the worker as they welded. It was not difficult to become inflamed while welding.

The old man was overheated whenever I saw him, and so I always reminded him to hydrate whether with the water he brought to work or with the Gatorade that all of our jobsites mixed up each morning during the hot summer months. One afternoon, I noticed him returning from somewhere at the end of our lunch break. When I asked him where he had found a place to eat nearby, he told me that he had just found a tavern. We were not allowed entry to dine within the casino because of their dress code, and we were in a fairly secluded location, which was why I asked where our crew could eat. I could tell that he'd been drinking his lunch, which was out of character for that man. He told me that he was in utter confusion and despair. Several nights before, he had arrived at home after work to an empty house. His wife and stepdaughter were not home, and all of his furniture and household items were completely gone. His wife had left him with no warning at all, and she had stripped him of everything except his clothing and personal hygiene items. She didn't even leave him a chair to sit on or dishes and utensils so that he could eat. He had fallen off the wagon and was drowning his sorrows in the taverns.

I felt bad for him and was worried that he would pass out working in the heat in a dehydrated state. When I drove back to the crew with our next few pipe pile, I told the foreman about the state of our welder and what he had been going through. We would all keep an eye out for him and make sure to check on him from time to time.

My surgery date arrived, and I was to be off of work for two weeks to recuperate. I had just made it home from the hospital and was resting on our couch when I received a phone call from the foreman of my jobsite. He told me that it was a good thing I wasn't at work because there had been a terrible accident. The company was shorthanded at the time, so the crew was told to spend the afternoon in our yard four to load up a semitrailer with bundles of sheeting.

They had to separate pairs of sheets, and to do so, the crane would tap one corner of a sheet against the ground by dropping it enough in free fall to make an impact. Upon impact, the second sheet would drop a bit. They would continue bouncing the lower sheet against the ground and sliding the sheet connected to the crane's hook out of the lock holding the pair together. Back then, we had open hooks on our rigging, and you had to be careful when separating sheets so that the hook didn't pop out of the hole that had been burned into the sheeting.

That was exactly what had happened when they were bouncing the sheeting onto the ground in their separating attempts. There became enough slack in the chains when the sheeting hit against the ground that the hook came out of the hole, and the sheeting was free standing. The men scattered to get out of the way of the falling pair of sheets. Unfortunately, the old-timer was too slow to clear the falling sheets, and they landed on top of him, crushing him to death. It was a horrible accident and an awful reminder that you had to keep your head in the game on a construction site. Accidents like that one were the reasons behind the installed OSHA standards of safety hooks. All rigging devices with hooks attached needed to have a latch installed that prohibited the release of any rigging applied to a hook. It then became necessary for anyone removing rigging from a hook to hold back the latch in order to remove the rigging. It was extremely sad that the old-timer lost his life, and to make matters worse, the wife who had left him without any notice and who had stripped him of his stepdaughter and all his belongings showed up immediately upon his death to reap the benefits of his pension from his union. I'm glad that I wasn't there to witness the accident; if it weren't for my surgery, I would have been.

My now husband and I were told to drive the yard crane to a town west of our city. We were to drive piling along the side of a company building so that they could expand. We would be driving the pile extremely close to the existing wall. My now husband was the foreman on our jobsite, and he headed out before me to check out the site to see where we needed to set up the crane to put the boom in and place our equipment and materials. The mobile friction crane was very slow, and I had quite a few cars trailing behind me. I was driving on a two-lane busy street. No one was passing me at my slow pace, probably because they couldn't see around the crane to do so.

I felt bad about holding up the traffic, so at the next area of the road that I had a bit of a shoulder, I steered the crane off the road enough to allow the cars behind me to pass by. What a mistake! The heavy weight of the crane sunk down on the side that the tires were no longer on the pavement. The crane immediately tipped to the side, and the tires that were on the pavement cocked up into the air. Then the shit hit the fan when the heavy counterweights that were mounted on the back of the crane caused the house to swing completely around. Then not only was the crane almost tipped over onto its side, but the front of the truck portion was raised high up into the air! It was a precariously dangerous situation. I was on top of a ridge with a plaza of businesses to the side below me, and I was afraid that the crane could roll down the hill sideways at any moment.

The boom butt of the crane was over the road, facing up to the sky, and the counterweights were over the edge of the ridge. I could walk beneath the boom butt and have clearance between it and myself. The cars would have no problem driving under the boom butt, but the drivers were afraid to do so. The traffic had backed up as far down the road as I could see. A police car finally pulled up, and the officer looked totally confused as to what was going on. After I'd explained to him that if the crane was to go anywhere, it would go backward down the hill. It was definitely not going to magically set back down on the road by itself. I told him to please direct the traffic to pass and move on. I then asked him to watch over the crane while I walked down to one of the businesses to use their phone so that I could call my foreman.

Back then, there were cell phones just coming into existence. The company had given them to some of the foreman. I couldn't get through to my foreman, so I called the office only to say that my foreman had driven on ahead of me to check out the jobsite, and I needed him back to the crane to assist me. They were able to get through to him, and when he drove up to me, he had a shocked expression on his face. I explained that I pulled over to allow the backed up traffic to pass, to which he said, "F—k those people. That crane is too heavy to be on the soft shoulder of the road. Once we hit the asphalt, you don't leave it for any reason."

I agreed and then asked if we should call the towing service our company used to haul our large air compressors to jobsites. I suggested that the tow truck could upright the totally tilted crane.

"Hell no!" the foreman stated. "We're going to jump this baby out of this soft soil, so hop up into that seat."

We had just begun dating, and I will honestly tell you that if any other man told me to just "hop up into that seat," I would have told him what he could have done with *"his"* seat and handed him the screwdriver in my pocket and told him that he could jam that into *"his"* seat as well! BUT since it was *that* particular foreman, I thought to myself, "What the hell, we'll give it a shot."

I had a hell of a time trying to climb up into a seat that was virtually looking up at the sky once I managed to get in it. As I'm writing about that awful gut-wrenching day, I'm just glad we *didn't* have cell phones back then. If everyone was filming that afternoon,

I would have felt even worse about it than I already did, and we would have probably broken the Internet!

He told me to step on the throttle and swing the crane into its proper position, which was the boom butt over the front. There was a cradle for it to be latched down in for traveling. I was trying like hell to get the counterweights over the rear end of the machine. I felt like I was sitting in one of those teacups on a Tilt-A-Whirl ride. I kept swinging, trying to get the momentum going to kick the house of the crane in line with the rest of the machine. The foreman had managed to climb up into the cab on the truck portion of the crane. He yelled back to me that as soon as I got that crane house swung around that he was going to gun it and throw it into gear to drive us forward.

As soon as it swung into the proper direction, he punched it! The whole front of the crane jumped ahead from its reared up position like a steel stallion. Sure enough, he jumped that crane back onto the asphalt. I couldn't believe it, but I was so lucky to be back on the road and headed to our jobsite. I didn't need the office personnel hearing about my major f——k up. I didn't want to give them any reason to keep me out of a crane seat. After that fiasco, my road etiquette went right out the window. I became a ruthless road hog, driving my sloth of a crane down the road at a whopping forty miles an hour.

We made it to the jobsite and prepared to drive pile the following day. We didn't make any mistakes as we drove piling extremely close to their existing building. After almost tipping my crane over sideways and possibly rolling down the hill with it, driving pile up close to a wall was a piece of cake.

I went to work on a bridge for the contractor who specialized in that field of construction. I'd completed many bridges with them and have written about a couple of them. The one I'm writing about now was very complicated and challenging. That bridge was and still is utilized heavily throughout each day. Our job was to widen it and pour a raised pedestrian sidewalk along one side of it. Our main problem was that there was no room in which to park a crane or to install its boom. The bridge had originally been built in an arch. It rose up and over two sets of railroad tracks far below. There were several trains that ran across those tracks throughout each day. On one set, the trains traveled to the north, and the other set took them to the south.

We had to work down below the bridge where there was enough room for all of our concrete forms, rigging, materials, and an area for the jobsite trailer and our vehicles. I had a long stick of boom so that I could reach the bridge above me. I couldn't see where most of my picks were up top, so I had a signalman. I followed his hand signals and did exactly what they told me to do.

The scary part of that job was when I had to track up and over one set of railroad tracks and sit between the two sets in order to work on one end of the bridge. My signalman would let me know as soon as both sets of tracks were clear of trains. I had to lay down hardwood lumber on the sides and in between the tracks to make a "step" for the crane tracks to climb over. My crane's tracks were very similar to those on a tank. I couldn't climb up at too great of an angle or my tracks would slam back down to the ground. I had to stay as level as possible because of the long boom I had attached to the crane. There were active high wires above us that I had to keep aware of and keep a safe distance from them.

The two trains traveling in opposite directions passed right next to each other at some point during the day. I couldn't hear the trains approaching because of my loud crane engine, but sometimes I could feel my crane vibrating from them becoming closer. Whenever a train was going to pass very close by me and especially when both trains passed by on either side of me at the same time, I had to keep my crane straight ahead and the boom angled up until they had gone by. The vibration was like being in an earthquake, and I had to wear earmuffs over my earplugs because the sound of the trains that close to me was deafening. As scary and dangerous as that job was, we executed it beautifully, and it went off without a hitch.

There are several photographs I've included that were taken of the jobsite that I'm going to write about. I was called to work for the out of state contractor that I'd been working the winter months with for several years. I was laid off by my usual company for the winter, and by working for the other contractor, I could keep making my wages and put hours toward my benefits. This job was to be different in that my ironworker husband had also been sent out from his union hall to work on the same project. In fact, my ironworker husband was to be my signalman as I operated a hydraulic crane. There were to be two hydraulic cranes in order to make dual picks, where both cranes were needed to lift the heavy portions of the large Manitowoc crane being trucked in. Once the large crane was put together, I was to be the oiler for the operator running it, and the hydraulic cranes would be returned to the rental company. Right from the start, that job proved to be one of the "jinxed" jobsites I've mentioned.

First off, it was a whole bunch of ironworkers, the crane operator, and myself. They all thought it was funny that my husband was working on the same project as his wife; the jokes were relentless. I was used to being razzed, so that didn't bother me. What did, however, was when they would hand out the paychecks each week, and they would give my husband MY paycheck as well as his own. I would say that I needed to see my check so that I could make sure all the information on it was correct (wages, hours, pension, and health insurance). I was told "not to worry about it." All the ironworkers would say, "Way to go, G—!" I tried like hell to get my check from my husband once we were home, but it would have been easier for me to pull his teeth out with a pair of pliers.

The incident of a "special" port-a-potty showing up just for me, even though I never dreamed of asking for one, happened on that jobsite as well. It insinuated to the men that I was a diva and too good to share a shitter with them. That move on the superintendent's part put my tits in a wringer. It created ill feelings from the men toward me, and I didn't appreciate it at all. One morning, we entered the jobsite to find a note placed on the crane's door. It notified the crane operator that a bolt of lightning was seen striking the crane's boom which stood high up into the sky. There had been a hell of a storm the evening before. We had to put a halt to the progression of the job so that we could track the crane out onto the street so that we had enough room to boom all the way down to the ground. We needed to do a thorough search of the entire boom and crane.

When the lightning entered the boom, it had to have exited somewhere. We were using a rental crane, so their erection specialist (yes, that was his title, and it even said so on his business cards—hey, I don't make this shit up) drove out to assist us.

We had a few ironworkers help in our search since they always put cranes together and, after a job's completion, dismantled them. They were well aware of what we were looking for. We finally found the burned area. The lightning had blown out through the boom cable on the last wrap on the drum. That meant that if we were not notified about the lightning strike, we could have lost our boom when we made a heavy pick. At that time, we were hanging heavy precast panels on the top two floors of our five-floor parking structure. We could have had a disaster on our hands.

It took us a few days to pull all of the old cable off and replace it with new cable before we could return to setting the precast wall sections that would cover the exterior of the parking structure. During that phase of the project was when my husband took me to lunch at the tavern the ironworkers were frequenting. On the way back to the crane, he insisted on driving me right up to the crane. I asked him to let me off of his Harley motorcycle, but no, he wouldn't hear of it. He ended up dumping his Harley about midway to the crane. They had trucked in big stone for the heavy crane to sit on, and as a rider of a Harley myself, I knew it was a no-no to drive the Harley on those rocks. He had the balls to yell at me to help him lift up his Harley as it was pinning me between it and the rocks. What he *should* have been concerned about was ME as I lay there, *crushed!* I had to work for the rest of the afternoon and was lucky I didn't break something. As I lay there, waiting for him and another ironworker to lift the Harley off of me, there were five floors of ironworkers clapping and yelling, "Way to go, you two!" *Nice.*

When we were setting the precast on the top floor, it was a lot harder for the ironworkers to keep the panels steady and landing them on their appropriate marks due to the wind. One afternoon, disaster happened when an ironworker's finger was crushed between two panels of precast. He had his work glove on, but his blood was pouring out of it. He was screaming in pain as his buddies walked him down the parking structure ramp and drove him across the river to the emergency room of the hospital the parking structure was being built for.

The accident ended his career, and he was lucky to have been able to keep his finger. They had reconstructed it and mended the nerves to the best of their abilities, but his hand would never be the same. He came to the jobsite to pick up his last paycheck and belongings. He had his entire arm rigged up in a cast that kept his hand in a particular angle. All of these needles ran through his repaired finger so that it looked like a human pin cushion! He had a long road of therapy and further surgeries ahead of him.

We finally came to the end of the job and had set the last piece of iron. There were several more pieces of precast to set and a lot of bolting up and welding to do. As was customary, they were having a "topping off" party after work on that day the last piece of iron was put in place. The superintendent invited all of us workers to a tavern immediately following our shift that day. The husband headed there with all his buddies while I went to pick up our daughter. I celebrated by getting our family takeout for dinner from our favorite neighborhood Mexican restaurant.

My daughter and I settled in at home for the evening. I had a shitload of ironing to do, so I took my plate of food with me to the basement downstairs to eat it while I was ironing. My daughter remained upstairs with our dog to watch some television. I remember hearing our front door open upstairs and knew it had to be my husband because the dog didn't bark, and I could hear my daughter talking to someone. My dog would have barked if anyone he didn't know came near our house, and the husband had used his key to enter. I remember also that I thought it was rather early for him to be home with the party for our jobsite going on.

As he came down the stairs, and I was going to tell him that his dinner was in the frig, he started in on me right away. It was "cunt" this and "cunt" that; he made it very clear that he had come home to fight with me. I'd been called a cunt and every other awful word you could think of so many times that they had no further effect on me. It was when he called me "stupid" that I had to agree. I thought, *I'm stupid for putting up with all of your goddamned shit!*

In that second, *I'D HAD IT!* I couldn't stand the nasty sewage spewing from his mouth anymore. I blasted him with my fist as hard as I'd ever thrown a punch, right into his dumpster of a mouth. Then it was on. The *red curtain* dropped down over my face, and fists were flying.

My daughter, hearing all the commotion, was at the top of the stairs, saying, "Stop hurting my mom!" The asshole turned his face up in her direction, and I saw a flash of anger on his face; he had a new target. I ran out from the laundry area and got ahead of him. I was running up the stairs as fast as I could to grab my daughter and my keys. I'd had to run for it too many times to count. I would drive us away from our home and get us somewhere safe until he left the house or passed out. I was afraid he would either hit our daughter to make her stop screaming at him or shake her and break her little arm.

As I was running up the stairs, I was hit so hard in the back of my head that it dropped me to my knees, and I saw stars blinking throughout my vision; blackness was creeping in from the perimeter of my sight, and I was afraid of blacking out. I couldn't. *I had to take care of my daughter. I had to protect her at all costs.* I prayed for God to let me get up, and I did. I had never been put down to my knees like that in the twelve years of *kumite* (full contact fighting in karate) I had done. When I stood up, he smashed me once again in the back of my head. That time I turned and planted a *yoko kekomi* (side thrusting kick) right in his chest to gain some distance between us. He smashed into the brick wall behind him. and that was when I saw my *iron* in his hand. He'd blasted me in the head not once but twice with my own iron. Here was the "light bulb" moment in which I realized this all important fact: if you manage to stand up after someone strikes you down when you're not looking. and *then they hit you hard again.* they don't want you TO "EVER" GET UP!

My head was throbbing, on fire with pain. My poor daughter having witnessed her dad smashing her mom in the head was shivering uncontrollably. I felt so bad for her and just wanted to get beyond the vicious encounter as soon as possible. Her dad raced passed us and left the house; I could hear his truck pull out of our driveway.

That was what I hated the most; we would be living our lives in peace with me tackling some household chores and then like an angry volcanic eruption of mental insanity, her dad would burst into our home, *drunk,* and God knew what else and demolish and destroy our lives within a matter of minutes. We would unexpectedly have to flee, and I wouldn't know if our family was going to be intact the next day or not. I usually was unable to sleep that night after finding us a place to stay at the last minute. Sometimes I was able to take the dog with us also.

On that night, shortly after he left, the police walked right through my front door. They told me that they had received a phone call from my husband claiming that I was kicking his ass and was a black belt in each of two forms of karate. They were there *to arrest ME!* I told them exactly what had happened and asked them if it looked like I had won the fight with him. My head was on fire and my right ear felt a weird kind of pain. When I put my fingers to my ear, it felt like I was touching an entire hand! My ear was so swollen that I knew what a "cauliflower" ear was that boxers get sometimes from a fight. It was fairly recent that I had found a quarter stick of dynamite placed directly beneath my bed just under the floor in the basement ceiling. I had removed the dynamite and gave it to a guy at work who took it up north to blow up an outhouse (WTF!). I didn't ask the ironworker husband where he got the dynamite or why he wanted to blow me up. There was no clowning gesture on his part like, *"Whoops,* you found the dynamite I had hidden underneath your bed, ha-ha."

I didn't rave, "You crazy bastard, are you out of your mind?" No, nothing like that. Crazy or absurd, it was just an everyday occurrence; no wonder I suffered from PTSD. Working alongside so many men throughout all those years, I found it in their nature to shoot to kill. They love to burn things up, chop things down, and blow things up whether that be an outhouse or a wife. That explanation is plain to see when you watch the news or notice your male neighbor's fascination with the constant mowing (down) of their lawns and inevitable tree trimming.

The police told me that if they were called out to a "domestic disturbance," they had to arrest someone, and since I was the only adult present, it was going to be me. My asinine husband, as drunk as he was, had the foresight to call 911 and got me jammed up with the police. All they had to do was look me up, and they would see my two previous assault charges on police officers. I told the officers, "I'm not going. I didn't start the fight nor did I want it to happen." Then I asked them, "Does it look like I won this fight?" once again. I told them that I was moving out of the house with my daugh-

ter the next day, so they let me stay in the house for the evening. They asked if I wanted to go to the hospital, but I did not want any more drama for my daughter, who I was trying to calm down. After I declined the ride to the hospital, I told them that I wanted my husband arrested. I told them that he had used the pay phone at the tavern up the street to call them. If he wasn't at that tavern, then he was most likely at the one a few blocks away. I explained that we were both working on the same construction site and that I didn't want to go into work and see him there. They told me that they would pick him up.

After the police left our house, my daughter began crying again. I told her that it was all over and that we would be moving so I wouldn't have to deal with fighting anymore. I told her that she didn't need to cry anymore, and she pointed at me in distress and said, "You have chimichanga all over your face!" and began to cry even harder.

My poor daughter was crying for my own embarrassment and humiliation. I had completely forgotten that when her dad had called me stupid, he had also taken my plate of food and not only jammed it into my face but smashed it all down the front of me—no wonder I blasted him one! So I was talking to the police with refried beans, rice, and a hell of a tasty chimichanga smeared all over me. I had no clue that I had insult added to injury as I spoke with them, and they had never let on that I looked like a mash up of Mexican buffet. WTF!

That night was a huge wake-up call for me. He had never struck me when I wasn't looking. We had always been face-to-face in our hand-to-hand combat situations. I knew then that I had to get us away from him because it was a matter of time before we would end up on the evening news as a domestic homicide. It was inevitable that on a night like that one, we wouldn't wake up to see the light of day. He would wake up to find that he'd murdered his wife and child in a drunken blackout the night before.

I didn't sleep that night as I kept watch over my daughter while she slept. When I was getting ready for work, I noticed that both of my eyes were the blackest they'd ever been, which was alarming because he hadn't hit me in the face, only on the side of my head and in the back of it twice. One of my eyes was only half open because it was so swollen, and the whites of my eyes were then beet-red with broken capillaries. I looked just like Sylvester Stallone in the movie *Rocky* at the end of his fight where he was calling, "Adrian! Adrian!" He was calling for his girlfriend, but his eyes were so beat up that he couldn't see shit.

Well, that was one morning that I couldn't put on any eye makeup. I needed the money to rent a van to move, and I wasn't going to not show up for my job because my husband was an insane asshole. I called my daughter's gramma and asked if she would watch her for me. As soon as I finished work, I wanted to get as much of our stuff that I could fit into a moving van along with my Harley, and we would be out of there. I figured that my husband was in jail, and I wanted to be far away when they let him out. I did not want another altercation with him. I was damn lucky that he didn't kill me with my own iron, and I wasn't going to give him another opportunity to try to kill me again.

When my daughter's gramma opened her door to let in my daughter, she was shocked at my appearance. I told her that we were moving out of our house and leaving town in order to put distance between us and her son. She asked me, "Can't you wait until M——— is eighteen?"

I told her matter-of-factly, "I'm not gonna make it." I was a "dead woman walking" in my own home.

I reluctantly went in to work, even though it was extremely humiliating to have the entire crew see me looking like I'd been in a head on collision on my way to work. When I opened the jobsite trailer door, there was my *husband,* still in the same work clothes he'd had on the day before! WTF! Those cops didn't go to either bar and pick him up. All the men just stared at me, except one iron-worker had the audacity to say, "Way to go G——, keep your woman in line!"

I thought, *Now there's a specimen that could use an iron to the back of the head!* My husband's expression was of confusion and disbelief. As I was walking toward the crane, a union brother buddy of mine came up to me and in a disgusted voice said, "Couldn't you get to the gun?" He was actually upset with me and walked away, shaking his head. I'd known him for many years, and we had gone through our apprenticeship classes at the same time.

It was in that moment I had lost his respect and friendship. He knew that I didn't take crap from anyone, and he expected me to include my husband. I had an extremely hard time performing my duties as an oiler because I couldn't see straight, my balance was off, and I had an excruciating headache.

After a short while, the crane operator received a notice on his walkie-talkie that the superintendent wanted to see me in the trailer. When I entered to speak to him, he told me that I was dismissed for the remainder of the day but that I would be paid. He apologized to me; he could see how drunk and aggressive my husband was becoming the previous evening at the topping off party. I stood before him with my face unrecognizable as the end result of the open bar that he had provided. I told him that I hadn't appreciated him handing my paycheck to my husband week after week, that I hadn't seen the humor in his ordering a "woman's" port-a-potty, and that after I completed that job, I no longer wanted to work for his company. After all the winters that I had worked for the same contractor that he did, he could lose my phone number. That job had just ended my marriage. After the long weekend of unexpectedly having to relocate and upend my life and my daughter's, I returned to the jobsite to finish the last few days I was needed there. My husband approached me and told me that the evening my daughter and I weren't there, he thought that we were just "shopping at Sears"—delusional! I simply stated that I was seeking a divorce. Once I was off that project and working back at my usual company, I heard about one more traumatic accident that happened on that parking structure. The crane operator was using the forklift I had operated while there. I never greased the rod that the forks slid on—ever. I refused to because when carrying a load with a greased rod, the forks slid back and forth and your load would fall off. I'd had it happen to me at a very inopportune time. I would just use my foot on the top of the fork and thrust the fork over with my leg or else I would use a sleever bar to wrench it over. The crane operator was too lazy to do that and sprayed lubricating oil on the rod. When he pushed the fork, it slid so fast and smashed into the other fork, cutting off one of his fingers that had been holding onto it.

Immediately after that blow to my head, I had horrible pain in my wrists and hands. When I went to a doctor, thinking that I'd developed carpal tunnel in my wrists from pulling and pushing on crane levers all those years, I found out that I had fibromyalgia. I had a brain stem injury from my iron hitting the back of my head from one of the blows and an area of mashed nerves damaged from the other blow. A lot of boxers and people who have been in car accidents end up getting it due to head trauma. It is a malady that continually worsens with the passing of time and has no cure. To this day, I have pain in all of my muscles and joints.

After my fibromyalgia diagnosis, I had blurred vision in my right eye; that was the one that was only able to open halfway after that life-altering final fight with the ironworker husband. When I went to an optometrist, I was told that my retina was hanging by a thread and would need repair once it had detached. The longest result and hardest to endure beyond the pain from the blows to my head was the deep depression that enveloped me. I felt like I dropped over the edge into a deep pit of sludge. I looked for help, and the first male therapist I found told me that women don't shoot themselves in the head to commit suicide because it was too messy; they overdose on pills instead. That was his reply to me when I told him that I felt like blowing my brains out.

Wrong answer! That is NOT what a man (or woman for that matter) should say to a depressed woman. I dropped him immediately as my therapist and went elsewhere. The next *male* therapist I saw told me to put on the boxing gloves he handed to me and that we were going to "duke the anger out of me." I declined, stating that I was trying *NOT* to hit out of anguish anymore. He told me that my depression was due to me containing my anger inside and not letting it out. I finally found a *woman* who helped me with therapy and medication for three years before I could deal with it on my own. I couldn't find work in the area that I'd moved to. I found myself having to drive back and forth to Milwaukee every day since that's where the jobs happened to be. I finally moved back there just in time for the stadium project to begin. The old one had been torn down and the area excavated to a flat surface. That job-site also happened to be a "jinxed" one right from the start. I was sent to operate a crane to drive the test pile for the new stadium. It took forever to pound in pile to the deep depths they wanted. One afternoon, we had just moved the crane to a new area they wanted a pile driven in. The markings had been painted on the ground by the engineers we were working with. All the markings were identical. We had just leveled up the pile I was holding in my leads, and I was waiting for the hand signal to tell me to strike the first blow when our head superintendent pulled up to us in his vehicle. He would check with the engineers from time to time to see how deep the pile were going to reach the maximum blows of the hammer we needed to drive it down. On that afternoon, however, he came flying out of his vehicle and told me to stop and *not* hit the valve lever to engage the hammer. He told us that the marking to drive the pile was in the wrong place. The marking I was ready to drive a pile into was the *live* electrical setting for the tall overhead lights that lit up the previous parking lot area. The light had been removed, and the excavator had covered its setting with dirt. If I would have hit that hammer, I would have been electrocuted and anyone remotely close to the crane would have been electrocuted too. It was lucky for us that the superintendent showed up at that exact second.

Our next debacle happened not long after that incident. We had continued driving the necessary test pile, and shortly after lunch one day, I could hear a slight hissing sound; that was never a good sign. I was operating a crane that had air tanks. The air pressure had to be kept up in order to engage the levers that allowed the machine to function. I told the foreman that I could hear a leak coming from the conjunction of air hoses directly to my right. I told him that I would need a few minutes to find the leak and what crane function was affected by it. It didn't take long for me to figure it out because I had been keeping my eye on the boom angle indicator, and it showed me that the boom was slowly inching downward. The hissing from the hose was getting louder and louder, which meant that the hole was becoming larger.

I told the foreman to call the mechanic and have him drive out right away with a new airline for the boom function of the crane. I stood up and pulled in all the levers with my two arms, pulling them in the upward position to slow the progression of the boom's descent. I threw out the master clutch so that no crane functions could be provided. As I slowed down the boom's momentum, I told everyone in the crew to go and move their vehicles so the boom would not crush them as it came down. We had just enough time to clear the area and set down pieces of plywood where the boom tip would be resting on the ground until it was repaired. If that airline had just blown out on us, we would have lost all boom function. It could have come down unexpectedly at a fast pace and crushed everything and anyone in its path—whew, scary!

We had a bizarre complication after that. After they computed the amount and length of pile needed to be put into the ground, we had brought in all our equipment and materials and began driving piling. We were having an unusually wet season, and the jobsite was a muddy mess. We had a heavy storm hit our area one evening, and when we arrived at the jobsite the next morning, we had quite a surprise waiting for us.

The giant hole that had been excavated for us to drive pile in was then a large pond! We also had cranes with drill rigs attached to them for those crews to drill caissons. The caisson holes were large in diameter and deep. The holes dug out for me to drive clusters of pile in were quite large and also deep. With the water covering everything, no one knew for sure where all the holes were. A foreman for the other pile driving crew and crane called to have a rowboat brought to the jobsite along with very long lengths of dowel. He would float across the paths we'd need to track our heavy equipment out of the water and up onto higher ground. He tapped with the dowel as he went, and when he found a hole, he pounded the dowel into the soil below the water next to it so that it would be avoided.

I waded very carefully out to my crane, feeling with my front foot as I went. When all of us operators were in our cranes and other heavy equipment, we followed the foreman in the rowboat and made it safely out of the water. The service crane on the site spent the rest of the day fishing out our welders, toolboxes, air compressors, and other equipment out of the flooded site. All of the pumps and hoses our company had were brought out to begin the long process of pumping all of that water out of the hole and dispersing it far from the jobsite.

We were all relocated to our yards for the several days it took to dry out our jobsite. The mechanics had to change all the oil and air filters on the equipment. Oil changes on the engines had to be performed, and all the heavy equipment had to be greased. The tracks on the friction cranes had to be oiled and greased also. It was a freak situation that took a toll on the timeline of our jobsite's progression.

We had finally been back at driving pile and drilling caissons when I heard a loud thud one afternoon. It felt like we were having a small earthquake that only lasted a few seconds. When I swung my crane around to pick up my next pipe pile to drive, I could see our other pile driving crew standing around their hammer and noticed that it was buried half way into the ground. There was a lot of swearing going on and yelling between the foreman and the crane operator. It turned out that the crane operator had been using a live brake, meaning that it was only the power of his foot on the brake pedal as he was lowering the extremely heavy air hammer. There was "power down" on the cranes that he and I were operating. That allows the operator to have far more control over the speed and continuity of the load as it is being lowered. It was very important when driving pile to set it in place as gently as possible because once it was lowered within reach, it would be manipulated by the hands of one or two pile drivers, depending upon the circumstances.

The hammers we used were so heavy that when you used a live brake (using the pressure of your foot on the brake only), it would most likely slide through the brake, and once it gained momentum, it was impossible to catch. If you *were* able to catch a hammer in freefall by stomping on the brake pedal, you risked a cable or some other form of rigging snapping; just the concussion it caused throughout the boom of the crane had a negative effect on its integrity.

The hammer that got away from the operator had hit the soil so hard that it was then buried half its length into the ground. They had to send for another hammer to be sent out to the jobsite and had to take an enormous amount of time disconnecting from the buried hammer and reconnecting to the newly arrived hammer. The foreman had to set and drive pile by himself while his two crew members dug the buried hammer out by hand. Once uncovered, the hammer had to be taken to the mechanics to have it blown out with an air hose, tested, greased, and lubricated.

Things were not going well on my crew either. I had met the foreman I had on that jobsite many years before on the big sewage treatment plant expansion that I've written quite a bit about. He was a carpenter who happened to be working for the same contractor who, in my future, I would end up building a lot of bridges for. We had become jobsite buddies, and I had become his confidant also as he was going through a divorce. He had even given me some jeans that his wife had left behind when she moved out from their home.

He had hired on with my usual company and begun work there as a foreman. He was one of those men (and there are many) who let that title go straight to his head. He no longer worked in any way other than to tell people what to do. Men like that (and once again, there are *many* of them) were kidding themselves. WTF! They made one dollar more an hour than their fellow pile drivers did because they did the paperwork for their jobsites. They were demeaning and full of hot air (meaning that they were full of shit!). Regardless of who it was, the crane operator made more money per hour and had a higher rate toward their pension and better benefits than the other crew members, which was why I chose to operate one.

He was having me drive the first pile in all the way to nearly the grounds surface. That made the pile driver welder have to lay on a piece of cardboard in the mud and attempt to weld while lying on his side. That pissed me off because it was totally unnecessary to have a man stay in such an awkward position and have the sparks from his welding encompassing his body. I kept arguing with the foreman (no longer my friend, by the way) to allow me to stop driving the pile at a comfortable standing position for the welder, but he would not allow it.

The other issue I was having with the foreman was whenever I was driving pile down in one of the deep pits, I needed to set my leads more solidly into the ground. Otherwise, when the hammer hit the pile, it was causing shock waves throughout my boom. It was causing the whole crane to rock. The foreman would make me lift them from a proper seat to where they were simply balancing on the surface of the soil, causing the rocking motion in the crane. He and I went round and round about how I felt uncomfortable with the leads sitting in the ground. He had become a hard-nosed asshole, and I should have left that job for another one because he wasn't listening to me regarding the safety of driving the pile.

The shuddering throughout the boom and the heavy rocking of the crane caused the middle brake to pop up, releasing the cable drum holding the pile I had been driving. My left foot was on the left brake, controlling the leads, and my right foot was pumping the right brake to control the hammer's cable as it spooled off the drum. Too bad I didn't have a third leg to squash down that brake on that afternoon. The pile fell out of the leads, dragging them along with the pile. The leads are very heavy and swung my crane through its brake, and I was up on the toes of my crane tracks on my way to dumping over into the huge hole that had been excavated for us to drive pile into. If the crane tipped over, I was dead meat. I swung to the left to avoid the hole as my boom was coming down, dumping my crane forward. I pulled up on the boom lever until everything stopped moving. That at least allowed me to keep from crushing the new giant air compressor the company leased for that job. The hammer was still pounding, but my hands held detrimental levers to keep the crane at a standstill until I could figure how to safely bring my tracks back down to the ground.

I had thought for sure that I was going to die out there that day. If I had dumped into that hole, I'd have been crushed inside by the heavy weight of the crane.

I stayed in the crane seat and waited for the mechanic to show up and help me to ascertain the best way to bring my crane back into a safe position. I kept the crane running in case I needed to pull levers if something shifted in order to keep it from collapsing. I had managed to maneuver the crane at his suggestions once he arrived, and we brought it back to a level position. It was scary as I boomed it back up and swung over to a cleared area behind me. I was operating with my stomach in my throat; the same feeling that I used to get when I would reach the summit of a roller coaster and then fly down the other side—I don't enjoy that feeling.

Once seemingly safe, we disconnected from the hammer and leads and called for a mechanic from the company we had rented the crane from. As I waited, I walked to my car to retrieve my camera I kept in my glove box to document jobsite issues to use as proof. I wanted to know why that third brake had popped up as soon as I'd been able to get out of that crane seat. I'd taken a look at the brake linkage. That constant shuddering throughout the crane and the constant rocking had been too much for that brake pedal to tolerate, and it had sheared the teeth clean off of the pedal. The teeth were what fit into the notches designed to set the brake at different increments. I told the head superintendent of my findings as well as our foreman and crew.

The crane's mechanic from the rental company went over the entire boom and found it to be sound. All of the cable had to be pulled off of the drums and replaced and that was always *a major pain in the ass* to do. It took us a few days to accomplish that greatest of feats, and then I was left on my own to replace the rigging back on the ends of the cable lines. The rest of the crew was dismissed to work elsewhere while I completed the necessary work on the crane. It was just before lunch one day when I was attempting to seat a becket on the end of a cable when it flew out of its constraints and whipped me right in the nose. It felt like a full grown man had punched me in the face! I know for sure what a punch to the nose feels like because between my series of full contact karate bouts and sparring with the ironworker first husband, my nose has been fractured three times. Remember this: when you strike someone in the nose, it temporarily mars their vision by causing the eyes to tear up and therefore causing a few seconds of blindness. That is a perfect blow for self-defense if you need to get away from someone (okay, that's your self-defense lesson for today).

I couldn't see because of my blurry vision, and to make matters worse, my nose was becoming the size of Jimmy Durante's—he was known as "The Schnoz." Our jobsite had always been a giant dustbowl with dust devils spinning across our jobsite throughout the day. I had blood pouring from my nose and face; the pain told me that I had open wounds. I wanted to get out of there and off of that filthy jobsite. When I could see clearly enough to do so, I searched for our head superintendent who I had seen earlier, checking on the jobsite's progression. It had become lunchtime, and no one was to be found. I left word with a foreman working for a different contractor nearby and told him I needed to leave to take care of my face. He was alarmed at my bloodiness and said he'd pass on the information. Once home, I was shocked when I looked in the mirror to see a piece of the inside of my nose hanging on the outside, OUCH! And WTF! Then, when I wiped off the blood from my face, I had a star pattern punctured into the lower portion of my jaw (I have a star patterned scar there to this day— *lovely;* a daily reminder of another near-death escape).

I made it back into work the next day with an extra-large nose, black eyes once again, and a hell of a headache. As I've previously mentioned, my sensei (karate instructor) would say to me, "This isn't a daisy-picking class!" and being a tough cookie, I got back to work. It was supposed to be the first day we got back into our pile driving regimen, but as soon as I checked out the crane and performed my greasing and lubricating duties, I was approached by the head superintendent. He told me that my foreman had called him the night before to tell him that he didn't want me as his crane operator anymore. I couldn't believe it! I reiterated my findings on the teeth of the brake shearing off as the cause of the accident. I also told the superintendent about our arguments the foreman and I had recently been involved in regarding the depth the leads were set at. I told him that the *foreman* was the one who needed to go!

I was so angry with that f——king prick that when the super-intendent told me to go work in the yard that day, I said, "No! I'm so angry that I shouldn't even be driving my car right now, never mind a crane! I'm going home." I was so mad that I forgot to grab my personal belongings out of the crane, and after I got to my car, I decided to wait until the foreman showed up so that I could jam my fist into his lying face! I waited and waited for that coward to show up until I finally said, "Fuck it!" and left for home. Some of my crewmates had shown up and asked why I wasn't inside with the crane. When I told them the reason, they sided with me, saying that they thought he was a motherf——ker too. I wished them luck and told them to watch their backs working with a carpenter trying to be a pile driver. The next day, after I'd cooled off somewhat, I began my day by going into the office and speaking once again to the head superintendent. I told him that I had given up all my summer plans in order to work the extensive long hours on that jobsite. I was counting on making all that overtime pay, and now that I was removed from that jobsite, I had lost a lot of money I would have made there. I told them that I would *not* work with that foreman again, anywhere. I would not even be in the same room with him until I knew that I could keep myself from kicking his ass. If he was my only choice I had to work with on a job, to lay me off instead, and I would go to work for someone else.

It took me two years before I could stay in the same room with him for a safety meeting, but I would never work with him again. At that point in my life, I was absolutely "assholed" out. I was done with male crap and bullshit. I'd had enough.

I learned a valuable lesson about that whole situation to "stick to my guns!" From that point onward, if I deemed something unsafe to do, I wouldn't do it, and instead, I would leave and go home. It wasn't worth arguing about or getting bent out of shape over. I never let someone get the best of me like that again either. Every day is a clean slate, and I move on. There are just too many assholes out there; to let them get to you gives them power, and f——k that!

Now to end the tale of that negative jobsite, I will add two interesting features of the positive variety. First, a woman came out to the jobsite to interview me, as I worked, for a newspaper. I've enclosed some of the photos and portions of the article here in this book. The second fact was that the old stadium that was torn down we found to be built upon one of the oldest dump sites within our city. When they excavated the property, the number of beautiful antique bottles that they dug up was astonishing! Members of the bottle association lined up along our fence line every day to purchase bottles from any worker who left the site with them in their possession. One backhoe operator found two complete intact oakwood barrels in perfect condition. They had been sealed in mud that preserved them. He cleaned them and kept one; he sold the other one to an antique dealer for two hundred dollars! They had been used decades ago to age whiskey or some such libation.

Anyway, I have in my possession some very old perfume, apothecary, beer, and soda bottles. I have old milk bottles that have the rim at the top that were hand blown. Unfortunately, during a long layoff period one winter, I sold my unique brown glass quart milk bottle with the hand blown rim for forty dollars because I needed the money.

Now on to a difficult portion of the stadium jobsite to write about. One of the worst construction accidents to have ever occurred happened when they were setting the iron, long after I'd been dismissed from the project from my usual company. I'd gone on to set iron and precast for another contractor during the time they were bringing in the cranes, jobsite trailers, and materials for the erecting phase of the new stadium. I'd been asked by a crane operator buddy of mine to be his oiler for that phase of the project which I'd agreed to.

As I was completing a jobsite that I'd been working on for quite a while, the stadium job began ahead of their preplanned start date. A union business agent in my locale asked if I would let another operator take my place at the stadium until my project was complete. I agreed as long as I could begin work there as soon as I finished where I was at the time.

When I showed up to enter the stadium project, they would not issue me a security pass, stating that they were not going to switch out employees. As upset as I was at the time to miss out working on a long-term project that would assure me a paycheck weekly for quite a while, it turned out to be better for me that I wasn't there.

I was working elsewhere, operating a crane, setting iron. One day proved to be too windy, so we shut down our jobsite. Many other jobsites that had cranes working on them shut down also. We used to shut down cranes in winds that were in the thirty five mile an hour range. It proved to be too difficult for the men to control the pieces of iron to set them in place when they were being blown around. It was too unsafe because wrestling a heavy piece of iron in those winds could have forced a man off the iron and back then they were not tied off to anything. It was structurally damaging to the booms of the cranes, and the loads lifted could cause the crane's boom capacities to become overloaded.

I drove to pick up my daughter on my way home from work, and my car was being blown about on the freeway. I could see the streetlights that lined the freeway swaying back and forth as if they were nothing more than tulips. As I drove past the stadium, something struck me as odd, but I couldn't put my finger on what it was. I needed to gas up my car for the morning commute to work. I took my daughter inside the gas station to pay for my gas. As I stood in line to pay the cashier, I was watching breaking news displayed overhead on the television.

A contractor at the stadium had hired a crane and its two operators to be built on the grounds. It was called "Big Blue" and would be setting the giant arched beams and other iron sections of significant weight. That crane was massive, and on the television, there was flashing "breaking news"; the crane was lifting an extremely large and heavy piece of iron that would become part of the roof when the crane toppled over, and as it fell, it cut through the cable of the crane that was holding the ironworkers in a man basket. They were being lifted to where they would climb out onto the iron and bolt the huge piece being held by Big Blue into place.

It was a nightmare; my daughter saw and heard the television, and she began screaming, "My dad! My dad!" as he had been working on that project for quite a while at that point. I told her that we would go by his house on the way home and leave him a note to call her and let her know if he was okay. In the meantime, I had calls coming in from both ironworkers and operators discussing what had led up to the accident.

Days passed with no word from my daughter's father. The news had announced details of the ironworkers who had fallen in the man basket to their deaths. One of the men was my daughter's godmother's husband, another was a young man who had left my jobsite early in order to gain employment on the long-term new stadium project. That man had boomed into the ironworker's locale in our area from a northern portion of our state. He was supporting his wife who stayed home, raising their two young twin sons. My daughter's godmother's husband had come out of retirement to work on one last job. The ironworker's union hall had called on whoever they could bring in to work on the stadium project because it was such a large, long-term project.

It was several days before we heard from my daughter's dad. He told me about that extremely windy day. The main contractor who was renting the expensive Big Blue crane had offered any worker willing to work in the high winds double time pay. Anyone not wanting to work could leave for the day. The contractor was adamant about keeping that crane working and not parked for the day, losing them money.

Half of the men took off for the tavern nearby, and the others went to work to make that double time pay. My daughter's godmother had taken her husband to lunch that day, and when she drove him back to the jobsite, he told her that an ironworker connector had called in sick that day, and as the union steward, he had to take his place up in the air, connecting that giant beam they would be setting. He told her he had a bad feeling about it and didn't want to go up in the air to connect, even though he had to.

The men were almost to their point of exiting the man basket. My buddy crane operator was hoisting them up in the air. That was the crane I was originally supposed to be the oiler on. Big Blue had hoisted the massive beam into the air. The winds were causing the load to sway out of the boom's capacity vicinity. The weight in the wrong place drew the crane over. As it was cutting across the sky, the long boom sliced through the cable holding the man basket. The men smashed together in the man basket on the ground, and the cable that had held them then free fell down around the cab of the crane that was holding the men. My buddy was so lucky he wasn't crushed by the weight of all that cable. If it had fallen on the window that was his roof, he wouldn't have made it either.

A friend of mine ended up being his oiler on that crane, and he had the horrific task of covering up the dead ironworkers with a tarp to keep everyone from gawking at them. He later told me that he had nightmares of the accident from that day on. The crane operator kept attempting to swing his crane away from where they were meant to connect the beam, even though the crane could barely move because of all the cable wrapped around it. It was as if he was trying to swing his then dead buddies out of harm's way. He didn't operate cranes after that awful accident. The man who was the oiler quit being an operator and drove a dump truck after that. He told me that he suffered from nightmares where he witnessed the basket of men crashing to the ground over and over when he slept.

The operator of Big Blue was in the hospital for some time and was lucky to have survived. If only he had said no to operating the crane in those high winds. As for my daughter's dad, he told me that the workers who had chosen to leave the jobsite that day were drinking in the tavern when they saw a news interruption on the television. Once they realized that their buddies that had stayed to work were killed, they drank themselves into oblivion. They were all so upset that they stayed drunk for the following several days. Every ironworker's worst fear was falling because it was a death sentence, and there it had happened to four of their friends. The bar was attached to a hotel, and the owner allowed them to stay in the bar or in a room rather than to have any of them attempt to drive anywhere.

The contractor didn't want to lose one day of work due to the high winds, but by doing so, in those winds, it caused an enormous amount of downtime on that project while investigators pieced together exactly what caused the giant crane to tip over. It took a very long time for compensation to be allotted to the grieving families. Every worker who was employed on the new stadium project was invited to go and watch the first sports event to be held in it. I've never been to that stadium and have no intentions of doing so in the future.

Not long after I had finished my stint at driving pile for that stadium, I had a life-changing event that was the final result of the two blows to the back of my head with my iron. My brain had hit the front of my head so hard it was what had caused my two eyes to be so black. I remember strangers asking me if I had been in a car accident (WTF!). I was told that I had a brain stem injury that was in an inoperable position.

One early morning, I woke up abruptly, feeling very strange. I felt an internal "CLUNK" in my head that caused me instant nausea and fear. I instantly knew that something serious was happening, and it wasn't good. I went in to work as usual when all of a sudden, it felt like lightning bolts were shooting through my head. With each step I took, it felt like shards of glass were pushing upward through my jaw and continuing through my face. At times, I felt like I had a wasp stuck inside of my nose, stinging me over and over. Other times, I felt like an ice pick was jamming from my brain out through my right ear. I would feel endless streams of ants tunneling throughout my face. I was operating the crane with both hands, utilizing levers while an imaginary spider fell onto my face and was walking across my eyelashes on my right eye. I thought, *WTF!* And as soon as I could, I brushed it free from my eye. That was how I found out that it was my nerves instead of a real spider.

Those horribly painful episodes would last anywhere from forty-five minutes to three hours. Every so often, they would last all day. I had to carefully tippy-toe around when the pain would hit. As soon as I was home from work, I would sit in my chair and not move. Otherwise, I would lay in bed. The quieter and darker the room, the better; it was like having a bad migraine on steroids. I went to several doctors and neurologists who all said that I had a brain stem injury and another spot on my skull nearby where my nerves were crushed together.

I was put on anti-seizure medication which I had to quit taking because it was making me feel like a zombie and wasn't helping with the painful episodes anyway. I went to an acupuncture doctor referred to me by my neurologist; they say it's a painless procedure—my ass! To make things even more painful, he told me that I needed to "upgrade" to an acupuncturist who threads electrical conduit from needle to needle. I tried that and ended up with electricity running between the needles the woman placed throughout the right side of my face. It hurt like hell, but she thought that with many more treatments, I may have received relief from the pain my nerves were causing in my head. I had a roadmap of bruises all over my face from the treatment, and it made me look like I just stepped out of a horror movie.

I had been diagnosed with trigeminal neuralgia. That's the main nerve that runs through each side of your face; it looks like a tree branch with many smaller branches and stems coming off of it. All of those branches and stems are nerves; they run every function of your face along with the muscles. Without them, the face has no feeling, and it hangs motionless. I had to go and fill in on a jobsite that had been ongoing throughout the summer. The usual crew had been called away to work on another short term project. They had been using the mini excavator to drill long rods through holes that had been burned in the sheeting wall lining our river in the area of our boat shop.

For many years, our barges had been docked there when not in use and tied up to the sheeting wall. The rocking motion of the heavy barges had weakened the sheeting wall, and they were securing it before it collapsed. The rods were drilled from over the river, back toward and underneath the ground the mini excavator was sitting on. The rods would be bolted through a beam that was set down below the grounds surface. Once secured through the beam, the soil would be filled back in covering it up.

It was only going to be me operating the mini excavator along with my helper, an apprentice pile driver who had been working with the regular crew for a very short time. He was there to rig up the long rod to the drill head mounted on the end of the boom of the mini excavator. He would help guide the rod into the hole in the sheeting wall so that I could drill it in.

I wasn't well, and I shouldn't have been working. I felt like something was off about what I was about to do, but I couldn't put my finger on it. I was on pain medication that I was allowed to take at work and heavy-duty pain medication for as soon as I was off the clock. I liked being crystal clear in my head, and on that day, I was not. I asked my crewmate if I was set up exactly how they had been working with the mini excavator, and he answered me, "Yes."

As I reached out the boom of the excavator with the long and heavy rod over the river, I felt the machine rocking back and forth, tipping slightly. I didn't like that at all, especially because I was so close to the edge of the sheeting wall that I looked down into the river. When I began to drill the rod toward myself, I could feel the machine pulling forward as the torque head turned the rod.

A lightning bolt flashed through my head, and it must have caused me to jam my arms forward. I had levers in both hands, so they were forced forward also. The next thing I knew, the mini excavator was tipped up and angled over the sheeting wall. The torque head holding the rod in its center was the only thing keeping the mini excavator from flipping entirely over the sheeting wall and dropping down into the river far below. I had the front windshield slid up over my head and locked into place so that I could have fresh air in the cab that day because it was hot outside. Everything I had inside of the cab with me that day fell down into the river. I was trying not to fly out of that window myself as I braced my hands on the edges of the window frame. I watched my gloves fly down into the water. I could see my hard hat floating up against a barge where the river's current had taken it. It was bumping up against a beautiful blue and white bowling ball; one color bled into the other one.

I could feel my butt rising off of the seat—I was going out of the window and into the freezing polluted river. I wouldn't be able to swim with the lasers of pain permeating my brain. I would drown, and what was worse was that the mini excavator would most likely land on me and take me all the way down to the thick sludge on the river bottom. I didn't want to go in that water!

I heard my crewmate say, "Jump to the side, I will catch you— jump to me!"

I went for it. I was going out that front window anyway, so I pushed from the machine toward my crewmate. I landed right on him, then I had to lay still because all of that motion made the pains in my head that were racing around even worse. The machine was still cocked up and over the sheeting wall, ready to drop in.

The crewmate ran to the nearby boat shop to get help. I could see in my peripheral vision a group of men running toward me from the boat shop where they'd been working. One man hopped into the Pettibone and drove it over to the flipped mini excavator. That machine I've written about because I lifted a lot of heavy materials and machinery with it. They shut off the mini excavator since I had no time in which to do so. They rigged the machine up to the Pettibone and were able to pull it back over the sheeting wall and away from its edge. I managed to get up and was assisted into the boat shop.

I could barely speak or breathe for that matter because of the enormous amount of pain I was suffering from. It hurt so bad that I didn't dare cry because it would have made the pain even worse.

By the time the pain subsided, the men had already moved everything away from the sheeting wall and had the mini excavator in a position to get trailered to the mechanics in the yard. Someone told me that my hard hat was next to a barge in the river if I wanted to retrieve it. I said, "Hell, no, I'm not going anywhere near that river. I'm going back to the yard and I'll finish the day there." I figured that I would just get a new hard hat once I got there.

Unfortunately, while I was in the boat shop, recuperating from my painful episode, the vice president of the company had driven down to our jobsite and asked why I wasn't operating the mini excavator. He had been informed of my close call with the river. By the time I walked into the yard, everyone had already heard about my accident. I was called into the office and was told that if I would have surgery, they would hold my job for me. If I chose to continue to look for relief any other way, I would have to go and work for another contractor.

I went home and began my search for a neurosurgeon. The man I ended up having to operate on me told me that the "clunk" I felt inside my head that started the lightning bolt attacks were due to the two blows to the back of my head with my iron. My main trigeminal nerve had fallen onto my artery so that when my heart beat, it was causing the electrical jolts through my jaw, face, and head. He performed brain surgery where he removed an area of my skull and carefully placed a piece of surgical sponge in between the nerve and the artery. That sponge made a cushion between them so that my heart could beat without causing me such tremendous pain. Nowadays, I have less episodes, and they are usually not as debilitating as they were before the surgery.

I was off of work for four months before the doctor released me to go back. It was a few more months before the company let me get back in a crane seat. The very first job they sent me to was right back to the river. I had to drill those rods over the sheeting wall. It took two weeks before I didn't feel like I was constantly tipping over, but one day, it finally stopped; my stomach quit flying up into my throat every time I reached out over the water with a heavy long rod. I remember thinking, *WTF! Why do I have to come back to work after all that time and be sent to the job that almost killed me?*

If I hadn't been forced to face my fear, it would have remained within me forever. It turned out to be a blessing instead of a curse to be reassigned there. One of the nicest things my coworkers in the yard did for me was to have gone down to that barge in the river and not only retrieve my hard hat out of the water, but they grabbed that beautiful blue and white bowling ball it was bobbing up against. They seemed so pleased with themselves for rewarding my return with that bowling ball. It was out of character for them to do something so sweet and selfless. I have that same bowling ball on a pedestal in my bedroom. I keep it as a reminder that I'm lucky to still be alive and to make the most out of each day because you'll never know if it could be your last.

One of my scariest and more interesting picks I had to make was during the darkness of night. A huge load was being driven in from out of state and wouldn't arrive until after dinnertime in the evening hours. It was a huge piece of equipment that was to be mounted on the roof of one of our tallest buildings in the city. Since I would operate by the illuminated hand signals I'd be given, I was asked who I would want to give them to me. That was a no-brainer question for me. I asked that my now husband (my boyfriend at the time) be the man to rig the load for me and give me the necessary signals I would need to pick the load off of the semitrailer.

We hung around the yard, preparing the rigging, grabbing some dinner, and waited for the arrival of the semitrailer. My now husband had been a pile driver foreman for many years prior to my entering the company as an operating engineer apprentice. He knew what the crane I was operating was capable of safely lifting. I knew that I could trust him not to take a chance on that crane tipping in any way.

The truck finally showed up, and armed with a flashlight, my now husband signaled me each movement he needed the crane to perform. All I could see was the humongous outline of the dark object in front of me. It was so heavy that he backed the semitrailer all the way up to the front of my crane. It was so tall that he needed a ladder in order to hook me up to the rigging on top. When I was ready to pick it, I was boomed up enough to be able to lift it straight up off the bed of the trailer so that the driver could pull out from underneath it. When he signaled me to hoist it up, I could feel the rear end of my crane getting light. That pick was extremely heavy and one of the heaviest I'd ever picked. The driver drove out from under the load, and I eased it down to the ground until it was just touching. In the morning, I would hoist it straight up and place it on the semitrailer, driving it to its destination.

It went as well as planned and was a great success for an extraordinary night pick. After that job, he and I were called the "A-team" and were sent on many projects together. I would make picks for him without hesitation or rejection because I knew that he had my best interest at heart. I knew that if he said the crane would have no problem with the pick I was preparing to make that it wouldn't. Any other foreman that I suspected didn't know his shit, I would be out of my seat, questioning him or examining firsthand the pick I was about to make and the rigging that was being used to make it.

I have stood on the brink of death several times now, three times I've written about, and twice my now husband saved me from physical ailments that would have resulted in death had he not intervened. It wasn't my time yet. Perhaps I'm still here to shed some light to others by writing this book. Hopefully, I've shared lessons that I've learned, such as you can change your mindset which will change your fate. You are strong enough to climb out of the hole that is an abusive situation. You can dare to challenge yourself in ways that you never dreamed or imagined. You can do whatever you set your mind to do. You can accept others for who they are and concentrate on improving solely yourself. One of the quotes I read several times each week to remind myself of its truth comes from news journalist Robin Roberts who has faced her personal battles publicly and thus bravely. She said, "We're all a little bit stronger than we think we are." She should know because she faced death herself.

I did not point out my first husband the ironworker in any of my photos, even though he is in some of them. I did not delve deeply into the difficulties he put our family through because when you live with an active alcoholic and/or drug addict, it always seems to be about "them." It isn't; -it's about YOU. It's a life lesson on how you choose to deal with any situation that comes your way on a daily basis. It's character building to take the high road and in that way you can live guilt free. As Michelle Obama said, "When they take the low road, we take the high road." You can either fly high with the eagles or you can play in the mud with the polliwogs—I choose to SOAR.

More about the "A-team" in the next chapter.

*The only way to get our crane out of the hole was
to dismantle it using a larger crane*

Separating the house from the tracks, I found a lot of lost keys and watches inside that turntable, some of them my own!

Trucked the crane to the other end of the island to put it back together and drive more pile for another building to be erected upon

Lifting the crane's tracks out of the hole

It's an ironworker custom to celebrate setting the last beam of iron by placing an evergreen in the center, the American flag on one end and their local union flag on the other end.

An example of walking the iron without being tied off; not allowed now; we were tying a new structure into an existing one

The long jib connected to the top of the tower was instrumental in reaching far enough across the iron to erect a helicopter pad on top of the hospital

The two photos on the left are showing the attaching procedure of the jib to the "rooster tail" at the end of the tower; the vertical tower allows the crane to track close to the structure

The iron in the bridge photo look like adult "Tinker Toys"; This is a good example of why I say that setting iron was like putting together a puzzle

The same jobsite in two separate phases of completion; it gets a whole lot more complex and complicated when more cranes are added to the project

WHEN IT'S GOOD, IT'S LIKE FLYING A KITE

Flying a kite refers to the feeling of hoisting a beam of iron high up in the air and successfully setting it in place or sailing a bundle of old pier sections up and over a well-established park tree without so much as touching a leaf. It's a feeling of zipping pile after pile into the ground, one after another, without skipping a beat. It also refers to skydiving, surfing fifteen-foot waves at Steamer Lane, or nailing the perfect kata with my favorite martial arts weapon, the Sai, or one of the other nine weapons that I currently train with—all those things are pretty damn cool. So in a nutshell, "flying a kite" is a *feeling*.

I'm going to start this chapter off by writing about one of my most "interesting" jobs: riding a bucking bronco forklift inside our casino. If that sounds fun, it's because it was! Our casino was expanding one of their many slot machine areas. They did not want to incur any downtime and, therefore, lose money. They came up with the brilliant idea of standing pieces of plywood on its edge and creating a wall with it. It was what separated me from the slot machine players on the other side of the plywood.

I was essentially inside one if their rooms so the forklift I was going to operate was on carpet, of all things. I remember thinking, *How classy for a construction site!* It was myself and my foreman; we had fans blowing on us to provide some relief from to enter the casino anonymously. The only thing that they specifically asked of myself and the foreman were to stay out of the casino because our construction attire was *not* up to their dress code.

I had hardly any clearance overhead of the hammer we set on my forks with special rigging. We needed to drive a lot of short pieces of H-beams into the ground. A circle of both carpet and concrete had been removed from where the beams were needed to be pounded the summer temperatures. The casino not only provided fans but a port-a-potty and security guards as well. The guards were to deter anyone attempting into place. We had special iron splice pieces to connect one piece of beam onto the one we'd driven. It was a long process just to get one beam driven down deep enough for specifications.

It was certainly one of cleanest jobsites I ever worked on, and for safety measures, I had to buckle into my seat belt anytime I was going to run air to the hammer. As soon as I threw the air lever, it was like releasing a bucking bronco out of the chute at the rodeo. "Ka-chunk, ka-chunk, ka-chunk!" Down the beam section it would go until the foreman gave me the hand signal to stop. While I was driving the beam, the forklift hopped up and down with the power the hammer exerted—it was a wild ride! That job holds fond memories for me because the only pressure put on us was to not hit the ceiling. We excelled there and made our head honchos happy and the casino even more money once the additional slot machines were added.

On this next jobsite I'm going to write about, I was QUEEN for a day (I know—it was only one *day* out of twenty eight *years,* but hey, I'll take it). This was my most unusual (and also my top secret—shhhh!) job. It happened on a Saturday morning while I was residing out in the country far north of the city I usually worked in. I was taking my daughter on a long drive to indulge in a little retail therapy in a city far from us. It was a nice warm sunny day, so I was wearing a sundress with some cute wedge-heeled sandals. Just when we were about to leave our house, I received a phone call from a foreman I had worked for under the bridge construction contractor. One of his operators hadn't made it in to work that morning, and they had planned on making a "double pick" that day. They had a huge beam to hoist into place on the bridge they were constructing. The pick would take two cranes (thus the "double pick") and, of course, two operators to run them. He asked me if I'd be willing to just pop in, hop in the crane to make the pick, and then I'd be on my way with a full day's pay of time and a half.

I told him that although I'd be close to his jobsite on my way to the mall, I was in a dress and sandals and had no safety gear in the vehicle I'd be driving. He said that the men would be so happy to make their overtime pay that day they would loan me a hard hat when I arrived, and no one would let on about me showing up to work in my girl clothes. He promised that I'd be on and off the job-site in about fifteen minutes.

On that note, I hold the world's record for *"best dressed"* construction worker! Even if it was for a short time only. Who didn't want to look like a Barbie doll, operating a crane in her sundress? I did! I did! it was unimaginable. At the same time that I was actually wearing clothing that I *liked* on a jobsite, I was walking across the dirty filthy ground, looking at my girlie sandals, saying, "Oo-oo-oo, my poor shoes!" with every step.

You know what, goddamn it? That's what we need—Construction Barbie! More specifically, Barbie crane operator! Can't you see Barbie wearing her nonconforming work boots (since her foot is formed in a continual *high heel* position) sitting in a big-ass crane? You know she'd be sporting a pink and possibly "sparkly" hard hat. She needs a good all-American working class job to afford to reside in her Barbie Dream House. She needs to finance a date now and then with the *genderless* Ken.

The men were so happy that they hadn't gotten up early on a Saturday morning for nothing that they didn't even make lewd comments when I exited my vehicle and tippy-toed across the jobsite wearing a dress and my festive wedge heels. The foreman thanked me for helping them out in their moment of need as he handed me a hard hat. I got in the crane and was ready to go. In no time at all, the other operator and myself hoisted the heavy beam together and successfully set it into place.

Everything went great, and the men cheered when I exited the crane, grateful to be able to make their overtime pay that day. I can bet that they never again worked with a crane operator wearing a dress! I can definitely say that I never wore a dress again while operating one.

When I returned to my car, my daughter and I were once again on our way to the mall to buy a commemorative dress to honor the occasion.

"Do you ride bitch?"

WTF! I remember thinking when my foreman asked this question of me. Was he calling me a bitch after asking if I rode? Rode what? Did he know that I rode my own Harley? I knew he was a biker. Was that question supposed to be a lesbian joke of some kind? He knew that I was divorced from my ironworker husband.

He was the first foreman that I had worked for on day one of my career. He had worked on many pile driving jobsites together with me, too many to count over the eleven years that I'd been an operator at that point in time. We were reunited on yet another expansion of the sewage treatment plant. We were to drive in pile to hold up another building they would be erecting on their property. I was driving the forklift over to the pipe pile to retrieve the amount of pipe needed for our immediate area we were working in. He had jumped onto the step next to my seat and asked me that question. Since I didn't know what to think about it, I just answered him, "No" and left it at that.

We continued working for the remainder of the day, and I hadn't given his question another thought. The next day at work, he explained to me that "riding bitch" was a biker term that meant that you rode behind the driver of a motorcycle. I told him that I'd never heard of that term most likely because I drove my own Harleys. At that time, I had a Sportster and was thinking about buying a Fatboy. My Sportster had begun to feel like I was riding a jackhammer, and it was time for me to get a bigger bike.

He asked me if I would like to join him after work the next evening for a ride in the country, west of the city. I thought that if the date went bad, I was screwed because I had to work with him on the jobsite to complete the project. At the same time, if I declined, he may feel rejected, and I would be screwed because we were working on the same project. Hell, I had to take his hand signals all day long and didn't want those to be him giving me the finger!

I thought, *What the hell, we'll go on a date, it won't work out, and we'll get back to working, and he won't ask me out again.* So I accepted his offer.

The henhouse must have been cackling because when I stopped into the yard at the end of the day to pick up some supplies I needed for the crane, the men were reading me the riot act. "You can't go out with him, you'll be another notch in his bedpost. Is that what you want? Is that how little you think of yourself?"

"That guy rides around with a different woman on the back of his bike every week!"

On and on *my concerned brothers* at work went. It was clear to me the little faith they had in me or "how easily corrupted into doing something I didn't want to do" they thought me to be. Clearly, they didn't know me quite as well as they thought they did after the many years we'd worked together.

I heard the roar of his Harley as he pulled up to my place. At the time, my daughter and I were renting an upstairs unit in the area her dad and his family lived in so she could be close to them. I was shocked when he handed me a rose that he'd daringly carried between his thighs while riding to my house. He mentioned the pain he'd endured from the thorns on the stem of the rose, not aware that he could have broken them off before he began his journey. I was impressed further when he handed me one of my favorite cigars, a Macanudo. In the first place, people usually frowned upon my cigar smoking, and here was a man who clearly couldn't give a shit if I smoked them or not. Secondly, they were not the cheapest cigars and also not the easiest to find.

It had turned out to be an awesome night for a Harley ride. Every time we entered an establishment, he held the door for me and basically was a perfect gentleman the entire evening. I had a fun and enjoyable time. When he returned me to my home, he asked for a kiss and then waited until I was safely upstairs in my apartment before driving away.

The next morning, when I walked into the yard office to pick up some gear, I looked at the men seated there and said, "Really? He was a perfect gentleman the entire evening. You guys know what I was living with, and I could have been happier a long time ago if I hadn't listened to you!"

They all bowed their heads and looked away from me like a bunch of naughty puppies who were guilty of chewing up my shoes. Not one of the men had anything further to say to me, and not one of them looked me in the eye.

I have to say that our jobsite became way more fun after our initial first date because we were both in better moods and were joking around. He asked me to go on a second date that Friday night. We went on his Harley to a concert at our lakefront, and when he asked me where I wanted to go next, I said, "Your house." We've been together ever since. That first date was twenty-five years ago as I write this, and tomorrow is our eleventh anniversary as a married couple. It's still crazy for me to think that I ended up marrying the first foreman I had on my first day of work as an operator. Whenever I've told him that we should have gotten together earlier, he says that it just wasn't the right time. Anyway, I think that's a hell of a love story to tell! Strange but true.

Once it was known to everyone that we were a couple, my life on a jobsite became a lot more easier because men quit asking me out; they didn't bother me in that way anymore, which was a relief. The company began sending us as foreman and operator to job after job together. We were sent on about five jobs together, back-to-back. I recently wrote about a night job where I had to pick the huge object off of a truck in the darkness of night. I wrote about us driving the yard crane out to a faraway jobsite where it almost tipped over sideways just off the busy road I'd been driving it on. We were sent downtown in the busy area of our city to drive pile in place to hold a human skywalk up above the road we were on. We shut down one lane of traffic to set my crane up in. The traffic was merciless, and a pile driver was assigned to signal me when I was clear to swing around and grab a pile to drive. I remember thinking that I was happy to not have to raise the iron on that job because of the stress the traffic caused me there.

We were sent to a church in a county far south of us. We were driving pile in a big mud pit to expand on a church there. I operated the forklift that had to bring in the pile from the semitrailers they had been loaded on and parked out on that city's street. I had to stay out of the mud so that I wouldn't become stuck. I also had to carefully maneuver around their active high wires and trees that lined the street.

After, we were sent to drill chance anchors inside a hotel room in order to shore up the end of the sinking hotel. I wrote about that job and all of the jokes and repercussions that came from working together in a hotel room. We drove chance anchors into the ground in a county to the northwest of our city. We worked out in a wooded area for the expansion of a John Deere tractor facility.

In another county in the heart of a small town there, we had to walk my crane in and out between a narrow area of space. The police station was on one side of my crane, and their firehouse was on my other side. My foreman kept his eyes on the high wires overhead as I tracked in reverse to grab a pile and then tracked in with it to drive it into place. The pile that we carefully drove in that narrow area enabled a 911 call center to be built between those two important buildings for that town.

We had been working together all day long, stopping together at the tavern on the way home to have a cold beer at the end of the workday. We would then go home and eat and sleep together and then start the whole routine all over again the next day.

One day after work, instead of taking me to the tavern with him, he dropped me off at home and went by himself. I thought, *Well, the honeymoon is over, he's spent his limit of time with me.* The next morning, before the workday began, I walked into the office to speak to our superintendent we'd been working for. I said, "I think it's time for me to work with a different foreman. M—is tired of spending so much time with me."

I was surprised when he began laughing as if I'd just told him a joke. He told me that he was shocked we'd lasted through so many jobs together. He further informed me that they'd had a bet amongst themselves in the office as to how many jobs we would work together before being asked to be separated. Really? WTF! Those clowns were using my relationship as their own pathetic amusement. By that point in time, I was used to whatever male behavior was thrown my way.

My now husband and I worked many more jobs together, just not as many in succession. We were referred to as "the A-team" and often heard, "Send the A-team" or "Put the A-team on it." It just became a title we grew accustomed to. I've often been asked the secret to maintaining our relationship after so many years. I joke with them that I was paid to work with him for eleven years before our first date, so in essence, I was "trained" to be with him all day long no matter the mood, the setting, or the environment. I can definitely say that the best thing that happened to me in my unique career was meeting the love of my life who is my "now" husband. This is a very short chapter because there are no perfect days at work—*any* kind of work.

There are, however, perfect *moments*, and that's why it's so important to take the best part of each day and hold onto *that* memory. Also, on the hardest days that seem to never end, it's best to get through them one hour at a time or even fifteen minutes at a time. One of my favorite mottos is, *"If you keep your feet moving in the direction you want to go, sooner or later, you will reach your destination."*

Another favorite is *"If you're building a brick wall, it's best to do it one brick at a time."* Whenever I'm working toward a goal, I do at least one thing that gets me closer each day to that goal. These ideas have been helpful for me and hopefully will serve you well also.

In all the time I asked for a wedding ring during the twelve years I was married to the ironworker, I never received one. My now husband not only got me a gorgeous diamond wedding ring, he also got me a second ring. My second ring I *could* wear at work because it was made out of tungsten steel. It was made with a unique giraffe pattern on it; it will never scratch or be marred in any way. Once I wore that ring to work, I was never asked if I was married again.

HASTA LA VISTA, ASSHOLES

Most of the assholes I've written about are no longer here, no longer on this Earth, and that includes my first husband, the ironworker. It's because karma is a bitch, and she will catch up with you sooner or later. That's why it's so important to leave your last encounter with someone on a good note and not involving some psychotic episode. You never know; it could be the last time you see someone.

On the other side of the coin, in a bizarre way, I have to "thank" all of the assholes I encountered throughout my career. It was their dismissive and condescending attitudes toward me that drove my determination to make it to retirement, in spite of them.

There are a few reasons that I chose to write this book. First off, it's been quite an adventure! Dare to live your dreams, you may surprise yourself. You can do whatever it is that you put your mind to—I'm proof of that. I learned that when I broke my first concrete bricks with my hands as a young girl in my initial karate classes. Hopefully, I've exercised a few demons by writing about some of the more difficult periods of my career. An important reason that I shared the more personal aspects of my life are to prove that there *IS* light at the end of the tunnel! If you find yourself in an unhealthy relationship, it's time to move forward and away from the negativity—no matter what, *stay in the light.* If I could improve my life by doing so, you can too.

I've introduced you to a unique career choice, and as I've mentioned, I'm not the only female who enjoys building and creating. It's fun to operate a powerful piece of machinery and cause it to do precisely what you want it to. Look up operating engineers union online and sign up or give them a call for a good job with good pay, health benefits, and a pension.

I want to dedicate this book to my daughter. I had to work through her childhood not by choice but by necessity. I want to also dedicate this book to my husband who made life on the jobsite more bearable for me out there. I want to thank him for giving me the opportunities to shine while out there. I also want to thank him for bringing laughter into my life each day, for laughter is an instant vacation. Lastly, I want to thank my girlfriend Terri for coming up with the name for this book.

She and I were sitting in the tavern one late afternoon after a particularly difficult day at work. We were enjoying a cold beer together when I mentioned that I should write a book about what we went through each workday. She worked outside in all temperatures as I did, and she worked with all men as I did. She worked for the city, and I worked on construction sites. She said, "Yes, you should… and call it *A Hard Hat in Hell!*" So I did.

It's a hell of a lot better out there nowadays for anyone working in construction and especially for the ladies who wish to do so. There have been a lot of changes in rules, structure, and attitudes. There are a lot of support systems in place, and any sort of harassment that is engaged in is career-ending. No one is expected to take crap from anyone.

There's nothing like the feeling of accomplishment you get when you look upon a big structure and can say to yourself, "I helped build that!" And always remember that "boobs are bigger than balls!"

A Hard Hat in Hell

by

Suzanne Szucs

Suzanne Traczyk earns more than $15 an hour as a crane operator, an occupation that is 99 percent male.

Engineer of the Year Awards were presented at the Madison Membership meeting to: District A: Suzanne Traczyk, Roger Hudzinski; District C: Donald Maguire; and the Apprentice the Year: Kenneth Bork. Tom Handschke was unable to attend.